MasterClass in History Education

Also available in the MasterClass Series

MasterClass in Drama Education, Michael Anderson
MasterClass in English Education, edited by Sue Brindley and Bethan Marshall
MasterClass in Geography Education, edited by Graham Butt
MasterClass in Mathematics Education, edited by Paul Andrews and Tim Rowland
MasterClass in Music Education, edited by John Finney and Felicity Laurence
MasterClass in Religious Education, Liam Gearon

MasterClass in History Education

Transforming Teaching and Learning

Edited by Christine Counsell, Katharine Burn and Arthur Chapman

MasterClass Series

Bloomsbury Academic
An imprint of Bloomsbury Publishing Plc

B L O O M S B U R Y
LONDON · OXFORD · NEW YORK · NEW DELHI · SYDNEY

Bloomsbury Academic

An imprint of Bloomsbury Publishing Plc

50 Bedford Square	1385 Broadway
London	New York
WC1B 3DP	NY 10018
UK	USA

www.bloomsbury.com

BLOOMSBURY and the Diana logo are trademarks of Bloomsbury Publishing Plc

First published 2016

British Library Cataloguing-in-Publication Data

A catalogue record for this book is available from the British Library.

ISBN: HB: 978-1-4725-2518-5
       PB: 978-1-4725-3487-3
     ePDF: 978-1-4725-2521-5
     ePub: 978-1-4725-3095-0

Library of Congress Cataloging-in-Publication Data

A catalog record for this book is available from the Library of Congress.

Typeset by Newgen Knowledge Works (P) Ltd., Chennai, India
Printed and bound in Great Britain

Contents

List of Figures and Tables

Figures

Tables

Notes on Contributors

Katharine Burn is Associate Professor of history education at the University of Oxford, where she leads the PGCE history programme, teaches on the MSc in Learning and Teaching and supervises doctoral studies in history education and teachers' professional learning. She is Director of the Oxford Education Deanery, a multilevel partnership with local schools, embracing a variety of professional development initiatives and research collaborations. Katharine is a co-author of *The Guided Reader to Learning and Teaching History* (2013) and of *Beginning Teachers' Learning: Making Experience Count* (2014). She chairs the Secondary Committee of the Historical Association and has co-edited *Teaching History* since 2009.

Ellen Buxton has taught history in two state secondary schools and is currently teaching at Cowplain Community School, an 11–16 school serving a socially diverse and comprehensive ability intake, in Hampshire, England. At Cowplain, 70 per cent of students opt to continue studying history at 14+ through to 16+ public examinations and the school is in the top 4 per cent in England for progress made by students in humanities subjects from 11 to 16. Ellen has published in *Teaching History*, completed a masters degree in history education at the University of Cambridge and contributed to history teacher conferences, training and masters-level courses as a visiting speaker.

Arthur Chapman is Senior Lecturer in history education in the UCL Institute of Education, University College London, UK where he works in initial teacher education and supervises masters and doctoral students. Arthur is Associate Editor of the *London Review of Education* and *The International Journal of Historical Learning, Teaching and Research*, a member of the editorial boards of the *International Review of History Education* and the *Curriculum Journal* and was co-editor of *Teaching History* in 2007–2013. He was an editor of *Constructing History, 11–19* (2009) and of *Joined Up History* (2015). He is Fellow of The Royal Historical Society.

Christine Counsell taught history in schools and is now Senior Lecturer at the Faculty of Education, University of Cambridge, UK where she works with history teachers to run an integrated PGCE programme. She has held Historical Association office as Deputy President and as chair of its Secondary Committee. Editor of *Teaching History* since 1998, she was made Centenary Fellow of the Historical Association in 2006. Christine has frequently assisted in drafting England's NC for history, including NC 2014. Her interests lie in ITT mentoring, students' historical knowledge and teaching history in post-conflict zones. She has lectured, trained and provided consultancy internationally, for schools, universities, governments and NGOs.

John Elliott is Emeritus Professor of Education within the Centre for Applied Research in Education at the University of East Anglia and Visiting Professor at the University Campus Suffolk. He is well known internationally for developing action research in the contexts of curriculum and teacher development, and is founding Chief Editor of the *International Journal of Lesson and Learning Studies*. From 2008 to 2010 he was president of the World Association of Lesson Studies. A selection of his work, titled *Reflecting Where the Action Is*, was published in the Routledge World Library of Educationalists series (2007). With Nigel Norris he edited *Curriculum, Pedagogy and Educational Research: The Work of Lawrence Stenhouse* (2012).

Michael Fordham is Assistant Headteacher at the West London Free School (11–18 comprehensive), London, UK, having previously taught history at Cottenham Village College and Hinchingbrooke School. In 2014, he was the Singapore Ministry of Education's Outstanding Educator-In-Residence. Michael's doctoral research was on subject-specificity in history teacher published discourse. He has published in the fields of medieval history, philosophy of education and history education and he has been an editor of *Teaching History* since 2010. He is currently Affiliated Lecturer at the University of Cambridge Institute of Continuing Education where he teaches the MSt in Advanced Subject Teaching (History). He writes regularly at www.clioetcetera.com.

Rachel Foster is Advanced Skills Teacher teaching history at Comberton Village College (11–18 comprehensive) in Cambridgeshire, UK and supports teachers, one day a week, at Voyager Academy (11–16 comprehensive) in Peterborough. Rachel mentors new history teachers training with the University of Cambridge Faculty of Education Partnership. Currently writing a textbook on the Crusades for 14–16-year-olds, she has published several articles in *Teaching History* and written a chapter in I. Davies (ed.) *Debates in History Teaching* (Routledge, 2011). Since 2014, Rachel has been an editor of *Teaching History*. Rachel frequently presents her work at national history education conferences.

Kate Hammond taught history for seventeen years in three UK schools, most recently leading the history department at Bottisham Village College, an all-ability state secondary school in Cambridgeshire, where she was also responsible for training history teachers through a variety of programmes. As part of the history mentor team working in partnership with the University of Cambridge she helped to develop its secondary Post-Graduate Certificate in Education programme, and has recently taken up a new post in Indonesia as a teacher trainer. She contributes regularly to *Teaching History* and continues to pursue particular research interests in the role of substantive knowledge within pupils' historical learning.

Michael Harcourt teaches history at Wellington High School, a medium-sized, culturally diverse, maintained school in the heart of New Zealand's capital city. He is currently a co-editor of the New Zealand History Teachers Association journal, *History Teacher Aotearoa*. With Mark Sheehan, he edited *History Matters: Teaching and Learning History in New Zealand Secondary Schools in the 21st Century* (NZCER, 2012). In 2015 he was the recipient of a Fulbright-Cognition Scholar Award in Education Research, which allowed him to spend six months at the City University of New York, pursuing his interest in culturally responsive history teaching.

Izzy Jones is Assistant Headteacher at William Ellis School (11–18 boys) and was formerly head of History and Politics at Parliament Hill School (11–18 girls). Both schools have a fully comprehensive intake and are maintained by the Camden Local Authority in London. Between 2011 and 2015, Izzy was seconded part-time to the UCL Institute of Education where she worked as a subject tutor on the History PGCE course and as History Subject Lead on the Teach First programme. She trained as a history teacher at the University of Cambridge and completed an MA in History Education with the UCL Institute of Education. Her most recent research examined connections between women's history and girls' gender identity.

Daniel Magnoff is Head of History at St Michael's College, London, UK, an inclusive, multicultural school with comprehensive intake. He has previously taught history both in selective grammar schools and in other all-ability state secondary schools in London. Daniel has worked with Ros Ashby, Arthur Chapman and David Wilkinson on projects aimed at developing historical reasoning in students at secondary school level. He has previously contributed to GCSE textbooks and published on medieval Icelandic literature. He is currently working on a long-term, intercollegiate project aimed at developing students' understanding of historical argument and academic process.

Allan Megill (BA Sask., MA Toronto, PhD Columbia University) is Professor of History at the University of Virginia. He previously worked at the University of Iowa and the Australian National University. His research fields are modern European intellectual history and the theory of history. He is the author of *Prophets of Extremity* (1985), *Karl Marx: The Burden of Reason* (2002), and *Historical Knowledge, Historical Error* (2007), as well as many articles. His academia.edu site, which includes a number of 'teaching documents', can be accessed at https://virginia.academia.edu/AllanMegill.

Ed Podesta is a history teacher and teacher educator who has worked in higher education, as well as in the state and independent sectors. He spent three years as Head of History in a large comprehensive school in Reading before undertaking a masters degree in education research methods. He has written an A-level textbook on the unification of Italy, published by Hodder, and is currently working, with others, on a series of textbooks to support new GCSE specifications. Ed blogs at www.onedamnthing.org.uk and has worked as a consultant for OCR, the BBC and PiXL. In September 2015 he became a senior lecturer in secondary education at Leeds Trinity University.

Rick Rogers has taught in schools in England, the Czech Republic and Vietnam, and most recently at Benton Park School, an urban comprehensive in Leeds. Rick was involved in the Frameworks Working Group and in other projects on frameworks with Denis Shemilt, Frances Blow and Claire Smith. He has published in *Teaching History* and *International Review of History Education*, written textbooks for Heinemann and Pearson and devised the

'Thinking Historically' exercises for a series published by Pearson in 2015/2016. Rick has presented at conferences for the Schools History Project, the SSAT (Schools Network) and, in Cyprus, the Association for Historical Dialogue and Research.

Mark Sheehan has been involved in history education matters for almost thirty years as a teacher, researcher, museum educator, advisor and textbook writer. As Senior Lecturer in the Faculty of Education, Victoria University of Wellington, he teaches and conducts research on critical/historical thinking, memory/remembrance, assessment and the place of knowledge in twenty-first-century curricula. He contributed a chapter examining debates about the place of history in the New Zealand school curriculum in Guyver and Taylor (eds) *History Wars in the Classroom: A Global Perspective* (2011) and, with Michael Harcourt, edited *History Matters: Teaching and Learning History in New Zealand Secondary Schools in the 21st Century* (2012).

Robert Somers is Head of Humanities at the British International School Istanbul, Turkey, where he teaches history and the International Baccalaureate 'theory of knowledge' course. He originally qualified as archaeologist, with an MA from Birkbeck, University of London, and worked in Bulgaria teaching English and managing cultural heritage projects before undertaking a PGCE at the University of Cambridge Faculty of Education. He taught for several years at Highfields School (11–18 comprehensive) in Letchworth, Hertfordshire, UK, which is where he carried out the classroom research reported in this volume, undertaken as part of his MEd in Researching Practice.

Carla van Boxtel is Professor of History Education at the Research Institute of Child Development and Education and the Amsterdam School for Culture and History of the University of Amsterdam. She is also director of the Dutch Centre for Social Studies Education and member of the management of the teacher training programmes of the University of Amsterdam. She is trained as historian and educational scientist. Her main research interests focus on the learning and teaching of history in schools and museums, particularly on improving students' historical thinking and reasoning. She has received several research grants and published in international peer-reviewed journals.

Jannet van Drie is Assistant Professor at the Research Institute of Child Development and Education of the University of Amsterdam. Originally trained as a history teacher, she has a special interest in the learning and teaching of history. She has published in the field of historical reasoning, computer-supported collaborative learning, the use of representational tools, classroom interaction, and content-based language learning. Together with Carla van Boxtel, she was awarded the EARLI Outstanding Publication Award in 2009 for their article 'Historical Reasoning, towards a Framework for Analysing Students' Reasoning about the Past'. She also works as a teacher educator and participates in the Dutch Centre for Social Studies Education.

Paula Worth is Key Stage 3 Co-ordinator for History and Lead Practitioner at Bristol Grammar School, Bristol, UK. She previously taught history at a state comprehensive school in Hertfordshire. She is Associate Editor for *Teaching History*, in which she has also published several articles. An academic supervisor for the Master of Education in Researching Practice at the University of Cambridge, she also works as an associate tutor for Bristol University's Post-Graduate Certificate in Education course. She currently works on a 'Raising Aspirations' programme designed to encourage pupils from schools serving socioeconomically deprived communities to consider reading history at university.

Michael Young, Emeritus Professor of Education at UCL's Institute of Education, is a sociologist and former chemistry teacher who works on knowledge and curriculum issues in education. He is the author of *Bringing Knowledge Back In* (2008), (with Johan Muller) *Knowledge, Expertise and the Professions* (2014), (with David Lambert) *Knowledge and the Future School* (Bloomsbury, 2014), and (also with Johan Muller) *Curriculum and the Specialisation of Knowledge* (2016). His current research is concerned with curriculum leadership in schools with Christine Counsell, Michael Fordham and Joanne Waterhouse and the education of engineers with David Guile.

Series Editor's Foreword

In this excellent volume there are perhaps three particularly interesting and impressive features. The first is a comprehensive and carefully crafted collection of eight expertly written chapters by teacher researchers addressing key issues in history education through enquiries emerging from their own classrooms. The second is that these teacher-authored chapters form part of a dialogue about history education with other high-profile professionals and academics who reflect on the themes emerging from the teacher-authored chapters, thus cleverly echoing and replicating the dialectical nature of the subject itself. Third, the three editors, all very well known and respected in History Education, use the final section to reflect on key themes evident throughout the book: (1) history education as education in a 'form of knowledge' and a call to strengthen this tradition; (2) history teachers and university-based history teacher educators working together as the foundation for effective teacher research in history education; and (3) the ways in which the present culture of genericism dilutes both disciplinary and substantive historical knowledge and threatens to distort the subject-specific professional knowledge of history teachers.

Part I thus presents the reader with an opportunity to engage with classroom-focused research in chapters written by teachers actively researching in the field. Refreshing in bringing to the fore through publication the excellent work being undertaken by teacher researchers, this part roots debates about history in the 'real world' of schools. These chapters are a much needed demonstration of the intellectual engagement that the best teachers bring to their teaching. Far from being simply part of a 'what works' debate, these chapters are clear evidence that teachers who bring critical engagement to the subject and curriculum through their research become leaders in the field. These are teachers who refuse to stop at simply being effective teachers; rather they seek to redefine 'effective' in order to move beyond a deadening compliance agenda to that of energetic curricular theorizing that will shape the future of history education. All the more exciting then is to have Part II constructed of reflections by national and international commentators whose academic and professional standing position them perfectly to identify and develop themes from Part I. In Part II, the debates from Part I are explored, and the interplay between history education and the wider contexts of history, education, curriculum and teacher research is made evident in eloquent and engaging chapters. As a reader, engaging with such powerful discussions is both a delight and a privilege. In Part III, the editors take up the baton of energetic debate with chapters both thought provoking and challenging and thus complete the subtly woven demand on the readers of this volume to be *part of the debate*. Readers of this book will find themselves irresistibly drawn into the arguments, and as with any 'good book', though perhaps rare even so, after reading the chapters will find those debates continuing in their heads, and perhaps their history departments, as part of a set of voices for whom history education is a live and crucial issue.

It is therefore a delight to have the History MasterClass as part of the series, and as series editor, my thanks to all contributors for an outstanding volume, and to the editors for shaping and bringing together such an important addition to the field of teaching and learning in history.

Sue Brindley
University of Cambridge Faculty of Education

Introduction

Christine Counsell, Katharine Burn and Arthur Chapman

The field of history education is increasingly enriched by a wealth of published, teacher-authored research. Through the journal *Teaching History*, in particular, it has been possible to cultivate, support and promote diverse innovation and reflection, research and debate, creating new conversations between teachers and scholars and advancing the role of history teacher as scholar. Through this creative cross-fertilization, over the last two decades, the editors of *Teaching History* have sought to disrupt the traditional scholar-practitioner divide in the interests of gathering together the voice of professional experience, the power of theory and the scrutiny of empirical research both to address long-standing problems in history education and to formulate securely founded responses to new policy initiatives.

The extent, range and quality of this teacher-authored research in history have been significantly strengthened by the growing numbers of teachers taking masters degrees, thereby enriching the pool of outstanding, research-active history teachers. More and more practicing history teachers are producing analyses of pupils' historical learning and new practice-led theorizing about history curriculum properties. The finest examples of such research increasingly take their place as important contributions to the published history education field.

When invited to produce a book for the MasterClass series, we therefore decided that there was no better way to support new masters students in history education than by showcasing extended examples of such research in action. The chapters by practitioner-researchers provide, quite literally, a 'masterclass' in how to do masters-level research. Some of our teacher authors present in detail the research processes leading to masters-level work that has already been published in a shorter form, others present new, post-masters research, while others share examples of the innovative enquiries that they regularly carry out, unrelated to formal qualifications. Across the collection, these teacher authors use diverse forms of empirical warrant. Moreover, through an initial literature review, each contribution is situated within this expanding scholarly field, thus providing for the future masters' student a stimulating gateway to existing works and diverse critical reflections on them.

International developments in history education are similarly rich in their research traditions, although no country other than England, to our knowledge, boasts such an extensive, subject-specific and influential tradition of history *teacher*-led published research and debate, forming a coherent, subject-based discourse that collectively builds an ever-changing, cumu-lative knowledge base for new history teachers. Our vision for this book was to bring the teacher-research tradition in England's history education field into critical conversation not only with history teachers from other countries but also with leading international scholars in history, in philosophy of history, in history education, in the field of teacher research itself and in the sociology of knowledge and curriculum.

Our book has three parts. Part I presents eight teacher-authored case studies of prac-titioner enquiry exploring diverse facets of history education. Some of these authors are already influential in the field of history education through other publications, while others are newcomers to the published field. Each has had to be selective in the features of their research that they present in depth; but across the book, the collection provides examples of different kinds of research questions and approaches, illustrating the development and deployment of various research strategies and methods, along with the analysis of data, pres-entation of findings and critical reflections on the process of researching practice.

In Part II, a variety of scholars act as discussants. These include practising history teachers who have been influential through research, publication, training or leadership. Each discus-sant provides a commentary on a different selection of three chapters from Part I, reflecting on the significance of these new works and relating them to their own specialist field. Part II thus fosters new conversations both among diverse history education experts and between history education experts and leading scholars in the fields of history, philosophy of history, teacher research and the sociology of education. By clustering the case studies in more than one way, we have allowed each case study to be considered within at least three discussions by experts with contrasting interests.

In Part III, the editors reflect on three broad areas that encompass the book's concerns. Arthur Chapman situates our teacher-authored research chapters in a wider tradition of research and practice focused on the development of children's understanding of history as a 'form of knowledge'. Katharine Burn considers how history teachers can most effectively learn, from the very beginning of their professional preparation, to embrace the dual per-spective of 'teacher as researcher'. Christine Counsell examines the vital role played by his-tory teachers' published discourse in renewing and mobilizing subject-specific professional knowledge in a culture of genericism.

Our book is thus designed both as an introductory reader for specialist history teachers tackling work at masters level and – given its new empirical and theoretical work and its dialogic structure – as a stimulating and informative reader for all history teachers, at any stage of their careers, for scholars with an interest in the field of history education, for policymakers and for many other stakeholders. Above all, we hope it will be an invaluable volume for any history teacher involved in mentoring, training, leading or supporting the development of other history teachers. Our aim is to celebrate a published conversation already taking place and to stimulate its renewal in the interest of improving the quality of the history education that students receive in schools.

Part I

Researching History Education

Historical Change: In Search of Argument

Rachel Foster

1

'There was some change . . .'

It was with some trepidation that I sat down to mark my set of AS history essays.[1] The question seemed straightforward. It required students to address the extent and nature of change in African Americans' lives during World War II. Over the course of teaching the lesson sequence I had grown increasingly uneasy as I became aware of my own uncertainty about how to construct an *argument* about change. Unlike the familiar products of students' causal arguments (e.g. Woodcock, 2005), the end product of an argument about change remained hard to envision. I had therefore turned to strategies tried and tested by the growing number of history teachers who have sought to help students to problematize historical change: graphs and scales to force students to take a position between two opposing viewpoints (Fordham,

2012); picture sorting (Dawson, 2004); word banks of analytical vocabulary to enable students to nuance their own analyses (Jarman, 2009; Counsell, 2011b; Fordham, 2012); and reading academic historians (Hammond, 2007; Jones, 2009) to help them to situate their arguments within historiographical debate.

My students' essays left me disheartened. The question (How far did African Americans remain second-class citizens by 1945?) concerned both the extent and nature of diversity *and* change. Most students began to analyse diversity using criteria of geography, class and gender but their analysis of change was limited to simplistic descriptions of what changed and for whom. Lauren wrote:

> In terms of political status in the south, there was some change during the war, for example before the war less than two per cent of the black population could vote, however by 1945 15% of the black population had been registered to vote which is a massive increase of 13%.[2]

The phrase 'some change' was particularly dispiriting. It was devoid of any analytic precision or power. Yet I had used every strategy I knew to encourage students to argue about change with precise and nuanced judgement. What had gone wrong?

A closer evaluation of students' essays suggested two related problems: a lack of any criteria by which to evaluate the extent and nature of change and a failure to deploy the analytic vocabulary provided. Inevitably, their essays collapsed into the problem that Counsell (2011c) identified – descriptive lists. But although the analytical shortcomings were clear, I could not articulate how students could develop their analysis. It was this need to theorize for myself what argument about change and continuity looks like that gave rise to my desire to experiment with ways to help students *see* the argument for themselves.

Literature review

Developments and debates concerning historical change in the history education community

For Counsell, change and continuity are 'elusive prey' (2011c, p. 107). Compared with causation, there is relatively little theorizing among history teachers about what constitutes a 'proper' change and continuity question, what it means to think historically about change, what a satisfactory answer to a question concerning change looks like, and how students can get better at analysing it (Jarman, 2009).

This uncertainty was exemplified in the treatment of change within England's 2008 National Curriculum (NC, 2008), which treated it simultaneously as a property of substantive knowledge – 'understanding of change is closely linked to a sense of period and an understanding of overarching themes and issues' (QCA/DCSF 2007) – and as a second-order concept to be problematized – 'Pupils should analyse the extent and pace of change, whether the change amounted to progress and for whom.' This duality is reflected in practitioner literature, within which three loose traditions can be identified.

One tradition, influential in the United Kingdom, particularly after England's 2008 NC was structured more explicitly than before around thematic narratives (QCA/DCSF, 2007), was articulated chiefly by Dawson (2004, 2008, 2009), whose work influenced Philpott (2008). Only implicitly concerned with the concept of change, Dawson's goal is the development of chronologically structured knowledge rendered coherent through pre-planned 'thematic stories' (Dawson, 2008). He sometimes calls this 'chronological understanding' (Dawson, 2004) and has attempted to link it to 'sense of period' (Dawson, 2009). Dawson's goal is essentially substantive: the construction and retention of meaningful historical narratives. Although Barnes (2002), Gadd (2009), Jones (2009) and Fordham (2012) share Dawson's goal of constructing and retaining meaningful overviews or narratives of long-term change, they treat narrative construction as a means of moving students into conceptual analysis by problematizing patterns of change and thereby keeping narrative possibilities open. Indeed, Jones (2009) has criticized Dawson's use of thematic stories as being too deterministic, and Howson (2009) has criticized him for not attending to conceptual development at all. For Dawson, the concept of change seems to be of interest only insofar as the construction of a framework of knowledge involves identifying similarities and differences between points in time. Although Dawson acknowledges that constructing stories is essentially an interpretative act, he is not (in his three articles on chronology) explicitly concerned with students' conceptual understanding of change, nor with any associated processes of reasoning about it. Thus while students are expected to identify, explain and connect changes, they are not required to problematize change as a concept nor build arguments using it.

A second tradition has been grounded in empirical investigation into children's conceptualizations of history. Its goals are superficially similar to Dawson's: its advocates share his concern with the development of meaningful frameworks (Lee, 1991, 2004; Shemilt, 2000, 2009; Howson, 2007, 2009; Howson and Shemilt, 2011), but whereas Dawson's approach is grounded in substantive knowledge (Howson, 2009), these researchers define frameworks as provisional factual scaffolds that are adaptive to students' changing constructions of the past (Howson and Shemilt, 2011). Their frameworks have a completely different purpose. Significantly, they argue that frameworks are modified not just by the acquisition of new knowledge, but by shifts in conceptual understanding. They therefore pay close attention to students' historical consciousness, defining progression as 'the acquisition of more powerful ideas' (Lee and Shemilt, 2003, p. 15). In particular, Lee (2005b) and Blow (2011a) have sought to define what student progression in conceptual ideas about change might look like. They have thus built on the much earlier work on change rooted in the early formulation and evaluation of the Schools Council History Project (SCHP) (Shemilt, 1980).[3] Arguing that basic, 'everyday' conceptions of change tend to be based on its construal as episodic, intentional events that punctuate periods in which 'nothing happens', their models of progressively more powerful ideas about change attach value to students' recognition that change and continuity interact and that these interactions form a process in which patterns of change (or development) can be discerned. For Blow (2011a), the most powerful conception of change is one that recognizes change and continuity as theoretical constructs and that treats any claim about the nature of change as an interpretative act. Some practitioners have sought to translate aspects of these concerns into practical teaching strategies. Jarman (2009), Jones (2009) Fordham (2012) and Murray et al. (2013) seek explicitly to change their students' conceptions of change, most notably by developing an understanding that change is a process rather than an event. For these practitioners, changing students' conceptual understanding is one of several goals. For Rogers (2008, 2011), however, it is the primary goal. Through the use of topic-based frameworks (2008) and causation maps (also applicable to change questions) Rogers seeks to develop students' awareness of the past as a continuum in which the interplay between change and continuity shapes patterns of change.

A third tradition is concerned less with students' ideas about historical change than with the kind of analysis they should be doing when addressing a question about change. While both the 2008 and the 2014 NCs in England have enshrined an analytical imperative by explicitly referring to the need to 'analyse' in relation to change, neither document defines what constitutes an analysis of change, nor offers a model of how students might get better at it (QCA/DCSF, 2007; DfE, 2013). This haziness is echoed in current curricular and assessment arrangements for 14–19-year-olds in England, Wales and Northern Ireland. These demand analysis of the extent and nature of change without offering a model of what constitutes lower- or higher-order analysis. Perhaps because of this, there is a burgeoning literature by history teachers seeking to theorize what it means for pupils to argue and to think analytically about historical change. Because they seek to problematize it, they take apart the idea of 'change' in order to define more precisely the analytical thinking that it enshrines. One such approach involves the isolation and definition of the constituent properties of change. Those most frequently referenced are extent, nature, direction and pace (Barnes, 2002; Foster, 2008; Jenner, 2010; Counsell, 2011b; Fordham, 2012). The practice and concerns of practitioners diverge, however, regarding the forms of analysis associated with these. The difficulty of thinking and writing about change is shown in Jarman's (2009) work. Wanting his students to explain change, he acknowledges that this frequently tipped them into *causal* analysis at the expense of characterizing the process of change itself. Other practitioners have sought alternative forms of analysis. Barnes and Jenner want their students to make a judgement about the nature, extent and rate of change, although Barnes conflates change with progress. However, while Barnes is concerned with his pupils' *identification* of patterns and processes, Fordham and Foster want their students to *characterize* the nature of change. Although suggestive of description, 'characterization' of change could be deemed analytical. Murray et al. (2013) are similarly concerned with students engaging in an analytic activity of 'characterizing', but with a special focus on continuity. Yet, like Fordham (2012), Murray et al. also lay stress on secure substantive knowledge interacting with successful analysis of change/continuity. Working to create an 'ever-expanding frame' of knowledge reference, they argue that explicit effort to analyse continuity across several centuries also sees pupils relating 'new knowledge to their previously embedded chronological frameworks' (Murray et al., 2013, p. 54). Palek (2013) explores his students' accomplishment in linking two second-order concepts – change and diversity – and thereby develops a new curricular goal, 'diachronic diversity'.

Other teacher efforts to develop the curricular power of historical change have focused on ascribed significance (both contemporary experiences and subsequent perceptions). Banham (2000), Barnes (2002) and Jarman (2009) share an analytical goal of judging the *significance* of change, whether through an appraisal of turning points (Banham, Barnes), determining the extent and nature of progress (Barnes), or through analysing the historical significance of change within its broader context (Jarman). In contrast, Jones (2009) and Counsell (2011b) promote sensitivity to people's subjective experience of temporality *in the past*, arguing that students need to consider how people in the past might have experienced change or built temporally construed meaning about their own past, present and future.

Some insights from the practice of professional historians

The recent proliferation of professional discourse seeking to theorize what it means to analyse historical change underscores the lack of shared professional reference points regarding the kinds of reasoning that such a question entails (Counsell, 2011c). There may also be lingering, latent uncertainty among history teachers concerning whether causal explanation should be the more important and perhaps ultimate accomplishment of all historical thinking and writing. Jarman (2009) has wrestled with the dilemmas that this creates. Acknowledging that his students were diverted from analysing change into a causal analysis of *why* change occurred, he argues, 'the nature of the essay task gets in the way of considering change directly; an essay is by its nature an explanatory medium and this implies some focus on causation.' The implication of his argument is troubling: that the very nature of the traditional school history essay impedes if not precludes an analysis of change.

This argument may have roots in the privileged place accorded to the task of explanation in historical thinking and writing. As Megill (2007) has argued, until as recently as the 1980s, many professional historians regarded 'explanation' (defined by Megill as the explanation of causes) as the central task of historical writing. Notoriously, Carr (1961, p. 81) went so far as to argue, 'the study of history is a study of causes'. The assumption that analysis is concerned with explanation meant that the task of description (often associated with narrative) could be denigrated as a lower order of thinking. Underlying this belief was a set of assumptions about what constituted a proper historical question. Thus Braudel's *Mediterranean and the Mediterranean World in the Age of Philip II* (1972), which addressed not a problem of causation but of change ('the only problem I had to resolve, was to show that time moves at different speeds' [Braudel, cited in Burke, 1990, p. 33]) was criticized by a reviewer as 'painfully lacking in "proper historical questions"' (Bailyn, cited in Megill, 2007, p. 102). Although this view was increasingly challenged in the 1990s by the growing influence and prominence of 'new cultural history' with its emphasis on 'thick description' (Megill, 2007), the idea that the primary purpose of historical writing is explanation still holds sway, and certainly so within school history discourse. Whereas within the Programme of Study of England's NC 2008, explanation and description were given equal status: 'Pupils . . . provide well-structured narratives, explanations and descriptions of the past' (QCA/DCSF, 2007), within the NC 2008 Attainment Target, 'description' was deemed lower level than 'analysis' and 'explanation' (ibid.). The privileging of explanation over description is also enshrined in England's General Certification of Secondary Education (GCSE) and the General Certificate of Education (GCE) subject criteria (Ofqual, 2011, 2012).[4] Megill's argument that analysis can occur in the context of description appears to have little resonance in most school history discourse. While several practitioners at Key Stage 3 (e.g. Barnes, 2002; Foster, 2008; Jones, 2009; Fordham, 2012) do regard analytic description as a legitimate goal of historical writing about change, not since Shemilt's (1980) theorizing on the earliest candidates for Schools History Project (SHP) examinations in the 1970s has there been any published theorizing about change as an assessed attribute in 16+ examinations and beyond.

Research design

Rationale for the investigation

Unclear about what constitutes analysis in a written argument about change, I wanted to theorize both the form that such analysis might take and its means of nurture. This theorizing began with my own planning and teaching of an enquiry (Riley, 2000) in the form of a lesson sequence for a Year 12 class of 18 students studying the US Civil Rights movement. This would then form the setting in which I could investigate qualities in students' thinking about change. With this goal in mind, I developed the following research question:

> *What properties in students' thinking about change and continuity were manifested in students'*
> *written work?*

Constructing the enquiry: some underlying principles

The theorization process began at the planning stage. It was informed by three broad principles.

The historiographical debate foregrounded in the enquiry

I first sought a model in academic historians' work. I did not necessarily intend to use historians' work as a model for students' *own* writing (already explored by practitioners such as Counsell (2004b) and Ward (2006)); rather, I was searching for an analytical language and discourse around which I could build a pedagogical strategy. In their historical surveys of the African American freedom struggle from Reconstruction to the early twenty-first century, both Fairclough (2002) and Tuck (2010) analyse the extent and nature of change. They write in a lively, accessible style that makes its use in the classroom not only feasible but advantageous.

Both Fairclough and Tuck make explicit the difficulty of evaluating the *extent* of change in race relations during the 1950s: that there was simultaneously progression, regression *and* continuity. The debate seems to lie in the characterization of the *overall* direction of change. Structuring the enquiry around this real debate would necessitate students' engagement with it.

I sought to foreground this debate by crafting an 'enquiry question' (Riley, 2000) that explicitly problematized the direction of change. I initially considered basing the question on Fairclough's chapter heading: 'How far were the 1950s "one step forward and two steps back" for African Americans?' Fairclough's analogy encapsulated an argument regarding the *direction* of change and the *process* by which it occurred. I wanted students to analyse the *nature* of change, however, and the question, while addressing progress, did not do this. Reading Tuck and Fairclough, I had been struck by the temporal dimension of their analysis, in particular the distinction that they make between experiences of change at the time and subsequent analyses of its significance. Their characterization of perceptible, tangible change and imperceptible yet potent change clearly constituted an argument about the nature of change. Why not use their analysis to drive the students' entire enquiry? In light of this, I refined the enquiry question into: 'What kinds of change could African Americans *see* in the 1950s?'

In order to introduce notions of perceptible and imperceptible change, in the substantive content of the enquiry I distinguished between 'trends' and 'events'. The first two lessons, as shown in Table 1.1, addressed cultural, economic and social 'trends'; the next two lessons focused on political, legal and social 'events'. The final lesson prepared for an essay responding to Fairclough's claim: 'One step forward, two steps back.' How far do you agree with this view of the improvement in African Americans' condition between 1945 and 1955? Andrews (1995) argues that students often fail to conceptualize argument as dialogic. As other history teachers have found, asking students to respond to an historian's claim (Fordham, 2007; Richards, 2012) can encourage them to enter the debate.

Metaphors were used as a means of conceptualizing change

The enquiry question had a strong analytic imperative but I judged that unless students could *see* the argument, they might not engage meaningfully with it. Mindful of Woodcock's (2005) argument about the interrelationship between the linguistic and the conceptual and given that my earlier efforts to introduce analytical 'change' vocabulary had had little discernible effect, I sought to help students to conceptualize change meaningfully, and to express that conceptualization more clearly in their writing. Counsell (2011c) and Fordham (2012) have emphasized the power of metaphors. Having already tentatively explored their use (Foster, 2008), I now experimented with them again. Finding the right metaphors would be crucial. A poorly conceived metaphor can impede analysis. It might encourage the distortion of events to make them fit the metaphor. It might offer weak analytic power. In the first instance (Lesson 2), I borrowed Fairclough's metaphor of a milestone to examine the nature of change resulting from Truman's presidency. By considering the function of milestones (e.g. to mark the distance travelled; to indicate future direction), students explored what kind of change *To Secure These Rights* brought.

Table 1.1 Enquiry outline

Enquiry question:	What change could African Americans see between 1945 and 1955?	
Lesson question	**Aims and objectives**	**Activities addressing change and continuity**
Lesson 1: How far did the social and economic climate change for African Americans after 1945?	• Describe and characterize the nature of the changes and continuities. • Judge the significance of the changes.	• Braudel-style waves diagram – categorization of changes and continuities into underlying trends and events.
Lesson 2: What kind of milestone was *To Secure These Rights?*	• Analyse motives for introducing reform. • Evaluate the radicality of the reforms. • Characterize the nature of change.	• Table: assessment of the radicality of each reform. • Conclusion: graph showing lines of development; students argue which line best represents the progress made.
Lesson 3: What was the most effective way of challenging Jim Crow 1945–55?	• Categorize the strategies used to challenge Jim Crow. • Evaluate the degree and nature of the campaigns' impact. • Characterize the nature of the change.	• Note-taking: assessment of the impact made by legal action and direction action. • Conclusion: Choose and improve from a range of possible conclusions.
Lesson 4: What kind of change was the 'Brown' ruling?	• Analyse the results of the Brown ruling. • Characterize the nature of the outcomes. • Judge the degree and nature of change.	• Card sort: impacts of the Brown ruling (positive/negative; short term/long term; symbolic/practical; latent/manifest). • Weather metaphor: debate the nature of change. • Conclusion: analytical word bank used to characterize the nature of change.
Lesson 5: What kind of change could African Americans see between 1945 and 1955?	• Analyse and characterize the nature and degree of change.	• Revision of Braudel wave diagram. • Card sort: trends and events plotted onto the 'wave diagram' to show changes and continuities. • Living graph: living graph created to show extent and nature of change. • Conclusion: analytical word bank used to characterize the nature of change. Final essay set.

In the second instance (Lessons 1 and 5), I wanted to address the *perceptibility* of change. Although concerned with much longer spans of time, Braudel's comparison of the history of events to 'surface disturbances, crests of foam that the tides of history carry on their strong backs' offered a useful picture of different types of change. It contrasted the visible, ephemeral, transitory movement of a wave with the underlying, imperceptible yet powerful movement of tides and currents. I wanted to see if Braudel's imagery could help students explore the relationship between more noticeable legal and political events (e.g. Supreme Court judgements) and longer-term socioeconomic and cultural trends (e.g. the Cold War).

Introduced in Lesson 1, students used their prior knowledge to assess the extent and visibility of change during the 1930s and World War II. At the conclusion of the enquiry students also positioned changes and continuities chronologically on a 'waves' diagram (see Figure 1.1 and Table 1.2), judging whether they constituted an event or a trend and the extent and direction of change they engendered. Table 1.2 gives a sample of the cards depicting changes and continuities that students were asked to position on the waves.

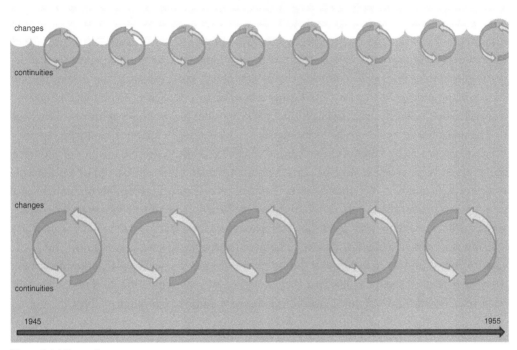

What kind of change did African Americans <u>see</u> between 1945 and 1955?

Figure 1.1 Waves diagram

Table 1.2 Sample of cards plotted on the waves diagram

From 1954, southern whites set up White Citizens' Councils to resist desegregation. 250,000 whites joined. They advocated 'Massive Resistance' to desegregation.	Black confidence continued to grow, as they realized that the Federal Government was showing sympathy towards them.	1947 *To Secure These Rights* was published. The report highlighted the huge discrimination African Americans faced and suggested radical proposals for ending inequality.	*Brown v. Board of Education of Topeka* (1954) declared that segregation in education was illegal.
1948 Executive Order 9981 guaranteed equality of treatment and opportunity in the armed forces.	The Cold War led to the persecution of any individuals or groups seen to have Communist sympathies. The FBI targeted civil rights organizations in particular.	Rapid urbanization continued in the North and South, meaning that fewer than 30% of black southerners lived in rural areas by 1960.	The number of African Americans registered to vote in the South grew from a few thousand to about 1 million.

Table 1.3 Bank of analytic words

symbolic	explosive	negligible	radical
embryonic	steady	profound	superficial
theoretical	latent	practical	overt
temporary	momentary	enduring	imperceptible

Finally, I wanted a metaphor that would help students to encapsulate and conceptualize the nature and experience of change resulting from an 'event'. Reflecting with a colleague, I began exploring how, within physical geography, change in the physical landscape is conceptualized as both event and process. I noticed that when explaining how change occurs in a landscape, geographers were seemingly concerned with describing and explaining the extent, nature, duration and process of change. Could geographical processes such as a volcano, coastal erosion, glaciation, a flood or blizzard help students to consider the processes of historical change?

The metaphor of a volcanic explosion represented a long-term but not necessarily perceptible change followed by a highly visible, explosive change. It also suggested the idea of enduring and profound change; the landscape is often permanently and radically altered by a major volcanic event. In contrast, glacial erosion represented underlying, imperceptible but nonetheless profound and enduring change. It also hinted at the idea of fluctuating change: glacial erosion varies as the glacier ebbs and flows. The metaphors were introduced in the final lesson, when students were shown images of a glacier, coastal erosion, a flash flood, a snowstorm and a volcanic explosion and asked to consider the *processes* and *outcomes* of change that they described. They then selected the metaphor that they thought best represented the kind of change that occurred following the Supreme Court ruling *Brown* v. *Board of Education of Topeka*.

Harnessing the power of analytic vocabulary

However useful metaphors might be in developing a better understanding of complex patterns of change and a more nuanced analysis of those patterns, students must still go back into the abstract in order to express such analysis. I therefore re-introduced analytical 'change' vocabulary, shown in Table 1.3, following the evaluation of the metaphors. In contrast with Woodcock's (2005) approach, I judged that in this instance the vocabulary might be more effective in strengthening their analyses if it expressed an understanding that they had *already* developed.

Nature of the research

The purpose of my research was descriptive and exploratory. I needed to engage in interpretation in order to discern and elucidate students' meaning-making (Crotty, 1998). I wanted to characterize the forms of reasoning in which students were beginning to engage so that I could define for myself the constituent properties of an analysis of change and continuity.

As a teacher researching my own practice, I was therefore of necessity using aspects of my own subjectivity in order to enquire into my object (Counsell, 2009a). Any meanings I discerned would be constructed out of an interaction between myself as subject and my students as object. The nature of the investigation – its context, the kind of phenomena under investigation and the kinds of knowledge being sought – therefore placed the research firmly within a constructionist epistemology (Crotty, 1998) and invited an interpretivist methodology.

The context of the investigation (a study localized in time and space) and its nature (naturalistic, descriptive) made the research fit Bassey's (1999) and Stake's (2005) criteria for a case study. It became an 'intrinsic case study' because the case was studied for its own sake. Rather than allowing me to generalize about wider teaching practice or student learning, the case could only point to possibilities or raise questions for future curricular and pedagogic theorizing.

Although it draws on elements from grounded theory and phenomenology, because of my concern with interpretation of meaning, the label 'hermeneutics' captures my approach most closely (Baronov, 2004). The hermeneutic circle, whereby parts and whole are continually reviewed in the light of each other, offered a holistic approach to data analysis, with its emphasis on close, iterative readings and the weighing of my own judgements in light of subsequent readings. It also allowed for my involvement as subject in the interpretation process, my concern to stay responsive to the data and to allow it to interact with my meaning-making process, my openness about the need to *construct* meaning and the need to make all this as transparent as possible.

Data collection

The data were generated naturally in the course of planning and teaching. In selecting ten students' essays for analysis I did not identify students who could be considered either representative of the class, nor of the general population, but sought a balance of gender and attainment, taking into account performance at GCSE, as well as their attendance record.

Methods of analysis

I planned to represent my findings as analytic themes (Boyatzis, 1998). Influenced to some extent by the system and transparency of grounded theory wherein the text is divided into discrete units of meaning that are first summarized (codes) before being translated into descriptions of their meaning (themes), I nonetheless judged that the process of fragmentation required by coding can result in losing the authentic meaning of the whole. Van Manen's (1990) hermeneutical, phenomenological approach is also systematic and transparent, yet acknowledges the creative, interpretative aspects of the analytic process. Crucially, his approach seemed to me to allow for reflection on the students' texts as a whole rather than as collections of atomized units of meaning. Van Manen suggests three ways in which themes can be isolated: the holistic approach (VM1), in which the text is taken as a whole; the selective approach (VM2), in which essential or revealing phrases are isolated; and the line-by-line approach (VM3) in which individual sentences are analysed. In order to discipline my reading process while preserving the meaning of the whole, I used both VM1 and VM2 analysis. Drawing selectively from processes in grounded theory, I developed initial codes when undertaking VM2 analysis as a way of creating a chain of evidence from the data to my themes. But rather than rigidly apply these processes to the data, I used them within the context of writing memos, as a tool to aid reflection. Writing memos helped establish connections between the data (Altrichter et al., 1993) and prompted me to think about the data abstractly (Charmaz, 2006), disciplining my analysis without inhibiting my ability to find meaning in the data as a whole. They also helped to establish transparency by keeping the role of my own subjectivity – as involved teacher with close knowledge of the students and the context – near the surface of my analysis and by showing the *process* by which analytic themes were derived from the data (Yin, 2003).

Findings

What properties in students' thinking about change and continuity were manifested in their written work?

Ideas generated from an initial holistic (VM1) reading of the data lacked analytical precision. I therefore re-read the data selectively (VM2), developing initial descriptive codes that remained close to the data, as shown in Table 1.4.

Table 1.4 Initial descriptive codes

Experience of change
Psychological/interior change
'Size' of the change
Pace of change
Visibility of change
Change as a process (e.g. describing *how* a change occurred)
Awareness of temporal dimension to judgements about change
Uses diversity as a criterion with which to assess the significance of change
Awareness that change can be progressive and regressive
Awareness of multifaceted nature of change (e.g. that a change can be both progressive and regressive)

Seeking to discern preliminary themes, I wrote a memo, then re-read the data holistically with these preliminary themes in mind, testing and refining them. From this iterative process of reflection three analytic themes emerged.

Theme 1: Reflection upon the direction and dynamism of change and continuity

All students showed awareness that change could be either progressive or regressive. While Hazel and Anna simply described change that they deemed 'positive' or 'negative', most justified their judgements by using criteria to characterize its nature, as will be discussed below. Some seemed to recognize that the direction of change could be multidimensional. This was most often manifested in descriptions of both the positive and negative nature of change, exemplified in Eden's description of the Brown ruling:

> Although the principal 'separate but equal' was stated as un-constitutional by the Supreme Court and that segregation in education was made illegal, the southern states ignored the ruling and the Supreme Court did nothing to uphold their decision. The response from anti-equality whites brought about negative change, one of these was the revival in Ku Klux Klan activity . . . Therefore any progress that was made was shadowed by negative change brought about as a reaction to this challenge of segregation.

Others sought to analyse the nature of the duality. Hazel, after critiquing the limitations of the Brown ruling, characterized its positive effects: 'the Brown case was highly symbolic because it showed that the Supreme Court was sympathetic to the civil rights cause.' Finn's response, 'to begin with the acts had positive affects, but then eventually grew into negativity and more powerful segregation', suggests an implicit awareness that the direction of change is dynamic and in continual flux. This awareness was shared by Jesse and Lauren, manifested in their descriptions of the pace of change. Lauren used pace to evaluate the significance of change: 'Urbanisation had been happening at a steady pace before this time, so this was not a radical change. It is however a profound change in that there is a high increase in the amount of people who were migrating from the "rural peasantry to the urban proletariat."' She also used pace when judging the extent and nature of change across the whole period:

> As to whether Fairclough's view of 'one step forward, two steps back' for the decade 1945 to 1955 is actually proved by the facts is another matter. The correct saying should be 'two steps forward, two steps back, one step forward.' This is because the actual evidence proves that it is a lot more complicated and although they managed a great number of victories in principle, in practice these were shunned by the white authorities of the states and even by members of the government.

Lauren's adaptation of Fairclough's judgement suggests that she conceptualizes change not just as an outcome (what changed) but as a process (how things changed).

Fewer students addressed the extent or nature of continuity, and more often described continuities rather than analysing their extent or nature. Frank, having discussed positive changes resulting from World War II, then proceeded to address continuities as a way of evaluating the extent of change: 'However, at the end of the Second World War social conditions in America still remained pretty poor for African Americans throughout the southern states, where segregation remained throughout.' By implicitly considering how a change could appear, at the time, to be a continuity: 'Legal segregation had made a positive but unnoticeable change in African Americans' lives and I think the change will become more noticeable when whites' attitudes had changed', Olive also demonstrated an implicit concern with continuity.

Theme 2: Use of criteria to make judgements about the significance of change

All students used criteria to describe or characterize the significance of change. Judgements about significance (in the sense both of importance and of meaning) encompassed both the extent and the nature of change. To characterize the types of criteria deployed, I re-read the data with my initial descriptive codes in mind, selectively reading highlighted data to see if new patterns emerged. Subsequently I wrote another reflective memo, out of which three sub-themes emerged.

The first type of criterion concerned the *tangibility of the change* (in the sense of being available to the senses). This was suggested by references to the ways in which change *appeared* to contemporaries (the extent to which change was *visible* to and *experienced* by contemporaries); the extent to which change was *concrete* or *outward* or *imperceptible* or *interior*; and the extent to which it held *symbolic* significance. This criterion was most often manifested in references to interior or psychological change. Most students, such as Frank, described changes in African American attitudes: 'After fighting in Europe they were being treated like heroes in Europe. This did a lot to the mind set of African Americans after the war.' Eden and Olive were more precise in their analysis. For example, Eden used vocabulary ('confidence', 'hope' and 'reassurance') to evaluate the significance of events by assessing the extent to which they resulted in both concrete and psychological change: 'Likewise other attempts to force southern states to comply with the Supreme Court's rulings failed, however it still gave African Americans hope as they realized that the Supreme Court was developing sympathy towards their situation.'

Others distinguished between 'practical' and 'theoretical' change. Katy used this vocabulary in her argument when discussing the significance of the *Smith* v. *Allwright* ruling:

> In theory the changes seemed a lot more significant and positive than they actually turned out to be in practise . . . This sounds really good in theory because it gives African Americans the right to vote [in primary elections] which moves their political status up quite a bit. However it didn't quite work out like that, whites did as much as they could to prevent this from happening without actually saying no, you can't.

Few explicitly addressed the contemporary appearance of change by examining the ways in which change was visible to and experienced by contemporaries. One student who did so was Anli. Discussing urbanization she concluded:

> Life in the South was steadily beginning to improve, yet this change was certainly hidden. As well as physical changes to the environment, African Americans' expectations of improved conditions had begun to develop after the war.

Anli also used African Americans' perception of change as a criterion for judging significance: 'The Montgomery bus boycott is what I consider to be a prime example of apparently dramatic changes, which were actually superficial and possibly disappointing.' She seems implicitly to distinguish between how change initially appeared to contemporaries and subsequent interpretations of its significance. Similarly Frank also distinguished between apparently insignificant change to contemporaries and his own interpretation of its significance: 'Although these changes probably would have been viewed by African Americans as insignificant it was improving their education which in the long run would improve what kind of job they could get and the amount they are paid.' Frank was one of the few students to address the symbolic significance of change, suggested by his comment that, 'Truman's decision to desegregate the army did a great deal to African Americans social standing as the American army was held in high regard throughout the country.'

The second type of criterion I called the *longevity of the change*. This was manifested in comments on the extent to which change was enduring and the extent to which the impact of change fluctuates over time. Eden and Olive used the criterion of endurance to evaluate significance, as implied by Eden's assessment of the FEPC: 'The idea of this would have brought huge change in practice but in reality the idea brought about momentary change.' Discussing how World War II changed attitudes, Olive argued, 'this change had huge potential; however, there were still too many racists that opposed desegregation . . . Therefore the change was quite temporary and although it improved immediately after the war, it still didn't stick.' Only Olive and Finn assessed how the impact of a change could fluctuate over the short and long term. Regarding the significance of Executive Order 9980, Finn argued, 'this enabled Blacks to be able to get more authoritative jobs such as a lawyer or a job relating to politics, meaning that in the long term they could affect the government and most importantly change the rules of segregation.' Although his judgement is simplistic and deterministic, nevertheless Finn displays appreciation of how a change could be insignificant in the short term but become more significant in the long term. Lauren's analysis was more developed, using the criterion of longevity to compare the significance of different kinds of change: 'The change that they then try to implement with urbanisation is momentary compared to the enduring financial uncertainties that they face whether they are in rural areas or urban areas.'

The third type of criterion, *scale and scope of change,* has potential connection with Palek's (2013) work on explicit interplay of change and diversity. It concerned efforts to measure extent of change by reference to those affected. This mostly took the form of an implicit distinction between universal change (such as a change in the law) and change selectively experienced. For example, Lauren used scope and scale to compare the relative significance of two changes:

> However, this ruling [*Sweatt* v. *Painter*] was for just an undergraduate student who wanted to study law. It did not change the entire school education system, whereas the Brown ruling tried to change the whole system for every school child. Although this did not happen as the NAACP wanted, the Brown case was still a significant victory, as it marks the end of 'separate but equal'.

Theme 3: Awareness that judgements about significance are ascribed and therefore dependent on temporal standpoints

Holistically reading students' essays, I was struck by the frequent attempts made to distinguish between their own perceptions and those of contemporaries. Although none explicitly acknowledged the influence of temporal standpoint on perceptions of change, the contrast some made between contemporaries' perceptions and their own suggests awareness of the ascribed nature of their judgements. At its most simplistic, this awareness was indicated by Katy's use of 'seemed' to describe change: 'the ruling sounded good . . . this may seem good at first'. The words 'sounded' and 'seemed' suggest an appreciation of how changes were perceived. Finn began to use this appreciation to make claims about significance. Arguing that changing ideas about race represented a significant change in African Americans' status, he qualifies his claim by characterizing the change as 'quite a theoretical change, as most did not see it happening, especially those blacks that lived in the South'. Olive, explicitly using her own standpoint to challenge the validity of contemporary judgements, constructed a more developed analysis:

> Economically, things seem to have grown worse for African Americans at the time of 1955. For example, as Fairclough explains, 'blacks were still largely excluded from manufacturing jobs and confined to low paid work.' This indicates that nothing had changed in terms of economic status. Despite in some areas, particularly the southern states, seeing a change, as their economic status improved, white Americans put up more resistance because there was still a huge amount of racism. This evidentially made the change in economic status damaging at the time and could be seen as a step back in the civil rights struggle, however, I think it could also be argued as a latent change because if the economic status improved this is an improvement.

Although she struggles to justify her judgement of economic change as latent progress, she appears to reflect critically upon the limitations of contemporary perspectives on change.

Discussion and recommendations

Through the data analysis process, three key reflective points emerged:

1. The end product of students' thinking, an essay, while essentially descriptive rather than explanatory, was nonetheless analytical insofar as students were discerning and characterizing *patterns* of change.

2. Students' analysis of patterns was characterized by discussion of the *interplay* between different properties and facets of change.

3. It was through their analysis of the interplay between different properties and facets of change that students began to construct an *argument* about change.

Students' essays could best be characterized as 'thick' descriptions: telling what was the case (Megill, 2007). Although they did display some elements of narrative – such as concern with character and setting – their essays did not take narrative's traditional form because they were not organized 'in a chronologically sequenced order' (Stone, cited in Megill, 2007, p. 94). They could be considered analytic because they were perspectival (they are not a 'neutral' act of data collection) and sought to describe patterns of change and were thus concerned with ascribing meaning. They are not 'mere' descriptions. While some history teachers recognize description as a legitimate task of historical writing (Barnes, 2002; Fordham, 2012), there remains a strong bias towards explanation, particularly in prescribed curricula and examinations (QCA/DCSF, 2007; Ofqual, 2011; 2012). This assumption that description is a lower order of thinking has perhaps limited teacher discourse about the constituent qualities of an analytic description and how these can be taught. A useful goal for future history teacher research might therefore be the theorization of such qualities.

Students explored *properties* of change (rate, pace, extent, nature) in their analysis and its different *facets* – its appearance and ascribed qualities. This was manifested in discussion of the perceptibility, perceived symbolism and significance, and changing interpretations of change. In their pattern-making, students seemed to treat these abstract conceptual properties and facets as 'strands': continuums within which they could situate a change in order to evaluate its nature. The main 'strands' were: change/continuity; positive/negative; perceptible/imperceptible; enduring/momentary; and theoretical/practical. At its simplest, each strand was treated as a dichotomous scale, with change situated on a single point along it. Marin and Hazel seemingly did this when they sought to judge whether change was positive *or* negative. More sophisticated analyses recognized that the ends of each strand could co-exist (Blow, 2011a), with interplay between them. This was implied in descriptions of change as simultaneously positive and negative, or by deploying different temporal standpoints to explore the changing significance of a development. Some students did not simply treat properties and facets in isolation, however, but interwove them by exploring their interplay. Eden seemed to do this when she characterized the creation of the Fair Employment Practices Committee (FEPC) as being a significant change in terms of the practical benefits that resulted from it but insignificant in terms of the enduring change that resulted. In doing so, she described complex, multi-stranded patterns of change. Jones sought to enable his students to construct a 'multi-stranded narrative of change' (2009, p. 20); in this instance a few students were constructing a multi-stranded *analysis*.

Existing history education literature often privileges the identification and explanation of patterns (Jones, 2009; Blow, 2011a; Howson and Shemilt, 2011). Some of this work appears to convey the implicit assumption that patterns are substantive, even if a more sophisticated conceptual understanding is needed in order to construct them or to render the patterning discursively explicit in particular ways. My findings suggest that while the patterns students described were substantive, they were also consciously conceptual because they were describing abstract properties of conceptual schema. In doing so, they drew upon a wide range of properties (e.g. Olive used properties of progress and visibility to judge the significance of economic change). This suggests that the focus of existing literature on conceptualizing change in terms of pace, extent, direction and nature, while useful should not be deemed adequate or definitive. My findings also indicate that if identifying and characterizing patterns is to be a *curricular* goal, then developing a broader range of *pedagogic* strategies that help students to *visualize* patterns of change might be helpful. In particular, further theorizing on the value of visual metaphors as a means of conceptualizing change could help to develop classroom practice.

Argument was manifest in an engagement with the claim asserted in the question (either through supporting or challenging the claim) and in the making and justification of claims about properties and facets of change and their interplay. By focusing on the *interplay* between different properties and facets students had to make *choices* between alternative positions in order to describe and characterize change. They therefore implicitly orientated their claims in relation to alternative positions. In this sense, their descriptions could be seen as perspectival (Megill, 2007). These findings point to a gap in existing historical-pedagogical literature – theorization of what constitutes argument in the context of an analytic description.

While there is a burgeoning literature that seeks to theorize the historical thinking that students can or should be doing when addressing a change-continuity question, little has been written about the end product of such thinking. If we want our students to think and write analytically about change, more professional-scholarly attention needs to be paid to defining what this could look like.

Historical Causation: Counterfactual Reasoning and the Power of Comparison

Ellen Buxton

2

Chapter outline

Introduction

'Fog over channel; continent isolated.' So, it is alleged, proclaimed a British newspaper in the 1930s. The rigidly imposed separation of continental and British experience extends, however, beyond meteorological phenomena. The limitations of this rigidity for history struck me as an 11-year-old after a holiday in the Loire. I returned with my head full of images of Chenonceau and Chambord, mingling potently with those of Hever and Hampton Court. Looking at portraits of Henry VIII and François I, I remember feeling that I better understood the posturing Henry. Unpolished though my thinking was, I understood envy and I recognized emulation. Yet when we studied Henry VIII at school, there was no mention of

François nor, more perplexingly, of France. Where had they gone? This was Holmes without Moriarty, Batman without the Joker. To know a man, says the proverb, is to know the company he keeps. Yet the few other countries deemed worthy of our attention had a transitory presence, fluttering into the national story like birds momentarily caught in a prevailing wind, and darting out, never to be seen again.

This was not, at its heart, a grievance about a lack of world history. At its core was a sense that I was missing, as well as juicy history, an analytical tool. It was with this very personal sense of the power of comparison that I approached the question of how to teach the causes of the French Revolution.

Causation in academic and school history

In 1739, Lord Chesterfield urged his son to read his Roman history because, he argued, '[t]he utility of History consists principally in the examples it gives to us of the virtues and vices of those who have gone before us' (Chesterfield, 1905, p. 2). Yet when he related the qualities of good history that he had discerned in Voltaire, the purpose of history ventured from the illuminating to the explanatory:

> He hath made me much better acquainted with the times of Lewis XIV . . . and hath suggested this reflection to me, which I had never made before – His vanity, not his knowledge made him encourage and introduce many arts and sciences. (1905, p. 234)

Chesterfield's conception of the purpose of history interested me because it lacks clarity. Alongside the exemplary purposes that Chesterfield believed that history served was a recognition that good history results in reflection on the causes of the condition of nations. In contrast, the historian E. H. Carr had no such difficulties in defining the subject's ultimate purpose. History was, he declared, unambiguously, 'a study of causes' (Carr, 1961, p. 81). Moreover, those who departed from causal analysis in favour of what he termed the 'functional approach' of *how* something happened, inevitably would find themselves returning to the question of *why*. It is interesting that both men, despite diversity of conviction, profession and period, argued that history carries a duty of explanation. Whatever one believes about other purposes of history, the idea that discerning causes is central to the structure of the discipline comes frequently to the fore. It is not surprising, therefore, that history teachers have devoted many hours to working out and debating what makes 'good' causal analysis and how it should be assessed (e.g. Burnham and Brown, 2004).

For Carr, good causal analysis involves the creation of a hierarchy and a decision about 'the ultimate cause, the cause of all causes' (Carr, 1961, p. 84). This, he argued, is the gold standard – the signature of the true historian. Certainly, many academic historians provide 'a cause of all causes'. A. J. P. Taylor's famous analysis that World War I was caused by railway timetables is a good example (Evans, 1997, p. 132).

This concept of the gold standard is present, too, in the professional discourse of history teachers. The ability to 'produce and explain effectively a hierarchy of causes and consequences' was, for instance, suggested as indicative of the highest stage of understanding of causation by the Teaching History Research Group (Scott, 1990, p. 12) and it remained high up the ladders defining student progress in the 'Attainment Targets' of successive national curricula in England (e.g. DES, 1990b; DfE, 1994; QCA, 1999). The following decade, Chapman described the creation of a hierarchy as the 'ultimate aim of causal analysis', adding that students 'needed to approximate to Carr's "final analysis"' (Chapman, 2003, pp. 47, 49). The ability to identify a cause that surpasses others is often seen by history teachers as indicative of a very high level of historical thinking (e.g. Woodcock, 2005, 2011; Evans and Pate, 2007). The student producing such an analytical account has, it is presumed, scrutinized all causes and formed a judgement as to which was the deciding factor.

The notion of an identifiable 'cause of all the causes' (Carr, 1961, p. 84) is not unchallenged, however. While, like Carr, Evans salutes the historian's professional reluctance to present a monocausal explanation of events, he advocates a model more complex than a hierarchical structure out of which can emerge one winner:

> Almost all historians are used to the idea that historical events are frequently overdetermined, that is they may have several sufficient as well as necessary causes, any one of which might have been enough to trigger the event on its own. Generally, however, they see it as their duty to establish a hierarchy of causes and to explain . . . the relationship of one cause to another. (1997, p. 158)

Note here: 'any one of which *might* have been enough to trigger the event on its own' [my italics]. Here is a notion of causes that are less rigidly determined in terms of their relative importance. But what is a trigger? Is it the culmination of one particular long- or medium-term cause, or can it be a seemingly unrelated event? If it is the spark that sets off the powder keg, where do we place it in our causal hierarchy? This 'spark' may not make its way to the top of the hierarchy, but the mere fact that it holds a position where it is deemed worthy of analysis alongside long-term causes is a key difference between Carr and Evans. Hughes similarly takes a complex view of causation. Her work begins by suggesting that the English Civil War had 'long-term origins' (Hughes, 1998, p. 4). She concludes, however, by noting that 'despite the deep-seated tensions and divisions in early Stuart politics and society, it is to Charles I's reign that we must look in order to show how and why these tensions erupted in civil war' (Hughes, 1998, p. 9). Here is the idea that the 'origins' of an event are distinct from its 'most important causes'. More fundamental shortcomings of the 'analytical clarity' arising from the quest for 'remote and categorical causes' have been suggested recently by Clark (2013), whose study of '*how*' Europe went to war in 1914 distances itself from 'the illusion of steadily building causal pressure'. Instead, Clark uses narrative to emphasize the contingency of 'short-term shocks to the international system'. His aim is to 'let the *why* answers grow, as it were, out of the *how* answers, rather than the other way around' (2013, pp. xxix–xxxi).

The continued nervousness about narrative in English school history (Lang, 2003) perhaps explains why there are few signs of Clark's approach in teachers' published discourse, but the teaching of causal analysis as a process of uncovering an extremely complex multi-causal web, containing triggers and long- and medium-term causes and inviting different kinds of prioritization, has certainly been explored extensively in their practice and publications. Howells wanted his pupils to 'understand the trigger' and attempt 'to connect the spark with the broader issues' (1998, p. 17). Chapman also sought to engage with the complexity of a causation question. In his 'Alphonse the Camel' exercise, it is from the point of the straw breaking the camel's back that we work backwards into medium- and long-term causes and the interplay between them (Chapman, 2003). Woodcock noted, 'History as it happens is an infinitely tangled web of cause and effect' (2005, p. 6) and argued from his own classroom practice that we should teach a much more nuanced and varied vocabulary so as to furnish students' independent causal analyses with more complexity.

Counterfactual reasoning: Devil's work or Heaven's helper?

Perhaps relating to these different conceptions of causation are varying intellectual tolerances of counterfactual reasoning. Both Carr and E. P. Thompson were unequivocal in their dismissal (Carr 1961). For Thompson, it was 'Geschichtswissenschlopff, unhistorical shit' (Ferguson, 1997, p. 5). Redlich, (1965) too, writing about the 'new' economic history, considered the use of counterfactualism highly dubious and not really history at all. More recently, other historians, however, have adopted a more nuanced view of the role that counterfactual thinking could and should play within historical argument. Megill, for instance, makes a distinction between the 'restrained counterfactualist' who 'moves from known effect to hypothesised cause' and the 'virtual historian' who 'exuberantly moves from invisible (but supposed) cause to an effect that never actually happened' (2007, p. 153). Glynn and Booth are similarly convinced that there is a difference between what they term 'certain kinds of explicit counterfactual analysis', which, they believe, 'can be useful', and 'loose counterfactual analysis', which, they warn, 'may rapidly become counter-historical, illogical and counterproductive' (1985, p. 90). Their language here is illuminating for, while they assert the validity of counterfactual thinking for explaining certain aspects of the problem of interwar unemployment, when a certain line is crossed, it becomes 'ahistorical speculation' (1985, p. 92). Moreover, the authors of the book they are reviewing are rebuked for engaging in the 'downright counterfactual' (1985, p. 93), and the reader is reminded that 'fantasy is no substitute for historical analysis' (1985, p. 90). Other historians appear more at ease with counterfactual thinking, noting the fact that all historians, when building a case for the priority of one cause over another, unavoidably judge the weight of that cause by asking, in effect, 'what if it had not existed?' According to Evans, for example, 'a . . . fruitful way of indicating the importance and limitations of chance . . . is to imagine what might have happened had things been slightly different' (1997, p. 132), while Ferguson (1997) argued in his celebration of the counterfactual that it is the land of the familiar as well as the enlightening.

In contrast to the concern voiced by some within the academy, many history teachers appear to be in broad agreement with counterfactualism's proponents or, at least, with those working with Megill's (2007) 'restrained' variety. These teachers contend that there is special legitimacy in using counterfactual reasoning to illuminate, for students, how historians argue about the relative importance of causes. The classroom activity/game of deciding which cause might have been removed, only for the event still to have occurred (e.g. Counsell, 1997, 2004c) is a staple of Key Stage 3 practice in England. History teachers use it to help pupils see that it might be possible to judge one cause as more critical than another. Wrenn (1998) praised Ferguson's (1997) work, *Virtual History*, as a resource for stimulating causal reasoning in school students. Indeed, Chapman (2003) cited Evans's work as inspiration for 'Alphonse the Camel', which encouraged pupils to think counter-factually in order to rank causes. It continued to influence Woodcock in his adaptation of Alphonse, as well as both Chapman and Woodcock (2006) when they collaborated in their lesson sequence on the Abyssinian crisis. Moreover, the special value of counterfactual reasoning for pupils is that it bears concrete fruit. Jumping too quickly to the abstract can make causal reasoning prohibitively difficult for some students (Counsell, 1997; Evans and Pate, 2007). This is not to say that such teachers are advocating the kinds of counterfactual thinking in which, to quote the example of Glynn and Booth, students should postulate about 'what might have been had Genghis Khan been converted to the ideals of Mother Theresa' (1985, p. 90) – an extreme instance, perhaps, of Megill's (2007) 'exuberant' variety.

But how does all this fit into a notion of *progress* in pupils' causal reasoning? Here, as a practising history teacher, I found Lee and Shemilt's (2009) research-based model of progression, based on major watersheds in pupils' conceptions, very useful. In contrast to the National Curriculum Council's 1993 guidance document (NCC, 1993), which identified what pupils might refer to in mature explanations (multicausal nature of events, different types of cause or consequence, relative importance of causes, inter-connectedness of causes), Lee and Shemilt offer a model based on the conceptual grasp of ideas that lie behind, or ought to lie behind, conventional causation work (Lee and Shemilt, 2009). Moreover, their model includes consideration of the role of counterfactual reasoning. A critical stage in their model is when students realize that there is a middle ground between determinacy and indeterminacy. At their 'Level 4',

the course of history ceases to be seen as a one-way street from the past we had to the present we have. Because the actual past and present are construed as . . . special cases within a set of causally possible pasts and presents, students are no longer forced to choose between an over-determined and an undetermined past-present. (2009, p. 46)

History teachers Evans and Pate (2007) expressed a similar concern both for deeper thinking and for shifting students' underlying ideas: 'pupils had met the standards of explanatory writing . . . (but) for us, this missed out all the things that sit behind writing and thinking' (2007, p. 26).

Designing a lesson sequence encouraging counterfactual reasoning

In order to investigate the potential of historically grounded counterfactual reasoning, I decided to design a lesson sequence for Year 8 (12–13-year-olds in their second year of secondary education) on the causes of the French Revolution (see Table 2.1). The remainder of this chapter explains the rationale for my investigation, the structure of my lesson sequence and my findings. The lessons took place in an urban, multicultural, multiethnic, 11–18 academy, with a comprehensive intake.

France is, arguably, underexposed in popular history. Only one of my pupils knew any kings of France. And why would they? As television schedulers had ignored France, so too had our schemes of work. Moreover, the eighteenth century was nowhere to be seen, apart from this sudden appearance in another country. Pupils had leaped from Cromwell to Victorian working conditions. How, I pondered, were they to grasp France as a *place* in the eighteenth century – an understanding vital for analysing the causes of the Revolution?

My solution was to provide them with an alternative contemporary model: Britain. Britain would illuminate certain features of France in the eighteenth century and the very particular

Table 2.1 Lesson-by-lesson breakdown of the two enquiries

Enquiry question	Lesson	
Enquiry 1: Why was Britain more successful than France in the eighteenth century?	1	Carry out role play leading to consideration of how 'sunny' eighteenth-century France could be said to be.
	2	Analyse role play. Use 'Diamond 9' to explore why France was less successful than Britain in the eighteenth century.
	3	Plan and write essay answering Enquiry Question 1: 'Why was Britain more successful than France in the eighteenth century?'
Enquiry 2: Why was there a revolution in France in 1789?	1	Launch Enquiry 2. Start by considering what problems Louis had in 1789. Examine 'Anglomania'.
	2	Do 'Alphonse the camel' and diseases exercise (Figures 2.3 and 2.4).
	3	Deconstruct the enquiry question (Figure 2.5). Carry out 'Add to 10' exercise (Figure 2.6)
	4	Plan and write essay answering Enquiry Question 2: 'Why was there a revolution in France in 1789?'

difficulties that France faced. The British model would also, I hoped, provide some chrono-logical continuity in British history by filling in the century-long gap. Moreover, the British example had the advantage of being historically apt. From the mid-eighteenth century, Britain occupied the French mind as never before. Indeed, Britain was, as one Frenchman put it, 'our model and our rival, our guiding light and our enemy' (Acomb, 1950, p. 151). Yet merely giving the example of a comparatively contented George III in 1789 seemed inadequate. The comparisons would have to extend further backwards. Although a little Whiggish, 1688 seemed the obvious point of divergence and a good starting point for a comparative study.

This was therefore to be an extended exercise in counterfactual thinking rooted in much wider and more thorough knowledge than is typical in Year 8, and embracing another country as comparison. I thus sought to extend the challenge for these 12–13-year-olds in two domains at once – *both* broader knowledge *and* more varied and sustained opportunity for counterfac-tual reasoning within an ongoing causal investigation – and to render those domains comple-mentary. The British model was to provide points of comparison on political character, social structure, fiscal success, military success and the nature of kingship. These points would then enable pupils to ask more pertinent 'what if' questions when arguing about the causes of the collapse of the *ancien régime*. For example, knowing something about the development of Parliament in England in the eighteenth century might trigger the question, 'What if the King in France had had a Parliament?' thus enabling argument about how critical a causal factor France's lack of that British tradition might have been. Similarly, it might prompt the question, 'What if France had won more wars in the early eighteenth century?' and so on.

The 'what if' questions needed to be historically grounded if students' counterfactual thinking were not to fall into implausibility. To ask, 'What if French kings had *not gone* to war in the eighteenth century?' would be to fail to grasp an eighteenth-century political landscape. With such a question, pupils might stray into a 'parlour game' where conclusions would be amusing but not illuminating (Ferguson, 1997, p. 4). This is not to argue that his-torians should only be concerned with what did happen; it is to argue that counterfactual parallels may be more useful if we ask, 'What *could feasibly* have happened if . . .'. I wanted to give these 12-year-olds enough substantive knowledge – both in the national context under study and in a contemporary European context – to be able to make counterfactual reason-ing useful for the purposes of causal reasoning. Knowledge would discipline and enable their counterfactual thinking. Knowledge would make it possible to work back from the event being caused (the French Revolution) to consider only feasible alternatives as they imagina-tively 'removed' or 'altered' a cause in order to weigh its relative importance.

I broke my seven-lesson sequence into two enquiries. The first part of the sequence focused on the early eighteenth century and led to the preliminary enquiry question, 'Why was Britain more successful than France in the eighteenth century?' From Lesson 4 onwards, we worked towards the second, main enquiry question, 'Why was there a revolution in France in 1789?' (see Table 2.1). I punctuated each enquiry with various activities designed to prepare for, implicitly encourage or directly elicit counterfactual reasoning.

The first enquiry began with an exploratory role play in which pupils formed teams of Britain (King, Noble, Merchant, MP) and France (King, Noble, Merchant, Peasant). In these national teams pupils made decisions about what to do in a variety of international situations from 1688 to 1776, and they had to cope with the financial and political consequences of these choices. Adherence to instructions on a set of cards (such as that shown in Figure 2.1) was vital. Were pupils to ignore the commands, they might opt for a policy of self-preservation and lose sight of the contemporary logic of continuous, painfully expensive and perennially unsuccessful combat. Like Dawson and Banham, I wanted my pupils to be thinking 'from the inside' (Dawson and Banham, 2002) becoming more and more familiar with events and noticing both the possibilities for and constraints upon international action.

After the role play and de-brief, pupils were keen to look at the historical questions that actually arose. There could be no doubt which nation had emerged victorious, and the French teams, so confident when first informed of their 'lot' in 1688, were particularly keen to supply the class with explanations for their failure. It was at this point that I introduced a 'Diamond 9' activity in which pupils organized the factors causing British success that we had discussed (Table 2.2) into a prioritized order.

We then played with different questions and saw how our diamonds changed depending on our focus (see Figure 2.2). As the start of a recurring theme in my lessons, I wanted pupils to be aware that answering one question about eighteenth-century comparisons was not the same as answering all questions. As in any prioritization activity, counterfactual reasoning was implicit in pupils' arguments for their various arrangements of the causes in the diamond, but I did not make a big feature of it at this stage.

The 'enquiry question' (Riley, 2000) on which pupils were to write their first essay was then formally introduced: 'Why was Britain more successful than France in the eighteenth century?' The purpose of this interim essay was largely to secure knowledge and to build

---

Congratulations on your coronation!

As King of Great Britain, you must be guided by the following principles:

It is your duty to:

1. defend the borders of Britain, making sure that she is not invaded;
2. make Britain rich, powerful and respected by other countries;
3. hinder (preferably defeat) Britain's enemies; and
4. make sure that Britain has money to spend. A King without money cannot do any of the above well.

You must also try to maintain your own popularity.

You are **dependent** upon support from Parliament. Without Parliament you cannot:
- raise taxes/ask for a loan;
- keep an army; nor
- make laws.

Figure 2.1 Sample card for exploratory role play: the King

Table 2.2 Facts for the Diamond 9 exercise

Why was France less successful than Britain in the eighteenth century?	
France	Britain
1. It cost France a lot of money to borrow money.	1. It was cheap for Britain to borrow money.
2. Neither the nobles nor the clergy (together the richest people in the country) paid much tax.	2. Everyone paid taxes. British nobles thought it was their duty to pay more than poorer people.
3. France had a series of disastrous harvest failures and bad weather. This meant that there were times when there was very little food for ordinary people.	3. Britain did not suffer from such bad harvest failures. This meant that there was always food for ordinary people.
4. The French people and Louis thought that the king should be respected and admired in the world. This meant following 'la gloire'.	4. The British people did not want their king to spend too much money on his appearance. They thought that this was using his money unnecessarily.
5. The French king had to spend money on his appearance to keep up the image of the monarchy.	5. Parliament and the government did everything they could to improve British trade. They, and lots of people in Britain, thought that this was the most important factor in making Britain great.
6. The French government and people were not as concerned about trade.	6. Most of the leaders of the army were nobles. This meant that some were talented and some were not. Britain had a very good general called John Churchill (Duke of Marlborough).
7. Most of the leaders of the army were nobles. This meant that some were talented and some were not. In France's case there were more *not* talented than talented.	7. The feudal system did not exist in England.
8. The feudal system still existed in France.	8. Britain had a very strong navy.
9. France had vulnerable borders.	9. Britain was surrounded by sea. She was not particularly worried about other countries threatening the land of Britain itself.

Why was France less successful than Britain in the eighteenth century?

- Pick out 3 of the 9 that you think were essential for Britain's LONG-TERM strengths.
- Pick out 3 of the 9 that you think were essential for France's LONG-TERM weakness.
- Pick out any that made these deep strengths stronger.
- Pick out any that made these deep problems worse.

Figure 2.2 Tweaking and testing the Diamond 9: picking out key factors

---

analytical awareness. I did not expect pupils to debate the term 'success', nor even to question the judgement implicit in the question. More open-ended and independent judgement was to come in the second enquiry. It was the second half of the sequence that would focus more directly on the causes of the revolution of 1789 and that was designed to equip pupils to reach their own judgements concerning a second enquiry question: 'Why was there a Revolution in France in 1789?' In this question they would be expected not only to grapple with the multiplicity of causes, reaching their own reasoned judgements about interplay and relative importance of causes, but also to show awareness of the subtleties of the question.

Enquiry 1 was not yet over, however. I wanted to use it to furnish pupils with a further, and contemporary, dimension to the comparison between Britain and France. I judged it important that pupils understood that contemporaries in both countries were vividly aware of each other, and therefore of other possible worlds. In class, we talked about the ideas of Voltaire and Montesquieu, who wrote both about England for the benefit of a French readership, and also about the Duc d'Orléans, whose penchant for English fashions so annoyed the King that he commented that he had become 'a shopkeeper' (Tombs and Tombs, 2006). I was worried at first that this would be too academic and dusty for Year 8, but with some storytelling and explanation they were quick to see why the English model would be attractive, and, moreover, what adopting English fashions would represent to contemporaries. Any counterfactual thinking that they were doing was not, therefore, *just* about, 'what would have happened if France had had a Parliament in 1789?'; rather it allowed them to see that these questions buzzed in the minds of contemporaries as well as historians.

At this point in my lesson sequence the *ancien régime* fell and we moved on into my second enquiry question. It was here that I introduced Alphonse. Chapman's 'Alphonse the Camel' has been enlivening history classrooms and history teacher debate in the United Kingdom since 2003 (Chapman, 2003; Woodcock, 2005, 2011). The expression 'the straw that broke the camel's back' is familiar enough to all of us, but Chapman's exercise allowed pupils to debate what counted as a 'cause of death', using counterfactual thinking to explore the complexity of causation questions and to facilitate analytical thinking. Is it the final straw or the prior burden? What about underlying problems or environmental factors? Could some things speed up or slow down the inevitable or was there never 'an inevitable' premature death? In my lesson sequence, Louis was the ill-fated French royal camel, whose death required explanation. At this point in the enquiry, I was keen for pupils to start thinking about the nature of each of these causes in its own right without distracting them too early with an explicit ranking of them into what they considered to be a workable hierarchy. As a class, we pieced together some broad causes for Louis's death in 1789. It was up to the pupils from then on to assign to each cause an ailment, disease or condition that they thought best summarized the effect that that cause had on 'Louis'. From chicken pox to rickets, these diseases were designed to encourage pupils to consider the *nature* of each cause before we went on to consider the language to express it (see Figures 2.3 and 2.4). At the same time, by considering the nature of the cause metaphorically, as diseases, they were, implicitly, starting to compare the causes through, for example, the speed or intensity of its effect.

After their attempts at diagnosing the misfortunes of Louis, time was spent 'unpacking' the question. Pupils needed to know that they were now answering a specific historical question: Why was there a revolution in France in 1789? (see Figure 2.5). But would the pupils realize just how specific it was? I wanted them to think about 'why *1789*'?', 'why *France*?' and 'why a *revolution*?' After all, some contemporary Frenchmen predicted the downfall of Britain, not France, after the loss of America in 1783 (Tombs and Tombs, 2006). Moreover, it is easy to see how pupils would see the similarities between the questions in Figure 2.5, rather than the differences. For example, the questions 'Why was Britain more successful than France in the eighteenth century?' and 'Why was there a revolution in France in 1789?' could easily seem, to Year 8, like the same question. Certainly each would appear, at first, to require the same sorts of material in its answer. Pupils might arrive at each question expecting to discuss the role of money, the King's personality and the unfairness of the social system. If these are what pupils

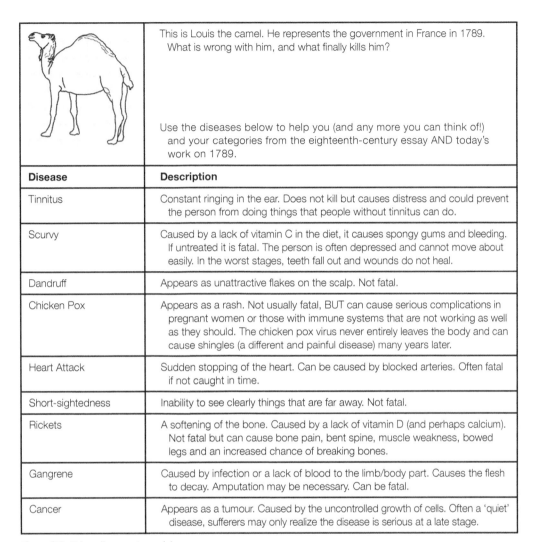

Disease	Description
	This is Louis the camel. He represents the government in France in 1789. What is wrong with him, and what finally kills him?
	Use the diseases below to help you (and any more you can think of!) and your categories from the eighteenth-century essay AND today's work on 1789.
Tinnitus	Constant ringing in the ear. Does not kill but causes distress and could prevent the person from doing things that people without tinnitus can do.
Scurvy	Caused by a lack of vitamin C in the diet, it causes spongy gums and bleeding. If untreated it is fatal. The person is often depressed and cannot move about easily. In the worst stages, teeth fall out and wounds do not heal.
Dandruff	Appears as unattractive flakes on the scalp. Not fatal.
Chicken Pox	Appears as a rash. Not usually fatal, BUT can cause serious complications in pregnant women or those with immune systems that are not working as well as they should. The chicken pox virus never entirely leaves the body and can cause shingles (a different and painful disease) many years later.
Heart Attack	Sudden stopping of the heart. Can be caused by blocked arteries. Often fatal if not caught in time.
Short-sightedness	Inability to see clearly things that are far away. Not fatal.
Rickets	A softening of the bone. Caused by a lack of vitamin D (and perhaps calcium). Not fatal but can cause bone pain, bent spine, muscle weakness, bowed legs and an increased chance of breaking bones.
Gangrene	Caused by infection or a lack of blood to the limb/body part. Causes the flesh to decay. Amputation may be necessary. Can be fatal.
Cancer	Appears as a tumour. Caused by the uncontrolled growth of cells. Often a 'quiet' disease, sufferers may only realize the disease is serious at a late stage.

Figure 2.3 Using diseases to explain causes

perceive to be the overriding causes of the collapse of the *ancien régime*, how do we expect them to notice the differences between questions if they have almost exactly the same answers? There is work to do in teaching pupils to notice the crucial differences between questions.

In my search for a practical way to solve this problem while also helping pupils to re-use their earlier analyses, I hit upon the creative use of arithmetic (see Figure 2.6). I wanted a model that would enable speculation, imagination and organization of ideas. Like Woodcock, I wanted to focus on using language to 'release the conceptual'; but arithmetic was to give me a further, tangible tool (Woodcock, 2005, p. 5). I explained to the class that an historical argument has to tell me how all the different factors and conditions created the thing you are trying to explain. That thing is a known – the final answer 'ten'. In our case, that is revolution.

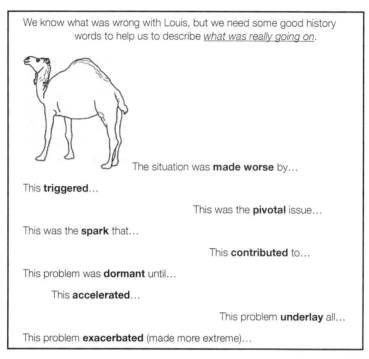

We know what was wrong with Louis, but we need some good history words to help us to describe *what was really going on*.

The situation was **made worse** by...

This **triggered**...

This was the **pivotal** issue...

This was the **spark** that...

This **contributed** to...

This problem was **dormant** until...

This **accelerated**...

This problem **underlay** all...

This problem **exacerbated** (made more extreme)...

Figure 2.4 Starting to transform useful historical thoughts into 'history words'

The question: Why was there a revolution in France in 1789?

Are any of these questions asking *the same thing?*

1. Why was Louis XVI unpopular in 1789?
2. What was wrong with the French political system in the eighteenth century?
3. Why was the French system so weak by 1789?
4. What was the key reason why the French were unhappy with their king?
5. Why was France less successful than Britain in 1789?
6. What was special about France in 1789?

Figure 2.5 Reflecting on the nature and scope of the causation question

What is not known is how we arrived at ten. Not mild disquiet, quiet grumblings or even revolt, but revolution. There are lots of ways to get to ten (cue, flurry of hands giving imaginative ways of reaching ten) and there are lots of historians who argue that France reached ten in different ways. Not nine, not eight but ten. The task of the pupils was to use all the factors we had discussed, weighting each one with how far it got towards France reaching ten and defending that weighting. It was in this weighting that the thinking about relative importance of causes had to become explicit, thus creating opportunity for various kinds of counterfactual reasoning. I knew from conventional 'card sorts' or 'Diamond 9s' that the moment pupils start to play with prioritizing causes, they inevitably find themselves arguing for priority with, 'if that hadn't happened/hadn't been the case, then X could not have happened'. It is impossible to judge how critical a particular cause was to securing the final effect – revolution in

Why was there a revolution in France in 1789?
We are going to write a sum to show how we got to 10. There are lots of ways that you could argue France 'got to' 10 or to revolution. You will have to think about: 1. how many causes you think there were; 2. how important each one was. For instance: Money + Unfair social system + Bread crisis = Revolution $5 + 3 + 2 = 10$ <div align=center>To work out how important each factor was, think about whether there could have been a revolution if it hadn't happened</div>

Figure 2.6 Getting to '10'. Using arithmetic to support causal reasoning

1789 – without at least implicit counterfactual reasoning. What I was interested to see, however, was how well my arithmetic activity would draw this out, what pupils would do with it, and what role the France-Britain comparison would play in shaping their reasoning.

The arithmetic activity was, however, like the earlier activities, merely another tool *en route*. Pupils concluded the enquiry by answering the enquiry question with a traditional causation essay, requiring analysis and argument, of the kind common in England's history departments (e.g. Laffin, 1998; Evans and Pate, 2007).

Researching my pupils' counterfactual reasoning

Those seven lessons became my 'case'. I developed three research questions (set out in Table 2.3) with which to structure my investigation, and used as data my lesson evaluations, a focus group and all the student work (oral and written), from the activities during the lesson sequence to the concluding essay.

Such data present challenges. Grant reminds us that history is often expressed in the language of the everyday. Therefore, pupil responses that sound historical may, in fact, be based on 'human sense': the meaning of words 'varies with the context in which they [are] used and also with the contexts in which speaker and listener have previously experienced [them]' (Grant, 2007, p. 201). On the other hand, certain genres may reveal self-consciously reflective historical thinking. Like other history teacher-researchers, such as Gadd, I judged it likely that pieces of independently constructed extended writing would offer peculiar access to pupils' thinking (Gadd, 2009). Moreover, as Evans and Pate observe, in history 'writing is never mere recording – it *continues* and *develops* the thinking process' (Evans and Pate, 2007, p. 25). Indeed, if, as Counsell (1997) argued, essay-writing is a 'knowledge-transforming tool', one which encourages

Table 2.3 Research questions and data

Research Question	Data
1. Which aspects of teaching through counterfactual example appear to have engaged pupil interest and assisted understanding?	• lesson evaluations; • work produced by pupils during the sequence of lessons; • oral responses of pupils recorded in lessons; • focus group, eliciting pupil responses to open questions.
2. When did pupils engage in independent counterfactual thinking?	• lesson evaluations; • work produced by pupils during the sequence of lessons; • oral responses of pupils recorded in lessons.
3. What properties of historical thinking can be discerned in pupils' final essays?	• pupils' final essays.

meta-thinking, and if the researcher is particularly attentive to possible meanings gleaned through several readings, then the essay may provide access to a pupil's most considered analysis.

To supplement the essays, I collected two other types of data. First, I arranged a focus group of four pupils who formed a cross-section in terms of attainment and (teacher-perceived) engagement. A focus group avoided the difficulties of an intense and asymmetrical relationship between interviewer and interviewee, thus allowing for a frank discussion of how engaged pupils felt with the counterfactual study (Limerick et al., 1996). Second, I collected pupils' raw comments made in my lessons. Such oral evidence that may or may not have been intended for teacher attention was particularly useful in enriching data sets for Research Questions 1 and 2.

To analyse the data, I chose van Manen's theming approach. The slow, iterative reading of texts allowing themes to emerge naturally seemed to be apt for this exploratory study (van Manen, 1990). While I would inevitably come to the analytical table with preconceptions concerning 'good' causal reasoning, I hoped that by rejecting predetermined categories I would allow subtler themes to surface.

Findings

Research Question 1: Which aspects of teaching through counterfactual example appear to have engaged interest and assisted understanding?

Of course, there is a difference between being engaged and being aided. One might expect some interplay between them, but to assume that one necessarily provokes or creates the other is to assume too much. Members of the focus group, interestingly, noted that the comparative study aided understanding rather than added to excitement. 'By comparing the two countries,' suggested one, 'and where they made mistakes, we could understand much better what the King did wrong'. Those elements of the lesson sequence cited as the most interesting were, by contrast, activities involving linking and ranking, in which counterfactual thinking was present but only implicitly. Counterfactual thinking here seemed to exist as a tool for a certain type of task – clarifying an alternative – rather than asking direct questions such as, 'What if France, like Britain, had had a parliament?' In written essays answering, 'Why was there a revolution in France in 1789?' it was clear that many pupils were drawing on previous knowledge from the earlier comparative study. Nargis, during the planning stage of her essay wrote, 'France was in debt. This was exacerbated by the fact that Britain *seemed* [her emphasis] more well-off.' Saeed, similarly, used comparisons with Britain in his final essay. '[B]ecause France was falling into debt, and one of her rivals, Britain was fareing [*sic*] well, Britain had much more popularity and power in all ways', he argued. Saeed also clearly felt that the comparison was useful. 'We knew that Britain was more successful than France', he argued, 'so we could compare more efficiently'.

This is not to say, however, that this limited conception of the usefulness of the counterfactual did not engage pupils. Pupils were enthusiastic about ranking activities during the preparatory enquiry and a flood of hands greeted my request that pupils shared their diamond 9s. Furthermore, in focus group responses, the majority cited such activities as the thing they found 'most interesting'. One pupil enthusiastically demanded A3 paper rather than his book because 'there are just *too* many links!'

Research Question 2: When did pupils engage in independent counterfactual thinking?

When ranking, pupils rarely mentioned counterfactual 'what ifs' explicitly, whereas both their oral responses and their written work throughout the enquiry were peppered with examples of counterfactual parallels. Many pupils focused on the differences in military strength between the French and British forces in their responses to the question of Britain's comparative success. Typical of the style of counterfactual thinking at play here was the pupil who suggested that 'maybe France should have been more trustworthy with their money and maybe would then have won their wars by training their navy better than Britain. But this didn't happen'.

Similarly, in an oral contribution during a card sort activity, Jane posited, 'Britain had a Parliament so we had an advantage that the French didn't, so we could get cheap money and could beat them in a war. It was easier for us.' Another pupil in the same activity suggested that British success was due to military strategy, 'because without that Britain could not have won the wars even if there was lots of money. So that must be most important'. This seems to be subtly different from thinking such as, 'if France had been able to get cheap money Louis wouldn't have had to go to the nobles' and, perhaps, could be said to betray an almost Carr-like belief that what happened was more important than what could have happened. This recurring theme in the responses of pupils may suggest that my initial hope that counterfactual thinking would display itself in historically grounded 'what could feasibly have happened if' questions brought mixed success. Some pupils did use counterfactual reasoning for ranking, but for the majority it appears that the counterfactual example was useful more as a comparison rather than something that directly supported ranking of causes.

This is not to say, however, that some pupils did not use counterfactual thinking for ranking. The essays, in particular, saw many instances of the language of counterfactualism in the form of conditionals in an 'if . . . could' or 'if . . . would' construction, echoing and substantially elaborating some of the urgent debates that they had while discussing the ranking exercises and arithmetic task with one another. One pupil, for example, in his essay on why Britain was more successful than France, argued,

> If Britain were less richer, France would've found it much easier to fund a better army, meaning there would be more places where French is spoken changing History for centuries. This is why I believe it is the most important reason for why Britain was more successful than France.

Research Question 3: What properties of historical thinking can be discerned in pupils' final essays?

Within pupils' essays I identified three main themes:

1. Recognition of a causal web

Many essays contained words or phrases that suggested connections, not just between events, but between causes of events. Most pupils explained links between one cause and another and acknowledged a web that was more complex and contained greater interplay between causes than a simple hierarchy. Saeed, for instance, noted:

> Firstly, France was in millions of livres of debt. This sent French economy to rock bottom, with inflation sky high. Louis had to think on his feet. He chose to raises taxes and put less money in the coinage. This made French people and merchants unhappy and untrustworthy, this led to rock bottom morale . . . this helped to cause the bread riots a trigger to the Great French Revolution (not so great for Louis).

Such webs often involved counterfactual thinking. Saeed continued later:

> If this problem never happened, the Estates General would never have been called and the Tennis Court Oath never sworn and the National Assembly never assembled, so the Revolution delayed, but it was like a ticking timebomb, something that was bound to happen but something else would eventually replace this issue.

With a slightly different analysis, Martin suggested,

> There was an extremely unfair social system in France. It involved the lower class of people being forced to pay dangerously high amounts of taxes when King Louis was spending large and important portions of money on his, what he believed to be, traditional royal appearance. This factor

links with the loss of money that grew harsher as time went on . . . My conclusion is that the unfair social system, linking with the money crisis to form one big conflict was the most important factor.

In both these examples, pupils are going beyond 'this *led* to that' analysis and recognizing what might be called a causal web – 'this is *related* to that'.

2. Recognition of the importance of temporal placement

Having considered the period in some depth, pupils could see the crises of government unfold. The later lessons saw some pupils attempting to define 'long-term' temporally. Saeed, for instance, wrote that a 'long-term issue arose into the King's list of problems from before the reign of Louis XVI, because the second issue was Power', while Tim suggested that the 'secondary reason was the ongoing problem of the country had hardly any money' with this dating 'back to the early eighteen hundreds'.

More complex thinking was offered by Joe who created an arithmetical representation to show how the *cumulative* nature of events should be seen differently from their individual impact. While, he argued, financial problems and 'bread riots' would be dangerous when combined with the King's unpopularity, the greater danger for Louis was when the two happened concurrently. In such circumstances, their joint weighting would be more powerful.

Joe attempted to use a form of algebra to show this:

- $5 \times (1^{first} + 1^{second}) = 10$
- $(5 \times 1^{first}) + 1 = 6$
- $5 = $ Money
- $1 = $ Bread riots
- $10 = $ Revolution
- $6 = $ VERY unpopular
- 2nd $1 = $ King's unpopularity

'So you see', he argued later, in his essay, 'it depended on when the events happened, what order they happened in, . . . to spark off the revolution in France in 1789'. For Joe, therefore, what mattered was not just what happened or even, necessarily, the broad order in which events happened, but the way in which the factors interacted with each other to create a new, unique set of causal conditions. While this level of analysis was not universal, it does perhaps indicate the breadth of possibility for encouraging deeper analysis that is inherent in exposing pupils to a parallel example pointing to counterfactual possibility. When a comparison is used to stimulate counterfactual reasoning, it will always underline the importance of the temporal placement of causes.

3. Recognition of the nature of causes (independent language and use of analogy)

Although influenced by Woodcock's provision of language to express causal relationships, I was wary of over-prescribing thinking by providing teacher-approved words with which to pepper the pupils' essays (Woodcock, 2005). I therefore deliberately encouraged independent use of language and explanation of choice of analogy. Although pupils were presented with a list of diseases that might prove useful analogies for different causes, the analysis itself was independent of teacher direction.

This had mixed results, however. For a few, it encouraged a literal diagnosis. For others, such as Neil, it seems to have encouraged consideration of the nature of the cause. Comparing fiscal problems to a degenerative disease, he wrote 'I think that links to money as they could not get rid of it like the chicken pocks [sic]'. He had thus determined that it was not only long term but, in these circumstances, unfixable. Similarly, Martin suggested that the money issue was like cancer because 'the consequences are noticed at a late stage, like Louis not visualizing the consequences of spending loads on his clothes'. He too seems to have considered the nature of the cause. Long term, undoubtedly, but beyond even being latent, its potency is only recognized in hindsight. Other pupils came up with yet more individual ways of describing the nature of causes. Saeed, for example, used the simile of 'a fungus', for the money problem. Noting that it was 'a small problem, only noticed when large and in your face and it ruins it's [sic] food'. Jemma mixed her metaphors, stating, 'the trigger for the revolution in 1789 was the bread point' because 'this had to be the cherry on top of everything and I think that this pushed people over the edge'.

This resourcefulness of language and analogy was not universal, but many did attempt to examine triggers and catalysts, suggesting thought about the nature of the cause beyond the comparatively limited, and largely teacher-imposed, categories of long term, short term and trigger.

Tentative recommendations

Prior to this study I had been wary of counterfactual thinking, fearing that unstructured 'what if . . . ?' questions would result in miracle counterfactuals that bore little relation to contemporary mores and capabilities. One of the most personally useful revelations that resulted, therefore, has been the positive impact that historically grounded counterfactual thinking can have on students' causal reasoning, engagement and historical knowledge. Looking to my future practice, for example, I might find it useful to explore how students' study of the Home Front could be enhanced by a parallel study looking at the home front in Germany. What benefits might this bring to any causation question concerning either the role of the Home Front as a cause of later developments, or to causes of the particular and divergent ways in which the home fronts each played out in the two countries?

More specifically, evaluating pupils' final causation essays has convinced me that counterfactual thinking can help enliven the link between social upheaval and place, and, moreover, that pupils enjoy the possibilities for comparison of place and period. Mohammed's response, embodying some of these facets, is worth quoting at length:

> Firstly, Britain had more money at their disposal than France, because they had a good record with the banks, therefore making it easier for them to borrow money. Because the king would have the support of parliament meaning that if they struggled to pay a loan then with the peoples'

cooperation . . ., they would be able to raise taxes to pay the loan back. Meanwhile France's kings had to burn their silver to get more money. Their financial state meant that they found it harder to borrow money and nobles were refusing to pay taxes. Money is important in a war because it pays for weapons, food, transport and each time England won wars they got more land and more money which meant they could fund more weapons and skill for wars. But could things have been different if England's financial state was the same as France?

Joe, in contrast, used counterfactual thinking to play with the role that the temporal positioning of causes played on their relative significance. 'How important something was', he declared, 'depended on when it happened.' 'So', he expanded, 'if the bread riots had come at a time when people weren't as angry about other things, they might not have been so serious.' From this and other examples in his final essay, I could tentatively suggest that Joe was on his way to the conception identified by Lee and Shemilt as their fourth 'level':

Although few pupils talk about 'necessary conditions' some explain that 'causes' make some things 'possible' and others 'impossible' and, thereby, validate counterfactual exercises as ways of analysing and evaluating causal arguments. (2009, p. 46)

Whatever the progress visible in pupils' historical thinking, it is interesting that they appeared to *feel* well-informed. As one student emphatically put it in the focus group 'we *knew* about Britain and France'. 'Knowing', is, of course, an enigmatic term. Is the implication that they thought they knew everything there was to know factually? Or that they knew the place in terms of a general feel? What is clearer is that many pupils appeared to enjoy the acquisition of related knowledge about two countries. The comparatively trivial detail about the differences between French and British gardens caused one pupil to comment to a friend that it was 'quite a cool fact', while even the most unlikely boys were eager to suggest reasons why Marie Antoinette's English-style muslin dress was different from the French formal court style.

Some aspects of the early analysis comparing relative British and French success were more long-lasting than others, however. The notion, for instance, that the French King paid money for 'magnificence' whereas his British counterpart did not permeated many essays, most of which blithely attributed this spending to the King's unbridled selfishness. In contrast, lofty notions about the importance of Parliament to fiscal responsibility and trust appeared sparsely. Furthermore, despite most pupils stating that Louis acted to maintain the appearance of power because the court was traditionally opulent, the notion of a bad King and a good, noble King was still a recurring theme. Perhaps my mistake was in adopting too black and white a depiction of France and Britain and then attempting to encourage pupils to see shades of grey in Louis's character. I had, in making British monarchs seem restricted both in power and in opulence, perhaps encouraged some pupils to follow a predisposition to attribute the fall of the *ancien régime* to Louis' abhorrent personality. A question that might destroy such a notion of the systems being binary opposites could be, 'Why did Louis fall and George III/the Prince Regent did not?' If a parallel is to be an analytical tool, it should, arguably, be chronologically co-existent with the period under study.

But perhaps the most exciting benefit of counterfactual example driven by a parallel setting acting as contrast is the potential for placing a British story into a richer context. The last
word must therefore go to Donne: 'No man is an island, entire of itself; every man is a piece
of the continent, a part of the main' (Carey, 1990, p. 344). A great advantage of knowledge-
enriched counterfactual exploration is that instead of geography dictating the parameters of
historical study, pupils can explore those parameters for themselves, and see Britain as 'a part
of the main'.

Knowledge and Language: Being Historical with Substantive Concepts

Michael Fordham

3

Chapter outline

Historians delight in words. Hobsbawm, in setting out to capture the essence of the 'age of revolution', instinctively went for language:

> Words are witnesses which often speak louder than documents. Let us consider a few English words which were invented, or gained their modern meaning, substantially in the period of sixty years with which this volume deals. They are such words as 'industry', 'industrialist', 'factory', 'middle class', 'working class', 'capitalism' and 'socialism'. They include 'aristocracy' as well as 'railway', 'liberal', and 'conservative' as political terms, 'nationality', 'scientist' and 'engineer', 'proletariat' and (economic) 'crisis'. 'Utilitarian' and 'statistics', 'sociology' and several other names of modern sciences, 'journalism' and 'ideology', are all coinages or adaptations of this period. So is 'strike' and 'pauperism'. (Hobsbawm, 1962, p. 13)

What is it that historians find in such words? As an historian, this passage conjures a thousand images for me. When I read words such as 'middle class' I think not of dictionary definitions, but rather of London coffee houses, Viennese concert halls and Parisian tennis courts. I call upon a lifetime of textual encounters in imagining the middle classes: Lucy Pevensie, Phileas Fogg and Marius Pontmercy are as much a part of this as are Charles Darwin, Emmeline Pankhurst and George Mallory. These images furnish the words 'middle class' for me, endowing them with a lingering residue that I call on in subsequent encounters with the term. Language and knowledge in this way stand in mutual support of one another, and, as I build fluency in one, I gain mastery over the other. As Counsell (2001, p. 7) put it, 'There must be a connection between the layers and patterns of the knowledge we hold, and our facility with language.' For me, as an historian, concepts – such as those outlined in Hobsbawm's passage – become meaningful knots in the fibrous substance of my knowledge.

As a history teacher, however, historical concepts necessarily provide for me both an opportunity and a challenge. Linguistic ability empowers: those of my pupils who can use concepts such as 'middle class' and 'conservative' are normally better able to make meaning of the past. Yet, viciously, I find in my practice too that a greater grasp of concepts depends on my pupils having sufficient pictures of the past with which they can render a concept meaningful. This circle was similarly found by Woodcock in his own teaching practice, when he noted that a concept, the meaning of the word associated with it and 'the understanding of the specifics to which it relates' are all fluid in their inter-relationships:

> Through reflection and new experiences, each will continually, symbiotically, mutate and evolve and continue to inform and reshape students' understanding. In one sense, therefore, it does not matter the extent to which a word provides a new idea or a new means of expression; both are vital, and neither marks the end of the process of conceptualization. (Woodcock, 2005, p. 14)

This idea that linguistic competence and historical understanding develop in symbiosis was one that resonated with my own experience. The role played by concepts in pupil progression in history emerged from my own practice as a matter worthy of further consideration.

It is necessary at this point to make some distinctions between different kinds of concepts. Ashby and Lee helpfully set out a distinction between 'substantive' and 'second-order' concepts in history:

> Substantive history is the content of history, what history is 'about'. Concepts like peasant, friar and president, particulars like The Battle of Hastings, the French Revolution, and the Civil Rights Movement, and individuals like Abraham Lincoln, Marie Curie and Mahatma Gandhi are part of the substance of history. Concepts like historical evidence, explanation, change and accounts are ideas that provide our understanding of history as a discipline or form of knowledge. (Ashby and Lee, 2000, p. 199)

On such terms, a substantive concept, distinct from a 'particular', refers to a phenomenon that recurs in different contexts in the past. One might, for example, talk of 'peasants' and know that this includes both the *ceorls* of early-medieval Wessex and the indentured serfs of nineteenth-century Russia. 'Slavery', as a substantive concept, might refer to the status of Spartan helots or black sugar farmers on the fields of South Carolina. Each particular context is unique, yet there exists sufficient commonality across time that we as historians find it useful to deploy the same substantive concept as a tool for making meaning of those moments. In this sense substantive concepts have disciplinary currency, allowing historians to express generalizations in a way that will be understood by others practising the discipline. Most of the words listed by Hobsbawm can, in some sense, be understood as substantive historical concepts, and indeed the most fleeting of glances across the pages of works of history reveals the prevalence of these words.

Second-order concepts, in contradistinction to substantive concepts, are 'those intellectual categories essential to the practice of history, such as cause, change and evidence. They shape the questions historians ask of the past' (Counsell, 2011a, pp. 206–207). Historians can be understood to be members of a social practice (MacIntyre, 2007, p. 187) in which claims to knowledge undergo a process of justification by a community of experts (Popper, 2003, pp. 242–243; Megill, 2007, p. 114). One of the things that unites historians in this practice is that they ask common questions about the past. Regardless of the substantive period, most historians address, for example, the causes and consequences of events, or seek to describe processes of change. These are the questions with which members of the discipline concern themselves. In this sense, learning history involves 'joining those "communities of specialists" each with their different histories, traditions and ways of working' (Young, 2010, p. 27).

It is perhaps for this reason that second-order concepts have provided powerful tools for history teachers seeking to grasp what it means to learn history (Counsell, 2011a, pp. 206–208). History teachers, through their published and unpublished discourse, have explored the ways in which second-order concepts operate as disciplinary tools within an educational setting, including emphases on causation (Howells, 1998; Woodcock, 2005; Buxton, 2010), change (Foster, 2008, 2013; Gadd, 2009; Jarman, 2009) and significance (Bradshaw, 2006; Brown and Woodcock, 2009). In all of these cases, history teachers have sought to elicit the curricular properties of these second-order concepts and to model ways in which pupils might progress towards more sophisticated responses to the kinds of questions that historians ask.

Such work, I think, is of great value to practising history teachers. It is my intention here, however, to argue that further attention needs to be given by history teachers to how *substantive* concepts are operationalized in curriculum, pedagogy and assessment in history. Drawing on an exploratory empirical study emerging from my own classroom practice, I propose here that, in contrast to earlier scepticism, history teachers may have much to gain by seeking to establish the role played by substantive concepts in the teaching of history, particularly in terms of thinking about pupil progress in the discipline.

Conceptual progression in history

The distinction between substantive and second-order concepts in history is of considerable importance to those interested in questions concerning pupil progression in the subject. Progression models serve a dual purpose for history teachers. On the one hand, they provide a powerful planning tool that allows teachers to think about the level of disciplinary complexity with which pupils are asked to engage at different stages in their history education. On the other, progression models can inform approaches to assessment, though we might do well to heed the warning of Lee and Shemilt (2003, p. 22) that a progression model is not the same thing as a mark scheme. If we, as history teachers, want to plan for pupil progression in our subject, and we want to be able to measure this in some way, then we need progression models that describe what it means to get better at history.

One might, in thinking about what it means to 'get better' at history, wish to make a distinction between 'aggregation' and 'progression' (Lee and Shemilt, 2003, p. 13). In some senses the aggregation of more substantive knowledge is meaningful: a pupil who can provide the basic facts about two historical periods is more knowledgeable than a pupil who can provide simple details about one period. This leaves open the question, however, as to what a more *complex* knowledge of the past might look like. A list of people and events is less sophisticated than an analysis that knits those pieces together into some greater whole, and finding ways to describe that which has been knitted is a crucial stage in defining progression in the subject. This is an end to which professional and academic reflection on the role of substantive and second-order concepts have been directed.

Early attempts at defining progression in history sought to use substantive concepts for this purpose. In part this relied on identifying pupil *misconceptions*. Peel, for example, highlighted three problems that pupils encounter when trying to use concepts:

> This dependence upon conceptual thought gives rise to three sources of difficulty in understanding history. There is first the tendency to over-generalise and to see similarities which do not exist. Secondly, since many of the names of historical ideas are words which carry existing, personal and concrete meanings, such as church, law, etc., there is a tendency for these meanings to be carried over erroneously. Lastly, much of school history is taught through texts and new words are often introduced for fresh ideas and institutions merely through contextual passages without a precise definition being given. This makes for erroneous concepts. (Peel, 1967, pp. 165–166)

A number of psychological studies were carried out in the mid-twentieth century that sought to explore how children progressed in their understandings of these substantive concepts, looking, for example, at how children built more sophisticated notions of concepts such as 'king' and 'committee' (Coltham, 1960; Wood, 1964; Peel, 1967, pp. 169–170). The predominant emphasis in research, however, was on the application of a Piagetian model to pupil progression in history (Booth, 1987), which led to scepticism about the ability of school pupils to handle abstract historical questions (Hallam, 1970, 1975).

Scepticism born of Piagetian research did not, however, bring an end to explorations of pupil progression in history: on the contrary, the latter part of the twentieth century saw a renewed interest in progression, although now the focus shifted from substantive to second-order concepts. In part, this was a consequence of the growing emphasis on 'procedural' knowledge (Schwab, 1978) in history curricula. New movements in history education – particularly the Schools Council History Project – shifted the focus from pupils' propositional knowledge to the structures of the discipline and the means by which historical knowledge was formed (Shemilt, 1980; Counsell, 2011a, p. 202). The transition to 'new history' in the 1970s and 1980s led to a growth in interest in how pupils progressed in their understandings of the syntax of the discipline, particularly in the form of second-order concepts. The largest empirical studies of this kind were the evaluation of the Schools Council Project 'History 13–16' (Shemilt, 1980) and Project CHATA ('Concepts of History and Teaching Approaches') (Lee, Ashby and Dickinson, 1995).

These studies set out to critique existing attempts to model pupil progression in history through the use of substantive concepts, particularly where this was premised on a Piagetian model of development (Lee, Ashby and Dickinson, 1995, pp. 50–51). Lee and Shemilt, for example, went on to argue that such an approach

> ran into problems about whether the concepts were in any clear sense 'historical', why some should be taught rather than others, and how they related to one another. Children seemed to approach them in so many different ways that patterns were hard to establish, and while a Piagetian framework appeared to offer the prospect of a very general pattern, it carried a theoretical burden that was arguably inappropriate for history. (Lee and Shemilt, 2003, p. 14)

Project CHATA, in contrast, explored pupil progression in their understandings of second-order concepts; this was seen as a particularly powerful tool for describing progress in a way that moved beyond 'aggregation':

> Work on pupils' second-order ideas began to provide evidence that it was possible to treat history as progressive in a somewhat analogous way to physics: pupils did not simply add to their information about the past, but acquired understandings that changed in patterned ways as they learnt about history. (Lee and Shemilt, 2004, p. 14)

From this research came empirically derived progression models that sought to describe, in general, the stages by which pupils progressed in their understandings of second-order concepts such as evidence (Lee and Shemilt, 2003), historical accounts (Lee and Shemilt, 2004), causal explanation (Lee and Shemilt, 2009), change (Blow, 2011a) and empathy (Lee and Shemilt, 2011). In some cases, such research has led to further reflection by history teachers (Brooker, 2009; Pickles, 2010); other history teachers have been influenced by the idea of second-order conceptual progression and explored it in other conceptual domains (e.g. Bradshaw, 2009).

The corruption of progression through assessment

The late twentieth century saw the influence of 'new history' reach its apogee in the United Kingdom with the introduction of the General Certificate of Secondary Education (GCSE) in 1988 and the National Curriculum (NC) in 1991. In the latter, second-order concepts were placed at the heart of the assessment model through which pupils were expected to progress. Although progression models used both in the 1991 and in successive versions of the NC became entirely divorced from research-based progression models (Lee, Ashby and Dickison, 1995), the idea of second-order concepts had nonetheless entered establishment orthodoxy. For example, under the 1991 NC, pupils were expected to progress in their causal reasoning from showing 'an awareness that historical events usually have more than one cause or consequence' (Level 4) to understanding 'that historical events have different types of causes and consequences' (Level 5) to recognizing 'that causes and consequences can vary in importance' (Level 6) (DES, 1990b).

The complexity of the 1991 statutory assessment models overwhelmed teachers in all subjects, prompting a thorough review of the NC in 1994 and a new version in 1995. An additional, more specific concern for history teachers, however, was the validity of single-domain conceptual progression models that separated different second-order concepts – such as 'cause' and 'change' – and that failed to integrate the substantive and the second-order. It was for these reasons that history teachers and history academics on the SCAA History Advisory Group responsible for writing the detail of the 1995 History NC replaced the numerous atomized statements across three attainment targets with a single attainment target containing holistic 'level descriptions'(DfE, 1994). These level descriptions were designed to be used only at the end of a 'key stage' and only on several pieces of work where both substantive knowledge and second-order thinking could be assessed in an integrated way. In a deliberate effort to prevent a recurrence of atomization and to include knowledge, each level description integrated substantive knowledge with judgements about the nature and quality of students' historical thinking. At the same time, the level descriptions still drew heavily on the idea that pupils make progress in their second-order conceptual understandings of history and included references to second-order concepts such as causation and change.

What happened next in the way these level descriptions were used by history teachers occurred largely as a result of developments outside of and unrelated to any history education policy or discourse, whether among teachers or other researchers. Both the 1995 NC (DfE, 1994) and the formal guidance following it (e.g. SCAA, 1996) had been based on the assumptions that integration with knowledge, in teaching and assessment, was essential, that it was wrong to try to use the new history 'Level Descriptions' (DfE, 1994) as a mark scheme for a single piece of work or indeed to use them at any moment other than at the end of a key stage for a holistic judgement on several pieces of work and that breaking them down into isolated attributes for the purposes of interim assessment was unthinkable.[1] Yet all these are exactly what began to occur in the early

2000s. In the history classroom, the consequences of this shift were particularly worrying. More generic research into 'formative feedback', or 'Assessment for Learning', had consistently shown benefits in giving pupils more understanding of how to make progress (Black and Wiliam, 1998). With school accountability systems increasingly placing a strong emphasis on demonstrating progression in smaller and smaller periods of time, history departments came under pressure to find ways to demonstrate and record progress that fitted with a whole school system, that could yield data frequently and that could be calibrated against a single scale. Level descriptions were thus called to a service for which they were never designed. The manner in which this was implemented in the history classroom proved troublesome (Burnham and Brown, 2004). Under pressure to show progress and to inform student learning with reference to a single scale, history departments were increasingly required to break down level descriptions into individual conceptual components and thereby to unpick the second-order-substantive interplay that the history teachers on the 1994–1995 History Advisory Group had sought to secure. By the mid-2000s, following common practice in mathematics and English, they were even required to invent 'sub-levels' to further divide these under the assumption that this would allow for greater discrimination in judging the quality of pupil work.

Dissatisfaction with the level descriptions or, rather, the way in which they were being corrupted in the name of assessment – particularly in terms of recreating the problems of the 1991 attainment targets by separating concepts and sub-dividing levels – led teachers to become increasingly vocal in the early twenty-first century (Counsell, 2004a, p. 2). Some history teachers, where free to do so, began to explore and argue for ways in which alternatives to the level descriptions might be used for the purposes of modelling and describing pupil progression. *Substantive* concepts offered one such route. Burnham and Brown, two heads of history working in comprehensive schools in contrasting settings, drew on their own practice to argue that

> the way a pupil uses a demanding abstract noun [such as 'empire'] will continually change as knowledge broadens and new questions are raised. Our job is to get pupils to carry on reflecting upon it, to allow its meaning to change throughout their time learning history in school and beyond, not to learn a single fixed definition and have done. (Burnham and Brown, 2004, pp. 8–9)

The association between conceptual development and the learning of vocabulary was already being explored in many history departments (Woodcock, 2005), but Burnham and Brown were specifically focusing on substantive concepts and were suggesting that a pupil's understanding of a substantive concept would grow as he or she developed a greater propositional knowledge of the past. Burnham and Brown argued that this could be a useful assessment measure. Making a point similar to that of Rogers (1987), they suggested that increasing sophistication in pupils' use of that substantive concept could be an indicator both of expanding substantive knowledge and of the growing complexity of the connections, similarities and comparisons that students were able to discern and characterize as a result of a widening substantive frame of reference. Here Burnham and Brown were effectively reaching back to the strong emphasis on substantive concepts in the 1995 NC, where, in a special curriculum component known as 'organisation and communication', students' grasp of substantive concepts such as 'parliament', 'government' and 'Church', 'state' and 'empire' had been singled out as a driver and measure of progress (DfE, 1994) and construed as a generalizing tool. Several history teachers had subsequently linked the 'organizing' role of these substantive concepts to activities supporting extended essay writing in which pupils were encouraged to see distinctions between the general and the particular (e.g. Counsell, 1997, 2000; Hammond, 1999; Jack and Fearnhamm, 1999). In trying to get back to the varied, teacher-driven professional judgement about pupil progress that had originally been envisaged, in 1995, for routine, everyday assessment, Burnham and Brown tried to explore how this emphasis on substantive concepts could be situated within a larger plan for progression.

Meanwhile, the role of substantive concepts and how students might acquire fluency with them have been examined closely in recent years in the Netherlands. For van Drie and van Boxtel, pupils give meaning to substantive concepts in a process of re-negotiation that comes from applying the concepts to new historical contexts. 'Negotiation of the meaning of concepts', they argued, 'seems to be very important in the teaching and learning of historical concepts' (2003, p. 28). In both cases, substantive concepts have been understood as being formed through a process of reflection and renegotiation in which pupil understanding of any given substantive concepts adapts as it is applied to new periods of the past. This attitude towards teaching is summed up in the recommendations of Haenen and Shrijnemakers, who argued that progression in pupil understanding of substantive concepts should proceed by 'constructing meaning by linking new information to prior knowledge . . . To truly make the new information their own', they argued, 'the pupils should be helped in organising and practising it' (2000, p. 29).

The 2014 NC for history may reflect, or may yet generate, a renewed interest in substantive concepts. In those schools in England where the NC applies, history departments now have a statutory obligation to place an emphasis on substantive concepts due to an explicit requirement for pupils to 'gain and deploy a historically grounded understanding of abstract terms such as 'empire', 'civilisation', 'parliament' and 'peasantry' (DfE, 2013). Although substantive knowledge was included as a curricular component in the 1995 NC (DfE, 1994) and although possibly coded references to substantive concepts had existed in the level descriptions, particularly in the requirement that pupils learn to deploy 'historical terminology', the 2014 NC is the first to explicitly state that developing a knowledge of substantive concepts is one of the primary 'aims' of an education in history.

For all these reasons, I suggest that there is considerable and urgent work on substantive concepts to be done by history teachers and other researchers in history education: we need a more thorough understanding of how pupils progress in their understandings of substantive historical concepts, we need to consider the place of substantive concepts within models of formative and summative assessment and, perhaps more importantly, we need to explore ways in which substantive concepts can be explicitly taught and revisited in sequences of lessons that can be structured in such a way as to effect the progression in pupil understandings that we desire. How do such concepts get embedded as a result of successive encounters with different instantiations of the same concept in different settings or periods? In particular, the role played by substantive concepts in securing pupil knowledge requires further consideration. A pupil who has studied the concept of 'empire' only in the context of Rome in the first century AD, for example, is likely to have a less sophisticated knowledge of the past than one who has studied this concept in multiple contexts. In this sense, substantive concepts can become devices by which particular period pictures might be collated and compared in building a more sophisticated knowledge base (Rogers 1987; Counsell, 2000). I offer this small piece of research as a contribution to developing these lines of enquiry. In particular, I shall set out some of the challenges that pupils seem to face in moving from the particular to the general in their use of one particular substantive concept: 'revolution'.

Developing a research question

As Donovan, Bransford and Pellegrino (1999, p. 10) argue, 'Students come to the classroom with preconceptions about how the world works. If their initial understanding is not engaged, they may fail to grasp the new concepts and information that they are taught, or they may learn them for the purposes of a test but revert to their preconceptions outside the classroom.' As a teacher in a comprehensive school, I needed to understand the very preconceptions about substantive concepts with which pupils come to my classroom. For this reason, I decided to frame my research in a descriptive mode, seeking to describe the ways in which pupils found meaning in substantive historical concepts and, from this, to draw out features or themes that might be helpful in future analysis of existing or desirable use of substantive concepts by secondary school pupils. The research question that I adopted to guide my small-scale empirical study was

What meaning do pupils find in the substantive historical concept of 'revolution'?

The lesson sequence

In order to create a situation in which pupils would discuss the substantive concept of 'revolution' at a level of some abstraction, a lesson sequence was constructed that asked pupils to compare a revolution they were studying in detail (the French Revolution) with other events in the past that have been called 'revolutions'. The lessons in the sequence were drawn into a unity by a single 'enquiry question' (Riley, 2000; Byrom and Riley, 2003), 'How revolutionary was the French Revolution?' The enquiry as a whole required pupils to examine the process of change during the French Revolution and then to compare this to change in other societies and at other times. The lesson sequence proceeded along the lines shown in Table 3.1.

Table 3.1 The lesson sequence

Enquiry question	How revolutionary was the French Revolution?	
Lesson	Lesson title	Focus of lesson
1	Who were the French in the eighteenth century?	Background to French Revolution including structure of French society in eighteenth century
2	What tensions developed in France from 1776 to 1789?	Growth of tension in France including the aftermath of the American Revolution and the economic crisis
3	Liberty, equality and brotherhood: How did the French Revolution evolve?	The course of the revolution from 1789 to 1815 including the terror and Napoleon's empire.
4	How revolutionary was the French Revolution?	Comparison of events in France to other named revolutions in history.

This scheme of work was taught to a mixed-ability class of Year 8 pupils, aged 12 to 13, who had recently studied the causes and course of the English Civil War. This lesson sequence created several opportunities for the collection of natural forms of data, of which the most useful were the recordings of classroom discussions between the pupils and me as their teacher. It was clear, however, that a form of augmented data would be required to provide sufficient grounds for answering the research question, and therefore two focus groups were formed with a purposive sample of five pupils, selected to be broadly representative of the ability spectrum of the class.

Research design

This study was primarily exploratory in character, seeking to identify possible starting points from which subsequent research might proceed. My interest here was to establish the meanings that pupils attached to the substantive concept of 'revolution'. The emphasis on studying meaning-laden experience is perhaps most prominent in the phenomenological tradition, and Van Manen (1990) provided one method by which this might be implemented. He argued that phenomenological analysis is best achieved through a process of theme construction, eliciting *leitmotifs* that characterize the data. In this cyclical process, data are analysed at different levels, from the sentence to the whole text, with the researcher identifying the themes that emerge from the data. In adopting this principle, my data analysis proceeded along the following lines.

1. Reading of the transcripts in light of the research question
2. Identification of important statements in a particular response
3. Construction of a 'theme' that characterizes the data
4. Reflection on the way in which the theme was constructed
5. Modification of the theme in light of reflection
6. Application of themes to the data, searching for 'illuminating statements'
7. Reconsideration of themes in terms of how well they fit the data.

Theme formation

After teaching the sequence of lessons outlined above, I conducted two rounds of focus groups with the pupils who were the participants in my research. In the first, I asked them questions about what made an event 'count' as a revolution, before moving in the second to ask them to compare different revolutions. In keeping with my seven-step method, I began by reading the transcripts in an attempt to tease out the kinds of meaning that pupils were finding in the concept of revolution. Consider, for example, the following extract from Focus Group 2 in which one pupil, Amy, was considering what made an event 'more' revolutionary:

> *MF:* If we start with Amy, why don't you explain which of those [events] you thought was the most revolutionary?
>
> *Amy:* I thought the Renaissance, the internet revolution, the industrial revolution and the Neolithic Revolution are revolutions because they all changed how we live today – without them, we probably wouldn't be alive. Without the Neolithic because, if we hadn't learn to farm, all the food we had would have been eaten and we would have died out; we wouldn't have done as well. And then the Neolithic Revolution sort of led on to all of the others; the Renaissance led on to the Industrial and then the Industrial led on to the internet.

A few readings of this text gave me the impression that Amy was using a working understanding that a revolution was something that had a considerable and significant later impact. There is some focus on how a revolution concerns change, but her emphasis is very much on how a revolution changes things later, not at the time. She also notes how these impacts can have a ripple effect, with one revolution leading to a later one, and thus she introduces an element of causal reasoning to her explanation. This reading led me to construct the theme '*a revolution has later impact*' from Amy's speech. Following the establishment of this theme, I then sought other examples of pupils determining the revolutionary nature of an event by reflection on its subsequent impact. For example, James went on to state 'a revolution is when something changed the way we live.' By reading through my transcripts with this theme in mind, I was able to identify further 'illuminating statements' in which this theme appeared to be operating. This approach, of identifying a theme and then searching for illuminating statements, was repeated a number of times, and these emergent themes and their associated illuminating statements can be seen in Table 3.2.

The next stage in my analysis was to begin the process of bringing these emergent themes together into more developed themes. In doing so, I came to the following five developed themes that seemed to encapsulate the meaning that the pupils in the study found in the substantive concept of revolution:

- Revolutions involve change
- A revolution contains a degree of novelty
- Widespread and persistent consequences flow from a revolution

Table 3.2 Themes emerging from the analysis

Emergent theme	Illuminating statements
Revolution involves change	'It sort of how thing change.''It changes into something else.' 'The Civil War has changed the most how Britain used to be, but now it's changed completely because [of] Parliament rule.'
A revolution has later impact	'I think a revolution is when something changed the way we live.''We don't really see our monarch as powerful because of the Civil War.' 'Because of 9/11 terrorism has been higher so security's been higher and there's more fighting and death around the world, because of one thing that's been quite big in the world.'
Revolution is perceived	'But now that we've seen this one, we think, "How did we not think of this before?" ''If say someone invented the wheel nowadays it would not be as big a thing as we've already got them on carts. We've got other things that are round that we already know about but ages ago the person who must have made the wheel, it's like the first thing ever made that was like revolutionary or so.'
Revolution as change in perception	'It's how people change and people change an outlook on life.''I think that something that really changes everything, like completely the tables have turned. Everyone's just focused on one thing and then it just changed.' 'When you're thinking outside the box you're completely changing how it looks, so you've kind of got to think outside the box and that's sometimes when you get revolutions.'
Revolution as a novel event	'Nothing like that's ever been done.''I think the other things, they kind of happened again and again and they weren't really a one off, except Cromwell's Protectorate.' 'He said he felt that the Russian Revolution was like a big revolution but there had been the French and the English Revolution before that, so why would that be a big change . . . ?'
Revolution as a later discourse	'And you don't really think "Why don't we have this massive respect for the Queen"; you don't think "oh because of the Civil War", you think, well, because somebody told me.''I know this sounds crazy but I think there's like genetic beliefs that families have and, following on from what Karen said about the Queen, we believe because we were told.'
Revolution as something of importance	'I think that Parliament nowadays with the Civil War is the most important thing or the most important revolution that has happened in since the 1600s and before that.'
Revolution as a cultural legacy	'I would say that to look for a revolution I would say we have kind of carried on the tradition for a long time. So the English Civil War, for example, we have carried on respecting government slightly more probably that we do the Queen.''And also I think the Gunpowder Plot, we still celebrate it today; so I think that's quite a big thing if something's very revolutionary because we have a holiday and everyone celebrates it every year.' 'We remember it a lot more.'
Revolution as an event of large scale	'I feel that one was big because we wouldn't know like without the internet.''It's like when 9/11 that's all over the TV so that's made a big impact.' 'Well I start looking at things that involve the whole country or the whole continent.'
Revolution as unusual	'It's pretty amazing that some people would actually try to go against someone who's got like armies.'
Revolution as progress	'I decide whether it did much good for the place where change happened.''The Neolithic Revolution changed how we lived and made us a better race, I suppose.'
Reasoning by agreement or confirmation	'As Karen was saying, it carries on down from tradition.''I think a revolution is also when – Edward put it in my head – when you think outside the box.'
Reasoning by challenge or contradiction	'No offence or anything but I sort of disagree as well because the Parliament would not have had that power without after the Civil War because parliament gained power after the Civil War.''I disagree with Edward. He said he felt that the Russian Revolution was a big revolution but there had been the French and the English Revolution before that.'
Identification of a process	'It's like following on, it's like an echo.''To look for a revolution I would say we have kind of carried on the tradition for a long time.'

- The meaning of a revolution can be negotiated
- A revolution continues to be discussed even today.

These developed themes were ideas that were central to the emergent themes thus far established. They were, to use Van Manen's term, 'knots' through which the web of meaning was held together. These developed themes characterize the ways in which my pupils were thinking about the substantive concept of revolution in the sequence of lessons and in the subsequent focus groups, and as such gave me the description of pupil understandings that I sought. The five developed themes were, in short, the answers to my research question, describing the meaning that my pupils found in the substantive concept.

Discussion

The briefest of glances over the table of emergent themes reveals that pupils, in moving from the particular to the general, were looking for *essences* and *properties* of a revolution: their statements suggest that they believed there was an 'ideal' revolution, in the Platonic sense, and that the extent to which a sequence of events might be termed revolutionary depended on the extent to which it matched up with a transcendent idea of 'a revolution'. When comparing revolutions across time, pupils were quick to search for different properties of revolutions that could be measured; they were, it would seem, working with the assumption that different events might be seen as more or less revolutionary by measuring the revolutionary characteristics of those events. As shown in the developed themes, the three properties that they returned to repeatedly were 'change', 'extent of consequences' and 'novelty'. Where an event could be shown to have all of these properties in some quantity, pupils were much happier accepting that event as a revolution. In some ways this is a fascinating (mis-)understanding. Some earlier work (Haenen, Schrijnemakers and Stufkens, 2003, pp. 29–32) suggested that pupils struggled to move from the particular to the abstract when talking about substantive concepts; I have some evidence here that, when they do make this shift, they might conflate the abstract with the absolute. This can, in some senses, be understood as a difficulty in the process of generalization.

It is interesting to note that, in the process of moving to the general, pupils were deploying criteria that called upon second-order ideas about the discipline of history. Although, at a simple level, pupils talked about change as an event rather than a process, they also, as shown in the themes elucidated, began addressing questions about the extent of change over time. Similarly, in considering the ways in which pupils looked for the impact of a revolution, they were drawing upon a notion of consequence, which involves addressing a causal link between any given revolution and the events by which it was followed. In asking about the novelty of an event, pupils were, in some sense, beginning to ask questions that drew upon notions of historical significance. Several questions here remain unanswered: it might be that the concept of 'revolution' is relatively unusual in being so closely bound up with the second-order concept of 'change'. To reflect on the extent to which a change is or is not revolutionary is to deploy and develop second-order thinking about change and continuity. On the other hand, it may just be that all substantive concepts are bound up with second-order understanding to some degree – those describing a process such as revolution being bound up with ideas about 'change' or 'consequence' or those describing a state of affairs or feature of a past society capturing a generalization about 'similarity' or 'difference'. I would suggest that further consideration might be given as to whether pupils require second-order ideas about history in order to move into thinking about a substantive concept in a more abstract sense. The evidence here would suggest, further, that asking pupils to move from the particular to the general in their consideration of substantive concepts might provide a window into how their second-order understandings are progressing.

Some idea seemed to emerge from this study that pupils were recognizing that to engage with substantive concepts necessarily involves engaging in a degree of dispute about their use. In part, perhaps, this comes as a consequence of the way in which the lesson sequence was set up: in considering whether some events are more revolutionary than others, pupils are bound to begin to question whether the term can be deployed appropriately in a given context. What the study could not determine was whether or not pupils realize that such terms are necessarily constructs, that is, inexact and always requiring debate because it is in the nature of 'generalisations' about the past to be a 'best fit' (Shemilt, 2009). While there is disciplinary currency in knowing their commonly ascribed meaning, equally, it is part of engaging in a discipline to be able to use the concept in a continuing debate about its own boundaries (MacIntyre, 2007). On the other hand, perhaps the students were conveying this indirectly: in their discussions pupils were willing to reach conclusions about the extent to which an event might be understood as 'revolutionary' by a process of rational negotiation. Consider, for example, that, when discussing whether or not an event 'counted as' a revolution, pupils were willing to recognize that any given event has a cultural legacy, and that subsequent societies might negotiate the meaning of the event in question. Edward, for example, suggested that 'there's genetic-like beliefs that families have'. In looking to explain whether an event might be understood a revolutionary, he was suggesting that meaning was in some sense dependent upon a tradition that passed down through generations. In short, he was recognizing that meaning was in some sense temporally and socially dependent, and not transcendent of these dimensions. There was, unsurprisingly, little evidence here to suggest that pupils understood that a substantive concept might be a form of disciplinary currency. This is an area in which further curricular and pedagogical development might prove fruitful.

Having framed this study as exploratory in nature, it is not my intention to attempt to generalize about the meanings that all pupils are likely to attach to a substantive concept: a much wider study would be required for that purpose. Rather, I wish, from this study, to offer a number of questions that, based on my findings in this context, would seem worthy of further consideration, in other contexts and at other scales. In particular, I would highlight the following as being of urgent interest to history teachers:

1. In what ways does the introduction of new propositional knowledge change the *meanings* that pupils attach to a substantive concept already encountered?
2. How might *changes* in pupils' understandings of substantive concepts be used to contribute to a model of pupil progression in history?
3. How might teachers *plan* for progression in pupils' understandings of substantive concepts over a key stage?
4. What *difficulties* do pupils encounter when shifting between different meanings of a substantive concept?
5. What is the *relationship* between pupil progression in their understandings of substantive and second-order historical concepts?

Conclusions

The small-scale scope of this study and the interpretative nature of the analysis prohibit the drawing of firm conclusions, and I would therefore offer the findings from this study more as a starting point for history teachers who wish to reflect further on the ways in which their pupils think about substantive concepts in their lessons. If substantive concepts are to be tasked with curricular and assessment roles – that is, as concepts around which a curriculum can be built, and on which pupil knowledge and understanding of history can be assessed – then further study is clearly required to explore the ways in which this might be possible and what difficulties might be encountered along the way. In particular, I would suggest that this offers an opportunity for collaboration between those interested in conducting a wider research study of pupil progression in history and those professionals who wish to explore the ways in which substantive concepts operate as curriculum components. The state of the profession, with its wealth of research-active teachers (Counsell, 2011a), suggests that this is an ideal time in which such a collaboration might proceed.

Frameworks for Big History: Teaching History at Its Lower Resolutions

Rick Rogers

Chapter outline

Introduction

Although, collectively, we may know a great deal about the human past, as Carr (1961) observed, no one person can hope to master all history in a lifetime. When understood only as information about the past, history can frequently appear as little more than 'one damn thing after another', and although pupils can learn a great deal about particular patches of the past (Ofsted, 2007), making intelligible large patterns out of the history that they learn can be prohibitively challenging (Lee, 2004, 2005a; Howson, 2007, 2009; Foster et al., 2008). This chapter is based on a working hypothesis advanced by exponents of 'frameworks' as an approach to 'Big History', which my own professional judgement supports. This hypothesis is that unless pupils learn to make historical sense at a low resolution, and thus explore patterns of change and development at the scale of the past as a whole, it is unlikely that history can be of use to pupils as a resource for understanding how the present (and future) connects with the past or as a tool for orienting in time (Howson, 2009; Blow, 2011b; Lee, 2011a).

Exploring this in my own classroom, I wanted to see how understanding history at the standard resolution normally adopted in England's Key Stage 3 (11–14-year-olds) classrooms could be improved by pupils *first* learning a narrative at very low resolution. I wanted this to furnish a more considered and contextualized treatment of the historical enquiries that students would later face in the average history classroom. This chapter begins with a brief examination of the problem and of a suggested solution put forward by Shemilt (2000, 2009). It then proceeds with a work-in-progress report on the development of a teaching approach through which I aimed to help my pupils make historical sense on a large scale. My account represents one teacher's first teetering steps along what may well prove to be a long and complicated path.

The problem of fragmentation

Pupils are not good at establishing a chronology, do not make connections between the areas they have studied and so do not gain an overview, and are not able to answer the 'big questions'. (Ofsted, 2007, p. 4)

Both from within the profession of history teaching and from outside of it, concerns are frequently expressed about pupils not knowing enough about the past (Wineburg, 2004; Cannadine et al., 2011). The concern raised by the government inspectors in England in 2007, in the epigraph above, however, is arguably a more serious one. Ignorance of this or that particular fact is not the pressing issue; a more serious concern is that,

the majority of adolescents leave school with bits-and-pieces of knowledge that add up to very little and fail to validly inform, or even connect with, their perceptions of present realities. (Shemilt, 2009, p. 142)

How can history education address the concern that pupils know something about fragments of history but appear unable to make sense of large-scale patterns in the past? My own judgement, as a practising history teacher, is that an answer to this question is urgently needed. If we are unable to help pupils to develop usable overviews of historical knowledge and understanding, we are likely to have little to say in response to the objection that it does not have any obvious relevance or use in their present or futures (Haydn, 2005). Were history lessons to involve making connections between past, present and future and asking fundamental questions about the human condition, we would perhaps have less difficulty in making a strong case for its central importance in a balanced curriculum (Howson, 2009; Lee, 2011a).

Frameworks for addressing fragmentation

Efforts to help pupils develop large-scale understandings of the past have a long pedigree in England. Through its focus on 'a study of development', they were at the heart of the Schools History Project (SHP) from its inception in the 1970s (Shemilt, 1980). In more recent years, a number of proposals have been advanced to address fragmented pupil understandings (Lee, 2004, 2005a; Howson, 2009). Kelly described strategies that aim to develop cohesive understandings and to go beyond 'timelines' that 'have no more narrative logic than an alphabet'. His work with pupils employed 'living graphs' in order to map patterns of change over time and to explore relationships between patterns of change across a relatively short period of time (Kelly, 2004, p. 2). Dawson developed a pedagogic approach based on 'thematic stories' designed to enable pupils to build thematic understandings and connections across time (2008, 2009). Other work developed by the Frameworks Working Group based at the Institute of Education, University of London and at Trinity University College, Leeds (Blow, Rogers and Shemilt, 2008; Rogers, 2008; Blow, 2011b; Shemilt, 2009), like the work of both Kelly and Dawson, has had a relatively narrow topic focus, while still aiming to develop understanding across multiple themes and over longer periods of time.

The classroom-based work presented here draws heavily on Shemilt's proposals for developing pupil 'big picture' understandings of the past through the use of temporal frameworks (Shemilt, 2000, 2009; Howson and Shemilt, 2011). In this tradition, temporal 'frameworks of knowledge' are *instruments* designed 'to accelerate learning' about the past' and are distinguished from '*objects* of learning', such as 'summaries', 'outlines' and 'pictures of the past'. They are also distinguished, by their function, from other instruments of learning such as 'grids' and 'timelines'. Whereas

> 'grids' serve to juxtapose and 'timelines' to sequence information . . . frameworks enable teachers and students to contextualize, organize and evaluate data against broad generalizations about human activity and experience. (Howson and Shemilt, 2011, p. 73)

Shemilt recommends scaffolding the development of big picture understandings using generalizations about large patterns in the past. He suggests four separate frameworks to carry the synoptic story of human development: 'modes of production, political and social organization, growth and movement of peoples and 'culture and praxis' (Shemilt, 2009, p. 161). The frameworks are structured around temporal markers indicating number of 'years ago', such as 60,000, 15,000, 3,000, 800 and 100 years (ibid., pp. 167–169). These are selected to embody turning points in each story, as shown in Table 4.1 for the culture and praxis framework. Each framework charts the progress of humankind in response to one main starter question. For the sociopolitical starter framework, such a question might be:

> Had you lived 60,000 years ago you'd have struggled to keep up with your parents and a few other families as they looked for food and kept clear of bigger bands of people you didn't know. If you got tired or hurt yourself you might be left behind. Nowadays you can fly in comfort to almost anywhere in the world without having to worry about being left to starve or being clubbed on the head and eaten. Why is life easier and safer now? (ibid., p. 166)

Table 4.1 Temporal markers for the framework: Culture and praxis

❯ 150,000 years ago	Living in the present and working as a team
❯ 30,000 years ago	Learning from the past and planning for the future
❯ 5,000 years ago	Using religion and tradition to stick together
❯ 160 years ago	Laws in all things: in heaven, nature and society
❯ NOW	Making sense of the world we have made

These frameworks are then addressed over sequences of lessons using two or three 'key questions' (Shemilt, 2000, 2009; Howson and Shemilt, 2011). For example, for the story of political and social organization, Shemilt suggests the key questions, 'How big is your group?', 'Who does what?' and 'How safe are you?' (2009, p. 167), each repeated for each block of time. Pupils are taught how to develop generalizations in answer to these questions.

Shemilt's intention is for the frameworks to act as a starting point and thus give pupils an overview that can later be developed and modified. Subsequent study of higher resolution history (through more conventional school history topics such as the Renaissance or the Cold War) can then be referred back to the frameworks, allowing the pupils to extend, amplify, evaluate and amend the original generalizations that they embody.

The next section explains how I adapted Shemilt's approach for the students in two of my Year 7 (11–12-year-olds) classes. I then reflect in more depth on some of the particular challenges that teaching 'big pictures' presents and how I attempted to address them. Finally, I outline how pupils responded to this approach and raise further issues that I hope other history teachers will continue to explore.

Developing Shemilt's approach for the classroom

My intention was to help pupils to develop a big picture of the past that would be 'usable', in the sense that it would promote some basic form of historical consciousness (Lee, 2004; Rüsen, 2005) and also in the sense that pupils who explored the framework should, at least, develop both some sense of chronology and of human development over time. The notion of historical scale was critical to these goals. I wanted the teaching to move pupils away from their tendency to judge all historical problems as if they were personal scenarios. I wanted them to realize that they needed better explanatory frameworks for talking about change and development over time than ones that relied *only* on the deliberate decisions and conscious intentions of individuals. I took the view that this particular aspect would, to a large extent, be the measure of the success or otherwise of the teaching.

In order to render Shemilt's four frameworks suitable for teaching 11–12-year-olds, I simplified each one. I decided that the detail was secondary to the overall *shape* of the story. I also chose to present the four frameworks together in a single overview, one narrative at the lowest resolution possible, so that pupils could think about how one framework related to another during parallel time periods (see Figure 4.1). In addition, I reduced each of the original frameworks into one key question, which, although crude, would become a way of focusing the pupils on these four key areas of human experience. Through these four key questions, I thus put Shemilt's four frameworks into child-friendly speech:

- How are we organized?
- How do we get our stuff?
- What do we think?
- Why do we move?

I deliberately phrased the questions in the present tense in order to make it clear that these issues were important in the past, are important now and will be important in the future. The simple present tense, often used to imply habit, was deliberately used to focus attention on the universal features of the human condition rather than on the differences between past and present. I thought it important for pupils to understand that the questions we would be addressing are about a past that connects to 'us' as well as to historical characters. This would pre-empt the common 'what's the point?' response.

The 'what do we think?' ('culture and praxis') strand was the only one that did not present a fairly obvious path of development. I therefore chose to focus on the broadening of the intellectual horizons of all of us rather than on other aspects of culture and praxis, which may be the preserve of those who constitute an elite, such as philosophers. Presenting a story in which human beings had increasingly been able to broaden their knowledge of their world beyond immediate experience, through language, then literacy, and through technology, not only created a cultural and intellectual developmental story but also fitted the stories in the other strands.

My version of Shemilt's frameworks was key to the kind of understanding that I wanted the students to develop and its physical construction required much careful consideration. A series of pictures for each question strand seemed the best way of delivering the material accessibly in a short time.

The next difficulty was deciding how the four strands would be chronologically divided. In the original frameworks, Shemilt had not used named periods; he had just divided time within strands by using turning points. While named periods are helpful for structuring our understanding of time, they can foster fundamental misconceptions: pupils can form the impression, for example, that periods are long time stretches when nothing changes and turning points are sudden shifts. Periods can come mean 'no change', while turning points

Figure 4.1 The Synoptic Framework

mean 'change'. If the Roman invasion of Britain in 43 AD is deemed a turning point, then, in the minds of some children, by 44 AD all Britons were enjoying life with roads, baths and eastern spices – all definitional period features of the period 'Roman Britain'. Then in 411 AD, the poor Britons were pitched back into a world of smelly villages, under attack by Nordic raiders. Periodization can convince some children that that is exactly how history happens. Problems arose, however, in trying to combine Shemilt's frameworks. Each of his frameworks had different turning points and finding common ones across all four proved to be impossible. I therefore had to employ named periods, despite my misgivings.

My problem then became: 'what periods?' The standard periods frequently used by historians were problematical for several reasons. First, they were too complicated. Up to the Renaissance they are straightforward enough but once we start talking about the 'early modern' period, the Industrial Revolution or the 'Age of Reason', it gets harder to see what starts when and how. Second, periods used in standard textbooks are typically Anglo-centric or, at best Euro-centric. In the ninth century, the Chinese had developed a trading empire that would not be replicated in Europe for a thousand years. Similarly, the Sumerians had developed a highly complex society while the inhabitants of Britain were still living in Neolithic tribal villages. Third, the danger of information overload from our standard periods was likely to present problems for all but the extraordinarily talented. Detail had to be shed while still retaining the coherence of the grand narrative. These considerations all informed my approach to periodization.

Fortunately, there were other examples to draw on. An American project, World History for Us All, offers a way of teaching world history that is genuinely a history of the world rather than, as so often happens in England's curricular tradition of teaching 'world' history, history from any part of the world that is not Europe (QCA/DCSF, 2007; DfE, 2013).[1] World History for Us All divides history into nine 'big eras'. Its curriculum is structured around three essential questions and seven key themes that move through time (Burke III, Christian and Dunn, 2012). While this could not be transplanted directly into a single synoptic framework, it suggested an approach to periodization that gave me the confidence to think of periods in a slightly different way.

The resulting framework that I devised (shown in Figure 4.1) consisted of five mega-epochs based loosely around organization and production. The first included all human experience from when *homo sapiens* began to migrate out of Africa to the onset of the Neolithic Revolution. The second epoch ran from the spread of agriculture to the rise of the first complex societies in Egypt and Mesopotamia. The third ended with the journey of Columbus to the Americas in 1492 and the fourth with the end of World War II. The last went from 1945 to the present. My titles reflected generalizations about the groups in which we lived during those times:

- bands (circa 170,000 BC to 10,000 BC)
- tribes (10,000 BC to 3,000 BC)

- kingdoms (3,000 BC to 1492 AD)
- empires (1492 AD to 1945 AD)
- multi-national organizations (1945 AD to the present)

Once the framework was complete, I created a booklet of questions highlighting key issues surrounding each picture in the framework. I also created a further page of over-view questions for each strand. These are illustrated in the section 'Teaching the Synoptic Framework'.

While I was putting together the booklet, what gradually became clear to me was that history at the lowest resolution is quite different from the history commonly taught in schools. I had assumed that lower resolution history would be like higher resolution history, only without the detail. I soon found that this was not the case. The history of the human race is so vast that concepts such as race, religion and even gender get lost within it when viewed at its lowest resolution. Concepts such as 'trade' become subsumed in the more generic idea of 'exchange'. I began to feel strongly that if I went into teaching this framework, without carefully consider-ing the difference between history at its lowest resolution and pupils' usual history fare, without considering the serious misconceptions that could arise or without clarity of purpose, then I might do more harm than good. As I did the detailed work of planning, these issues forced me to think deeply about why I was doing this, what could go wrong and how I might overcome the problems.

Reflections during the planning stage: emerging problems, emerging solutions

Before teaching the synoptic framework, I found myself trying to address several challeng-ing issues. While no quick or easy solutions were to be found, this period of reflection was crucial in helping me to clarify and refine both curricular goals and pedagogic means. Three broad problem areas, together with the tentative solutions that emerged, are presented here.

The first potential problem concerned the way in which pupils were likely to miscon-strue the framework. I anticipated a danger that pupils would see neither the framework's status as generalization nor its status as interpretation. I took the view that a framework was likely to be misperceived by children as an accurate and definitive record of exactly 'what happened' rather than as a generalized interpretation. It was more likely to be seen as 'fact' to be 'learned' than as an interpretation that could later be appraised and modified. At the same time, I did need the pupils to understand and remember the framework. The point of the framework in Shemilt's (2009) conception is that it is a starting point, a 'provisional factual scaffold' (Howson and Shemilt, 2011) within which pupils can move about as they encounter further material in mid- or high- resolution. Only if they had understood and retained it could they go on to *use* it in Lee's (2005a) sense. I therefore needed to find teach-ing approaches that would help pupils to retain the framework while also ensuring that they understood its nature as generalization and interpretation. I would have to manage that tension throughout my teaching.

Moreover, even in its role as a starting point, I wanted the big picture provided by the framework to deliver an understanding of history itself as much as to deliver content. The framework that I was going to use would represent history; it would have scale, resolution and chronological integrity. At the same time, understanding history as an academic subject involves understanding that there is always a viewer looking at and trying to understand the nature of the past, and that the viewer, too, is placed in time (Lowenthal, 1985). Where the viewer stands is critical: both physically, because distance to the picture determines what can be seen and in what detail, and metaphorically, because the attitudes that we bring to the discipline determine the kind of history we will write and the way we will understand it. How was I to convey the importance of this situated perspective at this elementary stage?

In order to address these related issues, I developed an approach to teaching about the nature of generalization itself. Generalization is crucial in big history. By virtue of its scale, a synoptic framework has to be a crude generalization. It is important that pupils grasp this if they are to avoid the assumption that in 1493 everyone suddenly started working in factories. But it is far from easy to teach pupils how generalizations work and what they are for. Moreover, I was acutely aware, as a teacher, that pupils can perceive information as being 'true' and therefore useful, or 'not true' and therefore not useful. Generalizations, however, can always be shown to be 'not true' by specific instances. If I were to teach pupils that human societies moved from agrarian to industrial societies, my worry was that in future history (or geography) lessons pupils would come across an example that contradicted this. If the pupils held the above view about the nature of 'truth' and 'not truth', it would undermine their prior learning. In order to understand the nature of the synoptic framework, the pupils therefore had to understand how generalizations work.

For an illustration of a generalization, I chose the boiling and freezing point of water. Most pupils would consider it a 'truth' that water boils at 100 degrees Celsius and freezes at 0 degrees. If one then asks what happens when we add salt, it becomes possible to open up discussion about what is meant by 'water', 'boiling' and 'freezing'. Some of the points may seem pedantic, surreal, semantic or just bizarre; nevertheless, discussing what we *mean* by the boiling and freezing point of water is a very historical thing to do: if history is an activity in which we make statements about reality and attempt to assess them against the things we know, then the discussion serves to illustrate the useful role played by generalizations in historical study. It is useful to know that water boils at 100 degrees Celsius and, similarly, it is useful to know that currency began to have an impact sometime during the era of early kingdoms. Each can be challenged or modified in analogous ways such as debating the meaning of terms or considering interaction with other elements. I also decided to reinforce pupils' developing understanding of generalization during a short unit on the Roman Empire taught immediately after the synoptic framework. This unit finished with the question, 'Does the Roman Empire being in the Age of Kingdoms mean that the synoptic framework is wrong?' The short answer, which many students were able to grasp, was, 'No, because the framework is a generalization.'

A second set of potential problems was likely to arise from the unfamiliar resolution at which the synoptic framework would present history to the pupils. In England and Wales, curricular requirements and history teacher practice generally differentiate between 'depth' studies on the one hand and breadth, outline or overview studies on the other (e.g. DfE, 1994, 2013; Kitson, Husbands and Steward, 2011). Breadth studies are rarely very broad, however. Most teaching material is therefore set at a fairly high resolution. Switching to the lowest resolution has neither been a requirement of the National Curriculum nor of examination rubrics. Nor had my own higher education prepared me. Courses at higher secondary and tertiary level are often set at the higher resolutions. Although university courses such as 'the French Revolution' or 'Mussolini's Italy' typically include some background they tend not to embrace much wider spatial and temporal contexts. At the lower resolution, history presents itself in different ways from those with which most of us, even with history degrees, are comfortable. In higher resolution, events and individuals appear as the agents of dramatic change, such as the rise of a particular religion. Yet if we take it at its lower resolution, Christianity, for example, was only one instance of the rise of organized monotheistic religions, arising through a gradual convergence of different social and political developments. As I planned the lessons, it occurred to me increasingly that specialization can perpetuate and deepen a fragmented approach. In planning these lessons, I was trying to break out of that fragmentation cycle myself.

Resolution, in turn, raises the problem of just what a big picture is. Other approaches to the problem of fragmentation have their merits and weaknesses, but because they remain laden with detail they can make it difficult for pupils to form and retain a big picture. Shemilt's (2009) big pictures are about gaining a sense of the past as a whole, they represent history over a long time span and they are structured by theme. By this definition, the history of medicine – a strand of a popular high school examination course first developed in England in the 1970s – is, arguably, a big picture.[2] It takes place over a long time, has a theme and, as the story develops, both the characters and the changes that emerge form clear links and interactions with those that come before and after. Yet, like many other history teachers (e.g. Osowiecki, 2006), I have found that a significant difficulty presented by the history of medicine is the amount of material that pupils have to retain in order to be able to tackle the questions posed in their final examination. Those examination questions are scarcely developmental in their focus, with the resultant danger that the parts become far more important to the pupils than the whole (Shemilt, 2009). In my synoptic framework, I needed the whole to be more important than the parts.

These considerations of resolution raised fundamental questions about the nature of my curricular goals and the character of teaching that would express them. *What* did I want pupils to learn? I took the view that with frameworks – or indeed any approach aimed at big picture formation – detail would have to be sacrificed in order to make the big picture more 'usable' or, at the very least, retainable. It takes a remarkable mind to be able to construct and retain a big picture of our history at the level of detail that is usually urged on teachers and students in public discussions of history education. Building and retaining a big picture at a lower level of resolution, where an understanding of the whole is more important than a recollection of its parts, seems a more reasonable ambition. It is also likely to be a more usable outcome of history education: a child who understands that the groups in which we live have got bigger in number and size and more complex over time has a contextual frame for any further study of (say) political developments. Once in possession of this understanding, that pupil may begin to see how any new learning in higher resolutions meshes with or is altered by what they have learned at lower resolutions and, perhaps, begin to build understandings informed by a meaningful interplay of different resolutions.

Reflection on the challenge of teaching history at low resolution led me to explore helpful analogies, such as Google Earth. At Google Earth's lower resolutions we can only distinguish between land and sea but when we 'zoom in' in high resolution, we see rivers and settlements, then buildings and, eventually, minutiae such as dustbins. In history, at its highest resolution, we can see (or attempt to see) inside the heads of historical agents but as we begin to zoom out, we lose sight of individuals and begin to consider a greater, and perhaps more histori-cal, scale. In the zooming out process individuals disappear and we can only talk of groups. As we zoom out further, the differences between these groups, such as religion or ethnicity, also disappear and we can only talk about mankind at the level of Braudel's (1972) 'longue durée', the deep processes of historical change that go far beyond the scope of individual lives. History at its lower resolutions is about the most fundamental aspects of human existence, about changes such as the Neolithic Revolution or the rise of urbanization in Sumeria and Egypt, which in turn led to more complex societies (Christian, 2005). There are no heroes here, no individuals on whom we can pin change.

The question of resolution also raised issues of terminology. The academic discipline of Big History has, in recent years, acquired a high profile (Spier, 2011) with a number of influ-ential works of meta-history (Diamond, 1997, 2005; McNeill and McNeill, 2003; Christian, 2005).[3] The lexicon used by these scholars differs from that of mainstream history. Concepts such as 'exchange', for example, which covers trade, ideas, science and diplomacy, allow us to fuse higher resolution historical processes into an overall theme. The concept 'groups', which gives us a term for nation-states, tribes and nation-state-driven empires, assists low resolu-tion thinking in similar ways: England/Great Britain/The United Kingdom may be cited as an exemplification of a low resolution development but our nation's history would be largely invisible in the big picture. It soon became clear to me that I would need to employ a much more generic lexicon than I had previously used.

The third problem concerns pupils' preconceptions about stories and how they apply these to learning about the past. In my experience, the devices often used to engage children can reinforce misconceptions. When we are young, stories are the currency though which we understand the world, and whether they revolve around not getting run over by a car or pigs doing better in brick houses, stories contain lessons. Children are sophisticated enough to absorb these lessons so that they learn to survive in our complex world (Connelly and Clandinin, 1990). However, if they bring this approach to the history classroom, then we may have a problem. Stories from history, told in much the same way as allegorical stories, are likely to be treated in the same way. Conversely, where there is no obvious connection on a personal level, pupils may find the past remote and irrelevant: How many British teenagers are going to invade Russia? The danger is that if pupils see all stories as having a tidy ending with a moral, then they fundamentally misunderstand the nature of time and this, in turn, could prove a major barrier to historical consciousness. It is tempting to hook children into history by presenting them with a series of engaging and interesting stories and this approach has much to commend it to a teacher (Harris and Rea, 2006). Focusing on the personal, however, has inherent dangers. The personal can come to resemble beacons within a flat image of history that lacks overall shape and direction.

It was this overall shape and direction, a sense of the past having a definable chronological integrity, that became prominent in my efforts. Many teachers might advocate using timelines for this but while timelines are useful learning tools, teaching chronology and teaching temporal understanding are distinct things (Blow, Lee and Shemilt, 2012). I wanted pupils to understand time as a continuum, rather than simply as a large collage of engaging scenes and stories. Howson (2009) has developed a visualization of temporal interconnections: a man in a pool with other pools linked by pipes to suggest the interconnections between past, present and future. I used simple models of shapes in order to direct student thinking away from breaches between past, present and future, and towards modelling time as a continuum. Using the rectangle in Figure 4.2, I constantly asked: 'What's happening the right-hand edge?' Whatever method is used, I am convinced that the nature of time should be taught explicitly. If we aim to build synoptic understandings, we have to build pupil thinking about temporality.

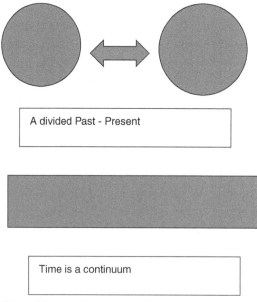

Figure 4.2 Modelling historical time

Teaching the synoptic framework

The considerations outlined above shaped my version of Shemilt's framework and my peda-gogic approach. I carried out the teaching in a school with a fully comprehensive intake in north Leeds, England, with a student population of approximately 1,400 11–18-year-olds. The framework was taught to Year 7 pupils (11–12 years) set by ability. Two groups in Year 7 were taught, one Set 2 of twenty-eight pupils and one Set 4 of twenty-four. In Set 4, only six did not have some identification for special education needs (SEN) and five pupils had full SEN statements.

In my teaching, I tried, as far as possible, to follow Shemilt's (2009) principles. As Shemilt recommends (2009), the framework was taught rapidly at the start of the academic year and then systematically referred to during all other history teaching as the year unfolded. During the rest of the year, teaching was as normal – a range of topics from the Roman Empire and medieval England – but I delivered it in a way that constantly reminded pupils of the larger context, using verbal references and setting short exercises that that made connections with the framework every four or five lessons.

Very early in teaching the initial framework, I noticed that I was starting to use a new vocabulary. Reflecting on it now, I recall how this new vocabulary crept up on me. For exam-ple, I found myself saying things such as, 'foraging bands settled down to be farmers and the massive impact of a sedentary lifestyle as opposed to the nomadic one became obvious'. I do not recall using terms such as 'nomadic' or 'sedentary' before. Terms such as 'tokens of value' or concepts such as 'exchange' also proved crucial to the kind of historical understanding that I was trying to teach. These terms had not been the usual currency of my history teaching, nor had I learned in this way at school or university. But having read 'big history', particularly Christian (2005), McNeill and McNeill (2003) and Diamond (1997, 2005), I saw how cen-tral this vocabulary was to the explanation of history at its lowest resolution. Even concepts such as urbanization, which do typically feature in ordinary history teaching, have differ-ent characteristics at the lower resolution. Urbanization certainly occurred in the Industrial Revolution but there were far greater impacts of urbanization with quite different connota-tions from 3,000 BC onwards. I realized quite quickly that in addition to teaching the big story of the synoptic framework, I would have to build in more time to explore terminology.

In order to support students' deepening understanding of the framework, I developed an approach involving 'expansion questions'. For each picture in the framework (see Figure 4.1), I devised a number of expansion questions. These were designed to expand and develop the answers that students could give to each of the overall 'key questions' for each period. For example the expansion questions for the key question, 'How do we get our stuff?' during the 'age of kingdoms' were as follows:

1. What stuff was really important?
2. How did these people get their stuff?

3. Why were people able to specialize in things other than urgent stuff production?
4. How did 'tokens of value' improve the process of getting stuff?
5. Why do we start to see large inequality in the group?

The first two expansion questions are fairly straightforward and might be dealt with in five minutes. I used them simply as a 'way in' for the pupils to think about the theme of the period. The next two are complex and fundamental to human activity. They could themselves form the basis of a unit of work. These two questions were deliberately designed to draw out two themes: that a token-based system of exchange led to a boom in trade and that the possibility of specialization led to advances in certain professions and trades. The fifth is a pointed question designed to raise the students' awareness that the concepts of 'rich' and 'poor', far from being historical universals, are actually recent and modern. These five expansion questions were addressed in one lesson, via a variety of techniques, including short discussions, source-based activities, picture stimuli and short presentations. The 'rich' and 'poor' issue was raised by a picture of two individuals, one from the 'bands' era and one from the 'multi-national organizations' era (see Figure 4.1). These illustrated the fact that the difference between one individual's wealth and another's in the 'Bands' era was a simple stone axe, whereas in the 'Multi-National Organizations' era, the difference in wealth could amount to billions of dollars (or other tokens of value). As all pupils had their own booklets, they were able to record their own answers to each question and I was able to check the extent to which they had understood. From the nature of the responses, which showed a growing readiness to generalize in the above ways, I felt that I was beginning to see evidence of a different way of thinking about history.

In order to help students draw aspects of their new knowledge together into different types of summary and in order to allow me to check their understanding, I gave students a set of 'overview questions' for each strand of the framework. These were answered at home, without help from a teacher. The following are the overview questions for the 'How are we organized?' strand:

1. Is your country a member of the United Nations?
2. Was a man living on this island in 35,000 BC a member of the United Nations? Explain your answer.
3. What has happened to our groups over time?
4. At what point would a member of the group cease to have the possibility of knowing every other member?
5. How have the possibilities of being able to communicate with every other member of the group changed over time?

Overview questions 1 and 2 are a matched pair. They reveal an understanding of how an individual fits into the world and the basic relationship of past-present. Most pupils gave the standard answer ('yes' for the first and 'no' for the second) but a small minority had problems. For the first question, errors were often just cases of misreading the question but errors in answering the second were concerned with problems in understanding the concept of

35,000 BC. The most common incorrect second answer was along the lines of, 'Yes, because everybody is in the United Nations'. The first question was deliberately phrased to plant an idea that would be unhelpful when answering the second; only pupils who genuinely baulked at the sudden inclusion of 35,000 BC would get the answer correct – a clear illustration that they were at least alert to the difference between past and present. The question proved diagnostically useful. I was able to note those students who had answered incorrectly and I made them the target for clear chronological questioning during the remainder of the teaching.

The third question, although simple in its aim, introduced the notion of gradual change over time. Most pupils answered correctly with, 'they got bigger' or some other idea of change over time, albeit a slightly flawed one. For example: 'They got more powerful', 'we became richer', or 'we got smarter and developed better things'. Those failing to provide an adequate answer either misread the question or offered counterfactual answers such as 'they got smaller' for which I could offer no explanation. The fourth asks about the impact of group size and many students understood that a kingdom which can be spread over hundreds (sometimes thousands) of miles and contain millions of people is the first barrier in history to communication with every other member. This question was a fairly good indicator of the pupils who could think on an historical rather than a personal scale. It sowed a seed that would be re-visited later when we tackled questions on literacy as a tool for organizing or on tokens of value as a medium for sophisticated exchange systems.

The fifth question was the most difficult but also the most revealing. It required pupils to assess two distinct changes over time and to show how the two relate to one another. The first was the increase of group size and the second was improvement in communication technology. Group size during the eras of 'Kingdoms' and 'Empires' weakened the possibility of communication, but technology in the era of 'Multi-National Organizations', particularly the last twenty years, has meant that communication between group members is possible regardless of group size or location. My expectation was that this kind of complexity would be beyond most Year 7 students and I was right. Most went for the idea that technology has made it better, which I did not expect, having already primed them with the notion that group size was important. Those who did mention group size found it difficult to explain its relationship with modern technology.

Examining the results of the teaching

At the end of the year, in addition to my own reflections on pupils' responses, I wanted to ascertain what impact, if any, the synoptic framework teaching had had on the students' historical thinking. Although the experiment was as much about me grappling with teaching issues as it was about the progress made by the pupils, I felt that some indication of which understandings had endured would be interesting. I chose to examine two areas in which, in my experience, pupils can struggle. One was in seeing time as a continuum and being able to orientate within that continuum; the other was seeing history from a personal rather than an historical perspective. I used several assessment tasks and questions. In addition, seventeen of the fifty-two pupils were interviewed. The sample of seventeen was taken from across the ability range and included two pupils who both had statements for special educational needs involving learning difficulties.

The first task of the interview gave me hope that the teaching had achieved something. The pupils were given five pictures and asked to 'sort them out': I deliberately made no mention of 'order', 'time', 'chronology' or 'sequence'. Immediately and without hesitation, fifteen of the seventeen pupils put the pictures in chronological order in a row from left to right. When asked why they had done this, twelve gave answers that showed that they thought that chronological sequencing was what was expected of them in history. Only seven of them got all the pictures in the right places but as my primary aim during the teaching had been to cultivate an approach to the material (i.e. a disposition to realize that chronology matters), I concluded that the teaching had had some impact on their thinking. In the past, I had made the mistake of thinking that a couple of lessons on dates and the occasional timeline would suffice and would enable the pupils to think chronologically. Other research in which I have been involved had shown that this is not necessarily the case and that chronological sequencing cannot be regarded as the default position for this age group (Rogers, 2008). Yet without chronological thinking, other aspects of history become more difficult and lose much of their value. Concepts such as change or causation cannot work without it.

I was also curious to find out what they had understood of the terminology. All fifty-two pupils were asked to explain what a 'period' was and what a 'turning point' was. All but three of the fifty-two gave an answer that showed that they knew that periods were a part of time. A third could explain 'turning point', albeit some with somewhat vague answers. Two further pupils gave answers to the question about periods in a manner that *implied* knowledge of turning points.

During much of the teaching, whenever we had addressed the historical significance of tokens of value (money) or of literacy, the pupils had generally given personal responses. Typical responses had been that money was used to buy things and literacy was learning to read and write in English which helped you to get a job. When asked about the importance of literacy in the assessment tasks at the end of the year, however, a quarter of pupils did give an answer of an historical nature. One such was

> Because the king when he wanted to know taxes could keep track of them and in the churches and when they were selling they could keep track of everything.

The rest gave answers that reflected their personal experience, such as, 'so people can get jobs and earn money'. When asked about the importance of tokens of value, just under half of the pupils gave historical answers which included some notion of change or development. One example was:

So they could trade and get different stuff from different places like bananas and pineapples. So they could move around the country and technologies improved because of tokens of value.

One of the most revealing parts of the interview came with some questions that aimed to explore, by deliberately presenting pupils with errors, the clarity of pupils' thinking about sequencing. I was interested in their disposition to note not only the order of events, but the scale of time and the distance between events. One of these questions asked pupils to assess how nervous the Romans were about the powerful Norman army of William the Conqueror. The relevant dates were given and the questions were phrased in ways that implied that they were straightforward, rather than trick, questions. Some pupils responded as follows:

Teacher: How far were the Romans (750 BC–476 BC) afraid of the Norman Army (c. 1066)?
Pupil: The Romans would not have been worried.
Teacher: Why?
Pupil: They had a much better army and a bigger empire.

This kind of answer would have been acceptable if the question had related to a 'What if?' scenario but it was carefully worded so that the only reasonable answer was that the chronological disparity rendered the question invalid.

A crude judgement about the success or otherwise of the framework teaching, based on numerical data generated from an analysis of answers to the tasks and interview questions, might be that half the pupils had developed an historical perspective on the past that was based around a chronological approach. There was qualitative evidence, however, that might support more expansive claims. At some point during the interviews, every pupil interviewed, except one boy with general learning difficulties, gave an answer that demonstrated some understanding that history is about matters beyond the personal and that history is developmental and has temporal shape and structure. They did not fall into the trap, as many had done during the baseline assessments from the Magna Carta Project, of seeing the past as separate from the present (Rogers, 2008).[4] Nor did they fall into the trap of making crude bilateral comparisons between past and present, such as, 'the past is like that and the present is like this'. The synoptic framework teaching had clearly had some effect in raising a heightened awareness of a big picture of history.

Earlier studies have suggested that temporal frameworks can be tools for helping pupils tie material together into a coherent whole (Blow, Rogers and Shemilt, 2008; Rogers, 2008). The synoptic framework teaching reported here suggests that the same thing may be possible on a larger scale and with slightly broader aims. There is, however, nothing conclusive: 'mights' and 'maybes' will not fade until a full academic programme of research on the effectiveness of such approaches has been undertaken. One small experiment in a Leeds classroom can prove little about the efficacy of a frameworks approach but it can suggest what could be achieved. Children can learn history at a low resolution and learn to place details within large-scale contexts. If all we want from history education is to fill little vessels with facts about great men and women and the dates of great events then this approach is likely to have little value. If, however, we want children to develop an understanding of the historical scale and structure of human experience and the ability to put what we teach them into temporal context, then using temporal frameworks may have a major role to play in history teaching. As academic 'Big History' gains popularity, history education can learn much from the resolution, scales and terminology that it uses. It seems to me that we need to lose some detail in some parts of our teaching, and we need a different lexicon. Through a mix of these strategies, we may well be able to teach children to understand and retain a usable big picture of the past.

Evidential Thinking: Language as Liberator and Gaoler

Paula Worth

5

Introduction

I vividly remember my first argument with my head of History, in my first term as a Newly Qualified Teacher (NQT). He was checking my marking on a practice General Certificate of Secondary Education (GCSE) paper.[1] I had awarded Daniel the highest level for his answer to a question about the message of a political cartoon. Apparently, his answer could not score higher than Level 1.

'Why?' I asked, politely, mindful of my position at the bottom of the GCSE-marking food chain, 'he stated the message, referred to the source and used contextual knowledge.' 'The message that he stated isn't correct. Look at the examples of correct messages suggested on the markscheme', answered my Head of Department.

He crossed out my mark with red pen. As I struggled on through my NQT year, it became apparent that this approach of inferring a 'correct message' from a source, by checking it against the acceptable answers illustrated in the examination board's mark scheme, was part of a culture in my history department – and, I was to discover, in many others. It was a culture geared to helping pupils to achieve the highest possible marks in the examination. These 'correct messages' were often referred to as 'valid inferences'. We were supposed to root out invalid ones. I desperately tried to remember whether I had been teaching the 'correct messages' from the examples given on the GCSE mark schemes, as encouraged by my department. I had not. I had been accepting all sorts of inferences, wherever I had considered the reasoning and justification logical. In other words, I had concerned myself with processes of inference. I had looked for validity in the students' historical reasoning, rather than arriving at an assessment judgement based on a given set of acceptable answers.

What makes a valid inference for GCSE students in this situation? If I had taught the 'right' method or process, would Daniel have been able to arrive at one of the messages deemed correct? I had encouraged my students in Years 7 to 9 to make a variety of inferences, marking them highly if I considered their justifications historically defensible. I realized, increasingly, that, in much the same way that Pickles (2011) later advocated, I had been chiefly concerned with trying to move pupils towards effective historical reasoning. Excited and encouraged by the way in which pupils' thinking often unfolded and by my own learning about the kinds of historical reasoning of which they seemed capable, it was dispiriting to discover that I might have been selling them short. Should I, instead, have been moving them more quickly into rehearsing a limited canon of acceptable outcomes, or what my department called 'valid inferences'?

Yet the more anxious I became about my methods for teaching evidential thinking, the more convinced I became that my department's apparently prescriptive version of 'validity' closed down legitimate pathways. I reflected further, that, in logic, 'validity' is to do with how one argues. Validity in historical thinking must inhere in the form of reasoning pursued. Yet, in pursuing this line, did I risk instilling relativism? Was I creating a class of irrationalists who would allow any answer or, worse, a class of cynics who would permit no answer at all? How could I allow pupils to explore a myriad of *possible* interpretations while avoiding excessive uncertainty, lest they run, screaming, back to the mathematics classroom?

To answer these questions, I needed to explore not only advantages and disadvantages of my teaching methods but my own curricular purposes in requiring pupils to use primary sources. I needed to look at how academic historians establish and use evidence and at the various goals, approaches and justifications of history educators. Thus I hoped to determine for myself whether an answer such as Daniel's showed a high or a low level of historical thinking.

A history teacher's journey through the literature

Historians and sources

How historians use sources to construct historical accounts is underpinned by the way in which they resolve epistemological questions about the nature of history.[2] As I reflected on how such questions might be considered by an historian – questions that might therefore have bearing on how Daniel should be taught and assessed – I grouped them into five broad issues.

My first issue concerned the 'validity' of any process of inference. In his 'professionalization' of history in Germany in the 1840s, Ranke argued that consulting historical sources carefully within their context could allow an historian to write objectively about the past. The outcome of such a method would be, as Acton (2008) argued in 1906, that critical scholarship on a particular topic could finish. All sources would be synthesized into an account that would say what actually happened through a corpus of ascertained facts. In 1961 E. H. Carr cast doubts on such empirical assumptions. Having returned to Carr in order to sharpen my thinking about historical causation during my postgraduate training year, I now reached for his writing on sources and evidence. The credibility of scientific methods to deliver 'value-free' history had clearly been shaken by social instability preceding World War II and Carr postulated that an historian's choice of sources is affected by his sociocultural context, shaping the way he 'fishes' for evidence (1961, p. 18).

But whereas Carr thought that sources still restricted the construction of historical accounts, the work of postmodernists was to place yet greater emphasis on the role of the historian. As a recently qualified teacher, I found myself joining the continuing iterations of these debates (e.g. Evans, 1997). Postmodernists resist the quest for totalizing explanations because 'truth is always relative to the . . . intellectual frameworks of the judging subject' (Butler, 2002). White (1985) conceptualized historical interpretations as 'emplotments' composed in the present. In this view, interpretations are literary texts that can be judged according to their fit with current notions of the acceptability of narrative structures, rather than their relation to unchanging truth. White and other postmodernists such as Jenkins (1991) prompted Evans' staunch defence of more traditional aims of attaining historical truth, albeit a defence made with decreased confidence: 'if we are very scrupulous . . . we . . . can reach some tenable though always less than final conclusions' (1997, p. 253). As a history teacher wrestling with these problems, I was intrigued to find both resonance with and an extension of this position in Megill, who, a decade later, reaffirmed Evans' position on 'responsible epistemology', yet asked the historian to leave conflicting attitudes 'suspended in . . . an unresolving dialectic' (2007, p. 2).

On this first issue, an example may be helpful. How far is it possible to justify the inference: 'most Romans believed in a number of gods'? In the continuum in Table 5.1, I tentatively suggest that the question has led less to a polarization of views than to historians

Table 5.1 Historians' views on the possibility of justifying an inference

Inference: 'Most Romans believed in a number of gods'.
Question: *How far is it possible is it to justify this inference?*

Possible to justify					Impossible to justify
Ranke (1840s)	Elton (1960s)	Evans (1990s)	Carr (1960s)	Munslow (1990s)	White (1980s)

admitting to varying possible degrees of truth. How would Daniel have scored if he had referred to Munslow to explain and justify his inference process, suggesting that his form of interpretation was a suitable narrative re-emplotment of its message?

My second issue concerns Daniel's predicament if the results of his efforts at inference clash with a definitive or canonical answer. If, for the purposes of a public examination, 'validity' is deemed to inhere in the product rather than the process of reasoning, that is, if there is a canon of *correct* 'messages' that can be found in a source, then Daniel was, perhaps, rightly marked down. Yet who determines which products are 'correct'? Is Daniel suffering because he has not got the right message according to a canon, be it a canon laid down by an examiner or by history teaching convention?

A further question, arising from this, led me to my third issue. If, as Megill suggests, historians should not sacrifice the pursuit of historical objectivity for their own ends, then how exactly should historians bracket their own context? Ranke (1981) believed he should detach himself from present-day concerns in order to understand the past. Carr (1961) challenged this by arguing that historians, the agents in the constitution of history, will always be affected by their own sociocultural context. In even greater contrast with Ranke's historicism, White's view (1985) of historical texts is present-oriented: the narrator inevitably imposes a present-day agenda. Historians are therefore faced with two competing extremes: Ranke's objective ideal of 'extinguishing the self' – an ideal still dominant, according to Burke, in the empiricist, English-speaking world (2002, p. 25) – and White's approach of imposing the subjectivity of self.

These reflections led me to consider language, both the language of the source, its context and period, and Daniel's own use of language within the interpretative process. These became my fourth and fifth issues. In the Anglo-American analytic tradition, language functions like labels attached to concepts. If language is thus rooted in the real world, then interpreting a source could be a systematic two-process method involving comprehension and evaluation. But a history teacher with knowledge of the 'linguistic turn' of the 1960s (Tosh, 1996, p. 128) is likely to question this. Wittgenstein (1972) famously cast doubt on the ability to derive a fixed meaning directly from a word, proposing, rather, that words function within language 'games' that should be analysed to discover what the agent may have been *doing* in saying what they said, thus anticipating Austin's 'speech acts' (Austin, 1980, p. 52). Derrida suggested that language is a crystal of cultural assumptions that need deconstructing (Kearney, 1994). Rather than unbiased containers of fact, words are cultural constructs and new modes of interpretation may be necessary as a result. 'Truth' uncovered from language is constituted through its relationships rather than being in itself (Butler, 2002). At one extreme, the relativism of the 'linguistic turn' could leave the historian with an anarchic mess of 'arbitrary signifiers' (Evans, 1997, p. 112), where any interpretation goes. Where does this leave Daniel? This became my fourth issue: How should Daniel assign meaning to a word found in a source?

Yet there are many options within this fourth issue. One might take a lead from an historian and philosopher of history such as Megill, and adopt a cautious, careful, contextualized approach to interpreting language in sources. More specifically, one might, like Skinner, pull traditional and continental approaches to language together. Skinner (2002) accepted Foucault's argument that language is a constraint, but he also viewed it as a resource. Skinner used Wittgenstein (1972) and Austin (1980) to present a hermeneutic method that focuses on the meaning of words and on their function within language games. Situating sources within their intellectual context in order to make sense of what their authors were *doing* in writing them, Skinner suggested that meaning and intention cannot be separated: concentrating on the 'speech act' will allow the historian to view what the words are 'doing' in their context, and how the context has shaped the author's use of the word. Skinner's approach challenges the traditional, categorical distinction between description of text and explanation of context. If Daniel had used more of the author's intellectual context to decipher the message of the political cartoon, would the result of his reasoning have been acceptable?

My final issue concerned how a student should use language to capture inferences made from sources. How should Daniel write up his inference? What if *his* use of language also comes with its own contextual baggage? Language used to communicate inferences in Western historical accounts is originally borrowed from legal discourse (Megill, 2008), where conclusions about reliability and truth dominate (Burke, 2002). Continental and postmodern linguistic analysis is less certain about the 'rules', having taken seriously Munslow's (1997) question: Who will write up historians' conclusions unproblematically for everyone to read? This set me wondering: Could a hermeneutic method involving interplay between subject and object, rather than a separation, offer a middle ground between Megill's quest for objectivity and White's subjective emplotment?

Working through these considerations, I wondered how far the spotlight that Skinner and White have shone on the issue of language as a 'gaoler' and 'liberator', on language as power and language as resource, has been used by history educators in English schools. And, insofar as these perspectives may have been neglected, what might they offer as resources for teaching and assessing pupils' emerging evidential thinking?

History educators and evidence

In this section, I identify several turning points in how history teachers have tackled the teaching of evidential thinking, noting where emerging problems have led to new conceptions of curricular goal and pedagogic method. I end by considering progression in evidential thinking.

Apart from rare, documented appearances of sources in classrooms as early as 1910 (McAleavy, 1998), a source-free approach seems to have dominated classrooms in Britain until evidence-focused, post-Carr history was popularized by the Schools Council History Project (SCHP; SHP from 1984) after its foundation in 1972. Despite challenging the Eltonian model, SHP proponents were arguably committed objectivists and rationalists. In his 'Evaluation Study' of the first years of the project, Shemilt (1980) argued that adolescents must understand that 'historical knowledge (is) grounded in reason' (1980, p. 2). In 1978 Lee suggested that only certain kinds of questions were 'worth asking' (1984, p. 5). Asking the 'right' questions to determine the reliability of sources continued to be held up as a key purpose of using sources throughout the 1980s (Sylvester, 1994). When the 1985 GCSE criteria and first History National Curriculum in 1991 made SHP history establishment orthodoxy (DES, 1990b; DfE, 1994), it can be argued that what students were being required to do was fundamentally Eltonian. Pupils were expected to ask the right questions in order to achieve reliable history (DES, 1990b; NCC, 1993). The 'interpretations' element of the 1991 National Curriculum (DES, 1990b), however, could be seen as a counterweight to the rationalist assumptions of the SHP in that it encouraged pupils to recognize the effect of context upon the construction of subsequent, that is, historical, accounts (McAleavy, 1993; NCC, 1993).

In the early 1990s, there were murmurs of mutiny among some teacher practitioners against certain (perhaps unintended) consequences of the SHP 'evidence revolution'. Lang (1993), while strongly supporting the use of sources, reacted against a set of practices that had developed in the wake of SHP, which led pupils into two fallacies, first, believing that bias was always synonymous with distortion and, second, missing the point that an author's bias itself can be the object of an historian's study thus rendering a biased source *useful* in certain respects. As a result of these misconceptions, too many pupils were cynically casting off their sources. In 1998, McAleavy built on Lang's challenge by emphasizing the need for pupils to cultivate healthier forms of scepticism by encouraging pupils both to read and to build fuller syntheses instead of relying on isolated source 'exercises'. McAleavy also agreed with Lang that pupils often needed more focused help (than was common at the time) in understanding that evidence can be used to support propositions not intended by the author, often known as 'unwitting' testimony.

A shift of emphasis among practitioners ensued when the Lang (1993) and McAleavy (1998) critique influenced several practitioner-led solutions to the problems of atomization and student negativity about bias. In different ways, LeCocq (2000) and Byrom (1998) sought to render student activities more constructive. LeCocq (2000) experimented with delaying an emphasis on bias, so that pupils discovered the utility of biased sources before getting sidetracked by the opprobrious connotations of the term. Byrom (1998) ignored bias altogether and focused on synthesis. Gorman (1998), Riley (2000) and Banham (1998, 2000) all developed the 'enquiry', meaning a sequence of lessons governed by a single 'enquiry question', as a planning method: instead of wading through endless exercises on 'reliability' and decontextualized 'source work', their students used a collection of related sources to answer one 'enquiry question'.

Lang (1993), McAleavy (1998) and later Smith (2001) also argued that the provision of more contextual information could help students to avoid formulaic answers (or 'stock evaluation'), although they did not develop a position concerning *at what point* context might best be used during pupil explanation and interpretation of sources. Card (2008) used her practice to show, in some detail, how pupils can be taught to use historical 'clues' to evaluate contemporary images, and Pickles (2010) later examined the relationship between knowledge and evidential thinking, but her research focused on students' direct reference to content, ignoring implicit use of knowledge. The open question remaining for me was: At what level should contextual knowledge be used – at the level of a word, a sentence, or the whole source? The problem of the 'decontextualized gobbet' was later extended in a different direction by Woolley (2003) and Counsell (2004b) who recommended reading much longer extracts to promote not only better evidential thinking but access and engagement. Counsell built directly on McAleavy (1998) by suggesting that longer texts motivated pupils, that they could be used to help pupils understand context and that contextual knowledge was vital for the attempt.

LeCocq and Smith relegated 'comprehension' to the bottom of the progression ladder, in line with early NC non-statutory guidance that 'pupils do not have to understand every last word to get the gist' of a source (NCC, 1993, p. 62). Yet if analysis depends on comprehension, then simple comprehension of meaning may lead to simplistic analysis. Finding issue with small parts of the source, on the other hand, may lead to *more* ways of interpreting the source and to interpreting the source in *different* ways.

A further feature of the teacher-led discourse that re-worked the original SHP approach was the history education community's own twist to wider work taking place on language and literacy. Several teachers explored ways of teaching pupils to become explicitly reflective about the strength of the claims they wanted to make. Wiltshire (2000) taught her pupils to communicate their evaluation of sources through the use of 'language of uncertainty', prompting a debate led by teachers such as Carlisle (2000) on how best to do so. Such approaches were not dissimilar to the earlier calls of Wineburg (1991) in the United States for greater attention to the use of 'hedges' in historical writing. In such ways, various history teachers have explored ways of teaching pupils to communicate degrees of certainty and uncertainty in increasingly nuanced claims about what might be inferred from sources. Yet I was still left with questions about how to help pupils such as Daniel to communicate their comprehension of a source *before* analysing degrees of certainty that may or may not be affected by provenance. How could I help Daniel with the 'earlier' step of communicating his comprehension of a source – that is, if, indeed, it is an 'earlier' step at all – through re-presentation or distillation?

In the United States, in 2001, Wineburg published a work, much cited by history teachers in England, which reflected the debate, among historians, about bracketing versus accepting context. Wineburg argued that historical thinking required the reconciliation of two contradictory positions: first, established modes of thinking in the present cannot be sloughed off; yet second, if we make no attempt to do so, we are doomed to a presentism that reads the present into the past. Thus Wineburg recommended maintaining the tension between familiarity (pupils using continuities in humanness to 'reach across the distance') and strangeness (pupils facing up to the very different, often alien, world of the past). Wineburg saw the former as 'our psychological condition at rest' (Wineburg 2001, p. 69). Therefore, using sources to uncover and reconstruct other intellectual contexts requires an 'unnatural act'. It is, according to Wineburg, a high-order accomplishment. Meanwhile, the Canadian history education researcher Seixas (2000) raises an interesting, possible curricular implication of any acknowledgement of the relationship between past and present: Should pupils themselves directly study ways in which their own, present and subjective contexts shape interpretation of the past?

Thus a myriad of approaches to teaching evidential thinking has emerged in the wake of the SHP revolution, yet how should these forms of thinking be taught developmentally? Two dominant types of progression models for evidential thinking can be found in the literature in England: a tradition designed to support planning and assessment, enshrined by successive national curricula (DES, 1990b; DfE, 1994; DFEE, 1999; QCA/DCSF, 2007), and research-based models of progression, developed first by Shemilt (1980, 1987) in relation to adolescent thinking about evidence, then taken up by the CHATA project (e.g. Lee and Shemilt, 2003).

Shemilt's SHP evaluation (1980) began the tradition of listening to children in order to discover what kinds of ideas about history they operate with and how these develop. The resulting empirically based progression models used mixed qualitative-quantitative research methods but were essentially positivist in their approach to establishing children's thinking (e.g. Shemilt, 1987). For project CHATA, Lee and Ashby (2000) analysed the evidential ideas of 320 children using tasks based on evidence. They noted key impediments to progress such as students confusing 'sources' and 'information', rendering such students helpless when faced with contradictory sources. Conversely, progress becomes possible when, for example, students understand sources as testimony and as relics, and when they realise that 'historians can make inferences that do not depend on anyone telling the truth' (2000, p. 201). Shemilt and Lee later collaborated to create tentative new progression models (e.g. Lee and Shemilt, 2003) based on empirical data emerging from CHATA. Careful to admit that progression in concepts occurred at different times and that stages in pupils' ideas were developmental rather than aggregative, Lee and Shemilt suggest that 'higher-level' thinking about evidence will use context to historicize a source and to understand what the source 'meant to those by and for whom it was produced' (2003, p. 21). This advocacy of reconstructing an intellectual context resonates with Wineburg's (2001) study with American students.

Daniel's GCSE answer certainly demonstrated some questioning, and some knowledge, but did he put them together? *How* did he put them together? Did Daniel first comprehend, and then evaluate, or did he use one in the service of the other?

Rationale for my research

If assessment arrangements and certain professional traditions in England have generally pri-oritized objectivity in student use of historical sources, I wanted to find a different approach, one that would encourage discussion about how *pupil* context affects interpretation. I wanted present and past to be in dialogue, thus 'opening up' notions of validity. Could being open to different conceptions of truth be liberating?

It is not surprising that comprehension is often seen in classrooms as a matter of simply discovering meaning 'within' the word: progression ladders have typically placed comprehension on the bottom rung (e.g. Portal, 1990; OCR, 2009). As explored in the above discussion, the interpretation of language is more complex, however. Skipping over comprehension as a simple 'mining words for meaning' can miss paths where present and past can meet: What does a word mean to us now, in the present context, and how can we find out what it meant to the author, then? How should pupils attempt to 'recreate' the author's intellectual context, as recommended by Skinner (2002), in order to interpret those words?

Focussing on 'social acts', by evaluating authors' language and intentions, could connect present and past (Gardner, 2010, p. 65). Deconstructing sources involves interpretation originating from two contexts (present and past), and comprehension may then involve a level of evaluation. If comprehension is compromised by 'light' readings, as opposed to the deep reading recommended by Wineburg (1991, 2001), then analysis could also be compromised. Wineburg has shown that understanding what an author meant by a single word could require an 'unnatural act': comprehension becomes higher-order when context is needed to make meaning. At this point, I came up with the teaching goal of 'problematization'. To encourage deeper reading of sources, I wanted to make the comprehension process appear more 'problematical' than traditional historians and SHP tradition have sometimes suggested.

The English history classroom tradition of using sources has often linked explanation of an author's bias to his or her context and presuppositions. In my own teaching experience, this sometimes seems to result in pupils appearing to treat source and context separately, a tendency also noted as a problem in diverse research, policy and professional quarters (e.g. Portal, 1990; NCC, 1993, Smith, 2001, respectively). In designing my teaching sequence and ensuing investigation, I decided to proceed on the assumption that comprehending the source and comprehending the context both involve interpretation and both affect each other. A method that appears to perform a double connection of the context of the author with the word, and the word with the context of the historian, is hermeneutics. Relatively unexplored in Western historical thinking (Rüsen, 2002), hermeneutics is largely absent from British history education and, according to Wineburg, from American history education too (2001, p. 10). Wineburg suggests that such an omission needs rectifying. This can feel like a sea-change in a British context. Hermeneutics and her sister tradition, phenomenology, feel distant from the frameworks that appear to underlie history and history education in England and America but they may have much to teach us in reconceptualizing what we ask pupils to do when they read a source and the accomplishments that we might consider valuing. The phenomenological-hermeneutic interplay of subject (the historian) and object (the text and its author) conceptualizes meaning as multidimensional and multi-layered, thus problematizing comprehension (Palmer, 1969).

A potential criticism could be that a 'deconstructive' approach towards language would mire pupils further in a pit of relativism driven only by a subject (Seixas, 2000). Hermeneutics is constructionist, however, rather than subjectivist: there is interplay rather than separation between subject and object. Hermeneutic reading of a text still searches for an essence, but the location of meaning or essence is explicitly complex. I wanted to slow down the reading process and go beyond 'definition' in a presentist sense and discuss what words mean both today and yesterday. Crucially, to link an author's context to the reasons why they created that text, pupils must communicate what the author 'meant' in the source – they have to distil or re-represent the source. This process of 're-representing' a source would therefore need to be broached – a 'communication' stage.

My Year 9 classes were beginning to study World War II. I decided that Churchill was the controversial individual on whom to focus, one whose enduring reputation has been manifested in myriad ways in plentiful sources. My pupils might enjoy discussing him. Consequently, my two research questions emerged as:

1. What were characteristics of pupil thinking in their efforts to capture and communicate their under-standing of Churchill?
2. What kind of challenge did the task of making evidence-based claims about Churchill represent?

Overview of the lesson sequence

I designed a lesson sequence (Table 5.2) that would allow me to explore the areas of interpretation, language and communication in students' evidential thinking. I therefore needed to collect data at different stages to capture pupils' thoughts about evidence and to uncover the most demanding aspects.

The first task was to encourage pupils to look carefully at contemporary texts about Churchill. Much as Byrom (1998) had done with his Year 7 students, I wanted pupils to concentrate on source meaning *before* climbing into evaluation of reliability. I needed to problematize the words in some way in order to encourage pupils to read 'deeply'. I devised a task in which pupils had to identify generalizations in three sources. By talking about how they themselves had, at times, been labelled with generalizations, pupils could start to think about Churchill as a complex human being. All this was inspired by my reading of Ted Hughes' essay 'Capturing Animals' (1967) in which he reflected on the way in which his boyhood pastime of capturing wild animals changed the essence of the animal, once caught in one's pocket. Hughes wrote 'History becomes interesting . . . just as soon as we begin to see vividly, and sense the living presence of, the people who created it.' In order to work out which words could be construed as simplistic or stereotypical, pupils would have to use their own `humanness' (Wineburg, 2001) by reaching into their own present experiences of being labelled.

Wanting pupils to be self-conscious about how their own experience of language affected how they 'mined meaning' from words, I devised a 'word continuum' to foster

Table 5.2 Summary of lesson sequence

Enquiry Question	Learning Objectives	Activities
	By the end of the lesson, pupils will be able to. . .	
How is Churchill trapped by language?	• Identify and explain problems in using generalizations to describe someone • Identify generalizations in historical sources about Churchill • Illustrate inherent assumptions found in the language used by contemporary authors describing Churchill • Re-represent impressions of Churchill based on historical sources.	• Starter: 'Churchill' (the teacher) describes how he has been labelled. • Pupils and teacher discuss how they have been labelled and why generalizations are problematical. Link to context. • Identify generalizations in contemporary sources. • Put generalizations on 'word continuums' from positive to negative. Bring out different interpretations of the word. • Read Ted Hughes' poem, 'Capturing Animals'. Discuss why Hughes deemed the wild animals no longer wild animals once captured. Discuss how to write about people in history. • Pupils attempt to write about Churchill, based on source comprehension. • Plenary: discuss the enquiry question.
Does Churchill need to stay trapped?	• Identify and explain benefits in using generalizations in general and in history • Recall and reinforce knowledge about Churchill, his role and context • Make links between a contemporary source on Churchill and the author's background • Illustrate inherent assumptions found in language used by contemporary authors in historical sources.	• Starter: Watch obituary of Churchill. Discuss how Churchill was portrayed. • Identify generalizations in new sources and put generalizations on 'word continuums'. • Pupils attempt to write about Churchill, based on the new sources. • Introduce author biographies. Discuss reasons why the author used the generalizations. • On cards that represent the authors of the sources, pupils write comments about their relationship to Churchill and how this might affect their opinion. Put cards next to the word continuums. • Plenary: what do the author's words reveal/conceal about Churchill?
When can writing a word be committing a murder?	• Describe how Churchill has been portrayed in contemporary sources • Make links between a contemporary account and events occurring at the time • Examine role of author's bias in reaching a judgement about Churchill today • Use knowledge of Churchill, his context and the source's context in order to discuss the veracity of a source's remarks about Churchill and the value of the source reaching judgement today.	• Starter: High-attaining pupils perform the words used to describe Churchill in the sources, using a bowler hat and cigar. Remind pupils of the effect a single word has on the impression of Churchill. • Pupils complete a table linking events in the war to Churchill's reputation. • Discuss the effect of the author's bias on how useful the source would be for historians to create a description about Churchill in the present day. • Plenary: Which words 'murdered' Churchill by overemphasizing certain aspects at the expense of others?

| How can Churchill be set free? | • Explain one or more ways to justify a judgement about Churchill.
• Comment on the use of language used to describe Churchill.
• Create a description about Churchill based on the sources.
• Justify that description with reference to the sources, to their context, to events then and to events, situations and interpretive contexts since then and/or now. | • Starter: Discuss how pupils' own use of language to communicate ideas about Churchill is unique
• Synthesis exercise (pupils encouraged to be thoughtful about both the methods they are using and the words they will eventually use to communicate their conclusions)
• Pupils begin to create their own descriptions of Churchill.
• High-attaining pupils 'become' the authors of sources. Class discusses where to put authors on language continuum from positive to negative. Tease out differences of opinion. One pupil, as Churchill, walks along. Other authors 'act' the word in the sense of what the 'saying' was 'doing' and what was done 'in saying' (i.e. in the specific sense of Austin's 'speech acts').
• Plenary: pupils read descriptions and explain how they chose their words |

discussion about why a word such as 'dictator' is construed as negative (Figure 5.1). Such tasks helped pupils to begin a scaffolded deconstruction of language, enabling them to 'play' with words, reflecting on their own choice of words and trying out different interpretations.

The final part of the first lesson was crucial. In asking pupils to re-represent the source in their own words, a 'simple description' stage according to Lee and Shemilt (2003), I hoped that pupils' thinking *prior* to any consideration of 'bias' could be revealed. Next lesson, pupils repeated the process with new sources. This time I wanted them to do a Shemiltian 'reverse somersault' (1987) and see language as a *liberator* (helpful in understanding Churchill), rather than something that had 'concealed' a part of Churchill. I then brought in the author's context by providing bibliographies.

In the fourth lesson I needed to help pupils to bring their ideas together constructively in the form of conclusions about Churchill's leadership. I used Wiltshire's (2000) 'language of uncertainty', to help them to communicate their ideas. It was at this point that I introduced

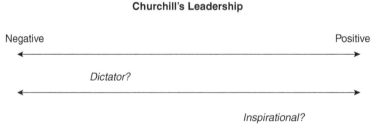

Figure 5.1 Example continuum on which pupils suggest different meanings of language

the enquiry question: How can Churchill be set free? This question would encourage pupils to stay focused on language that has 'revealed' or 'concealed' Churchill.

Research design

Epistemology: constructionism

I used the taxonomy adumbrated by Crotty (1998) to develop my epistemological approach to the research. As a teacher researching my own pupils' learning, a purely objectivist standpoint was not suitable. If objects (e.g., pupils' beliefs) were treated separately, I could not use my subjective knowledge of the context to draw insights about what those beliefs might signify. Yet a wholly subjectivist approach was not appropriate either. I wanted to find something from the data's 'essence' that would challenge traditional, professional conceptualizations of progression in evidential thinking.

Constructionism, in Crotty's (1998) sense, provided a middle way and a solution. It allowed me to *use* myself as subject to enquire into the data emerging from the object (my pupils' historical thinking), rendering my own subjectivity a positive condition for enquiry. This also created congruence with my object of study: pupils' thinking about sources. That subject and object interact to create meaning was a fundamental constructionist assumption of my research questions: pupils interact with historical sources and make meaning *from* them (rather than *imposing* meaning, or discovering meaning in the sources). Furthermore, pupils make sense of historical documents through a context-specific 'cultural lens' and I look at their achievement with a cultural lens too (Figure 5.2), resulting in two layers of interpretation and what Giddens terms a 'double hermeneutic' (Crotty, 1998, p. 56).

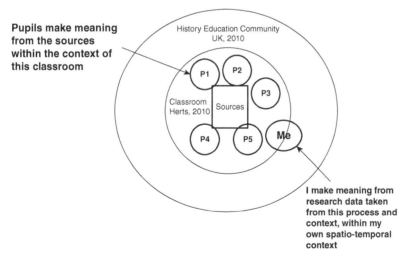

Figure 5.2 A double hermeneutic showing two layers of interpretation in the research process
Note: 'P' stands for 'Pupil'.

Methodology: case study

The study's clear boundary of a five-lesson sequence lent itself to case study (Stake 1995; Bassey, 1999). The study took place in a 'natural' context (as shown in Figure 5.3), where the boundary between the object of study (pupil thinking) and the environment (the classroom) was unclear (Yin, 2003). The purpose of my study, in its analysis of pupils' beliefs, was to examine interrelationships within a 'bounded system' (Stake 1995, p. 2), not to establish a causal explanation. Rather than using feedback to refine teaching intervention, as in action research, I sought only to find out how pupils *responded* to my interventions. I was doing this as a basis for theorizing the character of my pupils' thinking (RQ1) and generating possible new curricular goals (RQ2). I therefore determined that the case study was exploratory and theory-seeking (Stake, 1995; Bassey, 1999).

Loosely borrowing elements from a grounded theory approach allowed me to build a theory inductively, accounting for individual meanings in an idiographic, iterative approach (Glaser and Strauss, 1967). This allowed me to ground a theory *in* the data, rather than impose a potentially restrictive existing theory *upon* the data. Unlike full grounded theory, however, certain traditions within phenomenology acknowledge more strongly the role of the subject (the researcher) in interpretation. I decided that a phenomenological approach would also help me come to a more holistic understanding of the characteristics of my pupils' thinking (RQ1) and would be more appropriate in enabling me to characterize or name their accomplishments (RQ2).

For RQ2, I used a disciplined hermeneutic approach to examine the interplay between aspects of pupil work and the overall achievement bound together in the whole essay. The

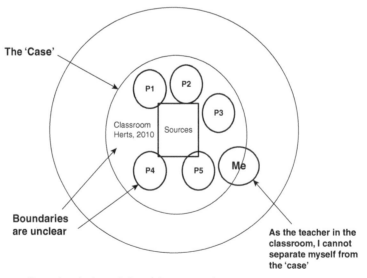

Figure 5.3 Diagram illustrating the boundaries of the case study
Note: 'P' stands for 'Pupil'.

hermeneutic assumption that interpretation is problematical recognizes that pupils' achievement can be understood in more than one way. Dialectical movement between part and whole helped me to find out what my pupils *intended*. I interpreted pupils' reactions to historical documents by moving between their responses and context in the double hermeneutic shown in Figure 5.4.

Research methods

Table 5.3 provides an overview of my data and analysis methods. First, I used pupils' work as data. Reading essays allowed me to draw themes inductively from pupils' writing to determine how pupils communicated their thoughts (RQ1). Hermeneutic readings helped me establish what they found most challenging (RQ2). Second, I used semi-structured interviews and focus groups, helping me probe pupils' thoughts about evidence in a style advocated by White and Gunstone (1994). I conducted interviews with ten pupils, five from each of the two Year 9 classes selected. I conducted focus groups with eight pupils; four from each class. Third, I used a research diary to record pupils' efforts in capturing their understanding of Churchill (RQ1) through discussion in class. This enabled me to use and to reflect on my own subjectivity as classroom teacher in determining elements that pupils struggled with (RQ2).

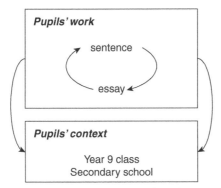

Figure 5.4 A double hermeneutic illustrating my interpretation of pupils' essays

Table 5.3 Summary of research methods, data and analysis

Research question	Data	Data analysis
1. What were characteristics of pupil thinking in their efforts to capture and communicate their understanding of Churchill?	• pupil work • interviews • focus groups • research diary	• theming and coding • relational diagrams • scattergram
2. What kind of challenge did the task of making evidence-based claims about Churchill represent?	• pupil work • interviews • focus groups • research diary	• theming and coding • hermeneutic readings

The external validity of a case study is limited by being space-time-specific (Bassey, 1999), yet I wanted my study to be useful in informing others' research or offering ideas to history teachers similarly wanting to reconceptualize and challenge existing curricular priorities and meanings in evidential work. For Stake (1995), the 'thick descriptions' possible in case studies can produce 'naturalistic generalisations', through the *possibility* of translating the research into similar situations (hypothetical replicability). In order to increase confidence in my findings, I used a triangulation of interview, pupil work and research diary. I conducted the case study with pupils in two attainment bands ('A' and 'B') thus generating diverse pupil data, admitting differing perspectives on the curricular and disciplinary issues in play.

Data analysis

Thirty essays were selected according to convenience sampling: I chose essays that were complete and that provided an equal mix of A and B bands. I subjected my data to content analysis, inductively generating themes and codes to answer RQ1. I use the term 'themes' as raw categorization of data emerging from initial analysis, and 'codes' as recurrent themes, organized systematically using Boyatzis' structure (1998). I created code descriptions (Table 5.4) to support the validity of my claims, avoiding reductionism and keeping emergent themes 'strong in reality' (Bassey, 1999, p. 23). Following Brown and Dowling (1998), I used diagrams to explore how codes emerging from essays could be organized and connected.

To answer RQ2, using interview and focus group transcripts, I inductively generated themes concerning *pupils'* perceptions of what they found challenging. I then subjected six essays, written by pupils with a range of abilities, to hermeneutic readings in order to build my interpretation of how pupils responded to the challenge of making evidence-based claims. In this second interpretation I sought to find new and multidimensional understandings of the challenge through a 'wholistic' reading (van Manen, 1990, p. 93). I decided to present these hermeneutic readings as qualitative narrative accounts (van Manen, 1990), rather than strict categories, in order to capture complex essences of pupil thinking. In accordance with ethical guidelines summarized by Stutchbury (2013), I obtained informed pupil and parental consent, anonymizing all names.

Table 5.4 Example of one code presented in the coding framework

Broad theme (category)	Sub-theme (code)	Code description
Pupil thoughts about language used to describe Churchill	Temporal context of language	Authors come from different contexts so Churchill's reputation will change due to new connotations being attached to words. Sometimes even a year may make a difference – for example, Britain's success in war may take a dramatic turn. Therefore the word the author used may have been shaped by context.

Findings for RQ1: What were characteristics of pupil thinking in their efforts to capture and communicate their understanding of Churchill?

Analysis of 30 essays led me to record 56 'codes' ('codes' were elements appearing to recur across more than three essays). Six categories emerged from the 56 codes that helped structure the phenomena into broad types (see Table 5.5).

I further classified the six categories into two overall forms: pupils' thoughts about the *author's* interpretation of Churchill, and their thoughts about their *own* interpretation (column 1, Table 5.5). This distinction was fundamental: in my teaching, I had wanted pupils to appreciate the strangeness of the author's intellectual context by comparing it with their own 'secondary' interpretive context. Four of the six categories are presented here.

Category 1: Pupil thoughts about the language used to describe Churchill in contemporary sources

All pupils could identify some 'generalizations' in a source (e.g. 'dictator'). They were all able to use their own contexts to explain how these generalizations were different from other kinds of language in the source. Pupils made more comments about the problems than about the benefits of using generalizations. Twenty-two pupils considered generalizations negative because they could neither describe the 'whole of Churchill' nor 'capture his complexity'. A further twenty-one pupils considered generalizations negative because they demonstrated bias and were therefore untrustworthy, but nine pupils judged bias useful in showing how authors reacted to Churchill.

Table 5.5 Recurrent themes ('codes') emerging from analysis of pupils' essays

Category	Content (pupils' thoughts about)	Category description
1	Author interpretation of Churchill	Pupil thoughts about the language used to describe Churchill in contemporary sources
2		Pupil thoughts about why contemporaries used certain words to describe Churchill
3		Pupil thoughts about how to determine the trustworthiness of the author's description of Churchill
4	Pupil interpretation of Churchill	Pupil thoughts about what method(s) or tools they should use to come to their own description about Churchill
5		Pupil thoughts about the content of their own description about Churchill
6		Pupil thoughts about what words to use to describe Churchill themselves

Twelve pupils categorized the meaning of a generalization as good or bad. One pupil wrote 'the enemy will say bad stuff'. However, seven pupils problematized this categorization by suggesting that connotations of words change according to temporal context. One pupil suggested that although the word 'dictator' has negative connotations in democratic societies today (as it suggests unrepresentative leadership), the word may have had a different meaning for people in the past. This suggests that some pupils saw the word 'dictator' and instead of comprehending the word at face value, saw it as embodying differing interpretations. Discussing the word led some pupils to consider how connotations of the word today might differ from those pertaining during World War II. For example, one pupil said 'dictator . . . can be good in war'. Another pupil said 'at the time, the UK didn't know what to do or who had a plan, after Neville Chamberlain'. Some pupils appeared to be asking what the word 'dictator' meant to the author and his audience.

Five pupils problematized the categorization of a word's meaning as positive or negative by suggesting that the connotations of words change according to different people's perceptions. One pupil contrasted his view of the word 'arrogant' with an author's. Six pupils qualified what they thought the generalization that they had identified actually meant. For example, one pupil went into detail about what a 'warmonger' is. Thus, while nearly half saw categorizing a word as a simple process, a minority of pupils questioned their comprehension of words before evaluation. Comments at interview bore this out by showing a reflexive awareness, for example: 'my own time period will affect my answer', and 'we're not in a war so we will think of it differently'. Thus some pupils understood the effect of current or personal context of the interpreter upon language.

The idea that a minority of pupils were grappling with both present and past contexts *before* evaluating sources is borne out by other findings. Six pupils explained in essays that labels such as 'dictator' can be 'recycled' through time and that repeated use might make more people believe the term to be apposite. Some pupils noted that uses of language can be so sensitive to temporal context that even a year may make a difference: one pupil argued, 'Britain's success in war may take a dramatic turn'. A minority of pupils appeared to use context to comprehend *what* the author was saying, before using context to make suggestions about *why* they said it.

Finally, I used a diagram to link codes within this first category. Figure 5.5 demonstrates that if pupils judged that a generalization was positive or negative, they would then evaluate the source in the light of this categorization. If, however, they problematized the categorization to suggest that words have different connotations in different contexts, different interpretive avenues opened up.

Category 2: Pupil thoughts about why contemporaries used certain words to describe Churchill

In their essays, most pupils attempted to explain why the author had used the generalization. This is supported by interview and focus group data, where pupils recommended explaining why authors said what they said as an important tool to use in constructing an analysis of Churchill. The reasons pupils gave in their explanations can be grouped into the five

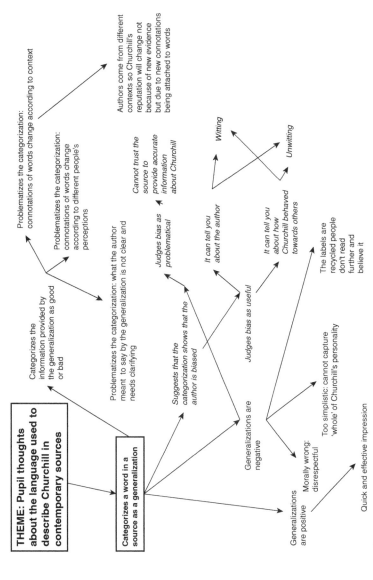

Figure 5.5 Relational diagram illustrating how codes can be linked within Category 1

codes in Table 5.6, each presented with its frequency. The majority of pupils found four or more reasons why an author used a certain word, from the author's individual background and from the wider context. Communication of explanations differed. Thirteen pupils used simplistic explanations; for example, one pupil said 'because all Nazis hated Churchill' and another said an author supported Churchill because he was American. On the other hand, twelve pupils appeared to use nuanced explanations, treating the meaning of what the author said as multidimensional. Five of these twelve pupils situated the author's motives in extended spatial or temporal scales. One pupil commented on the impact of the English Empire on interpretations of Churchill, and another went into detail about pre-war Nazi Germany. This appears to demonstrate that some pupils were rebuilding an author's context, from individual and psychological motives to international macro-forces.

In Figure 5.5, I show that, on the evaluative level, if pupils judged a generalization as negative, there was one thought that resulted: the pupil did not trust the source. If the pupil judged the bias as useful, they appeared to have two possible thoughts: it was useful to tell them either about the author or about how Churchill behaved towards or in relation to the author. This, again, opened up new areas of thinking where pupils could ask themselves: Was the testimony witting or unwitting? Did the author mean to say what he said? Codes in Category 2 were also presented within a relational diagram (Figure 5.6), and they pointed to the same finding. More links between the author and events occurring at the author's time of writing appear to make more nuanced explanations, involving a myriad of competing factors.

Table 5.6 Reasons used by pupils in their explanation of a contemporary author's interpretation of Churchill, with relative frequencies

Reason for author's use of generalization	No of pupils
Author's position in relation to Churchill	25
Events happening at the time the author was writing	23
Views and/or ideologies held by the author	22
The purpose and/or nature of the source	22
Author's awareness of audience	9

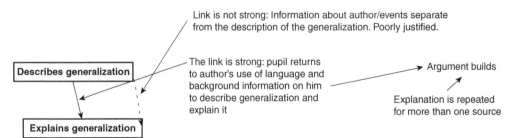

Figure 5.6 Part of a relational diagram illustrating how codes can be linked within Category 2

Some pupils, after identifying the generalization, then used information about the author to explain the use of the word by a constant to-ing and fro-ing between author and word. Other pupils appeared to *separate* the description of the generalization from its explanation.

When there is a strong link, pupil explanations keep on building; where the link is weak, however, the argument appears to have nowhere to go (Figure 5.6). The key part of a strong link appeared to be where pupils kept returning to the generalization used by the author in the explanation: there was interplay between describing the generalization (comprehension level) and explaining the generalization (evaluative level). Pupils linking description and explanation appeared to be operating hermeneutically as illustrated by the first extract from my hermeneutic reading of Jane's work, shown in Table 5.7.

By returning to the word after giving reasons why it was used, the pupils questioned their own understanding of the generalization, in their own context. However, for ten pupils there was a disconnection. Pupils separated events in the author's life from what they wrote in the sources, commenting on them separately. Instead of a hermeneutic circle (Figure 5.7), their interpretation was linear and led, at the most, to one link. Without linking the information about the author *back to the word*, they were unable to reveal why that word had been used in the author's context.

Table 5.7 Extracts from my hermeneutic reading of Jane's work

Jane

1. One challenge is determining the meaning of the source. In all three sources she analyses in depth, she appears to ask herself: does it suggest Churchill was a good leader, or a bad leader? When meaning is at first unclear, she uses other quotes in the source to help her, linking 'immoral malice' and 'traitor to England' with the generalization 'dictator' in order to help her build up a clearer picture of the tone of the source and of its overall message. Therefore, before she enters into an *explanation* of the author's tone, she appears to think that she needs to synthesize parts of the contents of the source in order to be clear about what that content means.

2. In responding to the challenge of 'recreating' the author's context, Jane 'surrounds' the author with contemporary events and people. She surrounds Joyce with Hitler, Churchill, Germans living under the Nazis' Third Reich, and Joyce's listeners. Temporally, she comments on the Battle of Britain and World War II, and spatially, she comments on both Nazi Germany and Britain in her explanation.

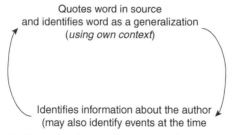

Quotes word in source
and identifies word as a generalization
(*using own context*)

Identifies information about the author
(may also identify events at the time

Figure 5.7 Hermeneutic method of interpretation used by some pupils

Category 5: Pupil thoughts about the content of their own descriptions of Churchill

Categories 4–6 concentrate on characteristics of pupils' thoughts about their *own* interpretations of Churchill. Category 5 focuses on pupils' thoughts about the content of their descriptions of Churchill. Twenty-eight out of thirty pupils believed that conclusions were possible despite the bias inherent in contemporary opinions of Churchill, although they justified their conclusions in different ways. Ten pupils suggested that because of Churchill's context (as leader in wartime), he needed to be a 'dictator' or 'arrogant', and used this to write positive descriptions. Six pupils appeared to deal with conflicting interpretations of Churchill by describing Churchill as a complex man who 'acts differently according to different people'. One pupil in the interview commented: 'if you give Churchill a straight label, you've . . . trapped him' and another justified the uniqueness of their own interpretation of Churchill by stating 'we can compare [Churchill] to another war leader later', suggesting that the pupil is aware of events affecting his own interpretation of Churchill.

Category 6: Pupil thoughts about what words they could use to use to describe Churchill

This category focused on pupils' thoughts about their description of Churchill at the level of single words or sentence. The writing of sixteen pupils demonstrated a level of caution in describing Churchill, and nine of those sixteen pupils made conscious use of the language of uncertainty. However, eight pupils' written communication could be seen to demonstrate elements of 'over-confidence' and seven pupils made one or more judgements about Churchill that were not linked explicitly to evidence.

Findings for RQ2: What kind of challenge did the task of making evidence-based claims about Churchill represent?

First, I present recurrent themes emerging from the analysis of interviews and focus groups. Second, I select essays demonstrating a range of interpretive strategies and interpret these essays using a hermeneutic approach.

Themes emerging from interviews and focus groups

Theming of this data provided me with *pupils'* perceptions of what was most challenging. The most difficult elements appeared to be the problem of 'determining the motive of the author' and 'communicating thoughts on paper'. In terms of the former theme, one pupil found it difficult to find out 'where he's [the author] coming from' and another commented 'you have to read between the lines'. For the latter theme, one pupil commented 'I knew what I wanted to say but didn't know how to put it' and another said 'I found it hard to phrase it'. Other challenging elements appeared to be 'coming to a conclusion' and 'justifying conclusions'. Less recurrent themes (recorded twice) included: processing a large amount of information; writing about Churchill without labelling him; cross-referencing information.

Only two elements appeared to be 'easy'. First, quoting source content; as one pupil explained, 'you had the information there'. Second, some pupils said it was easy to communicate their own opinion about Churchill: 'the sources gave me a good idea'. Finally, the theme of having to 'slow down' to read the sources emerged from data analysis. One pupil explained 'you have to read really carefully . . . two or three times' and another clarified 'we were looking deeper'.

Themes emerging from hermeneutic reading of six essays

Through several readings of six essays I explored the kind of challenge presented by the task of describing Churchill in depth. Five challenges emerged:

1. Comprehending and distilling meaning from a source
2. Using contextual knowledge to make meaning from a source
3. Maintaining clarity of purpose in consulting a source
4. Determining the value of a source as a response to a particular question
5. Constructing one's own interpretation of Churchill.

These themes were akin to van Manen's (1990) 'knots' through which the web of meaning is held together. In this section, and in the extracts from my hermeneutic readings presented in Tables 5.7 and 5.8, I will illustrate data interpretation that led to Themes 1, 2 and 5.

Table 5.8 Extracts from my hermeneutic reading of Mary, Clinton and Josh's work

Mary

Mary appears to suggest that a source is reliable when it is balanced and shows that Churchill is 'human'. Mary is judging the reliability of sources according to her own conception of Churchill arising from her own context, drawing upon her own thoughts about morality, human rights and 'the Truth'. She appears to be concerned with 'truth' in five places in her essay.

Clinton

Clinton comments: 'this backs up my point that maybe the British had given him a hard time'; 'it may also prove my point that he only wrote it because of his job'. Clinton appears to be aware that his assertions have a different status, depending on the strength of their claim, and it could be that this awareness prompts him to self-consciously build upon his assertions in order to increase the strength of his argument. His language, in places, is extremely cautious, always explicitly showing degrees of certainty/uncertainty by using words such as 'perhaps', 'might be' and 'implies'.

Josh

Josh is left with only one avenue in meeting the challenge of finding a 'true' and 'full' assessment of Churchill: 'if you met him . . . you could make your own deductions'. He returns to this argument in his final paragraph, concluding that 'no one can ever know'.

Theme 1, 'comprehending and distilling meaning from a source', is a challenge that involves considerably more thought than merely re-stating or quoting elements of the source. Quoting is arguably 'slicing' off content, rather than attempting to interpret its meaning. Students such as Jane (see Table 5.7, Extract 1) were treating meaning as multidimensional and requiring a successive trying out of associations between words in the source. These students thus rendered the task much more complex than if they were treating it as simple or static. Theme 2, 'using contextual knowledge', frequently saw challenge inhere in the building of multilayered explanations of the author and who or what they were responding to. Jane, for example (see Table 5.7, Extract 2) sees many different dimensions to Churchill, emerging from situating him in temporal and spatial context. Mary, on the other hand (see Table 5.8), considers the meaning of the source from her own context and uses this to dismiss certain sources. Theme 5, 'constructing one's own interpretation of Churchill' constitutes a substantial challenge where students, such as Clinton, link their various thoughts about Churchill together, using cautious, tentative language to express judgements that feel self-conscious in their attention to the status of the claim. Josh, by contrast, struggled to embrace this challenge at all and failed to construct his own interpretation because no source met his standards of 'truth'. He also appears to be impeded by an assumption that interpretation is synonymous with opinion.

Discussion and recommendations

Perhaps the most significant finding concerns the type of challenge presented by making meaning from sources *before* evaluation. Distilling meaning from sources appeared both creative and challenging, especially where pupils thought extensively about what an author *meant*. The different strategies employed by students to determine meaning potentially mirror the academic debate of whether meaning is 'contained' in a word through logic, or whether meaning can be deconstructed. Some pupils considered the meaning of sources to be static, conforming to a traditional Western-analytic view of language (Kearney, 1994). Others believed that the source could be interpreted in different ways, bearing out a continental and postmodernist approach to the word as a crystal of cultural assumptions (Butler, 2002). This difference suggests that the idea of 'comprehending' a source in order to garner 'information' is not a simple process. Should teachers encourage pupils to treat meaning as static or shifting?

The second important issue arising from the investigation is the character of challenge involved in *communicating* the meaning that pupils distilled. Building a multi-dimensional interpretation of multilayered source content within its context has the potential to increase the strength and warrant of that interpretation. In its most demanding and most successful manifestations, pupils were starting to link different interpretations of the source together to build a cautious, complex argument *about the difficulty of interpreting*, carefully substantiating these with different tentative readings of particular sources (rather than relying on formulaic generalizations about the general difficulty of interpretation). The high demand and historical value of this challenge is underscored, perhaps, by the failure of many pupils to attain it. Many pupils appeared to be overwhelmed by the multitude of possible interpretations. Future questions that the history teaching profession might therefore address include: Should pupils express their multi-layered findings? If so, how should high attainment be classified? Should pupils use language akin to 'law discourse' (Megill, 2007) with reference to universal laws, or should they deploy reference to Skinner's idea (2002) of establishing consistency of belief? What kind of reasoning about the interrelationships between these issues should characterize pupils' answers at the highest level? Perhaps a stage is missing prior to Wiltshire's (2000) 'language of uncertainty', one requiring pupils to think about how to express differing interpretations within one argument. Table 5.9 is a resource that I devised in order to show what helping pupils with such a stage might involve. The resource attempts to bridge two challenges emerging from my findings: determining the meaning of a source by using as much context as possible and expressing a judgement concerning what we might reasonably glean from that source in response to a question.

The third issue that may have value for in re-thinking appropriately demanding curricular goals is that some pupils blended different types of context, past and present, in order to establish and distil meaning in sources. Interestingly, they tended to do this at a stage *before* evaluation and the complexity of what they were doing casts doubt on the adequacy of the term 'comprehension' and its conventional treatment as a low-order accomplishment. In order to identify what constituted 'generalizations' in sources, all pupils used facets of their own context, such as personal experience and language use familiar to them, although only a few were explicit or self-conscious about such derivation. Some pupils, however, used their knowledge of the context in which the author was

Table 5.9 Possible addition to Wiltshire's 'language of uncertainty' (2000)

Part 1						
People	One person	Some individuals	Many people		Most contemporaries	
Space	At one point	At several points	Across most of the war		Throughout this time	
Time	In Churchill's office	In London	In Britain	In the Empire	In the enemy camp	

Part 2									
Final status	hints	might mean	suggests	implies	indicates	tells me	establishes	means	proves

Part 3

One person, at one point in the war (when Churchill had just become Prime Minister) thought that . . .

However, he was in Churchill's new office, which suggests . . . This source therefore hints that Churchill was . . .

Most contemporaries living in Britain, across most of the war, thought that Churchill displayed elements of arrogance. This means that Churchill was most likely . . .

writing explicitly to challenge this 'presentist' process (Wineburg, 2001). These pupils garnered a different view of Churchill. By questioning what the source meant in the author's context *and* in their own, and by considering how one modifies the other, these pupils were beginning to create a dialogue between present and past and thus to show the potential of such a dialogue in fostering and displaying student thinking. Indeed, in order to question connotations of words, some pupils said they needed more reading time, which appears to bear out Wineburg's suggestion that pupils need to 'slow down' to 'talk with' texts (2001, p. 69). All this counteracts the tradition that interpretation is a systematic two-stage process of 'comprehension' and 'evaluation' (NCC, 1993). Moreover, as pupils then moved into evaluation, their reflections on what the author was *doing* in describing Churchill built on the meaning that they elicited at the 'comprehension' stage. Encouraged to reflect in this depth and using hermeneutic strategies, some students kept returning to the meaning of a word, and, through questioning it, produced different interpretations of what the author was *doing* in creating the source. This bears out Skinner's argument against categorical distinction between description of text and explanation of context (2002).

In Figure 5.8, I attempted to show all themes arising from RQ1 and RQ2 together. I then built a very tentative theory (Figure 5.9) about how pupils' thinking developed when faced with the challenge of determining how language in history can be both a 'liberator' and a potential 'gaol'.

Overall, my findings suggest that 'comprehension' ought to be treated as far more problematical and demanding than is suggested by the examination mark scheme that prompted my investigation (OCR, 2009). Unexpectedly, this study also led me to conclude that Daniel's answer *did* show a low level of thinking, but not because his resulting inference was wrong; rather, because he did not justify it. He certainly referred to contextual knowledge, but he did not link this back to the meaning that he had inferred. By separating his inference from his contextual knowledge, his explanation stood linear, static and alone. Daniel needed more contextual friends – Lloyd George, or the Boer War – to help him build a multi-stranded argument.

If a richer conception of the challenge involved in source interpretation were to pertain in public examinations, then one attribute that ought to persuade an examiner is that a student has faced an unfamiliar world and explored it, through taking more than one avenue and with close reference to context.

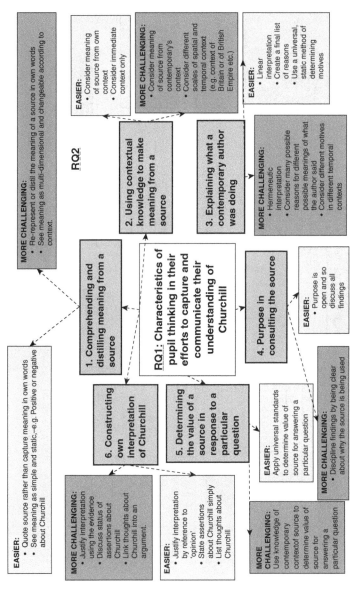

Figure 5.8 Illustration of how themes emerging from RQ1 can be linked to themes emerging from RQ2

Note: Themes emerging from RQ1 are represented by Boxes 1–6. Themes emerging from RQ2 are represented by the 'more challenging' and 'easier' boxes.

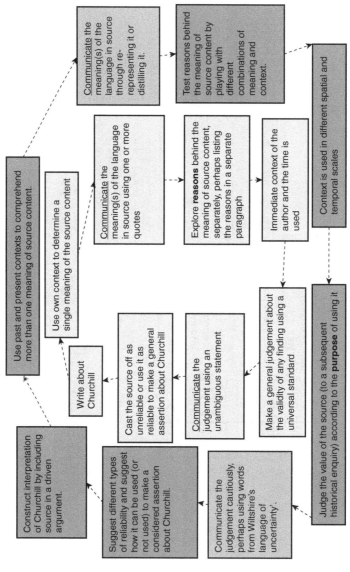

Figure 5.9 Tentative theory, based on the case study, showing possible processes in students' thinking.

Note: Higher-order historical thinking is shown in black boxes and lower-order historical thinking in grey.

Historical Interpretation: Using Online Discussion

Daniel Magnoff

6

Chapter outline

Introduction

There is an established tradition of history education in England that aims to develop students' understanding of the nature of history as a 'discipline' or 'form of knowledge'. The tradition seeks to shape their understandings of what historical knowledge claims are and of how they are made and can be evaluated (Rogers, 1979; Shemilt, 1980, Ashby, 2011; Chapman, 2011a; Haydn, 2011b). This tradition has had a significant impact on curriculum, pedagogy and assessment in secondary schools (Kitson, Husbands and Steward, 2011). At all levels of the secondary school curriculum, pupils are expected to study historical evidence, historical interpretation and a number of other 'second order' concepts (QCA/DCSF, 2007; Ofqual, 2011, 2012; DfE, 2013). History teachers have played a seminal role in realizing this disciplinary curriculum in practice through sustained traditions of curricular-pedagogic innovation and debate (Counsell, 2011a).

The last thirty years have seen considerable innovation in curriculum and assessment in the Advanced Subsidiary (AS Level) and Advanced (A Level) curriculum, covering the upper secondary age group (16–19-year-old pupils) (Chapman, 2011a). Although by no means typical of the history curriculum for 16–19-year olds as a whole, innovative courses, such as the Oxford, Cambridge and Royal Society of Arts' (OCR) 'History B' qualification, have been developed that take 'the nature of the discipline of history' and 'theoretical and methodological issues' (OCR, 2013, p. 3) as a central focus of study. There is also a strong tradition of innovative practice focused on developing pupil engagement and conceptual rigour in pedagogy and practice post-16 in ways that go beyond the often narrow requirements set by examinations (Historical Association, 2005). This is evident, for example, in the work of Harris (2001) and Fordham (2007) on developing pupils' understandings of argument and in the work of Laffin (2000, 2009, 2012) and Howells (2011) on developing pupils' understanding of historical methodology, interpretation and writing.

Despite these positive developments, concerns have been raised about how far existing post-16 curriculum specifications require pupils to develop meaningful understandings of how histories are written and of how historians work (Pickles, 2011). The majority of examination specifications approach historiography in limited and simplistic ways – viewing different historians' interpretations as a matter, for example, of conflicting 'opinions' or 'judgments' that students are to evaluate by indicating 'how far they agree' with short quotations in which they are expressed (Edexcel, 2012a). This fails to build on the more sophisticated tradition of teaching 'interpretations of history' in the statutory lower secondary curriculum in England (e.g. Howells, 2005; Hammond, 2007) and on earlier approaches to assessing historical methodology post-16, such as Association Examination Board, Syllabus 673, the London Syllabus E and the Cambridge History Project (Chapman, 2011a). Studies by university historians (Booth, 2005; Collins, 2011) and by teachers (Hibbert, 2006) looking at undergraduates' understandings of school and university history and observations made by students themselves (Alkis, 2005; Benjamin, 2005) all indicate that, for many students at least, the post-16 curriculum fails to prepare young people adequately for the challenges of studying history at university.

This chapter reports a pedagogic innovation – 'The Beatles Project' – that was designed to develop AS Level (16- to 17-year-old) students' understandings of historical methodology.[1] The project builds on prior attempts to develop students' thinking by connecting school and university history (Thompson and Cole, 2003; Chapman and Facey, 2009) and on efforts to use virtual learning environments (VLEs) – and discussion boards, in particular – to enhance historical learning (Moorhouse, 2006; Martin, Coffin and North, 2007; Martin, 2008; Chapman and Hibbert, 2009). Specifically, it arose from the History Virtual Academy Project (HVA) (Chapman, 2009a; Chapman, Elliott and Poole, 2012), intended to develop A Level (18- to 19-year-old) students' understandings of conflicts of historical interpretation and of the academic discipline of history. The 2011 iteration of the HVA revealed positive impacts on participants (Chapman, Elliott and Poole, 2012), and its architects therefore decided to design an intermediate intervention for students in the year below (AS Level). The Beatles Project was the result of those discussions.

In this chapter I explore and analyse the outcomes of the second iteration of the Beatles Project. I draw tentative conclusions about what might happen were historical methodology to be taken more seriously in the post-16 phase.

The Beatles Project: origins and aims

Both the HVA and the Beatles Project were collaborative projects; first, in the sense that they were jointly designed by teachers and lecturers working in schools and colleges and by academic historians and history educators working in universities; and, second, in the sense that they involved post-16 students in England interacting online with each other and with academic historians.

In both projects, the aim of the online collaboration was to stimulate and refine the students' historical thinking. A critical, forum-based community was designed to foster engagement and facilitate debate. Academic historians were invited to prompt broader discussion and to model aspects of mature 'historical thinking' (Wineburg, 2007). We aimed, through the Beatles Project, to develop students' understandings of the ways in which historians make selections from available sources of evidence when pursuing historical enquiries.

I was one of two members of the HVA team who developed the Beatles Project. The other was Dr Marcus Collins, an historian at Loughborough University whose specialisms include the history of permissiveness in the 1960s and the history of The Beatles. The participating students undertook the project in the summer term, just after completing their AS-level exams. They were drawn from three schools, two selective and one with a comprehensive intake. I administered the VLE through which the discussions were conducted. Collins commented on and contributed to the discussions. The online discussion forum was intended to temper the students' temptation to reject historical accounts as mere 'opinion' and to engage them with the principle that the discourse of history operates under rules of 'methodical argumentation, conceptual language, control by experience, and gaining consent and agreement by rational means' (Rüsen, 2005, p. 134). We wanted the students to move towards the understanding that there are good methodological reasons why historical accounts might differ.

The Beatles and the emergence of the permissive society in post-war England were chosen as the focus for the project on the grounds of accessibility: the students had, of course, heard of The Beatles and had some knowledge about them, arising from popular culture, but since they had had not studied them as part of their history courses, the students' views were unlikely to be affected by prior teaching and learning. In order to ensure that the students' had a firm contextual base from which to approach the tasks, a 30-minute virtual lecture delivered by Marcus Collins on The Beatles and the permissive society was made available to students on the VLE. Insofar as students would draw upon their background knowledge to supplement the overview from Collins, the topic itself could help reveal aspects of their preconceptions. We hoped that the students might become aware of such preconceptions in each others' responses and, perhaps, in their own answers.

The Beatles Project: structure and discussion design

Students were provided with anonymous logins that provided access to the project portal and were allowed to work individually or in groups of no more than four. On the project homepage, students were provided with the following instructions and introduction:

> The 1960s are frequently presented as a decade in which significant social and cultural changes took place in Britain. Many of these changes are often linked to the 'youth culture' of the time.
>
> The Beatles are the iconic '60s band' and are often treated as representative of the dramatic changes of the decade. The career of The Beatles also spanned the 1960s and is often considered to reflect the wider changes that took place.
>
> We would like you to imagine that you were writing an historical article on The Beatles looking at the career of The Beatles, and, in particular, at their song lyrics.
>
> Our overall question is this:
>
> *'Does an investigation of the lyrics of The Beatles' songs support the claim that dramatic changes took place in the bands' attitudes and values over the course of its career?'*

In the first week of the project students were asked to complete two tasks (see Table 6.1 for an outline of the full sequence of tasks). First, they were asked to spend no more than 15 minutes answering the following question before emailing their responses to their teachers:

> *'Historians set out to answer questions about the past. Please explain what you think historians do in order to answer their questions.'*

This question was intended to elicit students' preconceptions about historical methodology and to provide a benchmark against which progress in their thinking over the course of the project could be measured.

The second task in the first week focused the students' thinking on source selection. Before being asked to answer the overall question (Table 6.1), the students were asked to select no more than ten Beatles' songs from a list of fifty that they felt would best support a balanced and thorough answer to the question. They were asked to post this list to the discussion forum together with an explanation and justification of their choices. Finally, students were asked to comment on at least one other group's post, offering criticism or support for their

Table 6.1 The Beatles Project task structure

Week	Task	Week
1	1	Students answered the following question and emailed the answer to their teachers.'
		Historians set out to answer questions about the past. Please explain what you think historians do in order to answer their questions.'
	2	Students to watch and take notes on 30 minute lecture on The Beatles and the permissive society, delivered by Marcus Collins
	3	From a list of 50 Beatles' songs, students were asked to select ten that they felt would help them answer the overall project enquiry question:
		Does an investigation of the lyrics of The Beatles' songs support the claim that dramatic
		changes took place in the bands' attitudes and values over the course of its career?
		Students were asked to (a) post their selection to the VLE, providing a justification of their choices and (b) comment on at least one other group's post, offering criticism, support, or requests for clarification as appropriate.
		At the end of the first week, Collins posted a review of the posts as a whole to the VLE.
2	4	Students were asked to post a revised list of songs to the VLE, taking account of comments made in the first week, and to provide an explanation of their decisions.
	5	Students were asked to post a formal answer to the overall project enquiry question to the VLE (see above).
		At the end of the second week, Marcus Collins made a final post summing-up and commenting on the students' contributions.
	6	Students were asked to revisit and revise their response to Task 1 from Week 1 and to email this to their teacher.

suggestions, or requests for clarification as appropriate. At the end of the first week, Collins posted a review of the posts as a whole.

In the second week, students were asked to complete three tasks: first, to post a revised list of songs, taking account of comments made in the first week, together with an explanation of their decisions; second, to post a formal answer to the overall question (Table 6.1); third, to revisit and revise their response to the initial question in Task 1, explaining what they think historians do *in order to answer questions about the past*. Our intention was to track change and development in students' thinking by comparing revisions made over the course of the exercise. At the end of the second week, Marcus Collins made a final post summing-up and commenting on the students' contributions.

In denying the students the possibility of discussing every possible historical fragment relevant to answering the question, our intention was to force the students to make judgements about which material was of most value. In other words, we were posing the students a methodological problem (How to choose and how to justify your choice?) and we hoped to provoke metacognitive reflection as a result. We hoped that the process would challenge the tacit paradigms and assumptions that the students would bring to the task, which, we expected, would predispose them to approach the issue chronologically and thematically in terms of themes such as love, politics and social change. The criteria on which the students drew when making their choices would, we hoped, come clearly into focus when they commented on each other's posts: we hoped that students' song selections and justifications of their choices would differ. We also hoped that the process of discussion would encourage students to develop their answers and – especially if their song selections and the grounds on which they were based differed – help them to appreciate the value and role of peer-based criticism and review in disciplined historical enquiry.

There were, of course, potential flaws in this design. Like historical researchers, pedagogic designers have to make assumptions; and our assumptions about the sources that we were asking the students to work with were certainly open to challenge. Can songs be legitimately used to answer the overall question that we had set (Table 6.1), for example? There are significant problems in trying to use the lyrics of Beatles' songs as evidence of their fluctuating states of mind. Macdonald argues that for Lennon and McCartney, in particular, the lyrics were of secondary importance to their melodic and harmonic compositions and were often confused, trite and cryptic (MacDonald, 2008, pp. 22–23). Lennon, in particular, bristled at the notion of his lyrics being analysed rather than 'felt'. When he learned that English teachers at his old school were studying his song lyrics as part of their curriculum he deliberately wrote the nonsensical lyrics in *I am the Walrus* (ibid., pp. 266–267).

These problems did not strike us as insurmountable, however. We felt that the accessibility of this exercise – making a simple selection – might reveal something of the process of history-making to the students and provide a context in which they could develop, debate and test hypotheses. The absence – and perhaps the impossibility – of any definitively 'correct' answer to the problem could prove helpful in stimulating reflective responses uninhibited by the desire to be 'right'.

Evaluating the Beatles Project

The remainder of this chapter analyses data arising from the online discussions and explores the following three questions:

1. What kinds of ideas did students draw on when asked to explain the process by which historians create accounts?
2. How do these ideas compare with those that seem to have informed the students' own attempts to formulate hypotheses?
3. Did online discussion between students, their peers and an academic expert make a difference to what students said when explaining how historical accounts are created and, if so, in what ways?

Students' initial ideas about how historians work

Thirty-four students completed task one, explaining how they thought historians go about answering 'questions about the past'. The data sets were analysed using an inductive coding strategy (Strauss and Corbin, 1998). Posts were read and coded in iterative cycles until a stable system of descriptive codes had been developed that allowed all the students' explanatory moves to be categorized on the basis of similarities and differences in the ideas that they referenced. Six codes were developed and are detailed in Table 6.2. Individual posts were coded using as many codes as necessary to capture the complexity of the claims made.

Table 6.2 Types of student explanation of how historians answer questions

Response type	Exemplification[2]
Archival	'Historians should gain as much knowledge as they possibly could . . . Once they have attained this knowledge they can begin to establish their own viewpoints and opinions by piecing together all the evidence and knowledge they have gained through study.'
Impositionist	'Historians select specific information to mould history to their own purposes.'
Exam Technique	'Historians must annotate the question, underlining key words . . . they then draw up a table for both sides of the question . . . a well-balanced argument with plenty of facts and a good conclusion would be the perfect answer to any question.'
Hypotheses from others	'Historians need to interview other academics who have a more in depth knowledge before deciding which opinion they agree with and present their findings.'
Methodological	'Historians take part in debate with one another in order to consider alternative interpretations and perhaps alter their own opinions.'
Contextual	'Historians revisit past events to replenish the work of previous historians who may have written about the past through eyes which have been conditioned by their culture and society.'

Student responses coded as explaining variation in terms of *archival explanations* understood history as a process of harvesting as much material as possible in order to reach a conclusion and explained variation in interpretations in terms of limitations or variations in the archive available to historians. Students who made archival explanations tended to also hold that historical truth was 'out there' and that history was simply a process of collecting, collating and presenting veridical information. For example: 'Historians observe many sources, such as diaries, books or images. They then put all the facts together to create a big picture of the time they're focusing on.'

Student responses coded as explaining variation in terms of *impositionist explanations* put the historian rather than the available material at the heart of historical process, modelled historians as imposing their own preconceptions through the selection of material and understood interpretation as made possible by this. Although this was sometimes presented as deliberate and sometimes as subconscious, this type of explanation was most typically flavoured by the suggestion of professional dishonesty and the promotion of a private agenda (political, personal or materialistic).

Student responses coded as explaining variation in terms of *exam technique* appeared to conceive of historians as operating in the ways in which exam materials ask students to operate in order to reach 'balanced' answers that satisfy exam board mark scheme requirements. These responses typically substituted a distinct focus on what England's examination board, Edexcel, terms 'overall mastery of essay-writing skills' (Edexcel, 2012b, p. 7) for an engagement with methodology and context.

Student responses that were coded as explaining how historians worked in terms of *hypotheses from others* tended to model historians as relying on secondary material produced by other historians and reaching derivative conclusions based on this work. In some cases, responses suggested that historians carried out no new research at all.

Student responses coded as explaining variation in terms of *methodological explanations* held that empirical methodology was central to historians' construction of accounts. Students whose observations were coded using this category tended to make specific mention of the testing of hypotheses with selected evidence and of the role of peer-assessment and discussion in the refinement of arguments and theories. No mention was made, however, of substantive paradigms within which historians work – such as models of human behaviour, established chronologies, notions of identity, and so on (Fulbrook, 2002).

Student responses coded as explaining variation in terms of *contextual explanations* tended to be a more nuanced version of the 'impositional' stance. Here the process of history and selection of material was determined by the individual context of historians. The integrity of historians was not brought into question, but their hypotheses were seen as shaped, in part, by the paradigms within which they were working. Such contexts were presented as assumed by historians but as balanced by an empirical methodology through which claims were both formulated and tested.

Table 6.3 presents the incidence of these types of explanation in the student responses. Some answers contained more than one type of explanation.

These results support the findings of previous studies in which students were reported as explaining the process of history in 'archival' terms (Chapman, 2009a, 2009b) expressing naive objectivist assumptions about how historical truth is produced (Lee and Shemilt, 2004; Barca, 2005; Chapman, 2011b). Such responses are typified by the following Task 1 response:

> Historians would begin by studying secondary sources, gaining as much knowledge as they possibly could through this before moving onto primary sources and evidence . . . Once they have attained this knowledge they can begin to establish their own viewpoints and opinions by piecing together all the evidence and knowledge they have gained through study. This means they have a more clear image of the situation as to which they are examining and can make a rudimentary conclusion. The next stage could be . . . to interview either other academics, who have a more in depth knowledge, or in the case of more modern histories, survivors of the era, who would have first-hand experience and their own point of view. Once they have collated all their findings, they are able to conclude with a personal opinion and viewpoint, and the most established knowledge possible. They can then present their findings or work to a wider audience.

Table 6.3 The incidence of explanation types in student responses to Task 1 [$N = 72$][3]

Explanation	Frequency
Archival	16
Impositionist	16
Exam technique	15
Hypotheses from others	8
Methodological	10
Contextual	7

For this student, historical enquiry cannot be embarked on until the historian has harvested 'as much knowledge as he possibly could' and only at this point can historians 'begin to establish their own viewpoints'. Rather than constructing hypotheses that can then be tested against available evidence, the student talks as if the entire body of traceable material from the past needs to be analysed before an hypothesis can be attempted. To this end, other historians are consulted not as part of the process of testing hypotheses, but as a further means of acquiring answers wholesale from professionals 'who have a more in depth knowledge'. Claims can only be made once this process has been further supplemented by 'survivors . . . with first-hand experience'. However, even where claims are based on 'the most established knowledge possible' it remains no more than a personal opinion. Such inductive reasoning that side-steps the role of historians in testing hypotheses against evidence was common in the data set, unsurprisingly, perhaps, given the ways in which Advanced Level syllabi typically frame historiographical issues.

Many of these themes are echoed in other responses such as the following:

> Historians need to gather an in depth analysis on the question that they are trying to answer; they can gather this research by looking at information from past events. They can gather information from other historians. However . . . it is up to historians to further carry out more research and then base an opinion on the reliability of . . . old newspapers, magazines and television programmes which will help historians collect all the information needed to answer questions about the past.

Here again the student is reliant on the assumption that the relics and records of the past are simply inert and self-evident forms of 'information' and the path to enlightenment is achieved through a quantitative process of absorption. Again, this process can be supplemented by weighing up the 'information' from other historians before reaching an answer. There is no indication of any understanding of what historians might do with this information, nor of the evidential reasoning that could be based on it and there is no discussion of how historians formulate the questions that cause them to consult archives in the first place.

Archival, impositionist and exam-focused explanations were by far the most common in the Question 1 data set. Standing out, in particular, was the suggestion that historians should 'do the right amount of research', 'ensure all perspectives of that time are considered', or 'simply examine everything that they see' and, frequently also, the suggestion that historians are not always as objective or diligent as they should be, illustrated in the following 'impositionist' response:

> Historians should research and consider all viewpoints and arguments on the event, however some historians may be selective and only read what they want to read, giving an unbalanced view and some could argue this would be bad history.

On this model, again, selection is understood as a weakness; however, such impositionist responses represent an advance on archival answers in the sense that research is understood as driven by historians themselves rather than by the traces of the past. Many of the impositionist responses tended towards relativist positions – to treat historians' views as opinions and to treat all opinions as equally in/valid; however, some impositionist responses contained more sophisticated ideas. In the following example, the student supplements suspicion of historians' preconceptions with an awareness of the use that historians make of counterfactual analysis:

> Historians interpret historical sources in order to explain and portray their possibly biased views on historical events. By selecting specific information and representing the sources as fact they often mould history to suit their own purposes . . . Many historians theoretically change the key events in order to theorise other possible outcomes.

A few students were able to articulate more sophisticated accounts of how historians work, such as the following example, which acknowledged historians' preconceptions but also recognized historians' agency in asking questions of the past, the role of debate as a progressive process and 'methodological' controls on preconceptions and assumptions:

> It is important to note that when studying history, there are different ideals, morals and values at play, and thus our own view on events can and will distort and warp the opinion of those who were involved with what is actually being studied.
>
> The goal of historians is not solely to present the past in their unquestionable way of thinking, but to explore other causes and consequences of . . . events, their effects on the present, and how their importance has been viewed differently in the past. Historians welcome debate; whether to showcase their arguments further, or to help work towards a better answer with the help of other viewpoints.
>
> We think it is also important that historians apply their method of analysing other historians, to the analysis of their own work, and as an extension of this, improve their own understanding and reasoning. We all put past events into the context of today, therefore, being able to re-evaluate prior arguments allows historians to see the bias or slant they may have put on their own research.

Although the responses often reflected naïve epistemic assumptions, such as those reported in earlier work (Lee and Shemilt, 2004; Barca, 2005; Lee, 2005b; Chapman, 2011c and 2012), many of the student responses also demonstrated flashes of insight and indications that rapid progress might be made through curricular emphases and pedagogies explicitly focused on developing methodological understandings.

How did students approach the Beatles task?

The initial response to Task 2, in which students selected and justified a list of ten songs, was extremely positive both in terms of participation rates and the students' attempts to explain their position. The students organized themselves into fourteen separate groups, providing a range of song choices and justifications (Table 6.3). What can be learned about students' tacit understandings of how history is made from the ways in which they approached the task and how far did their ideas change over time?

The students' selection of song choices, as analysed by Collins in his feedback to the students, reflected a number of patterns (Table 6.4). In terms of authorship the overwhelming preference was for songs influenced by McCartney. This is perhaps a reflection of the relatively accessible lyrics of these songs, suggesting that the students had either side-stepped more difficult material or selected the songs that lent themselves most easily to manipulation as evidence to test their hypotheses. It should also be noted, however, that although most of the songs available were written in the middle part of The Beatles' career, the songs written at the beginning and the end were over-represented in student choices, suggesting that many of the students used chronology to frame their hypotheses (Table 6.5).

Students also tended to adopt a thematic approach in the selection of material, omitting material that did not fit easily into overarching patterns. Collins analysed the groups' justifications of their song choices, identifying two categories of response. With one

Table 6.4 Song choices by author, Task 2

Song writer	Songs available	Mentions by students
Harrison	2	1
Mostly Harrison	2	4
Equally Lennon and McCartney	2	9
Lennon	14	25
Mostly Lennon	9	22
McCartney	10	43
Mostly McCartney	12	30
Other	1	5
Total	52	139

Table 6.5 Song choices by year, Task 2

Year	Songs available	Mentions by students
1962	1	13
1963	8	22
1964	3	8
1965	10	19
1966	5	14
1967	10	20
1968	5	17
1969	5	10
1970	3	16
Total	50	139

exception, the groups chose to adopt a three-stage model to organize their material. For many, the songs progressed from an innocent and youthful perception of love to a more cynical and 'pessimistic' outlook on human relationships before arriving at a period of 'didactic' grand philosophical gestures. For others the pattern was the same, except that the middle period was one of political awakening. Both groups, however, struggled to accommodate the late-era *All You Need Is Love* within their models. The one exception to this pattern adopted a 'bipolar approach' interpreting The Beatles as 'oscillating between hope and despair from song to song' (Collins) rather than adopting a thematic model based on a coherent pattern.

The groups who developed models explained the change in The Beatles' output in terms of The Beatles' biography or in terms of the social context of the 1960s. Those groups who explained developments in the lyrics biographically did so using the theme of 'the maturing of young men in exceptional circumstances', in Collins' phrase, in terms of the incremental effects of recreational drug use, or in terms of the slow disintegration of the band itself. This last point suggests that some students were using hindsight to attribute patterns, for example, by interpreting *Come Together* as an attempt by Lennon to heal rifts in the band.[4] Students who grouped songs based on social contextual themes construed a number of songs as expressing social-revolutionary consciousness (*Revolution, Taxman, Paperback Writer*), in terms of assumptions about the pervasiveness of LSD in society (*Tomorrow Never Knows, Lucy in the Sky with Diamonds*) and, in the case of one group, in terms of a 'working crisis' in Britain in 1964 (*Hard Days' Night*).[5]

Eight out of the fourteen groups engaged in discussion with each other about the choices that groups had made, which was encouraging; however, most students were reluctant to offer criticism of each other's interpretive decisions.

Four of the posts were very brief statements of largely uncontentious agreement such as the following:

> I agree with what you've written and I think it's expressed really well . . . what didn't change at any point was that The Beatles members were always truthful with their lyrics and can be relied on to have clearly expressed their view regarding topical issues which is why it is so easy to see their changing attitudes over time.

Perhaps we can see evidence of the archival notion that records report straightforward truths, here, and the attendant notion that the job of the historian is straightforward and simply a matter of transcription. It would have been interesting to see how this group would have replied to a group with whom they did not agree.

The remaining four posts did offer a degree of criticism but did so mainly in terms of the mechanics by which the students had approached the task:

> You have a really good coverage and range of songs over The Beatles' careers. You back up your justifications with well-argued context but you could possibly focus a little more on how the lyrics are changing the songs overall.

Rather than assessing the other group's post in terms of the claims it advanced, this group evaluated using purely formal criteria similar to the 'exam technique' responses discussed above and to the approach taken in exam board mark schemes (Edexcel, 2012b, p. 7).

In the second week of the exercise, after Collins had provided feedback, nine of the fourteen groups posted a final list of song choices and a completed the answer to the overall question (Table 6.1). Four of the nine groups did not change their song choices and one group replied to feedback by saying,

> Even though you have enlightened us and explained our errors we will still keep this choice of songs . . . it is still clear that one of the main aims of The Beatles was to put emphasis on different inequalities within class division of our society.

Four of the remaining five posts did make use of the critical debate engendered by the forum. However, they tended to use responses to their original posts to strengthen rather than to revise their original claims. To exemplify:

> We would swap *Love Me Do* for *Taxman*, because on reflection it's clear that *Love Me Do* and *Twist and Shout* exemplify the same point – the original careless fun loving nature and attitude of the band. As a result one of the songs becomes invalid . . . We would also swap *Tomorrow Never Knows* with *Help!*, because we feel that *Tomorrow Never Knows* and *Lucy in the Sky with Diamonds* represent the same theme of 'hippie' and 'druggie' culture, whereas *Help!* displays an attempt by The Beatles to distance themselves from the frenzy and chaos surrounding them.

One group, however, did show signs of reconsidering their position as a whole and were able to use the exercise to revaluate their earlier methodological approach metacognitively:

> Looking back at the statistics for what were the most popular songs and then comparing them to our chosen song list, I can see that we did in fact choose the most predictable and popular songs (as many others did), possibly because they were already familiar to us and because they were iconic songs it seemed the best option . . . Overall I think maybe we should've put more thought into the songs we decided to analyse and look at different dynamics, maybe focusing more on the period where they changed and looked at defining moments (i.e. when they became more rebellious with their sound after experimenting with drugs and visiting in India) and we should've looked for any one moment the band began to grow apart and the signs their time as a group was starting to come to an end. It was important to look at different types of songs throughout but at the start we focused on all the upbeat songs and at the end the more mellow ones. However, this could reflect the band's maturity and turmoil.

Three students completed the final task, revising their answers to the question about how historians seek to answer questions about the past. Two of these students demonstrated signs of moving on from opinion-based relativism to an understanding of the paradigmatic and empirical factors involved in the construction of historical accounts. While these students struggled to articulate these new understandings in a nuanced way, the fact that they were beginning to demonstrate awareness of issues of this kind argues for the value of pursuing and further developing the approach adopted in this project. One student, for example, stated that the 'project' had 'affected the way in which I think in this area' and noted that they had moved *towards* the view that 'it is the amount of evidence that is obtained that can help support your line of argument' and *away from* the view 'that there is no correct answer, as everyone has different interpretations based on the material that they have found'.

There were encouraging signs that the project had helped at least one student move to a more sophisticated understanding of the challenges involved in answering historical questions:

> It is about finding a balance in the amount of material required to get an objective understanding and the total amount of information available. It would be impossible to analyse everything, so an historian would have to determine the most important and relevant items and cross-reference them in order to draw logical conclusions. This project helped me to realise the sheer amount of potential information that could be researched and, therefore, the necessity to narrow the scope . . . in order to feasibly be able to analyse the songs.

Conclusions

In many respects the data generated by this project confirm existing research into how adolescents think about epistemic and methodological issues. The majority of the responses at the beginning of the exercise articulated simplistic archival and impositionist explanations for what historians do. These explanations represented historians as essentially passive or they understood historians' decisions, where they occur, as subjective and determined by bias. The past, on this kind of account, speaks for itself and historians have no need for methodologies and ought simply to transcribe the veridical voice of the past. Such epistemic naivety is perhaps unsurprising, given the limited attention that most specifications give to developing understandings of how knowledge of the past is created and the impact that specifications have in shaping teaching and learning. It points also to a failure to appreciate the role of reasoned argument in history that is likely to inhibit students' ability to understand historical debates and their ability to make rational choices between competing claims more generally.

While the students were aware of the temptation to read patterns into the past, very few of them were able to apply this understanding reflexively when constructing accounts: there was a great deal of 'imposition', as we have seen, in how the groups selected and presented material in Task 2. Perhaps we can understand this as progress, however; the task design made it harder for the students to maintain an archival stance and, as it were, forced them to move to the formulation of hypotheses: it was not possible simply to harvest all traces of the past and let them speak for themselves.

We had hoped that the online discussion would allow students both to develop their ideas and to come to an appreciation of the procedural value of review and debate within academic communities. It is apparent from the analysis above that we were largely unsuccessful in achieving this aim: nine of the 14 groups remained wedded to their original convictions and the debate that did occur was largely unproductive in the sense that it did not yield novel ideas and arguments. Although five groups did refine their arguments only one of these groups developed new ideas and revised their original approach in light of the peer and expert review.

Although *prima facie* a discouraging outcome, I would argue that the fact that the exercise was successful in engaging a minority of the students in reflection on historical methodology argues for the further development and evaluation of exercises of this kind. As I have noted above, there is little incentive in England's existing examination regime post-14 for teachers to maintain a focus on historical methodology. My findings draw attention to the magnitude of the task. Successful innovative strategies that aim to develop younger pupils' understandings of historical methodology have been reported by Howells (2005) and Hammond (2007) demonstrating that students at Key Stage 3 (11–14-year-olds) can be drawn into evaluating historical interpretations by considering historians' methodologies and paradigms. This work and my findings should serve to encourage further innovation and development.

How might the 'Beatles Project' be refined and developed? Perhaps the students could be guided to think more explicitly about the challenges of finding a workable methodology before being asked to make decisions and engage in discussion (Chapman, 2011c). Although we asked students to develop and justify a methodology before formulating a hypothesis, in practice many of the students did not do so. Perhaps a preliminary task asking students to evaluate contrasting methodologies, such as the comparison of cliometrics and microhistory developed by Hammond (2007), would have been valuable at this stage. It is probable also that opportunity for metacognitive reflection on the parameters of the question would have been valuable: students could have been asked to debate what might count as 'change', to consider criteria for 'dramatic' change and to reflect on how and how far 'attitudes' and 'values' can be inferred from song titles. By debating such questions students could perhaps be encouraged to develop a framework through which responses to the enquiry question could be judged and assessed. Is it enough, for example, simply to select songs from the beginning, middle and end of the period or is it more profitable to explore 'defining moments' as suggested by one group? It is possible that making such challenges more explicit earlier in the process would stimulate discussion and encourage students to become metacognitively aware of their own preconceptions. Drawing on this awareness, teachers might have more success in encouraging them to question their own initial positions rather than defend them unflinchingly.

Historical Significance: Giving Meaning to Local Places

Michael Harcourt

7

When we look at the world as a world of places we see different things. We see attachments and connections between people and place. We see worlds of meaning and experience. Sometimes this way of seeing can seem to be an act of resistance against a rationalization of the world, a way of seeing that has more space than place. To think of an area of the world as a rich and complicated interplay of people and the environment – as a place – is to free us from thinking of it as facts and figures. (Cresswell, 2004, p. 11)

Introduction

The concept of 'place' traditionally belongs to the domain of geography rather than history. Where history teachers pay more attention to this concept, however, they might perhaps be able to develop and deepen students' historical thinking and the way in which they relate to local, everyday places. This possibility first struck me when I heard the Canadian environmentalist David Suzuki (2010) describing two different relationships to the same place, a forest in British Columbia. A helicopter pilot took a group of company executives scouting for a new logging operation and overheard them discussing pulp, truck access, employment opportunities and profits. The same pilot took Suzuki and several First Nations friends on an identical fly-over and observed how different the second discussion was, with its stories of burial grounds, hunting grounds and other places of cultural and historical significance. The way we act in a place can depend on how we attribute significance to it.

This chapter explores the impact of making an historical sound walk on the way in which students experience everyday, urban places and on how they participate in the meanings attached to them. In planning this enquiry, I wondered whether by creating a sound walk that made evidence-based, criteria-determined judgements about historical significance, students could 'map' the past, turning abstract, 'empty' city *spaces* through which humans moved into *places*: locations at which humans paused to make meaning (Yi-Fu Tuan, 1977, p. 6). This chapter reports my investigation of that question, examining how the concept of historical significance might be explored without treating places as mere backdrops for historical events and how this approach can reveal the broader social canvas of history that permeates discrete historical events.

Sound walks and significance

At its simplest, a sound walk is a recorded tour around a site. The audience listens to the recording at each intended location with an iPod or MP3 player. Sound walks, or 'geo-temporal narratives' differ from museum audio-guides because they actively connect the listener to their surroundings. They do this by making explicit use of ambient sound, the material landscape of a location and often the oral histories of people who live and work there (Plinder, 2001; Butler, 2006, 2007). This means that a sound walk is only fully appreciated when experienced at the location of recording.

For a national NCEA (New Zealand Certificate of Educational Achievement) internal assessment, my Year 11 students (approximately 15 years old) made a sound walk using 'disciplinary' criteria for determining historical significance. Drawing on recent research and practical theorizing, I interpret historical significance as a procedural concept within the discipline, an intellectual tool that students can use to think about the past more powerfully (Partington, 1980; Hunt, 2000; Counsell, 2004c; Bradshaw, 2006; Lévesque, 2008), recognizing that decisions about what is worth studying depend – more or less explicitly – on particular criteria, which are themselves open to debate. The purpose of this sound walk project was for students to explore the kinds of criteria that have been applied to judgements of historical significance and how they might be used to 'narrate, layer and intervene in the experiences of moving through [a place]' (Butler, 2007, p. 360). The students' completed audio files were saved to a website for family, friends and other interested local residents to download and experience on-site.

A central theoretical influence on my research was the online digital humanities project Hypercities, which uses Google Earth to create narratives exploring the different layers of city spaces.[1] Hypercities draws on Baudelaire's conceptualization of the *flâneur*: 'a person who walks the city in order to experience it' (O'Hagan, 2011). After experimenting with Hypercities for some time, I stumbled upon sound walks and was struck by the resonance between their approach to exploring city spaces and the spatial and participatory methodologies that Hypercities promotes. Presner (2011) argues that Hypercities collections are capable of 'animating the landscape', generating an 'awareness of the complex layers that are ever present in any historical landscape'. Could a sound walk project similarly help students engage with everyday places and their pasts more deeply?

The New Zealand context

An *explicit* focus on historical thinking in the New Zealand history curriculum is a recent development (Harcourt, Fountain and Sheehan, 2011). Previous national curriculum committees, teacher conferences and professional development had tended to focus on understanding changes in national assessment and increasing historical content knowledge (Fountain, 2012). However, the introduction of a new National Curriculum in 2007 (Ministry of Education, 2007) saw historical thinking concepts recognized in official documentation. Historical significance is therefore one of the concepts that teachers in New Zealand are beginning to discuss with each other and explore with their students.

Students in most New Zealand schools can choose to study history as a distinct discipline only in the final three years of their senior secondary education (Years 11–13). This means that there is little time in which to develop students' historical thinking systematically. Year 11 history teachers 'inherit' students who have encountered the past within an integrated social studies programme (that includes history, geography, economics and current events). Their previous teachers may have had no training in the discipline of history and little engagement with pedagogical practices specific to the subject. Additionally, New Zealand students frequently express misgivings about learning New Zealand history. Often their first criterion for determining historical significance is that important history probably did not happen in New Zealand (Levstik, 2001, p. 87). A geographical, place-based approach to the past brings historical thinking into the local environment, making it more immediate. Such an approach seems particularly important in New Zealand, not merely as a way of making the concept of significance less abstract for students, but also as a potential avenue through which to explore indigenous understandings of the past.

Research questions and methodology

I wanted to examine how my class of Year 11 students would respond to a focus on using local places to think about historical significance. My first research question was: 'How do students make use of suggested disciplinary criteria in determining the historical significance of a *place*?' In order to answer this, I undertook a small-scale exploratory case study using qualitative data. My primary data set took the form of students' completed projects and I employed thematic analysis as 'a method for identifying, analysing and reporting patterns (themes)' (Braun and Clarke, 2006, p. 79) within the projects. Six sound walks were used as the basis of this analysis, selected to represent a variety of locations. Each one was transcribed with all ambient sound and special effects noted. The transcriptions were coded in a process of 'organising . . . data into meaningful groups' (Braun and Clarke, 2006, p. 88, cited in Tuckett, 2005). From my initial list of codes, two themes were generated. These themes, or 'patterned response[s]', became the basis for a 'story of [my] data' (ibid., pp. 82, 93).

I was also interested in exploring whether the experience of making a sound walk resulted in rich engagements for the students and in determining whether listening to their sound walks had a similar effect on an audience. Thus my second question was: 'To what extent do historical sound walks create rich engagements with places and their pasts?' The role of the audience was important because I wanted students' publicly accessible work to contribute to the ways in which local, urban places might be experienced. Unfortunately, it was beyond the scope of this research to encourage members of the school community to access the sound walks and provide feedback. Curriculum time constraints also prevented investigation into the effects of students listening to, and commenting on, each other's work (which remains an important direction for future research). Instead I invited the whole class to complete a questionnaire about the experience of making a sound walk. In the absence of any literature on the effect sound walks have on students' engagement with the historical significance of places, I developed three indicators that for me constituted a 'rich engagement' with a place:

- Looking at a location in a new way.
- Asking questions triggered by being in a particular location.
- Using a location to consider its past.

To gauge the effect that student-made sound walks might have on an audience I listened to the same sample of six sound walks at the locations in which, and for which, they had been recorded. My observations of students' work are obviously conditioned by my perspective and identity as a history teacher and are necessarily subjective. They nonetheless serve to illustrate what a person accessing students' sound walks could experience.

Preparing students for creating a sound walk

To prepare students to judge the historical significance of places, I used several key activities. The first was to send the class on a 'memorial hunt' to provoke their thinking about statements such as 'History operates on the basis that some events are more important than others' and 'Different people will have different ideas about which historical people, events, changes, places and issues are significant and which are not' (Lomas in Counsell, 2004c, pp. 31–32). Groups of students were allocated a different section of Wellington city within walking distance of the school, and they completed an 'urban archaeological investigation' recording all memorials and historical markers within their allocated zone. A data collection form required them to gather information on the type of memorial (e.g. whether it was a statue, a sculpture or a garden), on its location, as well as its prominence, on public accessibility and on physical condition. This prompted students' thinking about key aspects of historical significance and made possible a general discussion about questions such as 'Whose histories are memorialized in downtown Wellington and whose are not?' 'Whose histories are more or less prominent? Why might this be?'

The students were then introduced to Counsell's '5Rs' – a set of criteria offered as *one* way of determining historical significance (2004c, p. 32):

- *Remarkable* – The event/development was remarked upon by people at the time and/or since.
- *Remembered* – The event/development was important at some stage in history within the collective memory of a group or groups.
- *Resonant* – People like to make analogies with it; it is possible to connect with experiences, beliefs or situations across time and space.
- *Resulting in change* – It had consequences for the future.
- *Revealing* – Of some other aspect of the past.

Among the various sets of criteria developed by researchers and teachers (see, e.g. Partington, 1980; Phillips, 2002) Counsell's seemed the most accessible and widely applicable, and therefore provided a useful starting point for young people new to the discipline of history. I then gave students a series of short accounts of historical events from the New Zealand Ministry for Culture and Heritage website and asked them to highlight any judgements of significance within them, annotating them to show which criteria seemed to have informed the author's claim.

After they had practised analysing several historical accounts using given criteria, I introduced students to the methodology of a sound walk and took them to six potential sites (listed in Table 7.1). They were given a folder of quotations and photographs, serving primarily as stimulus material to prompt questions about the layered histories of each place, and asked to use these sources and the five criteria that they had practised identifying in class to develop some tentative judgements about the sites' historical significance.

At this point, however, it became increasingly obvious that there were limitations to students relying *solely* on the '5Rs' to judge the historical significance of a *place*. At the National War Memorial, for example, some students were having difficulty differentiating between the historical significance of World War I and the historical significance of the National War Memorial as a site worthy of investigation in its own right. It appeared to me that while the students certainly needed to realize that knowledge of distant events and broader historical forces is critical to understanding the significance of a particular place, they also needed a deeper understanding of the National War Memorial in itself. I judged that it was not enough to see it simply as a location for marking the occurrence of geographically distant

Table 7.1 Historical sites within walking distance of Wellington High School

Potential sound walk locations	Brief description of location
The National War Memorial	The memorial was first consecrated in 1932 and is regularly the site of remembrance events.
Trades Hall	This building has for many decades been associated with the Left. It was famously the site of an unsolved bombing in 1984 that killed a trade unionist.
Te Aro Pa	An early nineteenth-century archaeological site on the same street as the school. The site is the remains of a Maori village that was slowly encroached upon and depopulated during the colonization of Wellington.
Suffrage steps at Parliament	These steps commemorate the actions of Kate Sheppard and other suffragettes, whose efforts were instrumental in New Zealand becoming the first nation to grant women the right to vote in 1893.
Haining Street	This street was New Zealand's most infamous Chinatown in the late nineteenth and early twentieth centuries. It is well known for the race killing of a Chinese man, Joe Kum Yung, in 1905.
Formerly the site of Mount Cook Prison	A prison built in the 1880s on approximately the same site as the school grounds. The school and its immediate surroundings have been associated with the penal system since the 1840s and is the site of one of the colony's first hangings in 1849.

events. Confusion at the National War Memorial led me to think that a genuinely geographic approach to *placing* historical significance required more careful consideration of the concept of 'place' than simply conflating it with an event (Brown and Woodcock, 2009, p. 10). Drawing on Taylor's outline of 'uncommon views of place' (Taylor, 2004, p. 7) and the work of Park (1995), a New Zealand environmental historian, I developed an additional set of criteria, presented using the acronym PLACE, intended to help students to engage more actively with the geo-historical significance of their chosen location.

- *Power* – The site reveals power relations in society. Its meaning for some people might have been silenced or marginalized in the past. Perhaps some people felt or continue to feel a sense of *belonging* there, while others are *excluded.*
- *Legendary* – The site is 'storied'. People tell legends there; it is used to sustain myths and memories.
- *Affected by change* – The site has changed considerably from one state to another.
- *Contested and connected* – The meaning of the site was, or still is, argued over. People feel a strong sense of connection to it, often for different reasons.
- *Evocative* – The site is one where you can 'feel' history. It is *eerie*, almost as though time has slowed.

The class now had two sets of criteria to help them create their sound walk.

Students were asked to choose one of the sites listed in Table 7.1 and were given two weeks of class time to gather evidence from primary and secondary sources that could be used to determine the historical significance of that place. This research was then used to create their sound walk narratives. Since teachers must support students' NCEA internal assessment by providing possible research questions, I offered them a bank of questions developed for each location from which they had to choose two. Each suggestion was based on the sets of criteria with which the class was now familiar, but in the end many students adapted the questions, or, with consultation, developed their own.

Findings 1: 'How do students make use of suggested disciplinary criteria in determining the historical significance of a place?'

Students' understanding of the historical significance of places is shaped by the kinds of criteria with which they are provided. This became clear from the two themes that emerged from my data, as shown in Table 7.2. Students made judgements *either* about the significance of discrete historical events and broad historical forces *or* about the significance of the place, but rarely combined the two. The majority made what I have called 'events-based judgements' by using criteria from Counsell's (2004c) '5Rs'. However, the use of place-based criteria seemed to be more successful in drawing students' attention beyond the single key event. Those students who used the place-based criteria looked at the role the location played in community life and the meanings that have been constructed and attributed to it. They made 'place-based judgements' of historical significance and were more likely to ask questions such as, 'What else happened here? Why did it happen here? What role did this place have in the lives of historical people? What are the important layers of the past here? Whose pasts are acknowledged here and whose are not?' However, making place-based judgements came at the expense of understanding the broader events and historical forces that always contribute to the meaning of a place. Students who used the '5Rs' were better equipped to understand these events and historical forces. My findings show that students who negotiated *both* sets of criteria developed a more complex, nuanced understanding of the historical significance of places.

Table 7.2 Criteria used by students to determine the significance of a place

Student	Location	Criteria used to determine significance	
		The '5Rs'	PLACE
Sally	Suffrage Steps	Resulting in change	
James	National War Memorial		Connected and contested
Leah	Haining Street	Revealing	Connected
Rachel	Haining street	Remembered and remarkable	
Sarah	Suffrage Steps	Resulting in change and revealing	
David	Trades Hall	Remembered and resulting in change	

The two students who used the PLACE criteria to make place-based judgements of historical significance did this by showing either how their locations were contested or how people felt connected to them. At the National War Memorial, James explained, 'still thousands of people come here who have no relation to anyone who is remembered at the memorial. There are many reasons why people might do this, but I think the main reason is that they feel connected to the idea of New Zealand defining itself as a nation'. To emphasize the connection of New Zealanders to this place he described a liquor company's advertising campaign that projected an image onto the memorial, explaining how 'the simple act of shining a logo upon [the memorial] could disgust the nation'. This student then examined ways in which the memorial is contested: 'Whenever an event is held here and even when it was first being built, there has always been someone opposed to what the memorial stands for, what takes place inside or the reasons why people go there'. To emphasize the contested nature of the memorial, James gave details about the lack of recognition in the memorial of wars fought between the Crown and Maori tribes in the nineteenth century. At a different location, Leah used the PLACE criteria to explain why New Zealanders of Chinese descent historically felt connected to Haining Street: '[It] was the first point of contact for many Asian immigrants; it was the place that helped immigrants to adjust to New Zealand life, but also had the comfort of the old life in China'. Her sound walk provided information about the role of Haining Street in sustaining Chinese cultural life and important social and economic networks. Leah concluded that 'a combination of . . . all these factors; support, comfort, familiarity, shows why Chinese New Zealanders are connected to Haining Street'. Although only James and Leah used my place-based criteria, their work stood out for their more 'layered' approach to their chosen place. No single event dominated or became the essence of that location.

Four students relied on the '5Rs' for their sound walk and those events-based criteria were more effective for judging the historical significance of an important moment in time. Again they made clear reference to the criteria they had chosen, beginning their sound walk with statements such as David's: 'This sound walk will focus . . . on two aspects of the bombing and Ernie Abbot's death: remembrance and aftermath'. In relation to the suffrage steps, Sarah stated: 'I will explain its significance by looking at how it resulted in change and what remarks made at the time about women's suffrage reveal about men's attitudes toward women'. Rachel reflected 'Why is this so historically significant, you ask? To me, the most outstanding factor is what Haining Street reveals about Wellington during that time'. This last argument continued with a judgement of historical significance that was very close, if not identical, to that advanced by the students who had used aspects of PLACE, indicating that there are some overlaps. The student who chose to focus on the murder of Ernie Abbot in the Trades Hall is particularly interesting. By relying on the '5Rs', David probed the significance of the 1984 bombing. Yet a story about the significance of the death of a trade unionist at the Trades Hall offers only one (important) meaning that can be ascribed to that place. To focus entirely on this aspect is itself a judgement of significance, made at the expense of a more comprehensive understanding of the role that the Trades Hall has played in Wellington and New Zealand throughout most of the twentieth century. It is this long history of trade unionism that may explain why it was targeted for an attack and that could have been brought out more easily with my PLACE criteria.

Comparing James' work using the PLACE criteria with that of David, who drew on the '5Rs', suggests that place-based criteria do seem to be effective in supporting certain kinds of thinking, but that when used in isolation, they can restrict other kinds of thinking. This hypothesis is supported by the example of Leah, the only student in my sample who used aspects of both criteria. As well as explaining the ways in which those of Chinese descent were connected to Haining Street, Leah also stated that 'remarks about Haining Street reveal negative attitudes towards the Chinese' and proceeded to describe the ways in which Haining Street became a symbol of the 'Yellow Peril'. She acknowledged the well-known killing of Joe Kum Yung and implicitly attributed significance to this event by leading her audience straight to his memorial plaque. But by incorporating elements of both the '5Rs' and of PLACE, Leah also succeeded in exploring the social history of Haining Street and its important role in the history of Wellington and New Zealand's race relations with the Chinese. Her sound walk was exemplary in bringing together multiple dimensions of the past that clearly showed the site's geo-historical significance.

Sound walks made at the suffrage steps at Parliament also highlight the importance of not treating places and events as synonymous. The suffrage steps memorialize suffragettes who successfully petitioned for women to be granted the vote. As some of the previous quotations begin to demonstrate, students were successful in using criteria from the '5Rs' to determine the significance of this major event in New Zealand history. However, determining the historical significance of the memorial steps as a *place* was more difficult and led to some confusion. One sound walk concluded with the statement, 'I hope you have enjoyed it and have gained insight as to the historical significance of this location'. Another finished with the announcement, 'hopefully this sound walk has made you realize how and why women's suffrage is historically significant to the places you have been taken in this walk'. Yet neither sound walk treated the suffrage steps as a place worthy of study in its own right because they both focused on the historical significance of the women's campaign independent of any particular location. Had they incorporated aspects of the place-based criteria these students might have been more able to explore the highly contested, complex memorial landscape in and around the Parliament grounds while still relating this to the broader women's suffrage campaign. Why students were reluctant to engage with the suffrage steps in this way needs further exploration, but it may be because the idea of interpretations of significance being embedded in the material landscape was a new idea, and more difficult to deal with than abstract events understood independently from particular places.

A place-based approach to determining historical significance led to a more archaeological attitude that examined different layers of human action. Murders, hangings, explosions and major legislative changes – actions typically understood as events – became part of the story and meaning of a particular place, but the historical understanding associated with that place was not determined by any single event. Students who negotiate aspects of both sets of criteria may be in a better position to show how and why particular locations become part of the tapestry of society, invested with complex meanings and caught up in complicated power relations. Additionally, their choice of criteria may have implications for the kinds of places they hold to be significant. For example, during a class discussion about why no one chose to study the Maori village, one student gave the reason 'because nothing happened there', suggesting that students may associate worthwhile history primarily with distinct events resulting in change at the expense of cultural, social and geo-historical forms of history that may focus on change as a process, or even on historical continuities (Blow, 2011a).

Findings 2: To what extent do historical sound walks create rich engagements with places and their pasts?

Here I define a 'rich engagement' as one that includes looking at a location in a new way, asking questions triggered by being in a particular location, and using a location to consider its past. These kinds of engagement are possible for both the creator and the audience of a sound walk. In this section I first draw on the results of the questionnaire and then reflect on my experiences as an audience listening to the sample of sound walks.

Students commented that the surprise of finding out about the history of familiar places changed the way they viewed those places. Making a sound walk made one student 'feel like I was surrounded by a lot more history than I thought. I always used to walk past this place – almost every day – and now when I walk past there I think about Joe Kum Yung'. A student who used to walk past the Trades Hall and 'not even notice it was there' claimed that 'Now, it's like: "Oh that's the Trades Hall, a bomb got blown up there"'. Another pointed out that the sound walk project 'made me have a deep understanding of my place because when I started this course I didn't even know Mount Cook Prison existed'. These comments suggest that the act of making a sound walk, created, at least for some students, a different, deeper understanding of particular locations.

Some students commented that the sound walk helped them to care about people in the past, an aspect of historical thinking that Davison refers to as the 'affective dimension' of historical perspectives (2010, p. 90). One student described being 'shocked' by 'how racist we were, specifically toward the Chinese. I never thought of New Zealand as a racist country'. Another commented that 'it made me care a little more about those who are ignored in the memorial' and another that 'it made me care about the place because there were quite a few personal accounts which gave the place some meaning'. One student thought the sound walk project helped her to 'feel more and empathize for Chinese New Zealanders because *being there* I could imagine the strong sense of community' [my italics]. Most students' answers suggested that the physical act of being present in a location and making a recording that used the material surroundings increased their capacity to care for historical actors.

Students were slightly less forthcoming in their feedback about the extent to which making a sound walk triggered new questions about a place. This may reflect the restrictive conditions of the Year 11 NCEA assignment, which discourages students from developing their own questions. However, when asked explicitly about the extent to which being on location to create their recordings prompted fresh questions, students claimed that 'I wouldn't have spared a thought for the place if it wasn't for making the sound walk' and 'I think by entering the Trades Hall and by seeing the plaque about Ernie I was asking questions about life back then and how they reacted to the event'. The most interesting comment was related to Mount Cook Prison: 'When visiting the place it made me ask questions about crime, the people there etc . . . These little questions helped to develop bigger, wider questions for my sound walk'. This last comment highlights the importance of using the initial field trips to promote questions about how each place could be linked to others and situated within broader historical trends. Simply visiting historical sites with students is often a powerful experience in itself and further work is needed to establish whether actively engaging with the material landscape specifically to create a sound walk prompts questions that other forms of assessment, and normal historical field trips, do not.

Making a sound walk certainly encouraged students in my sample to look at their locations in new ways and prompted some of them to ask questions that they would not have asked had they not been physically present at their location. When it came to engaging their audience, two particularly effective techniques struck me as I listened to them: specific strategies to connect them very deliberately with their material surroundings and proceeding sufficiently slowly to allow for unexpected interactions with people and the environment. Underpinning the success of both was the quality of evidence used to support the narrative.

I noticed that those sound walks that deliberately directed me around a site and pointed my attention to key changes between past and present created immediacy with the location. For example, in the Wellington Trades Hall I was told 'You might notice the chair nicknamed Abbot's Rest, made from timber salvaged from the bombing' and 'You'll have probably have noticed the almost eerie silence'. This student then made the point that 'depending on where you are standing now, there is a chance you would have died today if today was the 27 March 1984'. The impression created was creepy, an effect reinforced by evidence from eyewitnesses: 'According to several witness statements the vehicle parked outside the Trades Hall was actually knocked back several feet from the blast'. Sitting at the exact location of this explosion emphasized the horror of the attack and the sense that the victim could have been anyone living in Wellington walking past at the time or working in the building. In another location I was asked to close my eyes and to imagine smells, noises and sites of the former Chinatown. At the end of the description, I was told: 'Now open your eyes. The little Chinatown known as Haining Street has disappeared'. The strategy of deliberately contrasting historical Haining Street with the industrialized, material present encouraged my historical imagination in a way made possible only by my presence at that location, combined with the student's use of evidence to reconstruct the historical scene.

A sound walk about nineteenth-century New Zealand suffragettes used the material environment to create a different, but equally powerful, engagement with a place. After listening to the introduction at a memorial to the suffragettes, I was told: 'In front of the buildings in Parliament is a statue of one Richard Seddon, which should be visible from the bottom of the suffrage steps. Please make your way over and read the plaque . . . If Richard Seddon had his way, women would never have gotten the vote'. After further narration, I was directed back across the grounds to another statue where it was explained, 'John Ballance was a strong supporter of women's suffrage, declaring to Parliament that he believed in absolute equality of the sexes'. The physical act of moving from one statue to another while listening to a carefully researched supporting narrative implicitly highlighted opposing historical perspectives as well as the interesting judgements of historical significance made by the creators of the memorials. I found myself noting down questions such as 'Why did it take 100 years before the suffragettes were commemorated in 1993? Was there any argument about the nature of their memorial?' (The memorial was accurately described by the student as 'discreet'.) 'When were the Seddon and Ballance memorials constructed? What input did women have into the construction of these memorials?'

Successful sound walks were also created at a pace that allowed for unexpected interactions with people and the environment. In Haining Street, a student quotes a Wellington writer who remembers being warned as a child: 'If we went near that drab, narrow little street with its congestion of tumbledown houses, we might be kidnapped, boiled in a copper and made into preserved ginger'. Using the material surroundings to guide me slowly around the site meant that I was present when a local primary school bell rang and children began spilling into the street. The combination of the historical description of what children were once told about the Chinese and Haining Street with the sudden physical presence of European and Chinese children and their families added poignancy to the experience.

A similarly striking experience took place at the National War Memorial. By following a sound walk's instructions to pause at certain locations, I happened to be listening to details about the war and New Zealanders' connection to the memorial just as a group of young men walked by, the juxtaposition again enhancing the content of the recording. Other examples of serendipity that enriched the experience included the time of day, the weather and ambient sounds captured in the recording, such as church bells or children playing. Obviously, the slow and deliberate use of the material environment to support a judgment of historical significance can only create the conditions in which such unexpected conjunctions might occur; it certainly cannot guarantee them. However, in contrast to traditional text-based assignments, the chance of such an engagement with a place and its past is considerably more likely.

Although offering only a limited window into the experiential possibilities of sound walks, these examples show the value of certain techniques in engaging an audience. The students made a promising start considering the limited guidance I had given them, but future audiences (including their peers, family members and perhaps local residents) may not be as actively disposed to engage with them as I was. Treating the built landscape as a 'text' to be actively engaged with, developing an evidence-based narrative that makes a judgement about historical significance, while at the same time pacing the narrative to allow for circumstances along the way, is an ambitious task for novice, 15-year-old historical thinkers. Being an audience for the students' work alerted me to the modelling and practice they need to bring together all these dimensions of a successful historical sound walk. Perhaps most importantly, they needed to experience a good exemplar of a sound walk that we could analyse together, before starting work on their individual investigations.

Future directions for making sound walks

By spending more time on existing interpretations of historical significance, teachers can highlight the contested nature of places and help students to deconstruct particular sites *as* historical interpretations. By focusing on helping students use given criteria, I missed opportunities to support them more explicitly in developing arguments that challenged or supported particular interpretations of historical significance. With careful scaffolding, even these novice historical thinkers could have begun to think more critically, peeling back the layers of meaning already attributed to each site. Sound walks that incorporate this level of analysis are likely to have a more profound effect on an audience. Students could, for example, be better supported in rendering problematic the text on heritage display boards and plaques, the symbols within a sculpture, or even the memories and historical understanding of local people. Beside the former site of the Mount Cook Prison, for example, is a recent memorial to Maori prisoners jailed for protesting against the confiscation and surveying of their land in the nineteenth century. The memorial makes no explicit reference to the former prison, but its deliberate positioning at this site highlights ongoing contestation over land and the legacy of colonization. By focusing on existing interpretations of historical significance, teachers can highlight controversies about the meaning of historical sites, using the concept of significance as a thinking tool to make sense of these conflicting interpretations (Bradshaw, 2006).

Taking a local approach to history made students more enthusiastic about learning New Zealand history. The majority reported in the final questionnaire that their interest in New Zealand history had greatly increased as a result of the project. Half of them attributed this change to the short field trips to each site and half thought that it occurred during the library research phase. However, it is noteworthy that the only site my class visited that was *not* chosen for a sound walk was the Maori archaeological site (and only one student identified it as a possible second choice). This lack of desire to investigate a topic related to nineteenth-century colonization and Maori social history is curious and concerning. Why do some places capture the imagination of young people and not others? What are the consequences for nations such as New Zealand, grappling with the legacy of colonization, if certain places, their stories and their historical significance, remain unexamined?' These questions and their implications for classroom practice need further exploration.

Conclusion

When places that students walk past every day become the focus for historical inquiry, those places change. As one student phrased it, making a sound walk 'made me realize Wellington wasn't a boring place where nothing happened'. Gruenewald has argued that 'what we know is, in large part, shaped by the kinds of places we experience and the quality of attention we give them' (2003, p. 645). This research shows that in the process of making sound walks the quality of students' attention to places deepens considerably. It also suggests that the particular criteria used for determining historical significance have an impact on the way that students explore the history of those places. Relying solely on events-based criteria encouraged a focus on discrete historical events; additional use of more geographic, place-based criteria tended to promote deeper attention and more nuanced forms of engagement with the locality. Historical sound walks help to transform abstract city spaces into *places*, locations that are layered with memories, stories, emotions and interpretations. These places may then act as daily mnemonics, reminders of the histories beneath our feet.

Unmasking Diversity: Curriculum Rhetoric Meets the Classroom

Robert Somers

8

Introduction

Incorporated into England's 2008 National Curriculum (NC) (QCA/DCSF, 2007) as a 'key concept', the idea of diversity took on new significance for many history teachers. Although by no means entirely new – since 'similarity and difference' had featured in the original NC for history (DES, 1990b) – by 2007, 'diversity' appeared to play such a central role that it was said to 'underpin the teaching of history' (QCA/DCSF, 2007). But 'diversity', like many key concepts used within curricular rubrics, is a heavily value-laden term, and it could be argued that it has not received sufficient critical analysis. This chapter places the idea of diversity under a critical lens and attempts to overcome what are discovered as its Eurocentric limitations by exploring alternative theoretical perspectives.

The *Oxford English Dictionary* defines 'diversity' as the condition or quality of being diverse, different or varied. NC 2008, however, explicitly limited the word to cultural, ethnic and religious categories of diversity, making it compulsory for teachers to include the varied experiences and beliefs of people who lived in the past (QCA/DCSF, 2007). Two further statements seemed to shift the meaning of the word 'diversity' each time. First, NC 2008 linked diversity to racial equality placing it within a moral and humanistic framework. Second, it explained that diversity exists within and across groups and is located in the variety of past experiences and interpretations (ibid.). By clearly foregrounding differences rather than similarities inherent in the social world, NC 2008 privileged 'diversity' over its antonyms, 'uniformity', 'sameness' and 'identity', an emphasis that has recently been addressed in the 2014 revised NC (DfE, 2013), which reverts to use of the term 'similarity and difference'.

Alongside the substantive issues concerning diversity, several theoretical questions surfaced as I began thinking about the nature of this enquiry: How can we avoid simply studying ourselves when we engage with past and/or different cultural perspectives? Can we truly access diverse ways of thinking and living, or do we, as history teachers, taint everything we touch with our own ideological mind-sets? In other words, how can I engage or interact with the difference of the other without transforming her/him into myself, or into the same? (Scheurich, 1997).

For over half a century now, poststructuralist thinkers have been asking the same kinds of questions about diversity and multiculturalism. Post-structuralism and its related methodologies were not covered in the Masters programme I undertook at university, and were also absent from many of the textbooks and research handbooks popular to teacher-researchers. But because of the attention paid to the idea of diversity by poststructuralist thinkers (reviewed below), I was keen to employ poststructuralist perspectives in an attempt to unify both my literature review and methodological approach, synthesizing the substantive and theoretical issues in my investigation.

The empirical element of my research is rooted in a series of lessons based on three discrete periods of Indian and Anglo-Indian history: the Moghul period under the Emperor Jalaluddin Mohammed Akbar; the East India Company in the eighteenth century; and the Raj period in the late nineteenth century. A description of this scheme of work is outlined in Table 8.1.

The lessons were devoted to generating text in the form of interviews or written work, which could then be assessed using deconstruction analysis. I wanted to see if any rhetoric of diversity was apparent in the students' writing and speech, and if so, to deduce its source. My primary goal in these lessons was to engage and provoke students into interacting with the subject matter even though they had not previously encountered it. Six students were interviewed and their responses to my questions about the lesson sequence together with their work generated over a period of two weeks, as outlined in Table 8.1, forms the majority of the data set.

Table 8.1 The teaching sequence

Lesson focus		Resources	Outcome task
Lesson 1	Who was Jalaluddin Mohammed?	*Jodhaa Akbar* (Gowariker, 2008)	Akbar character outlines.
Lesson 2	How does Abu Fazl express the greatness of the Emperor?	Moghul miniatures	Data capture sheet
Lesson 3	How great was Emperor Akbar?	*Khwaja Mere Khwaja* and *Azeem-O-Shan-Shahenshah* (Akhtar and Rahman, 2008a, 2008b)	*Akbarnama* dedication
Lesson 4	How did the British take control of India?	Trading Game (Byrom et. al., 2004)	Discussion
Lesson 5	Can Kirkpatrick, the Resident of Hyderabad, be trusted?	Story from *White Mughals* (Dalrymple, 2004)	Role-plays
Lesson 6	How does Kim cope during the Raj period?	Story from *Kim* (Kipling, 1995)	Historical fiction passage

Literature review

Christine Counsell (2009b), in an online continuing professional development unit published by the Historical Association, tells the somewhat controversial story of the implementation of diversity within the NC – a history that began with the Schools Council History Project in the 1970s and was continued by the History Curriculum Working Group in the late 1980s, with the concept finding its way into the first National Curriculum in 1991 under the name of 'similarity and difference' (DES, 1990b). Counsell draws attention to the influence of media and politicians on the formation of the 1991 curriculum and their hostility towards another potential concept, 'empathy', implying that the institutionalization of 'similarity and difference' as a second-order concept was a compromise made to placate those criticizing 'empathy' (a claim supported by its disappearance from later curricular rubrics). 'Similarity and difference' was later replaced by the concept of 'diversity' in NC 2008 (QCA/DCSF, 2007). Interestingly, Counsell suggests that teachers would fare better by thinking about the concept under its former name, admitting that the explanation of diversity provided is rather vague. She does, however, suggest that the concept might be recast under the label 'complexity', but this brings to mind Spivak's comment that, '[t]o make a new word is to run the risk of forgetting the problem or believing it solved' (1976, p. xv).

In contrast with Counsell, Byrom and Riley (2009), in the same series of lectures, defend the use of the term 'diversity' in NC 2008. Riley, in particular, tells us that diversity is a rich and profound area of history that can be used to engage students in local, national and international history. He adds that the term 'diversity' may help teachers to avoid focusing on a narrow Eurocentric view of the past. Byrom is more guarded and suggests that we begin by working out 'diversity' practically in our classrooms in order to reach a better theoretical understanding in the future. However, both seem unwilling to explore the theoretical integrity of the term 'diversity' and instead focus on ways of implementing this concept in history lessons.

History teachers also tend to focus on the practical delivery of diversity rather than defining or theorizing it. Although Bradshaw describes the concept as a 'slippery fish' (2009, p. 5) and uses the NC 2008 Attainment Targets (QCA/DCSF, 2007) as a practical guide to navigation, he also casts it in a positive light. He pits the ills of grand narratives against the wonder of infinite diversity and warns us that we may have to shun traditional history schemes of work as they tend to hinder our appreciation of the diversity of past experiences. He is not alone in painting diversity in such bright colours. The editorial to the 'Diversity and Divisions' edition of *Teaching History* declares that the role of history is to nurture our sensitivity of diversity so that the nation's multivocal past can be justly celebrated (Kinloch, Kitson and McConnell, 2005). In the same edition, Gaze reminds us, in his article on the Black and Asian contributions to the World Wars, to 'view everything with diversity-tinted spectacles' (2005, p. 49). Wrenn (1999) also praises diversity in his article on citizenship and history, noting that good history teaching should naturally provide the opportunity to discuss stories from different social and cultural groups.

The teaching of different and diverse histories has, somewhat contradictorily, been seen by some teachers as being instrumental in developing a British identity. Walsh (2003) argues that one result of investigating topics related to the British Empire is that students will innately gain an appreciation of 'Britishness'. This view is also expressed by Guyver (2006), who suggests in his otherwise penetrating analysis, that an understanding of what it means to be British can be fostered by making lessons more relevant to minority ethnic groups, targeting their stories in the classroom.

It is clear from this review of the way in which history practitioners in Britain have used the terms 'diversity', 'difference', and 'identity', that teachers have been forced to plan quickly and have had little time to question 'diversity's' new role in history. This highlights a number of issues in the way the concept is approached. First, diversity is seen as a common good – an inclusive and moral step forward. Second, differences have been championed to the detriment of similarities. Third, diversity has been thrown together with citizenship and the categories of identity and multiculturalism, blurring the distinctions between them. I suggest that in view of these significant shortcomings further examination of the concepts involved is needed.

Unlike this lack of discussion of the theoretical basis of 'diversity', which characterizes its use in history teaching, the issue has long been debated by scholars in the fields of sociology, politics and religion. Three books in particular illustrate the current discussion surrounding diversity. In *Debating Diversity* (Blommaert and Verschueren, 1998), the concept is regarded as an ideology disputed at two extremes by cultural pluralists on the one hand, championing cultural difference in society, and white supremacists on the other hand, advocating the expulsion of minorities from society. In other words, diversity is acclaimed but not in its acceptance of unwelcome far-right groups. In looking at the rise of the political far right in Belgium, the authors claim that diversity is a resource managed by the authorities, whereas the managed, that is, the people, are given little say. Therefore, diversity is seen as a discourse, 'really about the "other", viewed from the perspective of the majority' (ibid., p. 15).

Conversely, in *Defending Diversity* (Foster and Herzog, 1994), the issue of diversity is linked to the philosophical debate concerning relativism. Diversity and multiculturalism are placed within a larger discourse about the nature of reality, in which pluralism challenges the Platonic, fixed idea of reality. Using Taylor's (1992) ideas on the politics of recognition as a jumping-off point, the authors in this volume are committed to respecting and negotiating difference. They collectively argue that a relativistic approach to education will cultivate an appreciation of difference and diversity rather than trigger more division in our society. In *Challenging Diversity*, however, Cooper (2004) exposes this humanistic argument. Using two case studies, the first focusing on anti-smoking legislation and the second on the prohibition of the construction of London's first *eruv*, giving Orthodox Jews more freedom during the Sabbath, Cooper discovers that underlying diversity are strong exclusivist tendencies. She notes that 'in its enthusiasm to challenge disadvantage and to celebrate variety, diversity politics comes unstuck when it is confronted with less attractive ways of living' (ibid., p. 40). In essence, she demonstrates that beneath the liberal sentiment of diversity lies authority's instrument of legitimate exclusion of undesirable elements in society.

Alternatively, Joseph (2002) links rhetoric on diversity to our capitalist ways of life in the West. Joseph reminds us that corporations use diversity as a strategy for increasing profit. She argues that we can see this in operation when businesses practise diversification and niche marketing. For her, diversity manifests itself in the corporate world when consumers are offered choice, a value cherished by many in the West. Capitalist societies, therefore, have a keen interest in upholding and promoting these ideals that support the free market economy. From Joseph we perceive that diversity, an expressly Western value, leaks into the workings of everyday life. And this, I would argue, materializes as diversity in the history curriculum.

These arguments not only demonstrate that the politics of diversity are highly contested but also illustrate why attempts to define and fix its meaning are so problematical. At the very least, an awareness of the debate surrounding the term is central to rationalizing its place in any national curriculum for history.

Multiculturalism, like diversity, is equally contested. At one end of the spectrum, the advocates of multiculturalism, representing the humanist and individualist traditions, radically endorse plurality and relativism. In *Multicultural Education* (Ramsey and Williams, 2003), the authors situate multiculturalism in a tradition with its origins in the American Civil Rights movement in the 1960s and 1970s. Multicultural education is thus seen as the next logical step, aiming to make us *all* sensitive to ethnic and racial differences, increasing our awareness of cultural traditions and experiences.

Another advocate of multiculturalism is Parekh. Surprisingly, his book *Rethinking Multiculturalism* (2006) shares many of the sentiments expressed in NC 2008. Parekh devotes a portion of his book to the topic of education, stating that multicultural education must challenge the Eurocentric content and ethos of the prevailing system of education. Unfortunately, by offering a best practice model for us to employ in our schools, Parekh serves only to establish another elite and exclusive system where alternatives, that is, those societies that value monoculturalism, are disdained.

Critics of multiculturalism have focused on the power relations lurking behind well-intentioned rhetoric. Grant and Sleeter (2007) note that all educational systems present themselves as the most evolved and progressive. The idea of multiculturalism in schools, therefore, seems paradoxical because it seeks to maintain the dominant society's knowledge. McCutcheon (2003) also identifies an 'us and them' discourse within multiculturalist rhetoric, which, he argues, is a tool that perpetuates the American way of life. Anyone inciting revolution rather than holding an 'Ethnic Day Barbeque' (2003, p. 154) is excluded from the public space. Those who are invited into the public space 'must already be operating by a set of socio-political values and standards that make it possible, attractive, meaningful, and compelling to "encounter," "understand" and "appreciate" the other' (ibid., pp. 153–154). All Americans are welcomed and given an opportunity to share sociopolitical values. However, when dominant values are questioned and true alternatives presented, those critics are quickly branded as exclusivist, fundamentalist or radical, and the whole weight of the political system is thrown against them. Similarly, Joseph (2002) argues that multiculturalism has been used in the United States to manage the assimilation of diverse ethnicities and communities into a more singular and unified entity. Badiou (2001) appears to concur, comprehending that when societies claim to respect difference within the larger context of upholding human rights, this inherently defines the identity and character of society. Badiou concludes that society's respect for differences applies only to those differences that are reasonably consistent with this identity. The postcolonial commentator, McGrane, states bluntly,

> Our culture knows that it is one among many . . . and further, it values this knowledge . . . it locates inferiority in ignorance of this relativity . . . The 'other' becomes an occasion for seeing the strength of custom. He manifests, above all, his own imprisonment within culture. (McGrane, 1989, pp. 120–121)

McGrane implies here that multiculturalism is valued by the West because it views pluralism and the acceptance of differences as a superior quality. Critically, for my study, this means that anyone holding different values – those who may not value 'diversity' as we do – is seen as ignorant and is identified as the lesser 'other'. But then can this properly be called multiculturalism?

Similar questions can be raised about the use of the terms diversity and multiculturalism in the 2008 National Curriculum for history. I suggest that the same power dynamic was in operation, that is, the desire to perpetuate the majority worldview through the exclusion of competing ideologies, and that history teachers themselves, albeit unknowingly, became channels through which this dominance was perpetuated.

Before these claims are taken any further it will be useful to survey how the idea of difference is theorized in wider literature. This allows us to evaluate whether its use in NC 2008 is problematical and also to assess whether its use as a replacement for diversity (as has happened with the use of 'similarity and difference' in NC 2014) might be an improvement, as Counsell suggests above.

Currie, in his book *Difference* (2004), playfully asks, '[w]hat could be more straightforward than the idea of difference? Is it the opposite of sameness?' (ibid., p. 1). In order to help answer this question, Barrett (1989) distinguishes three forms of the word used in critical theory. The first relates to its straightforward meaning in 'similarity and difference'. The second describes Ferdinand de Saussure's linguistic concept of difference and concerns the way in which meaning is constructed through linguistic opposition (see below). The third is effectively the recognition of diversity.

Let us turn to the second form of the category of 'difference' and its importance to critical theory as a whole. 'Difference' was picked up by academics in the 1960s through a re-examination of Saussure's structural linguistics. Saussure posited that 'in language there are only differences, and no positive terms' (1983, p. 118). In other words, meaning is created as a result of the differential relationship between two words – a cat is *not* a dog, for instance. Most relevant to this enquiry, however, is his idea that binary opposites or dichotomies (black/white; good/bad; male/female etc.) are the basic unit of difference. This insight reminds us that 'difference' as well as being similarity's opposite, and a synonym for diversity, is also a theoretical concept.

Derrida (1982) takes the structuralist notion of 'difference' and transforms it into *différance*, his neologism blending the verbs to differ and to defer. It forms the basis for the many critical interpretations of 'difference' that follow. *Différance* does not relate to the difference between entities, but the passage of the infinite and endless differentiation. Thus *différance* prevents signs (words) having static and fixed meanings. Drawing on his concept of logocentrism and the presence/absence binary opposition, Derrida writes that the meaning of any apparently 'present' sign is nothing more than the relationship between all the absent meanings that the term is not (ibid.). The meaning of the word 'dog', for example, is an endless play between associated alternatives; its meaning is produced through an infinite differentiation from possible alternatives (Hawthorne, 2008). In Derridean terms, therefore, meaning is absent, constantly deferred and unobtainable.

It is also valuable to look at how 'difference' has been employed by feminist theorists within gender and sexual theory. Cixous, for example, doubts language's ability to adequately describe the world we live in and asserts that binary opposites establish false and simplistic relationships between entities (Cixous and Clement, 1986). For Cixous, 'diversity' is inherently political. Irigaray (1993), moreover, uses the concept of difference to explore 'alterity'. Like Cixous, Irigaray seeks to unmask the power relations sitting behind binary opposites. 'Alterity' is, according to Irigaray, an oppressed state of 'other', where the politics of gender and sexuality reside. In Cixous and Irigaray, we see how poststructuralist and linguistic theory is wedded to cultural politics (Currie, 2004).

These poststructuralist writers illustrate how the concept of difference is problematical, political and theoretical. The challenge for history teachers is to be aware of these theoretical and political undercurrents when engaging their students with the concept of diversity and difference.

It would be difficult to complete this brief and incomplete review of the numerous manifestations of diversity and difference in academia without mentioning the impact of postcolonial thinking on the terms difference and otherness (for a fuller review see Currie, 2004). As we have seen with Cixous and Irigaray, the structural linguistic approach to 'difference' gives postcolonial writers a tool with which to redress the balance between Western authors appropriating the other in their research, and non-Western writers reclaiming some of the research territory lost to the West in the study of otherness. In unseating the binary opposition of similarity (identity) and difference, postcolonial thinkers challenge the essentialization of the other in Western research. Said (1979) famously names this discourse 'orientalism'. In this sense, much like feminist and queer theorists, postcolonial writers begin to break down the category of difference and explore its multidimensional presence in a world in which it had been largely absent. In fact, absence plays a major role in analysing the other. Spivak's famous question '[c]an the subaltern speak?' (1988), is highly relevant to my exploration of understanding diversity through history.

Finally, it is worth turning to the ideas of postcolonial author Bhabha (1994) and his remodelling of the category of difference into something which he calls hybridity, and which other writers have subsequently rebranded 'creolisation, in-betweenness, diasporas and liminality' (Loomba, 1998, p. 173). Interestingly, Bhabha's hybridity takes the concept of difference and places it right back into the debate about diversity, multiculturalism and identity discussed at the start of this review. He stresses the symbiotic relationship existing between the colonizer and the colonized. Within this utopian society, difference and hybridity replace all claims of a distinct and singular culture. Multiculturalism is finally replaced by a 'third space' where we 'emerge as the others of ourselves' (Bhabha, 2003, p. 209).

This review illustrates the highly contested nature of the concept of difference and its association with critical theory. It serves to introduce arguments concerning the rhetoric on diversity and multiculturalism in society, which I will seek to identify through a deconstructive reading of the interviews, work and talk of six Year 8 students in my history class.

Methodology

My methodological approach uses the tactics of deconstruction employed by MacNaughton (2005), when she draws on Derrida's ideas in her research on gender in early childhood. Derrida focuses on the relationships between binary oppositions – the fundamental unit of language – and identifies how one term in the pair is always privileged over the other, which he names the 'deviant' or 'parasite' (Derrida, 1988). Due to the fact that the privileged term defines the cultural standard of normality (Biesta and Egéa-Kuehne, 2001), it is unsurprising that the resulting hierarchy within the binary is not accidental, but rather socially produced

(MacNaughton, 2005). Deconstruction is therefore on the one hand, the tactic by which one can 'attend to the other' (ibid., p. 95), and on the other, a way to discern the contextual information that sits parallel to the text. The contextual information aids in unseating and decentring the binary opposition and reversing it, so that the privileged becomes the deviant. Ultimately, in contextualizing the binary opposition one can begin to determine the character and nature of knowledge held and controlled by the dominant ideology or institution. Martin McQuillan's (2001) simple interpretation lends itself readily to this study. He argues that there is just one rule that governs deconstruction, to allow the other, the different, the deviant, to speak.

Since Derrida, researchers and literary theorists have developed schema to clarify his deconstruction. MacNaughton (2005), in particular, has condensed it into a series of six successive questions, or tactics, whose cumulative effect helps to destabilize and reverse the binary opposition. I use this model in order to provide responses for my Research Questions (see Table 8.2), making it my primary methodological approach.

Research Question 1 attempts to identify the predominant themes in the text by visualizing patterns in word frequency using the *Wordle* program described below (Feinberg, 2009). Here, students watched excerpts from the Bollywood film *Jodhaa/Akbar* (Gowariker, 2008) while completing a data capture sheet in the shape of the Emperor Akbar. Students were given the question, 'Who was Jalaluddin Mohammed?' and instructed to write down anything they found noteworthy in the Akbar outline. The words and phrases generated by the students were analysed with the aim of identifying which binary opposites were at play.

Research Question 2, in presenting the way students describe the other, also looks at how pupils locate the other and involves identifying the politics of opposition within the text. The data for this question were collated from three separate sources, the first of which were transcriptions of interviews carried out with the six students. The second were the dedications that the students wrote for the *Akbarnama*, a task partly based on a suggestion by Riley, made at an Historical Association event in Cambridge in May 2009. The task involved students analysing Moghul miniature paintings from the *Akbarnama*, a portfolio of images created in the workshop of Abu Fazl, commissioned by Emperor Akbar. Using genre writing, popularized by Barrs and Cork (2001), the students were asked to postulate dedications to the paintings in the literary style of Moghul court poetry. The framework for the language came from two songs written for the film *Jodhaa*/Akbar (Gowariker, 2008), *Azeem-O-Shaan-Shahenshah*

Table 8.2 Research questions

Research questions	Data
1. What do students notice in the stories of the past?	Akbar outlines
2. How do students describe the other?	Student interviews
	Akbarnama dedication
	Kim Stories
3. Which binary oppositions are in play when students attend to the other?	Students' interviews

(Akhtar and Rahman, 2008a) and *Khwaja mere Khwaja* (Akhtar and Rahman, 2008b). The third source utilized texts written by the students, based on Rudyard Kipling's *Kim* (1995). They first listened to an excerpt from the novel and then watched a dramatization of the book that dealt with the same excerpt. The film was abruptly stopped and students were asked to complete the scene using the background details from their observation in their writing.

In contrast to the second question, Research Question 3 takes a more holistic view of deconstruction and employs the last three tactics by showing how each word in the binary opposition is dependent on the other for its definition. The interview transcriptions again provide the data used to answer this question. More details about the overview of the teaching sequence can be found in my original research dissertation (Somers, 2009).

Methods

Deconstruction analysis is a qualitative and text-based methodology and relies on the collection of textual data. With this in mind, it seemed natural to collate data from both student interviews and from classroom-based written exercises that could be subjected to lengthier analysis. I also limited the scope of the study by selecting a total of six students from the Year 8 history class who felt comfortable speaking into a recording device. As a result, the participants included four boys and two girls. Though this is an unrepresentative sample of the class, my aim was not to attempt a serious generalization from the results beyond the participants in the study, but to trace the discursive arguments raised in reviewing the literature, and to make tentative assumptions about the nature of the discourse on diversity in the study of history.

Interviews are the most widely applied method in this study. They provided the majority of the data required for the deconstruction analysis and became the basis for the responses to Research Questions 2 and 3. Rather than attempt a systematic coding of the transcriptions of interviews and lectures, I annotated the transcriptions during numerous close readings.

The textual analysis of the class work followed the same procedure, in that it also was a text appropriate for deconstruction analysis. However, Research Questions 1 and 2, lying outside the 'tactics' model, required alternative methods, and I experimented with using the free Web-based visual representation program, Wordle (Feinberg, 2009). Wordle creates word clouds giving prominence to words that appear more frequently in the source text. Rather than taking a wholly quantitative approach to Research Question 1 by analysing the frequency of words used by the students, I wanted to use a visual format that would retain a more open and fluid aspect to the data.

A word on validity

One cannot ignore the scientific discourse inherent in the notion of validity, making it a problematic requirement in social science research (Lather, 1993; Lenso, 1995; Scheurich,

1997). At one extreme, Scheurich calls validity an 'imperial project' (ibid., p. 87), while Lather is more practical and talks about her continual engagement with the issue (Lather, 1993). For the most part, all authors tend to agree that poststructuralist research needs to engage with validity through the notion of self-reflexivity and the question of voice.

Using Burr (1995) and Lather (1993) as guides, my response was to attend to the following factors. First, while making a determined effort to stay as close to the text as possible, I realize that my deconstructive reading is subjective and open to criticism and may be interpreted differently by others. Second, I tried to present a consistent position throughout all stages of my research, paying particular attention to epistemological and theoretical issues. Third, adhering to the conventions of academic research, I attempted to formulate a cohesive intellectual argument throughout; thus the validity of my research should be judged on the validity of my thesis.

Data analysis

Research Question 1: What do students notice in the stories of the past?

Using the word clouds generated from the Akbar outlines I could begin to make very guarded inferences about the types of words chosen by the students. First, it is unsurprising that students predominantly register adjectives in an attempt to describe the changing characteristics of the Emperor portrayed in the film, but it is interesting that the majority of the adjectives logged are positive. This in many ways reflects the manner in which Akbar is presented in the film, yet it is important to remember that students chose which words to note. In particular, the predominant use of the adjectives 'merciful' and 'respectful' implies that individual students made a collective decision to choose the same words. This may be due to the fact that the film solicits this type of response from a modern and Westernized audience. And if a film is to be successful, an audience must identify with a hero who holds qualities that are admired and respected. In particular, the words 'merciful' and 'respectful' represent values that are esteemed in Westernized society. In the same way, the most prevalent noun in the data, 'people', might reveal the students' preference for the writing about themselves as it occurs more than any other noun, adjective or verb. Alternatively, the relatively common occurrence of the word 'other' might suggest that students are collectively seeking ways to describe and address something outside of their identity. Therefore, their inability to successfully define 'other people', 'other religions' and 'other people' results in them generalizing the 'other' in a common and unified manner.

Research Question 2: How do students describe the other?

Before analysing the interview data, I presumed that descriptions of the Emperor would be concerning the other, the deviant and the strange. Michelle and Simon challenged my preconceptions. Michelle replies, 'I found it quite weird that he got married to a Hindu. And he didn't ask her to convert. Because like I'm Muslim and we normally have to.' The film, by presenting Akbar as merciful and respectful represents the normal, the same, the identical, that is, the student. However, the film inadvertently challenges Michelle's conception of the Emperor by presenting his marriage in a modern Westernized manner. This jars with Michelle's own experience, and Akbar, in this moment, becomes for her the other, the weird and the deviant. This episode affects Simon in the same way. He argues, 'they always did change, the women always did change religion', and in this moment the plot appears unreal, contradicting what Simon holds to be intrinsically true. Thus, locating the familiar and the strange becomes a tactic for identifying the similar and the other in the interviews, and Michelle's and Simon's responses are a turning point in my research as they help to unseat my own assumptions about where the 'other' resides.

A brief analysis of the Akbarnama dedications helps to clarify the issue of identifying Akbar as 'self', and everything else as 'other'. Michelle, Simon and Lucy adopt a personal relationship with the Emperor by using personal pronouns in their dedications: Michelle writes, 'always in my heart' and 'always here with me'; Simon comments 'You live in our hearts' and 'We praise you'; Lucy notes, 'You defended us'. Whilst it is clear that these students are replicating a particular style of writing, it is also clear that they are choosing to adopt a personal relationship with the Emperor, where the other three students do not. Some students, conversely, adopt the language of pre-existing literary genres, which may be an attempt to overcome an awkward and contrived moment. This form of intertextuality can be seen when David writes, 'Rainbow Nation', or when Ricky uses, 'Jai Ho', or when Michelle appropriates Mohammed Ali's 'float like a butterfly, sting like a bee' and Tina Turner's 'simply the best', and also in Simon's borrowing of the title song when he notes, 'You live in our hearts, we praise you'. In this way, one could argue that by borrowing accepted and known phrases and applying them humorously, students are developing a relationship with Akbar; they are courting him, and he in turn is becoming their other self.

Students also find 'other' in place. Students emphasize its differences from their own conception of place. For example, David describes the palace as 'really rich' and he cannot decide whether Kim's India would have been 'interesting or horrible'. Lucy describes the marketplace as 'dirty, or something like that'. Ricky talks of India as 'so beautiful and such a great country to experience'. Similarly, Michelle sees India as adventurous and somewhere to explore. These quotes seem to suggest that students already hold relatively stable ideas of India as a place, although David appears hesitant to commit to a decision on India.

In locating the other in students' speech and writing, one becomes aware that students' construction of 'other' is relatively unstable and is affected by their conception of normality and the context and moment in which they are writing and talking. Michelle's shifting construction of Akbar as 'same' and 'strange', and the location of Kirkpatrick as 'different' and 'rational' by David seems to confirm this point. However, the commonalities existing in the students' choice of words in describing the abnormal and strange suggest that students are approaching the other from similar starting points. The patterns evident in their language may suggest that such commonality stems from the shared environment of the classroom or, is the result of a mutual set of ground-rules which operates in the form of a collective set of values.

Research Question 3: Which binary oppositions are in play when students attend to the other?

The deconstructive reading and subsequent responses made to Research Questions 1 and 2 began to identify several primary binary oppositions manifest in students' speech. Though in fact these dichotomies are thoroughly enmeshed, I attempted to isolate them. One opposition is loosely termed free/bound, another is plural/singular.

The idea of 'free' is conceptualized in detail by David, who begins to define it by linking it to 'freedom of mind or religion'. He develops this idea by explaining its opposite, 'a controlled place' where 'you could only be a certain religion'. He says this place is 'not really spiritual', thereby implying that the free place is. The bounded and controlled place takes away the 'right to choose'. In David's interview, the free place represents Akbar's kingdom, which he links to peace and tolerance. This construction of the free place can also be seen when James talks about how the Emperor rules by listening to his people rather than doing 'what's best for money', which James considers 'evil'. James adds that Akbar 'was very tolerant towards other people'. This image of the tolerant and liberal society, in which Akbar listens to his people, seems to be held by Simon, too, describing Akbar as 'merciful' and saying that he ruled over his country 'without having to be actually forceful'. With Lucy the notion of the free is rooted, once more, in the kindness of the Emperor who allows his wife to 'keep her religion'. Lucy feels this is right because 'she wanted to stay how she wanted to be', 'because she *had* to have an identity' so that 'everyone knows . . . who you are'. Once again the bounded place is conspicuous in its absence, although it is becoming clearer that 'free', is for Lucy closely related to identity and the importance of the individual.

Ricky's definition of free is also revealing because even though he uses it in a different context, in many ways it supports the notion of free held by the other students. Ricky begins by invoking the bounded 'other' by stating that Kirkpatrick 'had to convert into Hindu [*sic*] so he could marry the Prince's daughter'. This element of coercion typifies a place where rules and tradition endure. Moreover, when talking about Kim, Ricky argues that 'he didn't really believe in the Hindu stuff', which further characterizes the bounded other as religious and dogmatic, but also trivial. In doing so, Ricky appears to suggest that Kim, who 'was half-English' yet, perhaps more importantly, secular, is able to transcend it. However, in relating Kim's life to his own, Ricky reveals his own conception of free, which is intrinsically linked to the other students' constructions.

The second binary opposition, singular/plural, most often comes into play when students are asked to express a preference, or describe why one source might be worthier than another. Interestingly, when the dichotomy is exposed it is expressed universally across the participants' responses. The plural is frequently manifested in the word 'both'. Having been asked the last two interview questions Simon responds, 'it is better to see it from both sides'. James comments, 'you can learn it from different points of view and get a clearer picture of what was happening'. Lucy says, 'I think it's good to see both.' David targets the singular by saying, 'there's never just one side to one person's story'. Michelle also sees the value of the plural as she answers, 'both ways, it's better'. In answering the penultimate interview question, Ricky claims, 'But if you see both sides of the stories, it will make it more interesting.'

In all these quotations more value has been placed on the word 'both', or on the plural, than on the singular. Simon qualifies this point by arguing, 'you can actually paint more of a picture of what was actually going on at that time'. In other words, Simon seems to suggest that the plural reveals more truth than the singular alone. However, a major contradiction appears to be in play here, which is exhibited when Lucy says 'you can get two different points of view and like kind of put them together'. This idea is reiterated when Ricky says, 'you can sum up your own opinion of what you think it was' and also when he comments, 'I would have to make my mind up myself what I would think it would be.' The privileging of the plural over the singular appears to serve a purpose. It appears that students see the value in the plural because they value choice. The students seem to value choice because they feel it empowers them to make a decision. In other words, choice gives the illusion of agency and ownership when the decision is made. As we can see here though, far from eliciting individual and original answers, the interview question generates a singular voice. Ultimately, one could argue, that in the common championing of the plural over the singular, the plural is inevitably silenced by the singular.

Discussion

It is a strange irony that for a word expressing plurality, variety and a sense of freedom and the acceptance of other life-ways, diversity has been found here to continually point to the singular, the self, the individual and to modern liberal society. Moreover, the colonization of diversity by notions of self is fostered in students' language when attending to the other.

The rhetoric on diversity and plurality pronounced by students finds much in common with the arguments raised in the literature review. Joseph's (2002) claim that diversity is a strategy for the expansion of capitalism is reflected in the analysis of Research Question 3, which identifies that the right to choose homogenizes individual agency in order to proliferate the Western liberal status quo. Blommaert and Verschueren's (1998) idea that diversity is a discourse about the other viewed from the perspective of the majority is reflected in language used by the students that locates and constructs the other. Lastly, McCutcheon's (2003) uncompromising picture of an 'Ethnic Day Barbecue' rings true when we reflect on how it is utilized in NC 2008.

In retrospect, when I look at the rationale for my lesson sequence I realize that I am as much a part of the system – that is, subject to privileging Western liberal values and promoting 'self' over 'other' – as the participants in this survey. My plan from the outset, as far as lesson content was concerned, was to deliver something *different*. I carefully *chose* the film for its gripping storyline which I knew would *interest* the Year 8 class. I also wanted students to engage with the cultural elements of the Moghul period because I *enjoyed* the craftsmanship involved in producing the Moghul miniatures. I purposefully created tasks that asked students to engage with the topic on a *personal* level. Pupils were *free* to *choose* on which Moghul miniatures to work and to decide whether Kirkpatrick could be trusted or not. Students were asked to create stories based on *Kim* because I wanted them to continue the story and participate. Even during the interviews there are many moments when I essentialize, generalize and privilege. For instance, I call the Moghul *salwar kameez* a costume, and I am keen to tell students that they are studying something *new* and *different*. I ask students to make recommendations giving them the option to *choose* and contribute to the discussion – and these examples are taken from just one interview! No matter how hard I try, I cannot stop myself uttering the same rhetoric of diversity, multiculturalism and inclusion. I am, in a sense, destined to bigotry on some level because my thoughts, speech and writing are rooted in language, and according to poststructuralist thinking, it is language that creates meaning in the world around us – not individually, but collectively.

This raises serious questions about the way we teach, attend to, discuss, and describe the other in history lessons. The other is found everywhere, whether we teach women's suffrage, Henry VIII, or a character from historical fiction. In effect, history is the study of the other in the past. One large obstacle we face in attending to the other is that we want our students to enjoy history. We cannot stop wanting to make our lessons interesting and engaging, but we need to be aware that we are unwilling participants in the transmission of diversity politics and as such we are guilty of imposing our vocal selves on a silent and vulnerable other.

Part II
Discussing History Education Research

Causation, Chronology and Source Interpretation: Looking at School History from the Perspective of a University History Faculty

Reflections on Chapters by Ellen Buxton, Paula Worth and Rick Rogers

9

'Such an interesting book, and so unlike the rest of his work: the theory is that it was written by his wife'. This was a former colleague's observation on E. H. Carr's (1961) *What Is History?*, and it captures the affectionate irreverence with which academic historians typically regard this one-time stalwart of historiography courses. No longer something one was forbidden to read, and displaced by Jenkins (1991) and Evans (1997), or more recently by Megill (2007), Carr's punchy but dated book has dropped off the university syllabus these days and rarely turns up even in UCAS statements and admissions interviews. It speaks to a form of history that no-one now practises – or at least that no-one sets out to own – and to read it today is to experience a kind of culture shock about the weirdness of mid-twentieth-century culture, and about the somersaults required of a critical mind that was well-versed in British Marxism but had no French-style linguistic philosophy.

It was thus a surprise to me to see Carr cited in all three of the distinctly cutting-edge essays that I read for this volume, but I think that reaction may tell us something about the different priorities of school-age history teaching and what we do in universities. In part, as I shall try to explain, there may be a degree of mis-fit between the forms of academic history presented in schools and those practised in universities, but it seems to me that there is also a great deal more self-conscious reflection on, and development of, the skills of the historian in secondary education than in higher education. That may make a certain amount of sense, given the persisting differences of mission and culture between schools and universities, but it underlines the challenges of transition faced by students, and perhaps it also raises questions for university lecturers about how we go about helping our charges to become better historians.

Of course, there is plenty of reflection on how students learn across the higher education (HE) sector: every history department offers some kind of skills training, and every degree scheme involves some sort of staged progression. But I would have said that the main form of historical education in universities remains, as it has always been, a mixture of modelling, performance and criticism. Just as academics teach themselves by reading, lecturing, writing, and receiving questions and comments from other scholars, so – broadly speaking – we expect undergraduates to learn in the same ways. We might push them to study a variety of types of history, and we certainly oblige them to look at historiography and methodology, but we do not break the skills of the historian down into their constituent elements, nor do we really try to teach those skills, as the three teachers in these essays have done.

I think most of us would be surprised at the sophistication of the intellectual tasks that children of 11, 12 and 13 are carrying out. Worth's students may not have realized that they were engaging in the development of their own hermeneutics, but they were brought to a point where they could grasp the notion that understanding a source involves creative input, and not simply skills of excavation. Buxton's pupils willingly transferred their attention from the French Revolution to the diseases of an imaginary camel, and they did so, just as they engaged in a parallel arithmetical exercise, partly because they could see the metaphorical relationship between these procedures and the interpretation of the past. And their methodological self-consciousness paid dividends: the mental leap made by Joe (Buxton, this volume, p. 39), in his algebraic representation of interacting factors, is the sort of thing one might wait a long time for an undergraduate to arrive at. When I first heard about 'meta-cognition', during a recent stint as a grammar-school governor, my instinct was to be sceptical – it seemed to matter more that pupils should know how to do things than that they should know about that knowledge – but now I'm not so sure: the two need not be separated, and the one could reinforce the other.

In a similar way, I had always had doubts about the disaggregation of tasks that, at university level, are performed together: the interpretation of sources; the integration of primary and secondary material; the examination of methodology; the cultivation of critical vocabulary; the organization of argument; the exercise of persuasion and so on. Like many amateur commentators on education, I guess my views are a product of my own formation. When I was at school, in the 1970s and early 1980s, we performed essentially the same task over and over again (Schools History Project notwithstanding!). The ambition of our project widened and deepened – more reading, greater complexity, longer essays – but there was no real change in its forms: over time, we simply got better at writing essays and talking about history. Certainly, we were challenged and criticized, and we tried to re-model our work in response, but we were not much encouraged to reflect on what we were doing, nor to spend time focusing on particular procedures to the exclusion of others. That would have been regarded as artificial (as if the endless production of essays was the most natural thing in the world).

From this regime, it was a small step to university, where the same techniques prevailed and, by and large, do so still. In my university, it would not be easy to persuade students to engage in role-plays, let alone more abstract exercises (I have been able to do this elsewhere), and yet initiatives like these are a fast route to identifying dynamics, understanding context, or enhancing the level of interpretation. It may be reasonable to expect undergraduate students to refine these skills for themselves – after all, as full-time 'research active' historians, we do not stand in quite the same relation to our undergraduates as teachers do to their pupils. Equally, by the time they are at university, students have acquired at least some of the cultural resources that should make it easier for them to read sources perceptively and creatively, to write deftly about patterns of causation, to locate events in time and space and so on; they can do this intuitively, at least to some extent. One unacknowledged function of the kinds of exercises described in the three papers, it seems to me, is to enable children to acquire and develop interpretative and expressive skills without drawing on a knowledge base that they cannot be expected to possess. And our students, of course, have done all these things at school; presumably they do not need to do them again. And yet our tendency to expect them to operate as mini-dons, writing short monographs from ever longer and more open-ended reading-lists, may not be the best way to advance their abilities. One observation that leapt out at me from Buxton's essay was the fact that, on the back of their comparative study, the pupils felt well-informed – 'we *knew* about Britain and France' (this volume, p. 41). These pupils will have known very much less than first-year undergraduates typically know after a term's work, but the latter often report feelings of ignorance, contrasting their sketchy grasp of what they have learned at university with their secure understanding of what they did at school. That confidence, borne of more restricted and defined activities, is important: with it comes greater readiness to reason, analyse and synthesize, the trademark skills of the history graduate.

So there may be an unexpected rupture between the innovative and methodologically self-conscious modes of teaching history study at Key Stage 3 and the comparatively unstructured regime at university. What about the nature and content of the discipline at these two levels? I suggested earlier that there could be some degree of mis-fit between the forms of history imagined and presented in these essays and what actually goes on in university departments. There are certainly continuities in the treatment of causation, source-interpretation, chronology and scale between school and university, but there are also some striking differences.

Rogers' fascinating project addresses a concern that is widely shared at HE level, particularly now that we are taking a global turn. 'Deep history' is all the rage in America (e.g. Shryock and Smail, 2011), and, even if it has not quite caught on here yet, more modest efforts to teach 'global' or 'world' history since the Middle Ages raise the same questions of scale (Pomeranz and Segal, 2012). Are we prepared for the different kinds of learning and assessment that these courses must entail? The answer is 'yes' in some British universities, like Newcastle, where 'world history' courses have been running for years, but it is not the case everywhere. And history departments have 'form' in evading the challenges posed by their own programmes. Ever since Bishop Stubbs invented the Oxford Modern History syllabus in the 1870s, long 'period' or 'outline' papers have been a staple of history degrees. They are notionally intended to enable students to trace large and important developments over long periods of time – or at least to be able to place specific episodes in a wider and longer context. Do they do this? More often, I think, they boil down to small islands of knowledge, explored in essays, tutorials or seminars and regurgitated in exams. Few Oxford students form a clear view of how the British Isles changed between 1042 and 1330 (British History II), or even 1800 and 1924 (British History VII); still less would they, or most of their peers at other universities, be able to sketch the major changes in Europe between 1000 and 1500, or across the world between the 'axial age' of the first great religions, and (let's say) the era of steamships and telegraphs. Of course, they can do many other things, and their grasp of the historical role of gender, of textuality, of culture and the relationship between representations and reality, is generally much stronger than it used to be, but let us not fool ourselves that we know how to do 'big history' at university. We do not, and our students graduate with huge holes in their knowledge of the sweep of time, even with respect to Britain and Europe, let alone the world. The fact that Rogers' 12-year-olds, however crudely, can make generalizations on the largest possible scale is both wonderful and chastening.

Worth begins with debates about historical truth and the role of the historian in producing knowledge that, for a time in the 1990s, seemed very threatening to our discipline, but have now lost their capacity to shock. As she indicates, thinking about language was both the cause of this upheaval and part of its resolution (if 'resolution' is quite the right word for the passing of postmodernism: we may be *post*-postmodern now, but that does not mean that we have answered all the criticisms of its exponents). Ideas born in the linguistic theories of Saussure and Derrida seemed to expose the radical uncertainty of historical knowledge, but historians have found ways of living with these insights. A pragmatic recognition that we can learn other languages and form some kind of understanding of what is encoded in them enables us to have some confidence in our readings. An acceptance that history is a social discipline, its assumptions – both methodological and substantive – established by inter-subjective validation has also allowed us to carry on. These days, historians are much more likely to note the kinds of insights that can and cannot be supplied by different ways of looking at the past than to consider the truth-claims of competing methodologies. It is axiomatic that everything we do is positioned, but most of us continue to believe that our work involves a dialogue with source material, rather than being a monologue. In today's universities, we probably expend more energy on getting students to engage with a range of methods and approaches than we do on developing their skills of source analysis, and these skills are turned towards the reading of secondary and tertiary material at least as much as original texts and artefacts. But source-based 'special subjects' and dissertations still represent the pinnacle of most degree-schemes, and yet the problem at the centre of Worth's essay – that comprehension, interpretation and deployment are fundamentally related – passes without comment, I think, in HE practice. A closer look at the concepts and procedures in play here would almost certainly help students faced with the arcana of the 'gobbet exercise'.

I have left Buxton's interest in causation, comparison and counterfactuals until last, because in some respects they bring us back to the world of Carr. It sounds a controversial proposition, but I wonder how much today's historians are really concerned with causation. We are much more likely to identify fields of influence – to 'deduce the most important circumstances', as Gibbon put it in the opening chapter of the *Decline and Fall of the Roman Empire* more than two hundred years ago – than to list causes, and still less to argue about their relative priority. Given the ever-widening frame of reference in which history is approached – not just politics and the 'constitution', nor even economy and society in aggregate, but through infinite forms of culture, environment and climate, embodiment and emotion, materiality and everyday life, cosmology and communication – we really do find it difficult to say that 'one thing is more important than another' (Rigby, 1995). Equally, if I look through the essay and exam questions I set for students, I find that more of them are about *characterizing* phenomena – that is describing and analysing them and/or assessing their interplay – than about considering their part in chains of causes and consequences. This kind of discussion may involve consideration of causes – notably through the medium of 'why' questions (often arrived at, as Clark (2013) does, through 'how' questions: Buxton, this volume, p. 25) – but that consideration is often peripheral or selective, and rarely concerned with establishing hierarchies. It may well be right for children to work at causation in a structured way, so as to enable them to identify patterns, dynamics, processes at a later stage in their learning, but perhaps there is more of a gap here between university and school practice than there once was (see also Wong, 2012).

And as it is with causes, so with counterfactuals. Richard Evans has recently remarked that these do not have the salience they once had, as the academy pulls away from political events, to consider social, cultural and transnational contexts (Evans, 2014, pp. 106–108). It is a moot point whether comparative history should be considered counterfactual: it certainly involves the induction of models and theories and the setting of these alongside variant realities, but that procedure might be considered meta-factual, or metaphorical; it is not 'against' what actually happened, but an attempt to find better heuristics for the conventional task of historical explanation. In any event, it is comparative history that forms the exciting centrepiece of Buxton's essay, and this remains an acceptable, even favoured, approach among historians and in university teaching. As we have seen, it generates fresh ideas and stimulates the confidence on which all further analysis depends.

So if Carr seems quaint to university lecturers, but retains a certain utility for reflective teachers (among many other resources), it is because he addressed components of basic methodology which are rarely confronted directly in universities. The pupils mentioned in these essays have been drawn towards levels and modes of thinking that undergraduates may have to re-learn, and via more indirect or self-directed routes. Perhaps that is the right thing – different stages in the education system can reasonably be about different things, and I do firmly believe (perhaps against a growing trend) that university students should be autonomous learners, with their own decisions to make about how best to combine a portfolio of skills and knowledge. Even so, at the very least, academic historians should be alert to these differences of training. The only remaining question in my mind, in light of these particular chapters, is what happens during the exam years.

On the Dual Character of Historical Thinking: Challenges for Teaching and Learning

Reflections on Chapters by Daniel Magnoff, Rachel Foster and Ellen Buxton

Allan Megill

10

The teacher chapters in this volume highlight a central characteristic of historical thinking and knowledge. I refer to something that distinguishes history as a field of reflection and scholarship from most other fields of knowledge that pupils (and all of us) encounter. Stated in the most general terms, this 'something' is the persisting presence of mutually contradictory entities or orientations. One might imagine, in the manner of Aristotelian or Hegelian logic, that contradictions exist only to be eliminated or resolved. This is what prevails in many disciplines, notably mathematics and the natural sciences, that pupils encounter in their school careers. In the discipline of history, however, things are different. There are manifold contradictions that historians do not resolve but instead leave hanging.

I do not have the space here to develop my notion that, at a structural level, history as a discipline manifests an 'unresolving dialectic', as I call it (see, briefly, Megill, 2007, pp. 2, 4, 41, 109, 111 and Megill, 2008, p. 20). Nor has this notion been systematically developed elsewhere. History is notoriously an un-theoretical discipline, and most historians would rather write history than inquire into its logical and rhetorical structure. As a consequence of its pedagogical focus, however, the present volume highlights a theoretical reality that is normally not noticeable in professional historiography, let alone commented on. The 'unresolving dialectic' of history contains multiple dimensions, and I cannot deal with all these dimensions in the present commentary. But I do not need to, because the teacher chapters in this volume offer a stellar opportunity for thinking about one important axis of history's unresolving dialectic: the tension between *experience* and *interpretation*. In the present context I use the term *interpretation* broadly, to cover all those processes by which historians attempt to analyse and make sense of the historical past.[1] Non-professional 'consumers' of history know perfectly well that works of history offer interpretations of the historical past. They know that these works offer interpretations of the past, not 'the thing itself', because they see that different historians offer different accounts of the 'same' historical phenomena. Consequently, the interpretive character of historical research and writing is glaringly obvious.

In contrast, historical experience often remains invisible to us. By 'historical experience' I mean the sensation that we pursuers of history sometimes have of a kind of direct breakthrough of the past into the present.[2] Historical experience is an experiencing, in the 'now', of a connection linking us to, or a gap dividing us from, the historical past. It is something that we *feel*. Still, the feeling requires knowledge of the historical situation and, in particular, a grasp of both the continuities and discontinuities between the particular past and the particular present that are at issue. Even among those who 'know', some people will be moved, and others not, by a particular historical artefact, situation or representation. Among instances of such historical experience, I think of Maya Jasanoff's encounter, evoked at the beginning of her *Edge of Empire*, with the incongruous presence of a 'vast Palladian villa' in the midst of present-day Calcutta (Jasanoff, 2005, pp. 3–4). I think of an amazing passage at the end of chapter 7 of Saul Friedländer's *Nazi Germany and the Jews: The Years of Persecution,* wherein, after noting Hitler's speech at the Heldenplatz on 15 March 1938, as well as the fact that seventy-nine Viennese Jews committed suicide in what remained of that month, Friedländer evokes, in addition, not a real suicide, but the suicide of an imagined character in the play *Heldenplatz*, by the Austrian writer Thomas Bernhard (Friedländer, 1997, pp. 239–240). This strange turn in Friedländer's narrative seems intended to generate a sense of shock, and hence of heightened awareness, in the minds of his attentive readers. Friedländer's own parents, Czech Jews who had sought refuge in France, were themselves killed at Auschwitz.[3]

Historical experience (or historical sensation; or the presence of the past) is elusive. After all, there never *was* a historical experience (except for experiences in past times of the presence of still earlier pasts). Historical experience (in the sense intended here) is always retroactive. In this respect historical experience mirrors historical understanding in general. As the philosopher of history Arthur Danto pointed out in his *Analytical Philosophy of History* (first published in 1965), the assertion, 'The Thirty Years War began in 1618', could not have been uttered in 1618 (Danto, 1985, p. xii).[4] 'The Thirty Years War began in 1618' is one instance of what Danto calls 'narrative sentences', which are defined by the fact that they 'give descriptions of events under which the events could not have been witnessed' (Danto, 1985, p. xii). Danto argues persuasively that such sentences are central to the *entire project* of historical understanding. No one in the past experienced history as it was, when it was. When experiences are *present*, they are not yet history, and when they are *past*, they are no longer experience. Only through narrativization – more specifically, through a particular *kind* of narrativization – does historical experience emerge. The tension, here, is between an un-experienceable experience of history on the one hand and, on the other hand, a particular kind of thinking. The best single term for designating this thinking is 'historical interpretation'. We need to treat this term quite broadly. The processes of thinking that make history possible are various. They include narrativization in the narrow sense – that is, the constructing of accounts arranged along a temporal axis. They also include analysis, representation, argument, and conceptualization. Only by the workings of these processes does experience get turned into *historical* experience.

* * *

The unresolving dialectic of history runs along different but connected axes. For example, there is the well-known tension between, on the one hand, historical investigation as a scholarly and scientific enterprise and, on the other, the political commitments that, I claim, are always present in historical research and writing, even when they remain entirely implicit. In modern historiography there is also a tension between an impulse towards universality and an opposing impulse towards particularity. But neither tension is prominent in the teacher chapters. The tension that *is* prominent (even when unstated) is the tension between historical experience and historical interpretation.

We can visualize this tension as follows:

Historical Experience <<----------->> *Historical Interpretation*

Historical experience is usually taken as a 'given' in historical writing. Indeed, it *is* a 'given', in the sense that it is a condition of possibility for the project of historical research and writing as these appear in the historical discipline today. Unless a prospective audience has within itself an *intuition* of historical experience, it will not respond to historical representations. Audiences lacking such a capacity can be reached only by other means, of a nonhistorical sort: myths, parables, 'fairy stories', acts of religion, ritual performances and so on. Nonetheless, in their everyday writing of history, historians explicitly invoke historical experience only rarely, preferring just to *assume* it. In general, they confine their evocations of historical experience to paratexts (most often prefaces or introductions), which they generally write after they have completed the main text of a work. The largest exception to this rule is when they wish to draw attention to historical realities that they find extraordinary in one way or another.

The task of initiating neophytes into historical understanding is largely a matter of 'working' the 'Historical Experience – Historical Interpretation' axis. Buxton, Foster and Magnoff focus quite explicitly on this axis in their chapters. Not surprisingly, their greater concern is with historical interpretation. They are less evidently concerned with historical experience, but if we read between the lines we can see that it does preoccupy them. In particular, a major challenge that they face in their teaching is the relative non-presence, in the minds of their pupils, of an already-established orientation towards historical experience.

'The study of history is a study of causes', E. H. Carr famously declared in *What Is History?* (Carr, 1961, p. 81). I have long had the feeling that Carr starts too far downstream, overlooking the difficulties involved in making justified causal assertions in history. Before history can be 'a study of causes' it needs to be a study of those things of which we speak when we speak of causes (if we come to speak of causes at all). Danto, a far smarter thinker than Carr, knew this perfectly well; and he also knew how difficult it is to engage in causal analysis in history (see Danto, 1962, reprinted with minor changes in Danto, 1985, pp. 143–181). I am fond of Danto's observation that 'the task of history is to establish the record of what happened when' (Danto, 1985, p. 285). I love the way he fixates on what is elemental, namely, that there were things that happened in the past. Further, although it was far from being his main concern, Danto's suggestion in *Analytical Philosophy of History* that we come to history only through a 'retroactive re-alignment of the Past' (Danto, 1985, p. 168) brings us close to the territory of historical experience, as does his suggestion that if we did not have knowledge of the past, we could not 'experience the present world as we do' (Danto, 1985, pp. 92–93). An adequate examination of the notion of historical experience is beyond the scope of the present paper, but I can at least indicate four *components* of 'historical experience', two of which are suggested by Danto's work:

a. some degree of knowledge (acquired by study, personal experience, family stories, media representations, etc.) of a 'past' that might potentially become a *historical* past;
b. the capacity to *look back upon* that past from a later perspective;
c. the feeling that the past in question is not, or is no longer, part of one's present, but is instead separated by a break or gulf from the present; and
d. some degree of motivation to reflect on, and to be moved by, the past in question.

As noted, Buxton's, Foster's and Magnoff's chapters are focused more on the cognitive than on the experiential side of the 'Historical Experience – Historical Interpretation' axis. In other words, they are concerned more with the processes of analysis and interpretation by which we 'make sense' of history than they are with the history itself or the experience itself. Clearly, it is an important, and also difficult, task to initiate young students into a specifically *historical* understanding. How are we to inculcate history 'as a "discipline" or "form of knowledge"' (to quote Magnoff)? In her chapter, I found Foster's approach in her lesson sequence on the US Civil Rights movement interesting. She aimed to get students to think interpretively about the direction, degree and perceptibility of change in the condition of African Americans in the period 1945–1955. Her efforts map quite well onto items (b), (c), and perhaps (d), above, the interpretive components by means of which historical experience emerges.

In reading these chapters (as well as other teacher chapters in this volume), I found myself consulting my own (limited) experience of the situation of persons of tender age who are (now) reaching adulthood via a childhood and adolescence replete with unremitting inputs of information. How, in this surfeit, are they to be brought into the dimension indicated in item (a), above, namely, some degree of awareness of what *might* become, for the pupil, a *historical* past? In this regard, I was much taken by Ellen Buxton's evocation of a childhood visit to the Loire Valley. Here she describes something that is not so much a historical experience as it is a kind of precondition thereof:

> I returned with my head full of images of Chenonceau and Chambord, mingling potently with those of Hever and Hampton Court. Looking at portraits of Henry VIII and François I, I remember feeling that I better understood the posturing Henry. Unpolished though my thinking was, I understood envy and I recognised emulation. Yet when we studied Henry VIII at school, there was no mention of François nor, more perplexingly, of France.

Buxton alludes to this childhood experience in order to make a plea for a greater inclusion of comparative analysis into English national history. However, I think that we can also read this passage as a reminder of the experiential dimension of historical understanding. Of course, not every 11-year-old will be able to travel to the Loire; and of those children who do, some will no doubt find 'boring' the experience of touring Chenonceau or Chambord – whereas this particular child was stimulated to compare her 'images' of the Loire chateaux with 'those of Hever and Hampton Court'.

I was also struck by the presence in Buxton's, Foster's and Magnoff's chapters (and in other chapters) of what I came to think of as a 'narrative of struggle'. What sort of struggle? To a large extent, it seems to be a struggle to get up to certain 'achievement' levels, such as the one proclaimed in 1990 as a goal by the Teaching History Research Group. The recommendation was that teachers should strive to equip pupils with 'the ability to "produce and explain effectively a hierarchy of causes and consequences"' (Buxton's chapter, quoting Scott, 1990, p. 12). I must first of all point out that I am a huge fan of the idea of introducing history pupils to counterfactual reasoning. For the most part, the students whom I encounter at my university, most of whom obtained their secondary educations at state schools (mostly schools of relatively high quality by US standards) do not have a clue that the making of causal claims *requires* counterfactual reasoning (but can they be blamed, if even the author of *What Is History?* was unaware of this obvious fact?)

I favour introducing school pupils to counterfactual reasoning firstly because it is an embarrassing gap in their knowledge that they do not grasp the function of such reasoning. The appeal of counterfactual reasoning, once the simple idea of it is grasped, is almost intuitive. But the point of counterfactual reasoning, or of any other reasoning in history, cannot be to arrive at 'the ultimate cause, the cause of all causes' (Carr, 1961, p. 84). To do *that* in a scientifically justified way we would need to possess knowledge of the Overall Shape of History. But it is surely far more prudent, and far more beneficial to students, to help them see how deeply and unavoidably speculative causal claims are – at least in history, where repeatable experiments are not possible. The lesson is not that we should not speculate: it is rather that we should by all means speculate where speculation is called for, but that we had better understand that whenever we try to provide explanations in history (in the sense of offering answers to the question, 'what caused it?') our speculations are doomed to *remain* speculative.

Collectively, we historians do 'know' that the assassination of the Archduke Franz Ferdinand, and the alliance system, and the mobilization plans, and the sense of insecurity felt by the German and Austrian political authorities, and economic rivalry and perhaps other things as well somehow 'led to' the outbreak of the war that we now know as World War I. But to declare that one knows 'the cause of all causes' is to reveal oneself to be either a political propagandist or an idiot (or perhaps both). Buxton speaks of 'using counterfactual thinking to explore the complexity of causation questions and to facilitate analytical thinking'. This strikes me as on the mark, the right lesson to draw – namely, that causal questions are complex.

For various reasons that I have never fully analysed (and probably won't), my orientation to the historical discipline tends to be rather cognitive: fundamentally, I look to extend my knowledge. It is no accident that I have written extensively on epistemological issues in history, or that I was assigned the task of commenting on three teacher chapters focused on argument, reasoning and interpretation. But I think that we also need to remember the other side of the 'Historical Experience – Historical Interpretation' axis. I have learned much from Frank Ankersmit on this score, as well as from such historians as Jules Michelet and especially Jacob Burckhardt, who highlight the aesthetic dimension of history. For this reason I rather liked the project that Daniel Magnoff writes about, which attempted to get pupils to draw conclusions from Beatles lyrics, although here, too, the pupils struggled.

Perhaps it is time for something of a rebalancing with regard to 'best practices' in secondary-school history standards. I am very much in favour of engaging pupils in analytical and interpretive exercises. These are a great contrast to the way that history was taught to me in secondary school in Canada many years ago, where the emphasis was rather 'positivistic', along the lines of 'here is the set of important facts that you need to know'.[5] It was far from being a bad mode of teaching, since eager pupils were given a set body of material to learn, which we could then attempt to reproduce and perhaps also to elaborate on in some slight ways. But this mode of teaching gave us no insight at all into how historians go about their work of attempting to understand the past (and to illuminate the present). Against the 'set agenda of facts' model, introducing pupils to counterfactual reasoning is an improvement. But . . . There is always a 'but', and here there are two: (a) introducing students to counterfactual reasoning is not an improvement if the pupils are told that there is a discoverable 'hierarchy' of causes; and (b) it is not an improvement if historical experience is left entirely aside.

In my view, we ought to allow more space for what is experiential. Given that 'historical experience' is a considerable cultural achievement, requiring (a) knowledge of the reality of a particular past, (b) the possibility of retrospection, (c) a sense of separation from, but also a connection with, the past in question and (d) the motivation to *reflect historically* on that reality, it is difficult to ask such a thing of school pupils. But we can try, and perhaps a certain cultivation of the experiential side of the experience – interpretation axis can help.

In particular, it seems to me that there is something that can offer a kind of preliminary possibility for historical experience, namely, the *artefact*. Admittedly, artefacts raise a danger for historical understanding, in that it is easy to approach them aesthetically, treating them as if they were works of art, rather than historically. (To be sure, it would be worse if historical artefacts were to be met by indifference.) The historical artefact does not exist as a *historical* artefact all by itself. Rather, the historicality of the artefact has to go *pari passu* with historical interpretation (in other words, to the *experiencing of the artefact* we need to add *the processes of historical interpretation*).

Beatles' lyrics, treated in the right way, can turn into a historical artefact. So can photographs, even when accessed only electronically. So can old books, digitized and downloadable as PDFs. For example, many instances of the famous Baedeker travel guidebooks, published in a growing number of editions and languages from the late 1830s onward, are available as PDFs, and could well serve as objects of analysis and interpretation concerning the development of travel in Europe in the nineteenth century. (The rise to ubiquity and fame of the series – to such a degree that 'Baedeker' became a synonym for 'travel guide' – coincided with the vast mid- and late-nineteenth-century expansion of European railway networks).

Such objects *become* historical. They do so not by virtue of having the capacity to provide definitive answers concerning causes and their hierarchies, but by virtue of the possibilities they offer for illuminating *past* experience (here, the life experiences of that part of the population that travelled by train in the nineteenth century). For pupils, such objects offer the possibility of *historical* experience, a sensation, however fleeting, of 'the actual' of a past time, with 'all the particulars of chance and change' that this implies.[6] Remember: it is an 'actuality' of a past time *from a present point of view*. But not just *any* point of view. If the experience is to amount to an encounter with *historical* experience, there needs to be a teacher, or a small team of teachers, engaging with the students, raising the right (interpretive) questions, and encouraging them to try to think of the meaning of artefacts for people in the past and, historically, for us now.

Exploring the Relationship between Substantive and Disciplinary Knowledge

Reflections on Chapters by Michael Fordham, Michael Harcourt and Daniel Magnoff

Kate Hammond

11

In reflecting upon the chapters by Fordham, Harcourt and Magnoff, I propose to consider the key ideas emerging from them, first, in terms of what pupils should learn and, second, how we can best assess that learning. Approaching these chapters as a secondary school history teacher, I want to reflect upon the ways in which they challenge and extend current classroom practice, and thus continue to reshape the field of history education.

The three chapters build significantly on existing debate about what pupils should learn in history classrooms. Fordham builds a strong case for devoting more attention to the development of pupils' knowledge of substantive concepts, arguing that substantive knowledge needs to be given greater prominence after a season in which disciplinary knowledge has taken centre stage. Harcourt's thinking about the range of devices currently proposed in the professional literature for helping pupils to consider historical significance leads him to propose a new set of criteria intended to equip pupils to tackle the significance of a place rather than an event. He reminds us that we may need to continue to probe our existing rationales for what students should learn, being ready to explore new territory in order to uncover possible deficits or distortions in our established plans. Magnoff argues that many pupils may need to be exposed more systematically and rigorously to the methodology of history, developing an understanding of how historians make the claims that they do, in order to prepare them better for the challenges of studying history at university level. At first glance, it might seem that each of these three teachers is clamouring for us to follow them down a particular path, each leading in different directions.

Yet, despite the differences in emphasis, there are important agreements on matters of principle about what pupils should be learning. I would like to comment on two areas of commonality.

First, the three chapters all explore the relationship between substantive historical knowledge and disciplinary knowledge. Although the existence of these two forms of knowledge has been widely accepted by history teachers for many years (Counsell, 2011a), their published work has often displayed a tendency to foreground one and background the other. Fordham's (2015a) analysis of the journal *Teaching History* reveals the top fifteen most cited history education articles in the last ten years; articles that clearly have had significant impact on the thinking of history teachers. Of these fifteen articles, nine have a second-order concept as their main focus, five have substantive knowledge as their main focus and only one has branched out to explore, directly, the relationship between the two. Work primarily concerned with the relationship between the two forms of knowledge does not seem yet to be as common as work that addresses either one form of knowledge or the other. It therefore strikes me that each of these chapters has something new to offer in our understanding of how substantive historical knowledge and disciplinary knowledge interact.

Of the three authors, it is Fordham who tackles this relationship most explicitly, questioning how a pupil's ability to grasp one form of knowledge might rest on their proficiency in the other. Emphasizing that this is an area that needs more theorizing, Fordham begins to ponder how a pupil's grasp of the disciplinary concept of change might affect their understanding of the substantive concept of 'revolution' and vice versa. Similarly, it would seem a reasonable hypothesis to suggest that a pupil who has an inclination to see 'diversity' in the past might be likely to have a corresponding disposition to discern nuance in a substantive concept such as 'peasant' or 'empire'. The interplay that Fordham sees between the two types of knowledge thus prompts him to suggest that pupils' understanding in one area of knowledge may well reveal much about their understanding in the other. Harcourt does not comment directly on this relationship between substantive and disciplinary knowledge, but it is evident from his pupils' use of his new PLACE criteria that disciplinary knowledge was having a profound effect on a particular type of substantive knowledge. When his pupils chose to assess the significance of a Wellington memorial using the '5Rs' criteria (Counsell, 2004c), their substantive knowledge of an *event* was developed; when they made use of the PLACE criteria, their substantive knowledge of an *environment* was developed. The deep entwining of disciplinary and substantive knowledge is evident once again. Magnoff's chapter shows how his pupils' understandings of the methods that historians employ in creating accounts of the past have had an impact on their assumptions about the substantive knowledge that it would be necessary to acquire. With a rudimentary, faulty understanding of methods, pupils selected Beatles songs for study from the beginning, middle and end of the 1960s; with more developed understanding of methods, they began to acknowledge that songs from 'defining moments' were the more helpful substantive material to pursue.

These chapters suggest that the relationship between substantive historical knowledge and disciplinary knowledge is tight and complex. I find this encouraging, for history education's published discourse is yet to consider this relationship with all the discernment that it requires. Fordham draws attention to the emphases of England's successive national curricula on disciplinary knowledge, and in my experience much of history teachers' long-term planning has focused on the development of disciplinary knowledge with the assumption that the substantive knowledge providing the context would look after itself. Yet here we are being challenged to think more carefully about effective combinations of substantive and disciplinary knowledge, and how history teachers might build both more powerfully if they are held in an optimal relationship. As history teachers, with our own historical knowledge that might be better characterized as 'broad' rather than 'deep' (Fordham, 2014b), we may need to identify how substantive and disciplinary knowledge come together most powerfully in particular historical topics. I would argue that in so doing we should deliberately draw on the scholarship and practice of professional historians who exemplify these relationships throughout their work. Indeed, it has long been the practice of several history educators to draw on academic history to inform their planning (Counsell, 2004c; Card, 2008; Laffin, 2009; Foster, 2013; Holliss, 2014) and these three chapters continue to encourage history teachers to do so.

A second area of commonality across the chapters, in terms of *what* pupils might learn, is an emphasis on history being understood as a construct. Harcourt's chapter shows this most clearly: his pupils are explicitly asked to tackle the notion of places being invested with significance, thus drawing their attention directly to the idea of history being constructed by those who choose to remember it. Those pupils who chose to use his PLACE criteria to help them analyse the memorials seemed to be able to talk most meaningfully about history being 'contested'. Magnoff took a slightly more indirect approach to making pupils aware of the idea of history as a construction. While the pupils' initial statements on how historians answer questions revealed that many seemed to see 'the past' as something to be discovered rather than constructed, this idea was consistently challenged by the process of debate in which they then engaged. Fordham began to question whether his pupils were beginning to see substantive concepts as constructs, and although he was unable to reach a conclusion on this point, he too suggests that pupils' awareness of the constructed nature of history is something that should be developed.

The majority of history teachers appear to agree that pupils should understand that history, as opposed to the past, will always be made up of constructed accounts (Husbands, Kitson and Pendry, 2003; Burn and Harris, 2014). Alongside the published discourse, my own experience of working alongside established and beginning history teachers across the UK for over fifteen years has affirmed a shared commitment to helping pupils understand history in this way. The emphasis in these three chapters on understanding historical accounts as constructions has, however, made me question whether history teachers' published discourse has paid enough attention to the ways in which we could build this understanding more systematically. Is it enough for history teachers to talk explicitly about the constructed nature of history when we are working on enquiries that lend themselves to developing such a view (such as Harcourt's historical significance sequence) or should we take greater pains to emphasize it in sequences that might, currently, seem to promote the view that our accounts are 'copies' of the past? The articles also prompt questions about the most successful ways of making this learning explicit. It would be easy for history teachers to confuse rather than enlighten here. Lee and Ashby (2000) have demonstrated that progression in pupils' understanding of history is complex, and have suggested that pupils need to have misunderstandings unpicked before they can move on to new ways of thinking. If history teachers, for example, were to start teaching a narrative as a contested version of events before pupils had sufficient knowledge of the period to anchor the narrative, would pupils end up uncertain whether there is anything that can be 'known' about the past? Conversely, if we take pains to develop a secure narrative and only then reveal it as a construction will pupils cease to trust us? With challenges like these to navigate, history teachers must share more of their attempts to teach the constructed nature of history and engage in further dialogue as to how pupils can be helped to succeed in this area.

Having considered how the three chapters might challenge history teachers about what pupils should be learning in our classrooms, I now turn to consider their insights into how we might improve our ability to judge progression in pupils' learning and assess their knowledge and understanding effectively.

The three chapters place an emphasis on *what* we should be assessing rather than *how* we should be assessing it. Fordham suggests that we should pay closer attention to the way in which pupils' understandings of substantive concepts change as they engage with new procedural knowledge, arguing that for too long we have neglected to assess substantive historical knowledge rigorously. In my experience, history teachers have understood instinctively the need to find some way of using pupils' substantive knowledge in order to judge the progress that they are making, but have struggled to determine what this might look like in practice. For example, one type of progression might be simply knowing more about the past, which might be assessed through a straightforward factual test or construction of a timeline (Carr and Counsell, 2014). Another type of progression might be the ability to use knowledge of one topic to shape knowledge of another (Hammond, 2014). Here, Fordham offers us a potentially powerful way of beginning to gauge pupils' progress by using their developing understanding of substantive concepts. If one pupil unproblematically equates Anglo-Saxon peasants with nineteenth-century Russian peasants, and another shows awareness that these groups of peasants are not quite the same thing while recognizing some commonality, we have some sort of progress. As Fordham notes, the history education community has much to do in terms of determining what sorts of progress are demonstrated as pupils use substantive concepts with increased sophistication, but this proposition offers an important first step in bringing substantive knowledge meaningfully back into the realms of assessment. It is a proposal worthy of more systematic consideration by history teachers.

Magnoff's research places more emphasis on the disciplinary knowledge that pupils should master, but I think that he, like Fordham, is calling for greater balance than there has been in recent years. Despite the deliberate attempt of the authors of the 1995 National Curriculum (NC) to end the separation of substantive and disciplinary knowledge emphasized in the 1991 NC (DES, 1990b), typical whole school assessment policies tended to push teachers into prising them apart (Burnham and Brown, 2004; Counsell, 2011a; Fordham, 2013). The tendency of GCSE examiners to atomize forms of historical knowledge in their assessment objectives has had a similar effect, as teachers have noted (e.g. Laffin, 1998). Here, Magnoff's work can be seen to be putting the pieces back together again and allowing pupils to study the past more holistically. By introducing his pupils explicitly to the methods of historians, he allows them to see how the various kinds of disciplinary knowledge that they would have tended to explore separately under the demands of the GCSE now come back together. This opens up for consideration some new ideas for assessment: should pupils be expected to show understanding of the historian's work in their A level studies? Is it more appropriate for them to show an *awareness* of this process in the work of published historians, or should they be able to *demonstrate* these behaviours in their own work to some degree? Should we expect to see pupils demonstrating these types of understanding at GCSE level or lower, and with what levels of complexity? Magnoff's work challenges history teachers to consider this area of learning more critically.

Although Harcourt's chapter might appear to be suggesting a new way of assessing pupils' learning through sound walks, I find myself struck by his question of 'whether actively engaging with the material landscape specifically to create a sound walk prompts questions that other forms of assessment . . . do not' (this volume, p. 131). Rather than simply offering history teachers a new form in which pupils' work might be submitted, he is suggesting that sound walks might open up a new area of understanding in our pupils that we have not yet considered in any meaningful way. His challenge is one we need to hear: What other areas of historical understanding have we yet to probe in order that pupils might gain a deeper and more satisfying picture of the past?

On reading these chapters, one final thought about the assessment of historical learning occurred to me. Each of these history teachers has made use of a form of thematic coding in their research in order to explore what pupils are thinking and doing as they engage with historical study. As they have done so, their observations reveal the kinds of features that differentiate the best responses from poorer ones. We might suggest that each teacher is engaged in the process of developing an informal mark scheme, although none mention that one was created explicitly. It seems to me that mark schemes developed through the careful reading and re-reading of pupils' work to ascertain *exactly* what they are doing that is worthy of credit should merit more of our time as history teachers. For some years now, the team of history mentors to which I belong, working in partnership with our university colleagues, has required our PGCE trainee teachers, employing this kind of process, to develop their own mark schemes for individual pieces of work. From my perspective, they are one of the most demanding, yet satisfying and successful, training activities we set. Wrestling with the intricate details of what exactly pupils are doing well has led to mark schemes that allow trainees to reflect far more meaningfully on their own teaching and, importantly, has resulted in feedback to pupils that has been of a high quality. Pupils are given a sharper understanding of what it means to think and write about history with greater sophistication. Surely we are at a point in time, particularly with the removal of level descriptions within the National Curriculum, when we should see history teachers developing mark schemes that are generated from deep engagement with individual pieces of pupil work rather than falling back on generic schemes. Our authors here have begun to show us how; many trainees are entering the profession equipped to do so. We all need to rise to this challenge.

Teaching for Historical Understanding: Thematic Continuities with the Work of Lawrence Stenhouse

Reflections on Chapters by Rachel Foster, Robert Somers and Paula Worth

John Elliott

12

Chapter outline

The role of the history teacher as a researcher

The chapters by Foster, Somers and Worth illustrate important aspects of Lawrence Stenhouse's (1975) idea of 'the teacher as a researcher'. Stenhouse argued that 'educational ideas expressed in books are not easily taken into possession by teachers, whereas the expression of ideas as curricular specifications exposes them to testing by teachers and hence establishes an equality of discourse between the proposer and those who assess his proposal' (p. 142). Stenhouse envisaged an educational science in which each classroom functioned as a laboratory and each teacher as a member of a scientific community. All three authors are practising history teachers concerned with the critical testing of curriculum entities.

Foster sat down with some trepidation to mark a set of history essays addressing the question, 'How far did African Americans remain second-class citizens by 1945?' Over the course of the lesson sequence she had become increasingly uncertain about the properties of an historical argument about change. Compared with causation, Foster claims, 'there is relatively little theorizing among history teachers about . . . what it means to think historically about change, what a satisfactory answer to a question concerning change looks like' (Foster, this volume, p. 6).

These questions, which the research reported in her chapter sets out to address, are pedagogically driven by the practical problems Foster experiences in teaching a particular type of historical analysis. Her theorizing about how to construct and nurture an argument about change began at the pedagogical design stage, drawing on an emerging discourse within the history education community, the insights of professional historians and the experimental use of powerful metaphors. This pedagogical design formed the 'theoretical' setting for Foster's research based on the question: *What properties in students' thinking about change and continuity were manifested in their written work?*

Her theorizing, embodied in a particular pedagogical design, was tested in action by providing a context for examining data about the quality of students' thinking. Foster's research exemplified Stenhouse's idea of the 'teacher as researcher' who theorizes about curriculum aims in the context of their practice and, in the process, transforms it.

Foster also exemplifies Stenhouse's view that in order to research their practice teachers need to communicate and report their work to one another. Teachers, Stenhouse argues, need to develop 'a common vocabulary of concepts and a syntax of theory' that is 'rich enough to throw up new and profitable questions' (1975, p. 157). In this respect, he suggests, professional research workers should be able to help. Foster's classroom practice is not an island cut off from academic discourse and teachers' professional discourse about developing students' understanding of the concept of historical change. It actively engages with both, although with respect to the latter she found that the concept of historical change was undertheorized when compared with the concept of 'causality'. She appears, however, to have found what she was searching for in the practices of academic historians, namely, 'an analytical language and discourse around which I could build a pedagogical strategy'.

Foster locates her research methodology as a form of small-scale case study, and appears reluctant to claim that her findings are generalizable to practice in other classrooms. She writes:

> Rather than allowing me to generalize about wider teaching practice or student learning, the case could only point to possibilities or raise questions for future curricular and pedagogic theorising. (Foster, this volume, p. 15)

I would suggest that some of Foster's methodological sources have led her to underestimate the power of case studies to generalize across particular classroom settings. As Stenhouse (1975, p. 157) argues, case studies of teachers' research in their classrooms can accumulate in forms that enable them to be scrutinized for general trends that can be expressed as propositional theories. As such, teachers' case studies of their classrooms can be accumulated to provide a source of dynamic, ever-deepening and universal insights capable of forming a basis for a pedagogical science. Indeed, the case studies of Foster and Worth bear witness to this process with respect to the level of engagement that they exemplify with other history teachers' research. The distinctive characteristics of Stenhouse's idea of 'the teacher as researcher' are no better illustrated than in the field of history teaching.

The problematical nature of historical concepts in structuring history as a thinking system

Foster's research is concerned with how to develop her pupils' 'understanding of the concept of historical change' in a context where there has been a lack of theorizing amongst history educators about what it means to think historically about change. Her research can be depicted as a process in which she tests her theorizing, in action, about what it means for her pupils to think about change, and in the process develops her theory of understanding further. It is a process in which theory and practice are joint objects of reflection and are developed interactively. Such is the process of action research.

Somers' study focuses on another problematical concept, that of diversity, which is used by history teachers to structure pupils' historical thinking in the context of England's history national curriculum tradition. Somers shows how the 2008 National Curriculum embodied shifting meanings of diversity, linking it to cultural, ethnic and religious differences, explaining that it exists within as well as across social groups and placing it within a humanistic framework of 'equality of value and esteem'. He points out that the 2014 National Curriculum has now reverted back to its original 1991 position of using the term 'similarity and difference', a position which many history teachers (e.g. Bradshaw, 2009) had, in fact, sustained ever since 1991, seeing 'similarity and difference' as structural properties of historical questions about 'diversity' and ways of teaching pupils to structure their resulting arguments.

In searching for the source of the instability and contestability surrounding the concept of diversity, Somers became interested in the work of poststructuralist thinkers. Such work, he claims, had often focused on deconstructing the rhetoric of diversity and multiculturalism in the Western world by reference to the power relations in society and their dominant legitimating ideologies, which shape the meaning and use of these terms. His review of poststructuralist thought helped him to explain the contestability of the concept of 'diversity' as an object of learning for history education. The outcome led him to conclude that the 'difference' of the other is defined by the mind-set of the powerful majority. How then, he asks, can history teachers access, and help their pupils to access, diverse 'ways of thinking and living' when everything they touch is tainted with an ideological mind-set that transforms *the other* into *me* or the method to *the same?* Somers regards these as the theoretical questions about the intellectual integrity of the concept of diversity that history teachers need to address in teaching it. He argues from his survey of the professional literature, however, that they appear to be unwilling to address these questions. They prefer to confine their reflection and research to practical questions about the delivery of diversity rather than to the theoretical questions about its meaning as an object of learning. Foster draws a similar conclusion from her survey of the professional literature on teaching about historical change.

Somers' own research was designed to address such questions by generating data – in the form of pupil interviews and written work – from a sequence of lessons in which pupils were confronted with *cultural difference* through lessons that focused on 'three discrete periods of Indian and Anglo-Indian history'. The data was gathered to address three research questions:

1. What do students notice in the stories of the past?
2. How do students describe the other?
3. Which binary oppositions are in play when students describe the other? (Somers, this volume, p. 143)

Answers to these questions formed the basis for a deconstruction analysis of the mind-set of the students and its determinants.

Somers concludes that 'the rhetoric on diversity . . . pronounced by students' finds much in common with the arguments raised in his literature review (this volume, p. 148). Hence, he argues, the claim that the rhetoric on diversity as a strategy for the expansion of capitalism, individual choice and markets is reflected in the students' responses to the third research question, while the view that this rhetoric constitutes a discourse about 'the other' viewed from the perspective of the majority is reflected in responses to Research Question 2.

Somers expresses some disappointment with his findings, given, he suggests, that his pedagogical design was aimed at breaking the rhetoric depicted in the literature and delivering a quite different, more authentic, experience of 'the other.' No matter how hard he tried, he could not help himself uttering the same rhetoric of diversity. Unfortunately we are presented with very little detail about his attempts to change his interactions with students and thereby break up the dominant rhetoric in the classroom. I find it interesting that he expected to fashion an emancipatory pedagogy in such a short timescale, one that would enable his students to render the rhetoric of diversity, which powerfully shapes their understanding of 'the other', problematical and to develop a deeper discernment of the integrity of the concept as an object of historical understanding. Such is the ongoing task of teachers' research in which curriculum theories are continuously tested and refined by teachers in classrooms depicted as laboratories. For Stenhouse (1975, pp. 157–158) such research is a painstaking process in which teachers develop a 'sensitive and self-critical subjective perspective and not with an aspiration towards an unattainable objectivity' that is totally free from bias and prejudice. The development of such a perspective on their teaching is difficult enough, Stenhouse contends, and involves the continuous testing of 'illusion, assumption and habit'.

Historical sources as complex objects of learning and the nature of understanding as a pedagogical aim

Foster, Somers and Worth evidence a shared concern with 'the development of historical understanding' as a pedagogical goal. Worth focuses on the process of evidential thinking involved, while Foster and Somers are concerned with the use of historical concepts to structure such a process, namely, those of change and diversity. Stenhouse argues that it is a mistake to see the concepts that structure thinking within a discipline 'as objectives to be learned by the student' (1975, p. 85). This is because they are problematical within the subject, providing a focus for speculative thinking, rather than an object of mastery. As such, the development of historical understanding will involve the attempt to understand both an historical event, person, or situation and the concept being used to explicate it.

Stenhouse's idea of 'the teacher as researcher' is grounded in a *process* rather than a *product or objectives model* of such development and this conception of the end of teaching is particularly reflected in the studies of Foster and Worth. Both are concerned with clarifying aspects of 'historical knowledge' in terms of what Stenhouse depicts as a *thinking system,* a structure to *sustain creative thought* rather than inert bodies of *information.* Their search for clarification 'of the aim of teaching history', in terms other than *objectives or targets* specified by a national curriculum, is integral to their adoption of a research stance towards their teaching. Stenhouse, in his critique of the *objectives model* of curriculum design, claimed that the use of the latter was a form of teacher proofing, inasmuch as the curriculum is 'to tend in the same direction whatever the knowledge and talents of the individual teacher and indeed of the individual student' (1975, p. 83). A *process model* of curriculum development is his response to the question, 'can curriculum and pedagogy be organised satisfactorily by a logic other than that of the means-end model?' (p. 84). He viewed a process model as a source of criteria by which teachers can critique and improve the quality of teaching and learning in their classrooms without 'reference to an end-means model which sets an arbitrary horizon to one's efforts' (p. 83). Unlike the latter, the process model places teachers in the role of researchers.

Worth's chapter amply illustrates the use of these different models in the teaching of history. Recalling an argument as a young, newly qualified teacher with her head of history, Worth sets the scene for systematic reflection about the process of inferential reasoning within the discipline of history. Like Foster she engaged with the work of academic historians in her search for criteria to judge the quality of her pupils' historical reasoning and her interventions to deepen and extend the process. Worth's literature review highlighted issues that are pedagogically relevant, namely,

1. Would consulting historical sources carefully within their context allow an historian to write an objective and value-free history? Or is an historian's choice of sources inevitably shaped by his own social-cultural context?
2. Is there a canon of 'correct' messages to be found in a source, such that the 'validity' of inferences can be judged to inhere in the product rather than in the process of reasoning?
3. How should historians 'bracket' their own sociocultural context of judgement? Should they struggle to detach themselves from any personal agendas or simply make them explicit and open to scrutiny in the process of inquiry?
4. How should meaning be assigned to a word found in a source? Are words simply 'unbiased containers of facts', which then may need to be explained by setting them in a particular sociocultural context? If so then 'comprehension' of the facts and 'evaluation' of their historical significance are different activities. However, if words are sociocultural constructs then historical sources need to be situated in their intellectual context 'in order to make sense of what their authors were doing in writing them'. In which case 'describing the text' and 'explaining its context' cannot be separated.
5. How should a student, such as Daniel, use language to capture inferences made from sources? 'What if his use of language also comes with its own contextual baggage'? Could a hermeneutic method, Worth speculates, 'involving interplay between subject and object', offer a middle ground between a quest for objectivity and subjective interpretation?

In reflecting on these issues, Worth began to construct criteria for designing and assessing an educationally worthwhile process of evidential reasoning that avoided the extremes of 'objectivism' and 'relativism'.

Interestingly, Worth pinpoints the emergence of a professional discourse about evidential reasoning amongst history educators in the years following the establishment of the Schools Council History Project (SCHP) in 1972 under the leadership of David Sylvester. This project followed five years after Stenhouse had begun to develop his ideas about 'the process model' of curriculum design and the 'teacher as researcher' within the context of the Schools Council Humanities Curriculum Project (SCHCP). As a member of the SCHCP, I was a witness to the interaction between the two projects. Stenhouse took a great interest in SCHP. He saw possible links between its curriculum aim, of developing evidential thinking in secondary school students between the ages of 14 and 16 years, and the SCHCP's aim with a similar age-range. The latter was aimed at 'developing an understanding of human acts, social situations and the controversial issues they raise' through a critical discussion of 'evidence' selected from the humanities disciplines. Stenhouse viewed 'evidence' in terms of its historical and legal as opposed to its scientific connotations:

> Evidence . . . often presents issues in concrete and living terms. Like life itself, it is usually ambiguous. The insight into a situation offered by evidence can be grasped only by the exercise of judgement in its interpretations. (Stenhouse et al., 1983 p. 18)

Both projects appeared to focus on the process of learning through inquiry. Sylvester also became interested in the work of Stenhouse and made a request to the Schools Council that the SCHP be based during its dissemination phase in Stenhouse's Centre for Applied Research in Education at the University of East Anglia. The request was turned down.

Worth shows that the proponents of the SCHP – what became from 1984 onwards the School History Project (SHP) – remained committed objectivists and rationalists through the 1980s. Students' evidential thinking was to be shaped by certain pre-specifiable learning outcomes; getting them to ask the 'right questions' to determine their reliability. In these terms, the SHP was incorporated into the 1991 National Curriculum and the GCSE examination for history. For almost twenty years, these features of the SHP became the orthodox approach to teaching history in schools.

Worth argues that two consequences of the SHP 'evidence-based' approach were students being led into the beliefs that biased sources were distorted and unreliable accounts and that the authors' biases were inappropriate objects of study for historians. She claims that the approach also resulted in the atomization of 'sources' as objects of evidential thinking 'through endless exercises on "reliability" and decontextualized "source work"', as opposed to synthesizing them in the form of a developed argument in response to a question. Worth's review of the professional literature pinpoints a reworking in the 1990s of the original SHP approach in the light of these problems of atomization and students' negative attitudes towards bias. Teachers began to experiment with 'a myriad of approaches to teaching evidential thinking' (this volume, p. 84) as they searched for solutions to such problems. In this respect, Worth interestingly maps out the emergence of teachers' research in the field of history teaching in England and Wales. She notes, for example, that 'various history teachers have explored ways of teaching pupils to communicate degrees of certainty and uncertainty in increasingly nuanced claims about what might be inferred from sources' (Worth, this volume, p. 82).

Worth pinpoints how the emergence of teachers' investigations into the development of students' evidential thinking marked a shift of focus among history teachers away from the implementation of an objectives model of evidential thinking to the development of more process-oriented approaches in their classrooms. One can only speculate about whether closer links between the dissemination strategies of the SCHP and teacher research carried out in the wake of the dissemination of the SCHCP would have accelerated the emergence of teacher research and the realization of a process model of evidential thinking in the field of history teaching.

In reviewing Stenhouse's conception of 'teaching for understanding' in the context of the SCHCP, I pointed out a similarity of perspective with Gadamer's theory of interpretation (hermeneutics) inasmuch as both viewed the exercise of judgement in relation to evidence as an integral component of the 'development of understanding' (Elliott, 2007, p. 26). For Stenhouse, it was only by evoking students' judgements in the form of their biases and prejudices, what Gadamer termed 'fore-understandings', in the process of discussing 'evidence', that students were enabled to 'develop their understanding' of an issue in the light of alternative interpretations which highlight aspects that they had ignored. From the perspective of the HCP, 'understanding' is developed in the process of reconstructing bias through discussing evidence rather than eliminating it. The assumption underpinning a feature of traditional teaching in the human field, namely that information needs to be understood before it is discussed and its significance as evidence judged, was challenged by the HCP. It cast 'the development of understanding' as a hermeneutical process in a form that was consistent with Gadamer's (1975) 'interpretive hermeneutics'.

Some 30 years after the publication of Stenhouse's major work (1975), we find Worth developing and testing a hermeneutic theory of understanding in the field of history teaching that resonates with that of Stenhouse in the human field more generally. Worth's review of the professional literature led her to identify an area of professional discourse she felt needed to be developed; namely, 'how pupil context affects interpretation' (this volume, p. 85). She felt that there was a need to find a different approach to engaging pupils with historical sources, one that would promote discussion of this issue amongst history educators. The argument with her head of history about Daniel's GCSE answer had clearly motivated at a personal level her review of the professional discourse. The review prompted her to ask questions about the process of Daniel's thinking about sources in generating his answer.

Worth decided to design a highly innovative teaching intervention in the UK context, based on the assumption 'that comprehending the source and comprehending the context both involve interpretation and both affect each other'. Pedagogically she aimed to establish a double connection in pupils' thinking 'of the context of the author with the word, and the word with the context of the historian' (the pupil). This interplay of subject (pupil) and object (text and author), Worth claims, will render historical sources complex objects of learning, inasmuch as they reveal the multilayered and multidimensional aspects of meaning and thereby problematize the comprehension of sources. Using this kind of hermeneutic learning process, she designed a sequence of learning tasks on contemporary texts about Churchill.

Worth's research consisted of gathering data about pupils' thinking by reading their essays, interviewing individual pupils, setting up focus groups and keeping a research diary to record pupils' efforts to develop their understanding of historical texts through classroom discussion. The latter in particular, Worth claims, 'enabled me to use and to reflect on my own subjectivity as a teacher in determining elements that pupils struggled with'. Concerned to ensure that the process of this research was consistent with her pedagogical aim as a teacher, she was able to use her subjective experience as a teacher as a positive condition of her research. She argues,

> As a teacher researching my own pupils' learning, a purely objectivist standpoint was not suitable. If objects (for example, pupils' beliefs) were treated separately, I could not use my subjective knowledge of the context to draw insights about what those beliefs might signify. Yet a wholly subjectivist approach was not appropriate either. I wanted to find something from the data's 'essence' that would challenge traditional, professional conceptualizations of progression in evidential thinking. (this volume, p. 89)

Worth acknowledges two layers of hermeneutic interpretation taking place in her classroom; her pupils making sense of historical texts through a context-specific 'cultural lens' and she researching their achievement through a context-specific 'cultural lens' as well. This 'double hermeneutic' is implicit in Stenhouse's view of teacher research as a form of action research. The latter is research conducted in the context of action aimed at 'teaching for understanding'. Worth, however, misleadingly claims that she was not engaged in a process of action research, which she defines as using pupils' feedback data to change teaching interventions. Rather, she argues, she was gathering data about how pupils responded to her interventions as a basis for 'theorizing the character of my pupils' thinking . . . and generating possible new curricular goals' (Worth, this volume, p. 90). In doing so, however, she acknowledges that traditional beliefs and assumptions, which shape teaching and learning in classrooms, are challenged and new curriculum goals are generated. New forms of action to realize these goals therefore have to be proposed and tested, and through that process such goals will be further clarified. Sustainable theorizing about aims takes place alongside and in parallel with designing and testing action strategies to realize them in practice. The joint development of theory and practice was a significant feature of teachers' action research in the context of Stenhouse's HCP. Worth appears to view them as separate processes which might possibly explain why her study says very little about how she might refine her pedagogical design of the lesson sequence. This is not, however, consistent with the rationale she gave for keeping a research diary.

According to Worth, her findings show that 'comprehension' of sources should be 'treated as far more problematical and demanding' than is suggested by the mark scheme that prompted her research. However, she also reports how the study unexpectedly challenged her assessment of the quality of Daniel's answer to the GCSE question. He did, she contends, 'show a low level of thinking' but not because his inference was wrong but because he failed to justify it (Worth, this volume, p. 102). Although he referred to contextual knowledge, Worth argues, he kept it separate and failed to link it back to the meaning he had inferred. Worth's study does indeed help her to redefine the criteria she employs for assessing the quality of pupils' evidential thinking in terms of process without reference to pre-specified learning outcomes. I would argue that Worth is indeed involved in a process of jointly developing a curricular theory about the 'what' of the curriculum and a pedagogy that specifies how students are to be engaged with it. Her denial that she is engaged in action research is, I would contend, indicative of the extent to which current accounts of action research in classrooms are shaped by purely instrumental conceptions of practical rationality.

The development of pupils' historical understanding renders the outcomes of learning unpredictable

Foster and Worth draw on a process model of the development of historical understanding rather than the objectives model that has underpinned the National Curriculum and assessment system in England and Wales. This, as I have argued, is consistent with Stenhouse's view of 'knowledge' as a thinking system. He claimed (1975, p. 82) that when *education* is conceived as an induction into such systems of thought 'it makes the behavioural outcomes of the students unpredictable'. This is clearly demonstrated in the case studies of Foster and Worth. Both studies highlight the importance of the essay for the assessment of historical understanding conceived in terms of a *process* as opposed to an *objectives model* of curriculum design. This is highly consistent with Stenhouse's rationale for the role of the essay in assessing the quality of pupils' understanding conceived in process terms (see Stenhouse, 1975, p. 82). He defines an essay in broader terms than a written text as an endeavour in which a pupil tests his/her powers. It may include a written text but can also take other forms, such as a painting, an oral performance, or playing a piece of music. Endeavours, he argues, are not attempts to meet a pre-specified outcome or product but an expression of individuality and creativity. As such, they take account of the indeterminacy of knowledge that stems from the constitution of knowledge structures as resources for thinking rather than as systems for classifying and retrieving information. Stenhouse claims that essays call for an evaluative response, not in the form of an objective test or standardized marking scheme but in the form of a critique informed by the teachers' understanding of the nature of his/her subject. An essay is not right or wrong, he argues, but to be judged qualitatively in the light of criteria appropriate in its field. Evaluation is not an objective process like 'marking' but a form of constructive criticism (critique) aimed at helping pupils to improve their work. Within the terms of this *critical model* of assessment, Stenhouse contends, 'The quality of the teacher is inseparable from the quality of his/her judgement of students' work' (p. 83). He recognizes that this sets problems in public examining, but argues that there is no escape from them into standardized marking systems that distort the nature of knowledge and understanding.

Some concluding remarks

What is remarkable about these three pieces of research is the thematic continuities they exemplify with the work of Lawrence Stenhouse some four decades ago. I have tried to depict these in this commentary. However, there is one major discontinuity that puzzles me, namely, the lack of analysis of the role of discussion in the development of historical understanding in classroom settings and the pedagogical problems of sustaining it in practice as the core learning activity. The chapters clearly suggest that their authors set out to engage their pupils in discussing historical texts and sources, but treat this as rather unproblematical for them as teachers. There is little suggestion that as history teachers they have difficulty handling worthwhile discussions of historical sources with their students, and what these consist of. For Stenhouse 'the development of understanding' implies the realization of certain pedagogical principles governing the teachers' role in handling discussion. These appear to have been a neglected dimension in these research designs, and I would simply ask, why?

School Subjects as Powerful Knowledge: Lessons from History

Reflections on the Chapters by Rachel Foster, Ellen Buxton and Michael Fordham

Michael Young

13

Introduction

The three chapters by Foster, Buxton and Fordham are impressive examples of the long tradition of school-based teacher research by history teachers in England. In many ways, at least for the case of history, they are ahead of anything that curriculum theorists are suggesting. They raise issues that have curriculum implications well beyond history as a school subject and make a significant contribution to the educational case that with well-qualified teachers, school subjects are not, as is traditionally supposed, elitist, but can be the basis for a curriculum for all pupils.

In this chapter, I begin by reflecting on my own re-assessment of the role of school subjects and how the concept of subjects that I defend in this chapter differs sharply from the traditionalist view associated with recent government reforms in England. I illustrate this difference with a discussion of Johan Muller and my 'Three Futures' analysis of the curriculum (Young and Muller, 2010) and the importance they place on the curriculum role of subjects as a source of 'powerful knowledge'. In the final section, I turn briefly to the three chapters by Buxton, Fordham and Foster and suggest how they not only offer a model of what I refer to as a 'Future 3' curriculum in history but have important lessons for any subject specialists seeking a basis for a curriculum for *all* students.

Subjects as specialized knowledge

Since the publication of my book *Bringing Knowledge Back In* (Young, 2007), I have been trying to work out the implications of a view of education that places the knowledge that schools can offer all pupils at the centre of any discussion of the purpose of schools. This has led me to a re-assessment of the role of school subjects (Young, 2010) as the basis of the school curriculum. Despite five years as a science teacher, teaching largely chemistry, as a sociologist I began as a subject-sceptic who over-naively saw subjects and the boundaries separating them as backward-looking and elitist, and any attempt to make them a requirement for all pupils as an imposition (Young, 1971) – in the words of the French sociologist Pierre Bourdieu, 'an arbitrary culture imposed by arbitrary powers' (Bourdieu and Passeron, 1977, p. 18). However, I gradually came to realize that although the critique of subjects has some truth in it, and although they may be experienced by some pupils as an imposition, neither subjects nor the boundaries between them are arbitrary. They are a form of specialization of knowledge with powerful educational possibilities. What I want to do in this chapter, therefore, is to outline how I came to change my understanding about subjects and why this might have implications for today's debates about their role in the curriculum. There are two important reasons for doing this. The first relates to the acrimonious debate about subjects between England's former Conservative-led Coalition and present Conservative governments and significant sections of the professional education community (Garner, 2013). Whereas government saw the diminishing role of subjects as something in need of radical reform, their educational critics, mostly on the Left and so opposed to the government on political grounds as well, opposed any signs of a 'return to subjects' as backward-looking and discriminatory towards pupils from disadvantaged backgrounds. This put me as a firm defender of a 'subject-based curriculum for all' in an uncomfortable position. I had always voted Labour and had many friends in the education community who endorsed the prevailing educational viewpoint. For the first time in my career in education, I had to accept that political beliefs and educational views were not necessarily consistent. My second reason for beginning this chapter with the change in my views about subjects is that I see important common ground between how I have come to think about subjects in general as a way of organizing the curriculum and the case studies of history teaching in this book. I think that they not only illustrate the possibilities of history as what I call 'powerful knowledge' but also suggest issues that other specialists need to explore if the idea of a 'curriculum for all' is to be more than a promise.

I began my approach to the question of knowledge in education by taking a social constructivist approach which aimed to put the curriculum in the hands (and minds) of teachers (for a biographical and longer, more scholarly account of this development, see Young, 2008a and 2008b). The one case that I was involved in where this idea was put into practice – in South Africa after the end of apartheid – demonstrated the problems with the idea of the curriculum being socially constructed by teachers. Education is not like democracy; it relies on specialized knowledge, which the poorly educated South African teachers lacked.

A three futures approach to the curriculum

Some years later, I wrote the joint paper with Johan Muller (Young and Muller, 2010) referred to earlier. It went back to the question of knowledge as the key issue for the curriculum and set it in a broad historical context. We drew largely on English sources and distinguished two periods, each with distinct assumptions about knowledge, what they implied about the curriculum then and now, and what this analysis suggested about possible futures. We called these periods Future 1 and Future 2. We traced Future 1 back to the beginning of mass education in the nineteenth century when knowledge in education was equated with a largely fixed tradition with which the elite of each generation was expected to comply, and the rest hardly mattered. It was out of this concept of tradition that school subjects emerged at the turn of the last century, so it is not completely surprising that radicals reject subjects as perpetuating an elitist past.

We characterized Future 1 as a period when knowledge was treated as largely given, and pedagogy, for most students, was based on compliance. Future 2, in contrast, described the education system's progressive response to the rigidities of Future 1 under democratic pressures for increased access and economic pressures for greater attention to what are now known as STEM subjects. What Future 2 tended to neglect, in weakening boundaries between subjects with programmes of integrated science and humanities, was that all learning, and STEM subjects in particular, depends on tradition; knowledge builds on knowledge, not just experience.

It was the later phase of Future 2, after World War II, on which our analysis focused. With no theory of knowledge to challenge the oversimplifications of social constructivism and a diminishing respect for the role of tradition in education, the only alternative to Future 1 was what might be described as an incremental and pragmatic relativism. This allowed the rigidities of the old curriculum to give way to market pressures and pupil choice and encouraged a weakening of subject boundaries for pupils who appeared unresponsive to Future 1. It was this weakening of the knowledge base of the curriculum for all but those in selective schools that led us to describe the emergence of Future 2 as a move from a curriculum based on an *a*-social assumption about knowledge that treated it as if it was beyond human agency to a curriculum based on an *over*-socialized view that saw knowledge as always open to external pressures and interests. Whereas Future 1 took not only knowledge but the social world underpinning it as given, the constructivism associated with Future 2 rejected any constraints imposed by the world and what we know about it, leaving knowledge and the curriculum increasingly determined by the market and those with power to change it.

The differentiation between Future 1 for high achievers and Future 2 for the rest became increasingly polarized from the 1970s onwards as the youth labour market contracted and an increasing proportion of each cohort stayed on at school. It was the expansion of curricula with a practical, pre-vocational or life skill emphasis of which the Coalition government were most critical and for which they blamed teachers and the education community. All they were left with, however, was a return to a modified version of a Future 1 that had been developed in another era. By the time the Conservative Coalition was elected in 2010, it had become clear, at least to some of us, that a different way of thinking about the curriculum was needed that took access to knowledge seriously for all pupils. Somehow the emphasis on the stability and reliability of knowledge that characterized Future 1 but without its rigidity needed to be brought together with an awareness of its social base that was an exaggerated feature of Future 2.

What is Future 3?

In this section I draw on the book that I wrote with David Lambert (Young and Lambert, 2014) to describe my idea of a Future 3 curriculum. It points to a possible curriculum of the future, at the same time as being an element of the curricula of today's schools, albeit to different extents. Some schools face pressures to lean towards Future 1 (by overemphasizing examination results) and some lean towards Future 2 (particularly schools that struggle with a high proportion of disaffected and often disadvantaged pupils and serious shortages of subject specialist staff).

Future 3 differs in its concept of knowledge from Future 1 and Future 2 in a number of ways. In contrast to Future 1, it explicitly locates knowledge in the specialist community of researchers in their field; as a consequence, it does not treat knowledge as 'given' or 'to be complied with' but as fallible and always open to challenge through the debates and research of particular specialist communities. Unlike the openness of knowledge assumed by Future 2, Future 3's concept of knowledge is open but not arbitrarily so. It is not responsive to *any* kind of challenge because it is bounded by the epistemic rules of the various specialist communities. It follows that a Future 3 curriculum rejects *the a-social givenness* of school subjects associated with Future 1 and the scepticism about subjects and their boundaries associated with Future 2. Instead it treats academic *subjects* as the most reliable tools we have for enabling students to acquire what I refer to as 'powerful knowledge' (Beck, 2013; Young, 2013). In other words, a Future 3 curriculum is a resource for teachers who seek to take their students beyond their experience in the most reliable ways we have. It implies that the curriculum stipulates the concepts associated with different subjects and how they are related, whether they refer to energy, matter, literature or historical change. It is the systematic inter-relatedness of subject-based concepts and the way that they take their meaning from how they are shared with each other that distinguishes them from the everyday concepts of experience that pupils bring to school; the latter always relate to specific contexts and experiences. The concepts associated with subjects, however, must be linked to the contents or facts that give them meaning and to the activities involved in acquiring and questioning them. It is the link between concepts, contents and activities that distinguishes a Future 3 curriculum from those that follow E. D. Hirsch's (1988) lists of 'what every child should know'. Future 3 points to the balance between the *stability* of subject concepts that is implicit in Future 1 and underemphasized in Future 2, *changes* in concepts that are underemphasized in Future 1 as new knowledge is produced, and *the activities involved in learning* that tend to be overemphasized in Future 2. The 'Three Futures' is not a new curriculum model waiting to be 'implemented' by schools; far from it. It offers *a way of thinking* about the most important issue a teacher ever faces, the question of knowledge. As I stated earlier, elements of Future 3, and of course Futures 1 and 2, are not new and are to be found to varying degrees in every subject and in the curriculum of every school.

What is powerful about 'Powerful knowledge'?

Although linking the two words 'power' and 'knowledge' is neither new nor specific to education, the idea of 'powerful knowledge' as an educational idea for distinguishing types of knowledge does appear to be relatively new; it has become part of curriculum debates within the last five years (Beck, 2013; Young, 2013; Young and Muller, 2014). Initially, I found it helpful to link the concept 'powerful knowledge' to the similar term that reverses the words, knowledge and power, namely 'knowledge of the powerful'. However, the two terms 'powerful knowledge' and 'knowledge of the powerful' use the words 'power' and 'knowledge' in very different ways.

I have used the terms to distinguish two different ways of linking power and knowledge when thinking about the curriculum. 'Knowledge of the powerful' focuses on which people or groups with power in any society or organization are in a position to define what knowledge is. In the case of the school curriculum, the concept 'knowledge of the powerful' refers to what knowledge is included and what is not and by whom. Karl Marx's version of 'knowledge of the powerful' will be familiar to many. It asserts, 'The ideas of the ruling class are in every epoch the ruling ideas'. It became a popular slogan in the 1970s among educationalists on the Left for several reasons. First, it focused on the question, 'who benefits from existing definitions and selections of knowledge?' Second, and specifically in relation to the curriculum, it addresses the question, 'Who has the power to exclude and include certain topics and concepts in the curriculum?' In other words it was a way of focusing on what seemed the intractable inequalities of the education system. The problem with analysing the curriculum in terms of the power and interests of those who design it or produce it is that it tells us very little about the curriculum or what alternatives to the existing curriculum might be possible; to use a phrase I owe to the late Rob Moore, 'it tells us about who the knowers are but not about what the knowledge is or might be'. The curriculum from this perspective is always predominantly a political instrument for maintaining power, not an educational instrument for supporting learning. A view of the curriculum or subjects representing 'knowledge of the powerful' contains an element of truth and challenges curriculum policy-makers and politicians and teachers. In practice, however, it is of very little help to any of them. As the sociologist Basil Bernstein (1970) once wrote, 'education cannot compensate for society'. In other words, he is reminding us that the roots of inequality in any society are not in the curriculum. At the same time he also reminds us that the curriculum is always potentially a disrupter of inequalities (Bernstein, 2000), so it is important to ask what different curricula can and cannot do, even if we cannot expect them to 'compensate for society'.

In contrast to the idea of the curriculum as 'knowledge of the powerful', the idea of 'powerful knowledge' refers to features of the particular knowledge itself and our relationship to it, what it can do for those who have access to it.[1] It is not concerned with who defines or creates the knowledge. Knowledge is 'powerful' if it predicts, if it explains, if it enables you to envisage alternatives, if it helps you to think.

If, then, these are some of the 'powers' of powerful knowledge, how might we distinguish it from knowledge that does not offer the potential knower any specific intellectual resources?

I will suggest three criteria for defining *powerful knowledge*.

(1) It is distinct from the 'common sense' knowledge we acquire through our everyday experience. Common sense knowledge is vital in our everyday lives but it is always tied to particular contexts. Our common sense knowledge develops through experience as we grow older; it does not need to be taught and we do not need to go to school to acquire it. It is limited, however, and it is primarily in order to overcome these limitations that we have schools and why the curriculum is based on subjects.
(2) Its concepts are systematically related to one another and shared in groups of specialists such as subject or disciplinary associations.
It is not, like common sense, rooted in the specific contexts of our experience. This means that 'powerful knowledge' can be the basis for generalizations and thinking beyond particular contexts or cases. The clearest examples both of the systematic structure of powerful knowledge and of its role as resource for generalizing are found in the natural sciences. Other forms of knowledge, however, such as the social sciences, humanities and the arts, form the basis of other academic subjects; they also have concepts that take us beyond particular cases and contexts in different ways and offer us different (because of the nature of the phenomena they are concerned with) capacities for generalization and understanding our relationship to the world.

(3) It is specialized.

In other words, powerful knowledge is knowledge that has been developed by groups with a clearly defined focus or field of enquiry and with relatively fixed boundaries separating them from each other. In education, these groups are what we know as disciplines and subjects. The specialist character of powerful knowledge explains, at least in part, why it is experienced as difficult to acquire and why acquiring it requires specialist teachers and much persistence on the part of learners. Neophyte learners have to learn what generations have struggled to know.

Powerful knowledge, subjects and curriculum specialization

In universities, *specialization of knowledge* takes the form of disciplines separated by boundaries with the priority of discovering new knowledge. Even those who work in inter-disciplinary fields such as town planning and transport draw on disciplines and collaborate with those from different disciplines until, in some cases, a new discipline is established with shared rules of enquiry (a familiar example of a still relatively new discipline emerging is biochemistry, which developed from biology and chemistry but there are many in the humanities as well). There are debates both about how far it is useful to think of disciplines as being the foundations for more applied fields – both in the pedagogic sense (some should be taught before others) and in the epistemological sense (can some disciplines be 'reduced' to others)? (Gibbons et al., 1994).[2]

In schools, this academic specialization has a number of aspects. First, it is subject-based and subjects are drawn from disciplines. This is not a straightforward process and has been the topic of little research. A useful concept to describe the subject-discipline relation is 're-contextualisation' (Bernstein, 1988, 2000). Whereas disciplines are primarily oriented to the discovery of new knowledge, academic subjects are primarily oriented to the transmission of knowledge and have to take account of the age and stage of development of learners and the knowledge that they bring to school. Subject knowledge is selected (from disciplines), paced and sequenced, according to rules that are often implicit but also shared.

Two final points about subjects and disciplines are worth mentioning. Their definitions of student progress and the development of knowledge are internal to the discipline or subject. On the other hand, they are always under what I have referred to as Future 2 pressures. An example is history departments in South Africa, which are expected to develop research and programmes in heritage studies.

School subjects; lessons from history

Any curriculum model, such as the one I have referred to as 'the Three Futures', tries to do two things. First, it aims to describe and locate historically key aspects of the world that teachers face every day. Second, such models, like any theory, enable us to envisage alternatives. Bernstein expressed this role of models as enabling people to think the 'un-thinkable' and the 'yet-to-be-thought' (Bernstein, 2000, p. 30); in Wheelahan's terms, such abstract theoretical knowledge serves as 'the means that society uses to construct its conversation about what it should be like and how it should change' (Wheelahan, 2010, p. 28). This is what Future 3 tries to do and the case studies by Buxton, Foster and Fordham flesh out what these ideas might mean for history teachers. As a sociologist who is unfamiliar with today's history teaching I was encouraged that their case studies demonstrated in specific ways, for history teachers, my more theoretical ideas about subjects.

Several points struck me which are clearly crucial to each author's approach to teaching history, but which have much wider implications for all subject teachers as well as for those of us who try and develop models of the curriculum. Each author emphasizes that students must have secure factual knowledge of any topic, so that they can move confidently to different topics within their subject. This is important because it stresses that the purpose of factual knowledge is not just its memorization and regurgitation. The second point I want to mention is their emphasis that history, like any subject, is not an unchanging canon from the nineteenth century, but a conversation, a field of debate and a range of arguments. Debates about causes will never be finally concluded, which is not to say that on the basis of current evidence there are no 'better' arguments. There is much, for example, for teachers of English to learn from these accounts, as they struggle with how to replace, or for some to reject, the old literary canon. The third and to me perhaps the most important lesson from the case studies is how they draw on and involve their students in historical scholarship. This calls into question the prevailing top-down model of how subjects are re-contextualized from university-based disciplines. In the examples that they cite, the disciplinary scholarship and debates among historians become part of history as a school subject and students find they can engage in types of historical argument practised by academic historians.

My last point is not made much of by the authors; perhaps because they take it for granted. It is that they are describing history teaching in a range of all-ability secondary schools, which in terms of the intellectual demands that they make on their students might have been selective schools. These, then, are concrete, practical examples of good subject teaching being possible 'for all', and not, as so often, restricted to those referred to as 'academic' students. Although these are far from isolated cases (Counsell, 2011a), as yet, they hardly impinge on wider debates about curricula for those labelled non-academic.

Conclusions

In introducing, in 2013, a national curriculum for England based largely on academic subjects, the UK's Conservative-led Coalition government must be given credit for opening up a debate about the purpose of schools, which successive Labour governments had signally failed to do. Linked to this is the wider question of social justice that government ministers continue to raise but which we rarely hear from the Opposition. Nick Gibb, the Minister for Schools in the current Conservative Government, refers to education as 'the major social justice issue of our time' and made a recent speech at the Policy Exchange on the theme '*Knowledge and power: the social justice case for an academic curriculum*' (Gibb, 2015). It is easy to claim that his argument is no more than sloganizing, and undoubtedly there is some truth in the claim. It is clear, however, that he is setting the terms for future debates and soon everyone will be talking about 'an entitlement for all'. That said, the government's policies, so far, are unlikely to be a basis for achieving their claimed goals of making an entitlement to a subject-based curriculum a possibility for all pupils; if anything, they could lead to the opposite. There are already two warning signs. Schools are beginning to advertise themselves as offering a knowledge-led curriculum and this has become a slogan, rather than a set of questions about how such purposes might be realized. A second issue that arises directly from the chapters by Fordham, Buxton and Foster is the question of specialist and well-qualified teachers. It is not irrelevant that the three authors of the case studies were educated as history teachers at one of our leading university Faculties of Education. It is important, as the government at least partially recognizes, that history teachers like any subject specialists have good first degrees in their subject. However, the three authors in this book are not just excellent historians; they have undertaken intensive studies of the didactics of history teaching with university-based specialists. Teaching is a profession, not a 'craft for graduates' as Michael Gove, the former Secretary of State, once claimed (Gove, 2010). 'Learning on the job' is important for any profession, but unlike crafts, not all professional knowledge can be acquired 'on the job'. Professions have to acquire systematic knowledge that draws on but is separate from their specialist subject studies such as, in this case, history.

As a sociologist and not an historian, there are several lessons I take from the three chapters by Buxton, Fordham and Foster. The first is a new role for curriculum theorists; we need to take the ideas developed by subject specialists such as these history teachers and use our Future 3 model of subjects to ask what the history teachers' examples might mean for geography, chemistry or French (for example). Ideally, curriculum theorists should be mediators and conceptualizers; too often they are prescribers. The second is that knowledge about the curriculum is a specialist form of enquiry that is the joint responsibility of curriculum theorists and subject specialists. With notable exceptions in history and geography (Counsell, 2011a; Firth, 2011), this interdependence has barely been recognized by either group. We have much taken-for-granted knowledge in both specialist fields, but this has only got us so far. Subject specialists have as much to learn from other specialists like these history teachers as they may have from curriculum theorists. Extending and establishing what I have referred to as Future 3 will be a collaborative endeavour if it is to achieve its goals, especially if we are serious about the claim that history and other subjects are, at least potentially, 'knowledge for all'.

Breaking the Ice: Encouraging Students to Excavate the Familiar Surfaces of the Past

Reflections on Chapters by Michael Harcourt, Michael Fordham and Robert Somers

Ed Podesta

14

The thing that I struggle with most in teaching is skating. Skating often happens when a class enters a familiar classroom, with a trusted and familiar teacher. They come in, sit at their usual desks, listen to the teacher's explanations, answer questions when asked and then complete their work in good order. At the end, each mind turns to break or to the next lesson and the pupils leave the room with their worldviews unchanged. Sometimes, when I feel a lack of purchase in the knowledge of the lesson and sense of drifting towards the end, I fear that we are skating over the surface, instead of digging down and finding out what is underneath. I see skating in my own classroom when pupil questions are lacking, when they are too concerned about cutting the edges straight on a picture that they are 'sticking-in', or when they rush to the end of an activity and put their hands up with a 'done it!', and I am at a loss as to how to interrupt their thoughts or to inspire re-thinking.

It is normal to jump to conclusions. It seems that there is a natural heuristic that encourages us to prefer simple explanations (Kahneman, 2012). Sam Wineburg (1999) makes a powerful case that we tend to think *a*historically and to see things from the past as being either like us or alien to us. It seems that this heuristic might also be self-reinforcing. Wineburg (2007) cites Tversky and Kahneman's 'availability heuristic' (1973) to explain how pupils might turn, in seeking support for their simple answers, to the evidence that is closest to hand and clearest in mind. This makes it easy to see why students might sail easily across historical questions, relying on ideas they already hold and grabbing new evidence that supports their preconceptions. For Wineburg, historical thinking is something that we have to be *taught*. In this view, deft historical thinking entails balancing the similar and the unfamiliar, suspending judgement, and making a conscious 'specification of ignorance' (Wineburg, 2007, p. 11) – in other words, recognizing what we do not know and not grabbing hold of what we recognize.

The three chapters that I am responding to here are all examples of teachers formally investigating what is happening in their classrooms, closely assessing what is being learned and asking questions about what can be done next. All three demonstrate the value – in combating skating – of activity of this kind: of deliberately scratching and disturbing the surface of historical teaching and learning, of digging deep and excavating the processes involved.

For me, Harcourt's piece offers direction in helping students see *why* we bother with significance. I have always taken Lee's view (1992) that the main purpose of school history is as induction into public intellectual criteria of history, and their use. Phillips (2002), Counsell (2004c), Bradshaw (2006) and others have pointed out the need to encourage and enable students to make their own judgements about significance and shown how the use of criteria can help scaffold student thinking. However, even this approach can still lead to skating. As Harris and Rea (2006) point out, abstracted reasoning alone is unlikely to convince students to invest real thought in a particular question. I have taught lessons in which students made judgements about significance after assessing the extent to which phenomena were 'remarkable' or 'revealing', using the evidence presented to them, and writing or made arguments in balloon debates and so on. And yet, I have found myself wondering if the significance activities actually signified very much for them. Before students can truly *make judgements* of significance, they must first *care* about the event, person or place whose significance they are considering.

Harcourt seems to have suspected this in setting out to explore the extent to which 'the experience of making a sound walk' about a particular location 'resulted in rich engagements'. Like Harris and Rea who advocate 'bringing in a local element which the pupils can envisage or relate to' (2006, p. 32), Harcourt hoped that place and local history could be used to 'develop and deepen students' historical thinking' (Harcourt, this volume, p. 121). The context of the 2013 National Curriculum in England and Wales (DfE, 2013), which requires a local history study, adds further reason, if it were needed, to take note of Harcourt's approach to the significance of a place. Harris and Rea's comments about meaningful history being 'about touching the "human" past and providing opportunities to see people as real figures trying to live their lives' (2006, p. 29) are very prescient given the evidence in Harcourt's piece that this approach to location 'increased' his students' 'capacity to care for historical actors' (Harcourt, this volume, p. 131).

Thinking about the significance of place raises the question 'What should the study of significance involve?' Counsell argues that the kinds of thinking that we want students to engage in when contemplating significance cannot easily be tidied up (Counsell, 2004b, p. 79), and she encourages all teachers to make the effort and form their own judgements about what significance entails. As an example, she offers four 'reflective and processing activities' (Counsell, 2004b, p. 79): (1) applying given or (2) self-devised criteria for judging historical significance; (3) discerning the criteria implicit in others' judgements of significance; and (4) challenging others' judgements about significance. In order to help scaffold student thinking in these tasks she offers a set of criteria designed to 'generate thinking' about significance, which Harcourt uses out in his chapter (Harcourt, this volume, p. 126).

Alongside these 'five Rs' Harcourt adopts his own 'PLACE' criteria designed to deal with the issue of the significance of a location (Harcourt, this volume, pp. 125–126). I would really like to hear more about and to debate how these criteria were developed: one could question the extent to which being affected by change makes a place significant, for example. We can perhaps imagine circumstances in which being affected by a great deal of change might be an indicator of *insignificance*. I also wonder whether the focus on the extent to which the site reveals power relations, as opposed to other types of relations or aspects of society, prejudges the question of the meaning of significance. There is clearly further work to do on devising and testing criteria that can help students think about the situated historical significance of a place.

The strength of Harcourt's work lies in revealing the way that judgements of significance depend upon the positionality of the person making them and upon the nature of the enquiry at hand. Lomas (1990) raised both questions but they have been rather neglected since – eclipsed, in my classroom at least, by the rush to judge the relative significance of events, people or developments, and, in the literature, by the more legitimate aim of broadening out consideration of significance beyond causal or consequential significance.

Does a focus on the significance of a place help us appreciate the extent to which signi cance varies with time? Harcourt notes that his students were more likely to ask q such as 'What else happened here?', 'What are the important layers of the p 'Whose pasts are acknowledged here?' when making use of the PLACE has the potential to draw attention to the events with which a place is con ways in which those events reverberate in memory and ceremony subseque about location has the potential, perhaps, to encourage students to understand number of senses and thus to negotiate similarity and difference (Wineburg, 199 too easily slide into contempt for, or identification with, the past, instead of dialogue. a focus on place can help us *encounter* the past and learn from it rather than simply (Wineburg, 1999, p. 93) and perhaps Harcourt's criteria and opportunities to apply them stem a rush to judgement and prevent students from skating over complexity.

Like Harcourt's, Michael Fordham's research encourages us to think about the history we teach in chronological themes and in repeating chronological patterns. Fordham is interested in finding out how pupils make sense of substantive concepts – how they come to know that the term 'peasant' can contain both the Anglo-Saxon *ceorl* and the Russian *serf* (Fordham, this volume, p. 45). Fordham is interested in understanding how substantive concepts could be used to help us think about what pupil progression *is* and about the processes that make this progression understanding *possible* – how new knowledge changes the meanings already attached to a concept in the pupil's mind.

Fordham's research data was gathered during a sequence of lessons structured through the enquiry question 'How revolutionary was the French Revolution?' and by comparative reflection on 'revolution'. He found that students tended to look for the 'essences' and the 'properties' of revolution and to create a Platonic 'ideal' of 'revolution 'characterized by second-order concepts focused on change, which they used to measure other 'revolutions'(Fordham, this volume, p. 55).

In one way it is natural for students to reach for the second-order conceptual tools that historians have used to help them understand the past (Lee, 2005b), and perhaps change is the tool that naturally springs to hand when contemplating 'revolution'. Fordham therefore raises the possibility that substantive concepts are bound up with second-order concepts and suggests that some second-order concepts are more closely linked with particular substantive concepts than we had thought hitherto. Fordham's analogy of 'knots' in pupils' understanding, tying together linguistic, substantive and second-order understanding and understandings of particulars directs us to the range of strands that we need to keep in mind when planning for long-term progress.

Harcourt builds on work calling for the use of a range of conceptual tools when considering 'significance', and Fordham's alerts us to the need to find new ways of approaching substantive concepts like revolution. I wonder whether Fordham's design – examining 'the process of change during the French Revolution' and then comparing this with 'change in other societies at other times' (Fordham, this volume, p. 51) – foregrounds change to the extent that it pushes out other possible issues. As an alternative, for example, we could, perhaps, focus on 'similarity and difference', asking questions such as 'Who took part in revolutions?'. An interesting question might be to think about *why* we use the term revolution to cover disparate events and *why* some things are understood as 'revolts' and others as 'revolutions'. It might be possible to explore revolutions as interpretations to consider when revolutions 'became' revolutions, asking, for example, when the Industrial Revolution became referred to as such. Of other revolutions it might be interesting to ask 'Could participants at the time have known they were in a revolution?' Burnham and Brown take a similar approach to the teaching of 'imperialism' over the course of a key stage by asking different types of second-order question about this substantive concept at different points in their teaching (Burnham and Brown, 2004, pp. 14–15).

I wonder if this could also be a way of negotiating Wineburg's jagged path between the similar and the different, in that it might encourage us to see that there are 'different' aspects to things that we thought we had understood. So, for instance, once an understanding of 'imperialism' has been attained, it could be questioned, refined and re-negotiated by looking at it through different second-order lenses and in different historical contexts. In my own classroom students are often very reluctant to return to topics or ideas and will complain that 'we've already *done* this', preferring instead to skate on to the next topic. If we take Burnham and Brown's approach, the substantive concept is re-problematized so that students become used to asking questions of things that they have 'already done'.

However, this process must be *meaningful*, so that students actively participate in it, rather than sit quietly whilst the lesson activities play out. In our search for meaningful history education Wineburg cautions us not to stay too close to the familiar and to things that look most immediately relevant to our pupils. Instead Wineburg wants us to move towards the strange, as this is the pole that will allow us to realize the limitations of our experiences and the breadth of those of the rest of humanity.

Rob Somers' chapter urges us to take cautious and well-planned steps when approaching difference (Somers, this volume, pp. 135–142). As Somers points out, other commentators have suggested that a more diverse curriculum might increase 'relevance'; however, making something 'relevant' can involve removing what is really different about it, by presenting it in accessible terms that are alien to it.

Somers' work also shows us that selecting less familiar pasts might not be as simple as it seems at first, especially in our multicultural and multi-identitied present. Individuals feel continuity with multiple and sometimes conflicting identities. They bring with them ideas and cultures, which mean that they feel the pull and possibly the confusion of the familiar, when we were hoping that they would be navigating the strange. Indeed, Wineburg's argument that students will tend to encounter new material through the lens of their existing beliefs and experiences is supported by the example of Somers' students, who drew on song lyrics and a boxer's catchphrase in their attempts to make sense of something they found strange (Somers, this volume, p. 146).

Somers' work also helped me to see that what is 'other' for me can easily be taken as 'familiar' by my pupils. I shared Somers' surprise at Michelle's perception of Akbar's seemingly modern and tolerant approach to his wife's religion as 'weird' and as contrary to her experience in which a woman marrying a Muslim 'normally' involved conversion to that faith (Somers, this volume, p. 146). Perhaps Somers is doing what Wineburg suggests – helping his students cast 'doubt on' their 'ability to know' people from the past 'as easily as we know ourselves' (Wineburg, 1999, p. 93). Somers *is* looking for meaningful relevance and a *real* question that students can truly engage with. His suggestion that his pupils were 'developing a relationship with Akbar' (Somers, this volume, p. 146) should perhaps give us pause for thought. Perhaps this is a relationship that we should aim to disrupt, so that students come to see that they need to find out more about Akbar's actions, goals, motives and experiences before they can begin to come to 'know' him.

At the end of his piece Somers seems somewhat disheartened by the responses of his students and by the realization that he cannot escape the historical context in which he is working. He notes, for instance, his failure to avoid 'the rhetoric of diversity, multiculturalism and inclusion', and that he was 'part of [the] system' and 'subject to privileging western liberal values and promoting "self" over "other"' (Somers, this volume, p. 149). In reply, I would urge the conclusion that history is never 'done' and every conclusion is merely temporary and awaiting revision and, perhaps, falsification, through further study, further exploration of the evidence and/or of new evidence. Initial ideas that seem to privilege a 'liberal Western outlook' are just that – initial. As the reactions of his students and the work of both Fordham and Harcourt show, what seems familiar at first can contain surprises and inspire further investigation. What we are attempting to cultivate in our students is pause for thought, a recognition that things are not what they seem at first. Perhaps we can see signs of that happening in Somers' students' words.

Redesigning History Education to Improve Pupils' Understanding: Implications for Theory and Research

Reflections on Chapters by Daniel Magnoff, Michael Harcourt and Rick Rogers

Carla van Boxtel and Jannet van Drie

15

Chapter outline

It is quite a challenge to enhance pupils' understanding of the nature and construction of historical interpretations and to teach pupils how to use interpretations to orient themselves in the present. Rogers, Harcourt and Magnoff designed their history lessons in innovative ways by having pupils create sound walks, by teaching a synoptic framework and by engaging pupils in online peer discussion about the use of historical sources. The authors highlight different aims of history education, such as the acquisition of a frame of reference, the ability to think historically about the way history is present in their own environment and the understanding of the nature and methods of history. Although Rogers, Harcourt and Magnoff are inspired by concepts and ideas that are central to international cognitive research and theorizing in history education, their contributions do not put much emphasis on the potential implications of their experiences and findings for this wider field. We think, however, that their contributions have much to offer on this point. In this chapter we will reflect on their three chapters from our perspective as researchers working in this wider field.

In our own research we work with the concept of historical reasoning (Van Drie and Van Boxtel, 2008). We argue that engaging pupils in historical reasoning is important, because it contributes to a deeper understanding of historical phenomena and the nature of history, and to the development of pupils' ability to think and reason historically in new situations both inside and outside school. We conceptualize historical reasoning as an activity in which pupils identify processes of change and continuity, explain or compare historical phenomena or actions of people in the past by asking historical questions, using substantive and second-order knowledge, and historical argumentation based upon a critical examination of sources (Van Drie and Van Boxtel, 2008; Van Boxtel and Van Drie, 2013). We are interested in how historical reasoning is the result of a complex interplay between pupils' substantive and second-order knowledge, historical interests and epistemological beliefs. In a number of studies we have examined the effects of tasks and teaching methods on the quality of pupils' historical reasoning using the tools and methods of cognitive science.

The three chapters that we explore pertain to issues that are important when theorizing and researching pupils' historical thinking and reasoning. The first issue is the kind of framework we need to teach in order to enable pupils to better understand history, contextualize, explain, identify aspects of change and continuity and compare historical periods and phenomena. Rogers provides an interesting entry into discussing this issue. His rich description of the challenges and dilemmas he faced when using a low resolution framework in the classroom, in particular, is very instructive and shows the difficulties of designing and teaching a usable framework. Harcourt and Magnoff explore important issues connected to the question of how to improve pupils' understanding of the methodology of history, particularly the attribution of historical significance and methods for using sources in order to create historical interpretations. Their findings and reflections not only challenge the way we conceptualize these understandings but also point to important ingredients of effective teaching approaches.

Teaching a usable framework

Rogers begins his contribution by elaborating on the problem of pupils' fragmented knowledge of the past. This problem was an important impulse for the revision of the history curriculum in our own country, the Netherlands. Just as in Rogers' work, the answer in the

Netherlands was sought in more low resolution history, although our curriculum is at a higher resolution than Rogers' framework. In the Netherlands the history curriculum includes a Eurocentric framework, also known as the 'ten eras framework'. This framework consists of ten clear-cut eras (with associated labels, such as the 'era of monks and knights') and a small number of characteristic features for each era, including developments in European history such as Romanization, the Enlightenment and Imperialism (Van Drie et al., 2009; Van Boxtel and Grever, 2011). Some eras include characteristic aspects of Dutch history, such as the Dutch Revolt resulting in an independent state. The framework does not include concrete events or persons. Next to this framework, schools are expected to use the Dutch Canon (consisting of fifty items, concrete persons and events from Dutch History) in the first years of secondary education to illustrate the characteristic features of the ten eras. Although there are both similarities and differences between the synoptic framework that Rogers used in his classroom and the ten eras framework used in the Netherlands, they are accompanied by similar possibilities and dilemmas.

Rogers' framework is divided into five eras and focuses on human development, organized through five general questions (e.g. 'How are we organized?'). The 'we' in the question aims to connect people in the past to 'us', emphasizing continuity between past and present. Although this makes good sense in terms of the aim of developing a framework on the scale of human development, it also raises the question of how this emphasis on continuity and 'sameness' can be brought into line with the idea that historical consciousness is demonstrated when pupils can *discern* differences between past and present and try to understand the actions of people in the past by taking into account the fact that they lived in *other* times and circumstances (e.g. Wineburg, 2001; Grever, De Bruijn and Van Boxtel, 2012; Smith, 2014). Developments stretching out over long periods of time may obscure the particular historical setting that shaped people's lives and actions. This raises a question: Can, or how can, a framework with a very low resolution be a useful tool to explain the particular actions of people in the past? In order to take an explanatory historical perspective we might need to construct an historical context drawn from a higher resolution framework. In our own studies we found that, when engaged in historical enquiries, pupils experienced particular difficulties in constructing an historical context in which to interpret historical events and the actions of concrete historical actors. Rogers combines a low resolution framework with teaching history at a higher level of resolution. It would be interesting to investigate how a framework with a lower resolution affects pupils' understanding of causation and the ability to construct historical explanations when studying particular historical events in depth.

In our studies on how pupils contextualize unknown historical documents and images from European and Dutch history, we found that knowledge of turning points that form the beginning and end of thematic stories, such as the Cold War or the rise and fall of the Roman Empire, is an important tool for pupils to orientate in time (Van Boxtel and Van Drie, 2012). Pupils used these temporal markers as anchors to decide the period to which a particular historical image or text belonged (e.g. 'it must be before 1989, because that was the fall of the

Berlin Wall marking the end of the Cold War'). From this perspective the rounded dates that are used in the ten-eras framework in the Netherlands (e.g. 'the era of monks and knights, 500–1000') are problematical and the way Rogers has chosen to use temporal markers makes more sense. In our study we also found that pupils who were able to construct an adequate historical context often made use of thematic stories, mostly labelled with a colligatory concept, such as the Industrial Revolution. Rogers discusses the labels he constructed for mega-epochs (e.g. kingdoms or empires). A grounded selection and labelling of the long-term *developments* that are included in the framework, such as the 'transformation from agrarian to urban-agrarian society' or 'industrialization', might, however, be just as important. This observation brings us to the question of the abstract terminology that often accompanies a lower resolution framework. In order to remember the periodization that is provided, pupils need concrete examples and visualizations connected to abstract propositional knowledge. More research is needed to explore how the more abstract terminology can be appropriated and understood by pupils.

Finally, Rogers raises a problem that is very recognizable in the Dutch context. He mentions that pupils are not inclined to see the synoptic framework as a framework, but, rather, as a record of what happened. In the Netherlands, pupils, and also many history teachers, seem to approach our framework in this way. Teachers often teach the same facts, dates and concepts that they taught before the framework was introduced and simply organize this material in the chronological framework of the ten eras. The ten eras and the characteristic features have become a curriculum – a tool to deliver content – rather than a framework to help pupils think about and model the past. Rogers used the framework more as a framework and also points to its potential contribution to pupils' understanding of periodization and chronology. In the Netherlands, teaching the framework demands so much time that pupils are rarely provided with opportunities to actually use it as a framework. What is a good balance between teaching the framework and using the framework? It would be interesting to see how the framework developed by Rogers is actually used by pupils when they are conducting an enquiry.

Using the methodology of history: understanding historical significance

One of the reasons why it is important to develop pupils' ability to think and reason historically is that they can apply it to situations external to the school setting. Outside school the 'thinking tools' developed within the discipline of history can be used by pupils to better understand how people attribute significance to the past and to attribute significance themselves. Two types of historical significance are relevant when investigating historical sites: the significance of an historical person or phenomenon (e.g. World War I) and the significance of a place connected to historical persons or phenomena (e.g. the National War Memorial). Harcourt found that the criteria he used to engage pupils in thinking about historical significance were not sufficient to understand the significance that can be attributed to a place, and he developed additional geo-historical criteria for significance. Although only few pupils combined both sets of criteria for attributing significance, their thinking and reasoning seemed to profit from this combination. The geo-historical criteria are useful to reflect on the operationalization of 'relevance for the present'. This criterion for historical significance is still poorly elaborated in history education literature (see also Savenije, Van Boxtel and Grever, 2014), probably because it is used less by historians that it is in heritage practices.

There are different types of study of historical significance in history education. First, there are studies that work from an identity perspective. Such studies describe pupils' beliefs and ideas about who and what they consider to be of importance in history and why. Such studies often seek to relate this to the social backgrounds of pupils (e.g. Barton and McCullly, 2005; Peck, 2010; Savenije, 2014). Second, there are scholars working from a learning and teaching perspective, who provide suggestions about how to teach historical significance in the classroom and who explore how the concept of historical significance is used as procedural knowledge (e.g. Cercadillo, 2001; Van Drie, Van Boxtel and Stam, 2013). It would be interesting to analyze the sound walks that pupils created in Harcourt's study from these two perspectives. Analyses and additional interviews with pupils might provide insight into ways in which pupils' identity and social background relate to how they ascribe historical significance. Such data might also provide an explanation for the finding that one site was not chosen for a sound walk (the Maori archaeological site). Working from a teaching and learning perspective, it is relevant to examine how pupils use the concept of historical significance as procedural knowledge. Which criteria do they use, and what kind of arguments do they develop? Harcourt's study provides us with some insights into pupils' thinking and reasoning. On the one hand, pupils' reflections on the assignment showed that for some of them it resulted in caring about certain issues and people in the past. This experience may contribute to pupils' understanding of why particular places are still important for people in the present and to their understanding of reasons why people have to commemorate. On the other hand, this 'caring' might inhibit pupils' willingness and ability to take a critical approach. Harcourt's study points to the difficulties that pupils can have in approaching historical sites as interpretations and as a kind of text that can be analyzed and critically examined.

Using the methodology of history: understanding historical interpretation

Daniel Magnoff investigated how the Beatles Project, in which post-16 pupils in England collaborated online with each other and an historian, affected pupils' understanding of what historians do in historical enquiries, particularly how they make selections from available sources of evidence. Pupils' understanding of historical methodology was investigated by asking them to write an explanation of what they think historians do in order to answer questions about the past. Pupils' investigation was guided by the overall question 'Does an investigation of the lyrics of The Beatles' songs support the claim that dramatic changes took place in the bands' attitudes and values over the course of its career?' In contrast with many other overarching questions used in the history classroom, which often focus primarily on substantive issues, this question focuses pupils' attention primarily on methodological issues. In addition, pupils were asked to engage in discussion with each other and with an expert and to comment on each other's answers and approaches, a process that aimed to contribute to their understanding of the practices that historians engage in when 'doing history'.

The analysis of pupils' ideas about how historians work showed that their understanding reflected naïve objectivist assumptions about how historians produce accounts. Pupils suggested that historians need to consider a large number of records and relics of the past and that they are then able to put together an answer. They also tended to approach historians' views as opinions. Here, pupils' epistemological beliefs seem to reflect what Maggioni, VanSledright and Alexander (2009) call a 'borrower stance', instead of a 'criterialist stance'. Historical accounts are not seen as reasoned arguments. Engaging pupils in historical enquiry and asking them to discuss the choices they made in using historical sources might not be enough to improve their understanding of what historians do when they create historical interpretations. In a whole-class discussion, teachers can explicitly reflect with pupils on the way they approach an enquiry task and on their beliefs about the nature of history (e.g. Havekes, De Vries and Aardema, 2010; Stoel, Van Drie and Van Boxtel, 2015). Such reflection may enhance the potential of the approach that Magnoff developed. Magnoff reports primarily on pupils' understandings and less on the content of the peer discussion and on the role of the historian who commented on pupils' contributions. Focusing on these issues might have provided additional information on changes in pupils' understandings during the project. Deeper analyses of the discussion between the pupils and of the contribution of the historian might also give us a better idea of the points at which pupils are likely to need support in developing sophisticated understandings. We must be careful when using pupils' written responses to a single question as indicators of their understanding of historical methodology. Pupils might not have mastered the vocabulary and writing skills necessary to articulate their understandings of methodology in a sophisticated way. Perhaps additional interviews in which their answers could be explored might reveal that they have more nuanced views than those suggested by their written answers. In our own studies we have found that pupils' end products did not always reflect the quality of their thinking and reasoning during tasks.

The authors of these chapters report how they carefully designed and organized a series of lessons, the ideas underlying their design, the problems and dilemmas that they faced, their own and pupils' experiences and the extent to which the learning outcomes matched their ambitions. This practice-oriented research is valuable for the teachers themselves to improve their practice and as a form of professionalization. Research contributes to a process of lifelong learning as teachers adapt to and reflect on changes in professional practice in the discipline of history and in the methodology of history teaching. Because these teacher-researchers share their theoretical frameworks, the design of the lessons and the findings, the research makes a valuable contribution to discussion and learning in the wider community of history teachers. The studies also contribute to the development of the wider body of design principles for the teaching of history. Finally, as we have argued here, the research is valuable for the wider field of history education research, since it generates new questions about the theoretical constructs that are used and provides new starting points for exploring ways in which history teaching can develop pupils' understandings of history. The three studies can be expanded with more fundamental research focusing on pupils' learning processes. For example, with analyses of how pupils use a synoptic framework when investigating history, how pupils discuss methodological issues in an online learning environment and how pupils develop their constructions of a sound walk. Both practice-oriented research as done by Rogers, Harcourt and Magnoff as well as fundamental research need to be conducted, not least because together they can help us understand why pupils reach or fail to reach particular understandings, how a particular curriculum or teaching approach works in practice and about how we can best support pupils in developing their historical knowledge and understanding.

Voices from and Voices about the Past: Connecting Evidence, Significance and Diversity

Reflections on Chapters by Michael Harcourt, Robert Somers and Paula Worth

Izzy Jones

16

Chapter outline

Drawing on my perspective as an experienced head of history in a comprehensive school, I examine the significance of the research presented by Harcourt, Somers and Worth in the context of the existing history education field. The chapter concludes with reflections that draw together the ostensibly diverse concerns of the three different authors.

Reflecting on three teachers' chapters

Harcourt's work draws on published practitioner work, mostly from the UK, which problematizes significance as 'a procedural concept within the discipline' (Harcourt, this volume, p. 122). He makes use of Counsell's (2004c) suggested taxonomy, the '5Rs', and echoes Bradshaw's aim to allow students to 'interact with two highly complex historical considerations':

1. *Historical* significance is 'not a property of the event itself'; it is ascribed by others (Counsell, 2004c, p. 30).
2. Historical significance is contested not decided. It is 'a debate in which they can make a genuine contribution of their own' (Bradshaw, 2006, p. 24).

Harcourt, however, does this in a different context, where teachers' discussions of historical significance as a concept are new and where history is studied as a discrete subject only by older students and only for three years. His situation appears similar in some ways to the situation Cercadillo describes in Spain, where 'insistence on a single or intrinsic significance is still quite common' (2006, p. 8). Harcourt's sound walks are an example of Cercadillo's focus on 'significance in the context of an historical account' (2006, p. 7). Cercadillo appeals to White (1984), whose exposition of a false dichotomy between narrative interpretation and dissertative representation may strike a chord with history teachers in England who experienced recent debates about the reform of England's National Curriculum for history (Evans, 2013). Harcourt and Cercadillo's work, taken together, thus has renewed relevance for the history education community in England. Both authors attempt to show their students that ideas about significance are central to the discipline of history and that their contested nature invites reasoning. Harcourt's sound walks provide a practical prism through which this can be addressed, especially where the places studied by his students have contested pasts.

Harcourt's desire to explore geo-political significance in order to engage students in local history is one with which I empathize, teaching as I do in an inner suburb of a global city. I easily forget that some of my students rarely visit central London and do not share my 'uncommonly rich and diverse' (Taylor, 2004, p. 6) connection with that place. This is why, on first reading, I found myself contrasting Harcourt's sound walks activity with Brown and Woodcock's series of lessons on World War I in which they explored questions about historical significance through their school's village, thus predisposing the pupils to see 'the immediate relevance to their own lives . . . families . . . street and . . . communities' (2009, p. 4). I later reflected, however, that these two works reveal a common complementarity between the multilayered ways in which their students think about place and the ways in which students see significance as a label to be wrestled with and debated, rather than a property of the place itself or the event or person represented. Moreover, like Brown and Woodcock's students, Harcourt and his students grapple with the inherently contested 'opposing . . . judgements of historical significance made by the creators of the memorials' (Harcourt, this volume, p. 132).

Harcourt's work is influenced by diverse scholarship on place, from teachers and historians, in England and New Zealand. He draws on Taylor's 'uncommon views of place' (2004, p. 7) and the work of Park (1995), an environmental historian from New Zealand. Yet his own curricular thinking develops in response to his students' construals. I, too, have found something special about that moment when ideas from my reading spring to life through a student's question or misconception. It is then that I am able to apply those historical ideas with clarity. I found, with some relief, on reading Burn (2012), that I am not alone among history teachers in experiencing this incremental process. Unlike Brown and Woodcock (2009),

Harcourt does not separate thinking about historical significance from thinking about historical interpretations. He draws on Cresswell's (2004) ideas about the multidimensionality of place and the ways in which places are a product of human construction as well as nature. Questions about location, tangible environment, sociopolitical and cultural context and meaning attributed to individuals – the last of which illuminates processes of representation and ideas about belonging and insider identity (Taylor, 2004) – form the 'multilayered' criticality that Harcourt notices in some of his students, and wishes in future to develop in all of them. It is through a human interpretation that significance has been ascribed.

***

Describing her effort to navigate a path between her ambition to develop and reward independent thinking and the responsibility to guide her students towards examination success, Worth reveals just how difficult this is in practice. In my experience, it can sometimes seem impossible. These difficulties, and efforts at solutions, are well-documented by history teachers (e.g. Laffin, 2000, 2009, 2012; Smith, 2001). Dissonance between history teachers' conceptions of rigour and the reductive formulae of examination remains a central professional difficulty.

In addressing this issue, Worth finds herself asking questions that are disciplinary:

- What do terms such as 'evaluation', 'inference', 'interpretation' and 'comprehension' mean, and in what ways are these things complex?
- What kinds of work with language will empower students to express the ways in which they comprehend and interpret sources?

The third question Worth does not explore explicitly, but she hints at it in her final paragraphs. This strikes me as central to employing her ideas successfully:

- What is the place of knowledge in understanding sources?

Some difficulties to which Worth draws our attention should be contextualized by the possible consequences of certain statutory rubrics. The 2008 National Curriculum for History (QCA/DCSF, 2007, p. 114) defined using evidence as a key 'process'. The definition of this as 'skills . . . pupils need to learn' as opposed to one of the 'key concepts that underpin the study of history' might have contributed towards some readers, especially early-career teachers, forming the view that evidential work was not complex, and served merely as a route towards 'real' historical thinking. Other history teachers (Pickles, 2011) have drawn our attention to the fact that comprehension, inference and cross-referencing are not simple tasks, and not best described as 'processes', let alone procedures. Worth, in highlighting the complexities of one form of thinking, returns us to the position summarized by Ashby – reached through many years of research and theorizing the place of evidence in school history – that 'a problem arises when "doing history" . . . takes precedence over developing an understanding of . . . historical knowledge through a developed concept of evidence' (Ashby, 2011, p. 139).

For Ashby, comprehension is connected with understanding the distinction between sources, which do not 'speak for themselves' (Ashby, 2011, p. 140) and evidence, which can be yielded from sources when they are scrutinized appropriately in relation to a claim or hypothesis. Worth acknowledges the need for that distinction but notes other challenges that can be hard to overcome. Her students are able to interrogate the sources for meaning but they lack sufficient proficiency in language to articulate their understanding with adequate precision. This seems to be related to their understanding of substantive concepts – such as 'dictator' – and how these can be contested in different contexts. This transcends work with evidence and may point to a variety of possible challenges. For Lee, it concerns a 'dispositional acknowledgement' that people thought differently in the past (2011a, p. 66), one essential to the deep understanding that 'transforms factual information into usable knowledge' (Donovan, Bransford and Pellegrino, 1999, p. 12). Pickles provides us with suggested validity tests for assessment that take on board these ideas, incorporating reasoned interpretation, empathetic and conceptual understanding and the appropriate application of knowledge (Pickles, 2011, p. 59). Other teachers, such as Hammond (2014) and Palek (2015), while not disputing the need for students to develop awareness of second-order issues, suggest that the reason substantive concepts such as 'dictator' are sometimes insecure is the result of inadequate familiarity with content, such as stories from the past which are central to the topic.

This leads to the third point that arose for me in my reading of Worth, which is summed up by Donovan, Bransford and Pellegrino (1999):

> [S]tudents need . . . a deep foundation of factual and conceptual knowledge and to understand . . . facts and ideas in a broader framework . . . it must be organized so they can access and use it, . . . to make cautious and realistic assessments about how far and in what circumstances it is applicable. (2005, p. 65)

I wonder whether this 'deep foundation of factual and conceptual knowledge' is the 'context' that 'a minority of pupils appeared to use . . . to comprehend what the author is saying' (Worth, this volume, p. 94). Such knowledge might include factual and conceptual frameworks, contested ideas or definitions *and* an awareness of the processes by which these might be studied. Worth's pupils were able to move to and fro between the author and the word, and, for some, comprehension and evaluation came to support each other. What we see here seems to be the kind of interplay between knowledge and evidential understanding that Ashby discusses at length, and which can be summarized as knowledge of (a) where and how a source was found, (b) its relationship to the line of historical enquiry, (c) its relationship to other sources and (d) the 'interplay between the interpretation of sources and history's existing [public] knowledge base' (Ashby, 2011, pp. 41–42). Worth's work thus demonstrates the complexities of students understanding what any source 'meant in the world from which it survives' (Dickinson, Gard and Lee, 1978, p. 9).

***

The conclusion to Somers' writing infuses me with optimism about the power of history to influence the way in which students think, but also makes me fearful of the unwitting consequences of our actions. But if our projection of ourselves onto the history that we teach is inevitable, then perhaps it is more helpful for history teachers to consider how the question of diversity, as content and as concept, fits into the bigger picture of the entire history curriculum.

The 2008 NC for history classified diversity as a 'key concept' (QCA/DCSF, 2007, p. 112). Its curriculum role brought together two traditions: first, a requirement for students to consider similarity and difference, originally made explicit in the 1991 NC (DES, 1990b), that is, to treat it as a concept demanding a certain type of analysis; second, a requirement to consider a range of content that 'provided threads which define diversity more explicitly' than before (Bracey, Gove-Humphries and Jackson, 2011). Somers' aspirations for his students' learning embrace both of these. Each, alone, is complex, and he tries to tackle both simultaneously. History teachers set themselves multifaceted curricular challenges all the time, but the sensitivity and controversy of some topics that could be deemed to sit under a 'diversity' umbrella mean that we are more conscious of the adverse consequences when we do not succeed, and that this needs to be considered from the earliest planning stages (Traille, 2007; Whitburn, Hussain and Mohamud, 2012).

To avoid feeling overwhelmed by this, I find it helpful to acknowledge that there are forces in society that influence the development of the young people with whom I work, which are at least as powerful as my 180 hours with them across three years. In the light of an account of these forces in the 'Ajegbo Report' (DfES, 2007), Harris (2013) searches for a framework in which two competing discourses around community cohesion and the broader purposes of history education might be brought together. Applying Harris' ideas to a single enquiry would be extremely complex and attempting to do so highlights the difficulties that Somers feels he cannot escape.

The only possible way in which one might achieve partial resolution of Somers' dilemmas is not to look at a single enquiry in isolation, but to consider it in relation to the content and thinking taught across all of school history. A key question, then, is where Somers' Akbar enquiry might fit within a broader programme of study. There is a long trail of literature in which history teachers have reflected on ways of configuring depth and overview (Banham, 2000; Counsell, 2002; Dawson 2004; Gadd, 2009). Banham's King John sequence includes work with contemporary source material, through which 'pupils are drawn outwards into wider knowledge of medieval life, institutions and values' (Banham, 2000, p. 23). There are times in this enquiry when King John is characterized in a certain 'traditional' way (p. 25) and where 'wider knowledge' of the medieval world might be discussed with the perspectives of modern society. I share Somers' concerns that such characterizations can be problematical because they are 'subject to privileging western liberal values and promoting "self" over "other"' (Somers, this volume, p. 149). It is possible, however, to construe this differently – as part of the ongoing challenge to judge what might be an acceptable simplification, 'central to many debates about how to teach history' (Harris et al., 2014, p. 249), and, in particular, the need to cultivate students' 'period sensitivity' highlighted by Counsell (2003). If it is impossible to escape the way in which we shape how students project the self into some figures in the past or the moral framework in which they are discussed, then these complex issues arising from how we constitute diversity for curricular purposes could be addressed across the longer time period that students spend studying history. What we *can* do is to strive for our curriculum design choices to reflect the 'differences within and between groups' (QCA/DCSF, 2007, p. 112) so that students are not *always* promoting a self that is from the same gender, ethnic, religious or cultural group. Even in a conventional Year 7 programme of study they might, for example, identify with Watt Tyler, Elizabeth I and Saladin. As for the transmission of values, this is part of a bigger, and ever-continuing, discussion about the purposes of history education that always goes far beyond one enquiry, whatever the topic.

Concluding thoughts: making new connections

Reflecting on three chapters with ostensibly differing curricular foci prompted me to make a range of connections – both connections between Harcourt, Somers and Worth and with wider material. I will conclude by summarizing these as three questions:

How can history teachers support students' identification with the past?

Wineburg's 'tension between the familiar and the strange' (2001, pp. 6–7) has the former providing comfort, the latter opening up the humanizing possibilities of history. Harcourt and Somers conclude that this is a tension their students find hard to negotiate in short spaces of time. This put me in mind of Lee and Shemilt's progression model of students' conceptions of historical empathy, defined as 'a way of explaining past forms of life that were different from ours, and a disposition to recognise the possibility and importance of making them intelligible' (2011, p. 48). Their model shows what teachers might be looking for in their students as they develop over several years through sequences such as Harcourt's sound walk or Somers' carefully chosen content and enquiry focus. I was further struck by the pertinence of a recent article by McCrory (2013), who sets out to draw together curricular notions of similarity/difference (or diversity) as content and as concept. Through intricately structured learning activities and the winning enquiry question, 'How many people does it take to make an Essex man?', she explores a way of helping lower secondary school students to know more about human differences in the past, to be able to *think* clearly about them as *differences* and to be better disposed towards seeing these in the future. Her work offers a way for students to begin to shift their encounters with the familiar through an excitement about investigating the strange. This could become illuminating within the curriculum focus both of Somers and of Harcourt.

How can history teachers empower students through learning the language of historical analysis, especially first-order, substantive concepts?

If historical knowledge involves knowing both about the past and about the basis on which historians' claims are made (Lee, 2011a), then as students move through this complexity, they will always need frameworks and common reference points in structures of substantive knowledge even if – indeed precisely *because* – they must be open to later having them disrupted or to rebuilding them as new narratives in response to other kinds of questions. They need some substance as starting points both so as to interpret and explain the past themselves and to grasp the status of others' interpretations and explanations. Teachers and researchers have provided diverse, potential foundations for this, ranging from the synoptic, provisional factual scaffolds theorized in Shemilt (2009) to Counsell's (1997) work as a classroom teacher suggesting that the organizing work of a substantive concept (such as 'peasantry' or 'empire') can be better understood and exploited by pupils struggling to write essays when linked to the organizing work of an analytic paragraph. Worth's and Somers' students, too, were needing to become secure in certain abstract, generalizing concepts, such as 'dictatorship' and 'empire' while simultaneously realizing their mutability and hidden voices. How teachers might build in this substantive dimension in a way that simultaneously provides *both* this secure mastery *and* a sense of the openness of such concepts is currently being taken forward by practitioner research. Palek's (2015) exploratory study of the relationship between substantive knowledge and second-order analysis looked for ways in which students' security in substantive concepts enhanced their capacity to engage in causal reasoning and argument. Hammond (2014) has recently examined the multilayered structure of students' substantive knowledge of a particular time and place for their relationship with larger bodies of substantive knowledge acquired earlier. All these relationships between the substantive security and the ways in which it must be disrupted by the disciplinary or second-order work of argument would suggest, as Worth seems to imply, that the way in which evidential thinking and interpretations of the past are separated from 'knowledge' in examination contexts should be revisited.

How, as professional learners, can history teachers best operate constructively within the external frameworks set by national examinations?

Like Worth and Harcourt, Palek (2015) and Hammond (2014) are teachers balancing the limitations of examinations and their ambitions for students' deep historical understanding. This reminded me of the work of Harris (2001) and Laffin (2009, 2012), who, writing a decade apart, show us how this can be done successfully with post-16 classes. The common features of all of these studies are the way in which their authors somehow align their own sense of what good history teaching is with the objectives of the examination syllabi, while using assessment not to chase examination mark schemes but to support dialogue with students about history itself. These teachers are highly attuned and responsive to the needs of individual students, both as budding historians and as future educated people, and they focus consistently both on pupils' secure knowledge and on how it is expressed, while also drawing on wider research. The experienced teacher also keeps an eye on wider research and engages critically with it through the prism of good history teaching, a task of practical and intellectual complexity that Banham and Hall (2013) exemplify. To be able to do all these things at once is a high aspiration for experienced and highly reflective teachers. I remember finding it a daunting prospect with my first examination classes, yet this shows the value of hearing Worth sharing the detail of her pedagogic planning process and her simultaneous, painstaking investigation. It allows us to arrive *with* her at her curricular re-think about the interplay and, therefore, about the relative status, of components of evidential thinking.

History's Distinctive Contribution to Critical Citizenship

Reflections on Chapters by Rick Rogers, Rachel Foster and Ellen Buxton

Mark Sheehan

17

Rogers, Foster and Buxton have theorized on how young people develop critical, evidence-based understandings of the past especially with regard to causation, continuity and change. These are core historical thinking concepts, and the authors provide a number of useful insights that illuminate how the use of such concepts can be translated from theoretical notions about teaching and learning historical thinking into innovative classroom practice. They are creative exemplars of teachers theorizing in some depth about their practice informed by (and contributing to) the historical thinking literature. This discussion will explore the fine-grained analysis of their practice that these authors have contributed to the field through the lens of critical citizenship. In particular it asks why these models of teaching and learning matter beyond the history classroom and is based on the premise that if young people are to learn think independently and participate confidently as critical citizens in a rapidly changing globalized environment, they need to be historically literate. That is they need to have access to historical knowledge and ways of thinking that equip them intellectually to engage critically with notions such as identity, place and heritage and to participate constructively in conversations about the past, the present and the future.

Developing the ability to think historically and be informed critical citizens is especially challenging in a New Zealand setting because only a minority of students learn to think critically about the past. The curriculum does not prioritize subject-specific knowledge (Ministry of Education, 2007) and allows teachers considerable autonomy in what they choose to teach. Although historical thinking is emerging as a prominent feature of senior secondary school history programmes in New Zealand (Harcourt and Sheehan, 2012; Davison, Enright and Sheehan, 2014), history is only offered as a senior school option. History is not a core subject, and in the compulsory curriculum (Years 1–10; ages 5–14) it is subsumed in the integrated subject of social studies where students are unlikely to engage with historical ideas.

Each of these three chapters contributes to young people developing the dispositions and attitudes of critical citizens through developing the ability to think historically about the past. Historical thinking about questions related to change, causation and continuity is at odds with the uncritical nature of popular approaches to history. It challenges 'common sense' beliefs and uninformed opinions about the past. Like all disciplinary knowledge, historical interpretations are fallible and open to question. It is an appreciation of the fallibility of disciplinary knowledge and its openness to alternative viewpoints (Young, 2013) that serves as a major contribution of historical thinking to critical citizenship and as such distinguishes critical citizenship from notions of citizenship that are based on dogmatic and fixed beliefs. Historical thinking requires young people to engage with complexity and uncertainty and thus plays a vital role in preparing them to engage confidently with an uncertain (and largely unknowable) future.

Rogers argues that young people need to develop a 'Big History' chronological framework of the past: exploring patterns of change and development across a broad timescale so that they can understand how the present (and future) connects with the past and develop a sense of historical consciousness that goes beyond the deliberate decisions and conscious intentions of individuals to an appreciation of broad themes and trends across time. The importance of young people having access to a chronological framework to make sense of the past has been a concern of history educators for years. Shemilt has noted that many adolescents leave school with 'bits and pieces of knowledge that add up to very little and fail to validly inform, or even connect with their perceptions of present realities' (Shemilt, 2009, p. 142). Although typically a focus on teaching chronology has been explicitly concerned with developing (or maintaining) the social cohesion of the nation-state (Guyver and Taylor, 2011) and transforming young people into citizens who believe they belong to 'imagined communities' (Anderson, 1983), the model of 'Big History' frameworks goes beyond this. Expanding the time-frame means that historical themes and trends are not bounded by 'periods' or 'ages' (that are often ethnocentric and can lead to misunderstandings about change). Rather, young people can develop big picture understandings and make generalizations about large patterns in the past (Shemilt, 2009, pp. 167–169).

Mastering a core body of historical information (including a sense of chronology) is a crucial stepping stone in learning how to think critically about the past. However, while developing a grasp of long-term historical trends has the potential to provide young people with a secure platform of foundational knowledge, informing their understanding of change over time, without the ability to interrogate these overviews in relation to the details from which they have been built, students can only treat them as information. From a critical citizenship perspective 'Big History' does not contribute to young people being able to think for themselves or make independent judgements unless (as Rogers argues) students develop the ability to problematize the notion of frameworks. This means that young people's sense of chronology must be premised on the understanding that narratives of the past (constructed on whatever timescale) are open to critique and often contested. So, in identifying patterns of change and development in the broad scale, young people need to be equipped to ask why some aspects of the past are included in the narrative and other aspects excluded. They learn these ways of thinking by mastering the intellectual tools that historians use when they produce and critique knowledge (Wineburg, 2001; Lévesque, 2008; Seixas and Morton, 2013). They understand that history is a sceptical, critical discipline and that historians typically see their role as 'puncturing myths, demolishing orthodoxies and exposing politically motivated narratives that advance spurious claims to objectivity' (Evans 1997, p. 4). In a classroom setting, young people need to be exposed to a variety of different accounts of the past and to develop the 'means to assess the relative strengths and weaknesses of these interpretations' (Seixas, 2000, p. 25). Rather than simply learning a number of historical narratives (whatever the timescale on which they are constructed), young people need learn how to think historically so that they can make their own informed, analytical judgments about the past and adjudicate between competing claims to historical 'truth', thus equipping them to participate confidently in society as critical citizens (Johnson and Morris, 2010).

Foster's chapter is in the tradition of teachers' theorizing about teaching and learning in response to particular concerns that emerge from their classroom practice. In this case her concern was that the way her students understood change was 'devoid of analytical precision'. The focus of her research was to discover how students could construct more refined and accurate understandings of the process of historical change, encompassing the idea (for example) that change typically includes progression, regression and continuity. A particular contribution that this model makes to developing critical citizenship, one that is central to Foster's work, is her specific critique of the way in which models used for examining change tend to become aligned with a focus on *causation* and so serve to distract young people from recognizing and making sense of the complexity of change. This has given rise to models of chronological change that are overly deterministic and do not require students to problematize change. Just as Rogers does, in pointing specifically to the need for students to understand the interpretive nature of 'Big History' frameworks, so Foster argues that if students are to analyse the extent, nature and direction of change (and to construct descriptions of the patterns of change that are genuinely evidence-based), they need to understand how to isolate and define the constituent properties of change (Counsell, 2011c).

Buxton argues that counterfactual history has the potential to provide insights into how to analyse and investigate causation. Although the idea of counterfactual history is controversial within the academic community (Megill, 2007; Glynn and Booth, 1985; Evans, 2014), it resonates powerfully in the wider public imagination and, as Buxton demonstrates, serves as a useful pedagogic device to engage young people in thinking critically about the past. The idea of counterfactual history, with its combination of strangeness and familiarity, appeals to the inherent curiosity of young people about the past – a curiosity that is not unrelated to the fascination that history holds for the wider public. Museums and heritage parks are popular sites of entertainment and feature films; television period-dramas and novels often draw on the past. Recent decades have seen an increasing interest in genealogy, in the preservation and restoration of historic buildings and in the erection of memorials to commemorate particular events. These popular approaches to history are enormously important in encouraging young people to think about the past at an emotional and imaginative level. They can bring history alive, making the events and personalities of the past seem much more real. However such popular histories – although compelling – seldom encourage people to ask difficult questions (Lowenthal, 1996; Timmins, Vernon and Kinealy, 2005). Typically they seek moral clarity and eschew complexity.

In contrast, Buxton's work not only draws on students' historical imagination, it adopts a comparative reasoning approach to counterfactual history that can develop young people's capacity to investigate and genuinely analyse questions of causation. She invites her students to engage with an historically grounded counterfactual model as a means of addressing the enquiry question 'Why was there a revolution in France in 1798?', and the question is framed by a comparison of eighteenth-century France and Britain that encourages students to place the events that they are studying within a wider context. The idea of discerning causes is central to the structure of the discipline, and the ability to identify a cause that surpasses others is often seen by history teachers as indicative of a very high standard of historical thinking. Buxton's comparative approach helps young people to gain purchase on the question, providing them with an analytical tool as well as helping them to appreciate the complex interplay of factors. She too is problematizing the particular historical concept with which her students are working, thereby challenging simplistic or deterministic models.

Thinking critically about the past is an essential disposition of critical citizenship but it is counterintuituive. Indeed, thinking historically has been described as an 'unnatural act' (Wineburg, 2001). For young people to be able to adjudicate between different versions of the past is not a straightforward matter. Typically they make sense of the past based on the narratives presented in the popular media and their beliefs about the past are often shaped by the concerns and preoccupations of the present. To learn how to think critically, young people need to engage with the disciplinary features of history so that they can shift from focusing on the superficial features of knowledge, to develop the habits of mind of experts who tend to think in terms of the deep structures or the underlying principles of knowledge (Gardner, 1985; Bolstad and Gilbert, 2012). What makes historians experts in their field is not only that they have a vast knowledge of the details of a particular event or historical period. Rather it is that they are uniquely placed to explain how human experience has been structured *over time* since that is the particular preserve of history. Expertise thus also depends on the capacity to use core concepts such as change and continuity or causation to structure historical accounts and explanations. It is these ways of thinking, so effectively explored and developed in these chapters, that contribute to young people being intellectually equipped to think for themselves and participate constructively in the democratic process, as informed, critical citizens who can make sense of a complex social world. Each of these teachers has been concerned that pupils should understand the ways of thinking that historians adopt when they produce historical knowledge – indeed that is the core business of teaching and learning history – and by doing so they have made an invaluable contribution to developing the qualities and dispositions that young people require to be critical citizens who can think for themselves.

Part III

Contextualizing History Education Research

Historical Thinking/Historical Knowing: On the Content of the Form of History Education

Arthur Chapman

1. Hereward the Wake was a good ruler over a country. He was ruler over the English people. He was born in the year 1076. He died in the year 1381.

   Thomas à Becket was quite a little boy when he became king. He was a good little king. He was born in the year 1080, and he died in the year 1400.

   Jack Cade was a good ruler and a good man. He was born in the year 1090, and he fought a great rebellion which was called Jack Cade's rebellion. He died in the year 1100 after many happy years.

2. The result of the Norman Conquest was very bad. The Normans won the English at a battle near Newbury. The battle was fought by the Normans in the year 1112.

3. The Magna Charta was a document which had to be signed by King John which was called the Great Charter. It was signed by King John because the Pope wanted King John to sign the document. It was passed in the year 1340. It was a great document. King John was a good king and a good man; he died in the year 1400 . . .

This passage, which continues on for a further five paragraphs not quoted here, is from Maurice Keatinge's pioneering *Studies in the Teaching of History* (Keatinge, 1913, pp. 108–109) and not, as one might perhaps expect, from *1066 and All That* (Sellar and Yeatman, 1975). It reports the answers to questions about 'historical characters and events' given by 'Muriel Howard', a 14-year-old English girl, 'educated in a secondary school', which, Keatinge noted, enjoyed funding from local taxation 'and from the State, as well as the privilege of State inspection' (Keatinge, 1913, p. 108).

I start with 'Muriel' in order to explore some of the challenges that arise in developing children's historical knowledge and understanding and also to underline the fact that these challenges are perennial and persistent – symptoms of the inherent difficulty of the task, rather than, as is often suggested, local and contingent difficulties arising solely from the erroneous framing of curriculum, pedagogy and assessment.[1]

Muriel is now, of course, long dead. We can learn a good deal, nevertheless, from her errors. Muriel's answers are inaccurate – often wildly so – and exemplify a 'problem' with history education outcomes that has been identified again, again and again. Like Professor Matthews' accountancy students, *dramatis personae* in numerous political speeches in recent years in England, Muriel simply does not know the things that she 'should' know (Matthews, 2009).[2] Muriel clearly also is 'not good at establishing . . . chronology', to deploy another familiar *topos* (Ofsted, 2007, p. 4): what belongs apart – Hereward the Wake and King John, for example – comes together in Muriel's writing, which was, it would seem, chrono-illogical to a remarkable degree.

Focusing on factual deficit and chronological lack scarcely begins to scope the dimensions of Muriel's history problem. Muriel's weak grasp of substantive political and anthropological concepts (Carretero and Lee, 2014) adds a further dimension to her difficulties: for Muriel, 'kings' lead 'rebellions' and die at the age of ten, having lived for 'many happy years'. In addition, the persons, events and occurrences in Muriel's text are all equally interchangeable. There is no sense of context in her writing, nor of the embedding of the historical figures that she discusses in the particularities of time or place: all exist in a flat narrative space redolent of the folk or fairy tale. There is still more to Muriel's difficulties, however, and, like those of many other children, they are a matter of presence as much as of absence: Muriel's answers have *form*. As Keatinge observes:

> Everything that has been placed before her is epic . . . For her nothing that is common or mean exists . . . All the kings, queens, or other personages, whether they bear their own names or those of other people, whether they live for ten years or for two hundred years, are 'good' men and 'good' women; all the battles and documents are 'great'. (Keatinge, 1913, p. 109)

Even if all Muriel's 'facts', chronological grasp and understandings of substantive political and anthropological concepts were unimpeachable and embedded in historical context, she would still be ignorant of the ways in which something that we might recognize as history is organized at a 'second-order' or structural level and at a textual level.[3] For Muriel, history is structured as chronicle (Burrow, 2009) in which disconnected moments in a nation's political history succeed each other as a series – in sequence but mostly without *con*sequence or intelligible *structural* interconnection. At the level of the moments themselves, unity is a matter of subject (the personage who occurs in each sentence) rather than episode, in the majority of cases, and structure a matter of predication ('was a good king', 'was quite a little boy') rather than narration. Muriel's text is rich in the language of 'appraisal' (Coffin, 2006a), however, it is entirely lacking in reasoning. Muriel's evaluations are pronouncements, or statements of received opinion, not reasoned historical judgements, and where the language of explanation is present (there is one 'because' in the 195 words quoted) it is used rather than grounded.[4]

Muriel's difficulties are, of course, of their time in important senses. Ideas about what history is and about what school history should be have changed a very great deal in the last hundred years. It is no accident, perhaps, that we can hear 'echoes' of *1066 and All That* in Muriel's writing: the latter is very probably a product of the kind of history education that the former sought to debunk. Although Muriel was probably not asked to 'Stigmatize cursorily

(a) Queen Mary' or '(b) Judge Jeffrey's asides' or to 'Outline joyfully (1) Henry VIII' or '(2) Stout Cortez' (Sellar and Yeatman, 1975, p. 85), it is not difficult to perceive the echo of analogous understandings of school history – as an exercise in memorizing and repeating judgemental recounts of past political actors and events – in Muriel's efforts to deliver what she thinks her teachers expect.

School history can, of course, be understood in the way that *1066 and All That* satirized and on the model of the history education that Muriel very probably experienced – as consisting of a 'monumental' narrative (Nietzsche, 1983), asserting and celebrating the achievements of past actors (Conway, 2005), transmitted to 'children sitting in rows, learning the kings and queens of England' (Faulkner, 2010). There are very good reasons, however, for doubting both the practical efficacy and the democratic viability of school history education understood in this way, and it is very doubtful, of course, whether an approach of this kind can, in fact, be called either history or historical (Evans, 2011; Cannadine, 2013).[5]

*   *   *

It is only if thought-compelling exercises can be devised that history is worth treating as a serious school subject and, it may now be added, it is only if this formal element be there that history can be of real value as moral training. (Keatinge, 1913, p. 110)

Such was Keatinge's response to Muriel, who he conceded was 'no doubt an extreme case' of what could happen as a consequence of 'postponing the critical stage' in 'secondary' education (Keatinge, 1913, p. 110). Keatinge's *Studies in the Teaching of History* – and extensive subsequent work in textbook production lasting over twenty years – was a sustained attempt to work out what school history might look like if it took history seriously *as a discipline* and a *mode of knowledge production* and aimed to develop children's knowledge *and* understanding of the past, their motivation to know and learn about the past and their ability to think about history in intellectually engaged ways (Chapman, 2014).

Over the last forty years, and more, a nationally and internationally influential tradition has developed in the UK that aims to achieve precisely these aims by understanding school history education as an education in a 'form of knowledge' or 'discipline'.[6] This tradition was inspired more by Jerome Bruner's argument that it was possible to for school 'subjects' to express the epistemological structure and logic of the academic subjects on which they were modelled in authentic ways and at an age-appropriate level of complexity (Bruner, 1966, p. 72; 1996, p. 19; Rogers, 1979; Chapman, 2010), and/or by Paul Hirst's arguments about 'forms of knowledge' as tools for curriculum organization (Hirst, 1974; Shemilt, 1983), than it was by the work of thinkers like Keatinge.[7] The model has proved internationally influential and helped to shape thinking about curriculum, pedagogy and assessment in the United States (Donovan, Bransford and Pellegrino, 1999; Wineburg, 2001, 2007; Donovan and Branford, 2005), in Canada (Lévesque, 2008; Seixas and Morton, 2013), in Australia (Taylor and Young, 2003; Parkes and Donnelly, 2014) and elsewhere (Nakou and Barca, 2010).

For this tradition, learning history involves acquiring knowledge and understanding of the past – 'first-order' or substantive knowledge of the past and of concepts essential to its comprehension and 'second-order' or structural knowledge and understanding of how history works as a form of knowing. The latter includes a grasp of the cognitive tools that are used to generate first-order knowledge (historical enquiry and historical evidence) and of the cognitive tools that are used to organize and structure first-order knowledge and understanding in usable and intelligible ways (concepts such as change, cause, significance, and so on).

This distinction – between first- and second-order knowledge and understanding – does not map onto the overused distinction between 'knowledge' and 'skills', although it has often been understood in these ways both by critics (Cain and Chapman, 2014) and by some practitioners of the 'new history' (Lee, 2014). Second-order knowledge and understanding is not generic and not something that can be mastered merely by practice as skills can be; rather, second-order understandings are developed through reflection and through historical problem solving, processes essential to *knowledge building* and *knowledge organizing* more generally (Lee, 2005b).

The 'second-order' is not secondary – in the sense of being a mere supplement to 'primary' factual knowledge.[8] It is better understood as *meta*historical knowledge and understanding – as knowledge and understanding *about* historical knowledge and understanding. Second-order knowledge and understanding is fundamental to the development of substantive knowledge in history above the level of isolated or aggregated 'facts': it helps both *to form* substantive knowledge (assisting in knowledge building) and gives substantive knowledge *form* (assisting in organizing and structuring substantive knowledge).[9] To illustrate and exemplify:

- Without an understanding of the concepts of time and chronology (Blow, Lee and Shemilt, 2012) and change and continuity (Blow, 2011a), it is difficult and probably impossible to develop a *narrative* understanding of a series of discrete events *as a sequence* of events. Without some grasp of these concepts, it might be possible to develop understandings of isolated episodes, as Muriel perhaps did, but this is a knowledge of fragments only and not knowledge of coherent narrative wholes. Sequences of events exist in time and colligating aspects of sequences into higher-order wholes (such a 'revolutions') entails temporal understandings with which to reflect on duration and alteration, aspects of change and continuity without which narratives are impossible, since without them there can be nothing to 'tell' (Rimmon-Kenan, 1983).
- Without an understanding of cause and effect, it is impossible to develop a coherent understanding of what makes events and developments events and developments *in a narrative*. Narrative requires 'plot' and causes and consequences are the ties that bind isolated 'story elements' together, *constituting them as a narrative* of which we can ask and answer questions such as 'Why did it happen?', 'What did that lead to?' and so on (Goldstein, 1976; Rimmon-Kenan, 1983).
- Without some understanding of what an historical account is, and of the range of different genres of historical writing and representation (Counsell, 2004b; Coffin, 2006a, 2006b; Chapman, 2011a), it is unlikely that students will develop competence and confidence in writing history – an essential tool for both the *expression* and the *integration* of knowledge fragments into intelligible and interrogable wholes.
- Without some sense of the role of enquiry and evidence in the construction of historical knowledge (Collingwood, 1994), it is unlikely that students will develop a coherent sense of what it *is* that they are

learning – of the *warrant* that differentiates 'fact' from myth or propaganda (Rogers, 1979) and of the degrees of certainty with which different kinds of historical claim can be held or advanced (McCullagh, 1984; Megill, 2007). Furthermore, without some understanding of historical epistemology, students will be unlikely to be able to deal confidently with historical uncertainty when it arises in their study of the past, as it inevitably must, or with controversy and disagreement – both of which are necessary in history classrooms, if the debates through which historical knowledge develops are to be modelled and understood, and both of which are unavoidable in our contemporary present where contrasting claims about the past arise with great frequency (Lowenthal, 1985, 1998; Ankersmit, 1994; Wertsch, 2002).

Much of the labour of history teachers, curriculum developers and history education researchers working within the 'form of knowledge' tradition over the last forty years has been devoted to trying to understand how to integrate first- and second-order dimensions of historical learning organically so that both develop together, in cumulative and mutually enhancing ways, and so as to enable historical knowing to be meaningfully realized in and through classroom practice (Lee, 2014).

*   *   *

The teacher-authored research chapters at the core of this book wrestle with the challenge of developing historical knowledge and understanding in contemporary classrooms. What resources do they draw upon and what questions do they pose and pursue?

A count of the books, articles and other materials referenced by each of the authors reveals that 363 items are referenced in their chapters as a whole.[10] These materials fall into types, the largest of which are as follows:

- 195 (53.7%) items of history education literature;
- 36 (9.9%) items of philosophy or critical theory;
- 29 (8%) works on research method and methodology;
- 27 (7.4%) government curricular documents;
- 23 (6.3%) works of historiography or philosophy of history; and
- 20 (5.5%) works of history.

The majority of the history education items (182, or 93.3%) are publications by British authors and 111 (57.2%) are articles published in *Teaching History*.

Insofar as it makes sense to make claims about a group of authors in aggregate and on the basis of a crude reference count, we can infer the following:

- Our authors' research is located firmly within a British tradition of teacher-authored history education research.
- Our authors are driven by practical pedagogical concerns (*teaching* history), but – and this highlights the limitations of the overused distinction between 'theory/practice' – they are decidedly theoretical in the optic that they bring to these concerns, as the relative incidence of philosophical or metahistorical works and of works of history in the reference count indicates.

As their chapter titles show, seven of our eight authors are concerned with conceptual issues and six of these seven with second-order concepts (such as change, evidence and causation). One author approaches history in an interdisciplinary manner and one author takes what one might call a 'third order' – or meta-metahistorical – approach, critically appraising an historical concept ('diversity').

The detail of our authors' arguments clearly shows, however, that it would be a serious misreading of their work to contend that their concern with historical thinking detracts from in-depth engagement with historical knowing. Buxton, for example, is clearly concerned with developing her pupils' conceptual grasp, and devises a series of scaffolds and strategies to achieve this; however, she returns again and again in her enquiry to the *grain* of the historical past, introducing more 'content' (eighteenth-century England) than many teachers might think it necessary to adduce in order to help her pupils grasp and grapple with the history *and* the historical questions that they were learning about (the French Revolution and its causes).

* * *

All our chapters succeed, in differing ways, in demonstrating the power of a disciplinary approach to planning and teaching history. There is extensive evidence, in the examples of pupil thinking cited, to support the contention that the pedagogic approaches that our teacher-authors develop can enable considerable sophistication in their pupils' historical knowledge and understanding. The contrasts between the *kinds* of historical knowing exemplified in these chapters and Muriel's 'epic' inaccuracies are both striking and telling.

Understanding how we can help pupils sophisticate their thinking and understanding the preconceptions that can act as barriers to the development of their thinking have been central concerns of history education research for many years in England (Shemilt, 1980, 1983 and 1987; Lee and Ashby, 2000; Lee and Shemilt, 2003; Lee, 2005b) and elsewhere (Wineburg, 2001 and 2007; Seixas and Morton, 2013). Progression is analogue rather than binary – a matter of *degree* and of *continua* of sophistication rather than an 'all or nothing' affair (Lee, 1991). It is sometimes urged against the 'form of knowledge' approach to historical thinking that it is futile and self-defeating – experts and novices are, the argument goes, radically different things, and it is simply not possible to get 'students to think like real . . . historians' (Willingham, 2009, p. 127). 'Like' is, of course, an ambiguous word that can denote identity or analogy and although critics of pedagogies that aim to develop 'thinking like an historian' tend to understand 'like' in the first sense, advocates of these pedagogies tend to understand 'like' in the second sense (Wineburg, 2007, p. 11). As has long been understood, the notion that children can or should be 'doing what historians do' is 'either pretentious "claptrap" or an imprecise statement of something more modest' (Dickinson, Gard and Lee, 1978, p. 13). There is ample evidence in our authors' chapters that reflective and metahistorically informed pedagogic design, focused on the development of 'historical thinking', can have very positive impacts on the quality – and on the qualities – of children's historical knowledge and understanding. Asking the question 'How can I help my students think *more* histori-cally?' can be a powerful tool for enhancing what children know, how they come to know it and how they understand what they come to know. It is also apparent that the question can be a powerful one in helping teachers interrogate and develop their pedagogy.

*   *   *

Wineburg argues that the 'specification of ignorance' is a key feature of disciplined histori-cal thinking (Wineburg, 2007, p. 11). Before we can find new things out, or come to new understandings of things we are already acquainted with, we have first to *recognize the limits* of what we know.

I will end by drawing attention to one of the limitations of the tradition on which this chapter has focused. Work in this tradition has tended to be *descriptive* (e.g. focused on mod-elling progression) or *small-scale* and *tentative* in its conclusions.[11] What is true of the wider tradition is true of the teacher-authored research chapters in this book that aim to continue, develop and extend it. Many of our authors – for example, Foster – show what *can* be done or that an intervention *can* lead to outcomes of a particular kind. Some of our authors – for example, Worth and Somers – are able to challenge claims about what is or is not *possible* or *desirable* by presenting warranted practice-evidence or conceptual argument. It would be very valuable to supplement work that can ground claims of these kinds with work whose research design and/or scale enables more *decisive* conclusions, and this is particularly so in contexts where curricular and pedagogic reforms are often urged in rather polemical ways on the basis of limited research evidence.[12] It is very valuable to be able to show, for example, on the basis of large-scale American quasi-experimental research, that classroom strategies that draw on research in the 'form of knowledge' tradition (Wineburg, 2001) and that aim to help young people 'read like an historian', have *demonstrable positive effects* on

> (a) students' historical thinking; (b) their ability to transfer historical thinking strategies to con-temporary issues; (c) their mastery of factual knowledge; and (d) their growth in general reading comprehension. (Reisman, 2012, p. 88)

Fordham is right to call, in the conclusion to his chapter in this volume, for further collabora-tive research on a large scale into the development of historical thinking and knowing. As we have seen, the small-scale work that our teacher-authors report in this volume makes a pow-erful contribution to innovation and improvement in history education. There is scope for combining innovative teacher-research with research designs that can yield conclusions of the kind that Reisman reports, as is clearly shown by recent work in the Netherlands that uses a 'quasi-experimental pre-test–post-test' design, *inter alia*, to test the power of a pedagogic strategy developed through English teacher-author research (Stoel, Van Drie and Van Boxtel, 2015). History education is a house with many mansions. Perhaps it is time to encourage more movement between rooms?

Sustaining the Unresolving Tensions within History Education and Teacher Education

Katharine Burn

19

While history teachers and teacher educators in England have long sought to challenge the 'distracting' (Counsell, 2000) and 'dysfunctional' (Cain and Chapman, 2014) dichotomies that plague public discussion of history curricula and pedagogy by politicians and the press, observing the ways in which colleagues working in other contexts and in different fields of education are similarly wrestling with the reduction of 'complex educational debates to bipolar slogans' (Alexander, 2008) has been both consoling and inspirational. While I have deliberately chosen to echo Megill's reference to the 'unresolving dialectic' of history to encapsulate the themes within this chapter, they are perhaps equally well reflected in Young's social realist campaign to resist a sterile reversion to 'Future 1' as the consequence of rejecting the relativism of 'Future 2', or in Elliott's recognition, in the chapters that he read, of Stenhouse's vision of the 'teacher as researcher'. Although Megill applied the concept specifically to history on the assumption that this characteristic made it unlike most other forms of knowledge, it may prove equally helpful in thinking about the nature of education (including teacher education) where further distinct constellations of tensions abound.

The beauty of Megill's adjective as applied to the discipline of history is the emphasis that it places on the need to leave the ends of each continuum – of which he suggests there are many – in perpetual tension: historical *experience* confronting historical *interpretation*; an impulse towards *universality* vying with an emphasis on the *particular*. There is no expectation of neat resolution; historians must learn to live with the 'persisting presence of mutually contradictory entities or orientations' (Megill, this volume, p. 159). Megill suggests that this presents relatively few difficulties for historians themselves – the majority preferring not to enquire too closely into the logical structure of a 'notoriously un-theoretical' discipline. Problems arise, however, for those obliged to think more carefully about that structure in order to make it accessible to young people in school. It is precisely because they are so concerned to find effective ways of *developing* historical knowing that the history teachers contributing to this book place such an emphasis on making explicit the apparently contradictory elements that they know need to be held together. While the interplay between them has to be creative, the teachers' overriding concern is that it should not be confused. While some degree of disaggregation is essential, as Watts clearly recognizes (this volume, pp. 154–155), in order to make the different components intelligible to beginners, there is no point in generating a series of essentially atomized objectives that, by their very nature, distort the nature of historical knowledge.

Recognizing the essential relationships between different concepts and processes

The fundamental relationship *between* first and second-order concepts is a recurring theme of this book, and indeed, as Chapman (this volume, pp. 228–229) has eloquently summarized, of history education research over many decades. While there is no need to revisit it here, it is worth highlighting other examples of history teachers' concern to understand the relationship between different elements of the historical process and hold them together effectively. One such example is Worth's exploration of the processes by which she can support the development of students' understanding of sources and capacity to make evidence-based claims. Her conclusion, supported by Skinner's (2002) argument against categorical distinction between description of text and explanation of context, explicitly challenges simplistic notions of a two-stage process or hierarchy separating 'comprehension' and 'evaluation'. The implications of this conclusion for history teachers are profound, given that so many of them are wrestling not only with the rigid formulations of examining boards, but also with inflexible whole-school teaching and learning policies in which Bloom's taxonomy of educational objectives (Anderson and Krathwohl, 2001) is enshrined as an ideal, with no respect for the nature of knowledge or the processes by which it is constructed in different subjects.[1] Given this context, Foster's careful analysis of historians' discourse and detailed exploration of the properties manifest in students' writing about change and continuity are similarly important in holding together within history education processes that others would artificially separate. Not only does Foster's research result in a powerful exposition of the importance of *combining* 'description' with 'analysis' (cognitive processes that are assigned to separate levels in hierarchical interpretations of Bloom's taxonomy), she goes further, calling for thorough consideration of what might constitute 'argument' in the context of that analytic description.

Planning for progression: getting the structure and the sequence right

Given this concern to hold together both the genuinely contradictory orientations that Megill discerns within history and other (more compatible) concepts and processes that policymakers have persistently sought to separate, it is hardly surprising that history teachers highlight the critical importance of the structure and sequence of curricular planning, determining the most effective order in which to introduce the different components to young people. While Fordham calls, for example, for further research in relation to securing *progression* in students' understanding of substantive concepts, Hammond suggests that more attention be paid in teachers' published discourse to the question of *when* students are made aware of the constructed nature of historical knowledge in relation to the development of their knowledge of particular historical narratives. Rogers' investigation of the effects of presenting 11-year-old students with a low-resolution narrative of the past as a whole, as the *prelude* to their study of history at secondary school level, allows him to test a particular hypothesis about the order in which young people's encounters with the past should be structured. Buxton's discovery of the power of comparative history in supporting students' causal reasoning has obvious implications both in terms of curriculum content and the sequence in which it is taught.

Structure and sequence (i.e. curriculum design) are of fundamental importance in tackling another apparent dichotomy, highlighted by Young: the challenge of providing genuinely powerful knowledge *for all,* and not simply highest attainers. Watts expresses surprise at 'the sophistication of the intellectual tasks which children of 11, 12 and 13 are carrying out' (this volume, p. 154); Young is delighted by the range of practical examples demonstrating the capacity of students in all-ability classes to engage effectively in the types of historical argument practised by historians. Those students are able to do so precisely because of the curricular theorizing in which their teachers have engaged, exemplified both in their carefully crafted enquiry sequences and in the analytical and creative tools that they design to meet precisely specified needs; tools such as Foster's geographical metaphors (this volume, p. 14) or Worth's modification of Wiltshire's (2000) 'language of uncertainty' (Table 5.9).[2]

Teacher as researcher: acknowledging the relationship between teaching and learning

As these examples illustrate, getting the structure and sequencing right depends on thorough knowledge of students' existing understandings and current difficulties, which means bridging another overdrawn dichotomy – the distinction between 'teacher-led' and 'child-centred' learning. History teachers cannot simply map out the journey that *they* want their students to take; they have to know exactly where those students are coming from and what resources they already have with which to navigate the terrain. Understanding the learners' preconceptions involves not just identifying *mis*conceptions to be addressed because the 'everyday' knowledge that they embody impedes the construction of disciplinary or 'scientific' concepts, but also recognizing where those everyday concepts can serve as an effective foundation for particular aspects of disciplinary thinking.[3] Fordham's discovery of his students' tendency to equate the abstract with the ideal alerts him to a potential stumbling block that will need to be removed in developing their capacity to generalize. In contrast, Foster explores whether students' existing understandings of the nature, extent and pace of change brought about by certain geographical phenomena will prove productive in developing their capacity to characterize historical change.

It is this need to know what ideas students bring to the historical questions asked of them and how they respond to the structured steps that their teachers hypothesize will help them to move forward that essentially *requires* teachers to be researchers. Hammond instinctively recognizes this in the parallel that she draws between the thematic coding undertaken by different teachers to determine what exactly their students were thinking and the processes of careful reading and re-reading of students' work that have to be invested in developing a task-specific mark scheme. History teachers' long experimentation with such mark schemes (as a means of effectively recognizing the development of substantive knowledge *together with* the second-order concepts that underpin and give such knowledge its form) (Burnham and Brown, 2004; Brown and Burnham, 2014) illustrates one of the ways in which they have sought to resolve some of the challenges for assessment of which Elliott (this volume, p. 182) reminds us in Stenhouse's *process* model of curriculum design.

Elliott's detailed discussion of the ways in which the work of Foster, Somers and Worth so closely reflects Stenhouse's conception of 'teacher as researcher' provides precise exemplification of aspects of the claim that Fordham (2015a) has made elsewhere about the realization of Stenhouse's ideal in history teachers' published discourse. The fact that Fordham's claim is based on a citation analysis of research published by history teachers in the professional journal *Teaching History*, demonstrating the extent to which they are also drawing on, developing and critiquing one another's work, also allows him to argue that they have created a 'sustained and coherent research tradition that transcends the boundaries of particular contexts and, as such, represents a coherent, codified body of professional knowledge' (Fordham, 2015a, p.13).

Shared programmes of research: combining the insights from educational research conducted from different perspectives and on different scales

To claim that history teachers' published discourse has overcome the weaknesses and limitations with which action research is often associated – its failure to build systematically on what is known and to make its findings public (Furlong, 2013) – is certainly *not* to claim that *all* that is needed is teacher research. Just as Stenhouse envisaged an essential role for professional research workers, so the practitioners in this volume explicitly draw on, call for more, and point to specific gaps in, what Van Drie and Van Boxtel (this volume, p. 207) have termed, 'fundamental research' in history education. Fordham's citation analysis again bears this out: while 42 per cent of the references cited by history teachers in their published research were works written by other teacher-researchers, 21 per cent were the products of empirical research in history education – by which he means 'large-scale empirical enquiries that examined history education through the lenses of the psychology, sociology, history and philosophy of education' (Fordham, 2015a, p. 11). In reflecting on the implications of his own small-scale exploratory study, Fordham explicitly calls for 'collaboration between those interested in conducting a wider research study of pupil progression in history and those professionals who wish to explore the ways in which substantive concepts operate as curriculum components' (Fordham, this volume, p. 57). Exemplifying a similar commitment to working together, Rogers' exploration of the use of low-resolution narratives is already located within a programme of research advanced by the Frameworks Working Group, originally established at the Institute of Education and Leeds Trinity University College. The collaborative project reported by Magnoff's was conducted as part of the History Virtual Academy Project (Chapman, 2009a; Chapman, Elliott and Poole, 2012) which brought together history teachers and university-based history education researchers along with professional historians.

Learning to become a teacher-researcher: a simultaneous not sequential process

While it might be argued that these are exceptional history teachers and that a research orientation cannot be expected of the majority, the very nature of teaching – the constant need to examine students' developing knowledge and understanding as they respond to the questions and activities devised for them – means that *every* teacher requires the capacity to interpret and make sense of what is happening within their own classroom. The profound but productive dilemma that Worth encountered struck her *not* as an experienced professional but as a newly qualified teacher. Magnoff was not much further advanced in his career when his concern about his AS level students' understanding of the process by which historians' interpretations are constructed prompted him to join a research collaboration.

This is precisely why the final report of the BERA-RSA inquiry into the role of research in teacher education concludes in the following manner:

> A focus on enquiry-based practice needs to be sustained during initial teacher education pro-
> grammes and throughout teachers' professional careers, so that disciplined innovation and collabo-
> rative enquiry are embedded within the lives of schools or colleges and become the normal way of
> teaching and learning, rather than the exception. (BERA-RSA, 2014, p. 6)

The force of this argument *seems* to have been accepted in England by the Carter Review of Initial Teacher Training, which begins with an outline of effective models of teacher development in which the notion of 'teacher as researcher' is explicitly endorsed (Carter, 2015, p. 22). Yet its subsequent recommendations adopt a more restricted conception of research engagement, closer to a 'theory into practice' model. Trainees, it is suggested, need 'timely opportunities to apply theory in the classroom' and although they are also encouraged to 'reflect upon their experience afterwards', this is a faint shadow of the genuinely *reflexive* practice that Elliott endorses. Similarly, its recommendation that 'a central portal of synthesized executive summaries providing advice on research findings about effective teaching in different subjects' should be developed is a pale imitation of Fordham's description of initial teacher education (ITE) programmes in which induction into the profession involves 'gaining some mastery over a body of professional knowledge, including identifying ways in which that knowledge base can and needs to be extended' (Fordham, 2015a, p. 14).

Carter's restricted recommendations are explained with reference to the challenges for trainees of 'learning how to teach as well as undertaking quality research in a one-year course, unless these two areas are skilfully brought together in a way that support each other' (Carter, 2015, p. 53). While skilful curriculum planning is certainly called for, successful integration also depends on close collaboration between the partners involved in any ITE programme. But obviation of the need for such planning by postponing beginning teachers' development as researchers – which is essentially what Carter does by suggesting that it is sufficient for them merely to become 'intelligent consumers of research' by the time they qualify – is a woefully inadequate solution that robs new teachers of the agency necessary to sustain professional commitment.

The contribution of engagement in research to teachers' sense of agency is highlighted by the review of teachers' perspectives undertaken as part of the BERA-RSA Inquiry (Leat, Reid and Lofthouse, 2015). Among the benefits cited are teachers' claims that their research resulted in renewed feelings of pride and excitement about teaching; reminders of their intellectual capability and its importance to their professional lives; reconnection within their colleagues and their initial commitment to teaching; and a feeling of power, in the sense of having a voice (McLaughlin et al., 2007). These attitudes all resonate profoundly with the moral purpose that Carter is rightly concerned to embed in teacher education, creating a 'strong sense of energy, collective purpose and professionalism' that he is anxious to establish and sustain 'from the point of entry to the profession' (Carter, 2015, p. 25). It therefore makes little sense to suggest delaying development of the capacity to engage effectively in teacher research until some later, unspecified, point in teachers' careers, by which time frustration with their lack of agency may well have driven them from the classroom. While subsequent research engagement may offer an 'antidote' to the more 'restrictive and negative aspects of their working environment' (Leat, Reid and Lofthouse, 2015, p. 275), it is surely better to inoculate beginning teachers against such feelings of constraint and powerlessness during the course of their ITE programme. That is why the final report of the BERA-RSA Inquiry argues that '*every* teacher should have the confidence, ability and capability to engage in research and enquiry activities when the opportunity or need arises' and urges policymakers to recognize the 'potential of *initial* teacher education for the development of teachers' research and enquiry skills and predispositions' (BERA-RSA, 2014, p. 12, my emphases).

Making sense of the missing dimension: the importance of subject-specific research

Despite all the apparently contradictory elements held in tension in this collection, there is one particular continuum – that running between generic and subject-specific pedagogy – on which the contributing teachers align themselves in a distinctly lop-sided fashion. There is much less evidence here of co-dependence or creative interplay. While this is perhaps unsurprising in a collection showcasing the research of passionate and knowledgeable history teachers, their frame of reference again echoes Fordham's (2015a) citation analysis of history teachers' published articles, in which only 9 per cent of the teachers' references were to works presenting generic educational research, including psychological research into how children learn.[4] While Fordham concedes that such generic research may have been less accessible to practising teachers than other kinds of subject material, he essentially concludes that they found little to interest them in it, at least in relation to their published discourse.

There are, I would suggest, two reasons for this. One is the fact that generic research findings – all too often hideously distorted or emptied of meaning through the processes of decontextualization and simplification – are *all* that have been formally offered in recent years to the majority of history teachers in England (i.e. other than to those engaged in high-quality specialist history ITE or masters' programmes in history education). The other reason is that such generic principles (even where they are well-founded and meaningfully exemplified) cannot ever adequately address their core concerns, since the key decisions with which history teachers wrestle are essentially curricular choices about structure and sequence in light of their students' current understandings.

The endorsement, by Carter (2015), of the importance not just of teachers' 'subject knowledge development' but of 'subject-specific pedagogy' is an encouraging acknowledgement of the fundamental importance of what Shulman (1986) termed 'pedagogical content knowledge' – but which actually finds expression not merely as pedagogy but as curricular theorizing. It is encouraging, however, precisely because of the profound *neglect* of the subject-specific dimension within education policy over the past three decades; a neglect that has been compounded in recent teacher education policies, despite the 'knowledge turn' (Lambert, 2011) now reflected in the school curriculum.

While the introduction of the first National Curriculum (established by the Education Act of 1988) might have been expected to bring the distinctive features of different subjects into sharp relief, concerns to establish standardized forms of assessment overrode essential differences between different forms of knowledge (as Fordham outlines, this volume, p. 49). Subject differences were further obscured by the introduction and expansion of the National Strategies, subsequently described as one of the 'most ambitious change management programmes' ever seen in education (DfE, 2011, p. 2). Where the National Curriculum prescribed (in varying degrees of detail over time) *what* was to be taught, the Strategies prescribed the format of that teaching through a series of training materials, establishing key pedagogical principles that, for many teachers, effectively defined the lesson structure of every lesson, regardless of what was to be taught. Although schools, and indeed individual departments, experienced and responded to such policy initiatives in very different ways (Ball, Maguire and Braun, 2012), in many contexts teachers were simply expected to comply. The trend towards genericism, characterized by Young (this volume, p. 188) as 'Future 2', reached its apogee in the framing of the 2008 National Curriculum – expressed, not in the subject specifications themselves (which members of the subject community *were* involved in drafting), but in the associated emphasis on essentially content-free 'Personal Learning and Thinking Skills'.[5]

Although this trend has essentially been reversed by revisions made to the curriculum from 2014, recent teacher education policies are tending to dismantle the stable subject communities that make it possible to introduce new history teachers not merely to a set of decontextualized research findings, but to an ongoing professional discourse, a narrative that outlines the journey that teacher-researchers, in conjunction with 'academic' history education researchers, have taken in refining their collective knowledge base. The thrust of those policies – reflecting an international 'practicum turn' in ITE (Mattsson, Eilertson and Rorrison, 2011) – has been to ensure that 'more training is on the job' (DfE, 2010, p. 23) and that schools, rather than universities, assume the leadership of that training. The rapid expansion of 'School Direct' provision and other employment-based training routes has seen a corresponding fall in the number of history training places allocated to 'university-led' providers (Burn, 2015).

The inherent irony of this attack on 'university-led' provision is that the commitment of university-based educators to nurturing teacher research has played a fundamental role in nurturing *and* sustaining the discourse that has enabled construction of the professional knowledge base on which Fordham (2015a) suggests history teachers' professional autonomy could now be based. It is as advocates of genuinely school-led professional learning that the editors of this book have worked so hard to support the publication of history teacher research, not only within this collection, but as long-standing editors of *Teaching History*, the professional journal of the Historical Association. It is the stability of the ITE partnerships of which we have been part that makes it possible to establish and sustain research-literate communities of history mentors able to induct novices into a living tradition, demonstrating in their own practice how to make critical use of other history teachers' research and contribute to it.

Our concern about the expansion of School Direct is not that it seeks to enhance the leadership role of schools within teacher education; that is an entirely appropriate responsibility for schools to bear. Nor are we opposed to trainee teachers spending most of their time learning in school, observing and guided by skilful history practitioners. Such experience is essential (Burn, Hagger and Mutton, 2015) – and already accounts for at least two-thirds of trainees' time, even on so-called university-led programmes. Our argument is simply that in handing responsibility for training to partnerships of schools (many of which are concerned only about their immediate staff recruitment needs), the scope for coherent planning and the long-term engagement of mentors within a stable subject community is lost. As Justin Champion, president of the Historical Association, reflected when a third of the history training places allocated to university/school partnerships were cut in single year:

> These cuts will severely damage the highly effective partnership between schools and universities delivered through the training and development of a stable community of school-based mentors. The rich knowledge of subject and teaching nurtured through these networks will be decimated. (Historical Association, 2014)

University departments of education cannot operate effectively and justify the employment of subject-specialist tutors unless they can guarantee stability in terms of trainee numbers. That becomes impossible if decisions about the number of training places to be offered are made annually by school partnerships with no obligation or financial imperative to fill them. The losers are not only new history trainees but their mentors, whose continued professional learning and research engagement is also most effectively nurtured though membership of a stable community, giving them access not only to university-based history education specialists but also to academic *historians* – the other resource on which their professional knowledge base has been shown to depend. It is teachers' engagement with historians' work that provides some of the richest thinking and most inspired planning reported by the teacher-researchers within this collection, empowering both them and their students. Watts' thoughtful reflections (this volume, p. 157) on some of the differences that he discerns between the kinds of causal questions being asked in school and those that he asks of his undergraduates illustrates just how important it is that these links should be constantly renewed and refreshed.

History Teacher Publication and the Curricular 'What?': Mobilizing Subject-specific Professional Knowledge in a Culture of Genericism

20

Christine Counsell

This chapter draws on history teachers' published work in order to weave two themes – first, the importance of subject-specificity and the reasons why, in England, history teachers' advances in professional clarity around disciplinary rigour have been undermined by genericism; second, the need for yet more work within the history education community on the role and nurture of substantive knowledge. While both 'form of knowledge' and choice of content remain vital issues, without a theory of how substantive knowledge builds over time and what its systematic nurture achieves for students over time, we will continue to exclude many students from the conversations of history. I conclude by linking the knowledge question to the problem of genericism.

* * *

A head of history wanting to examine her department's practice is not short of other history teachers' work to appraise. She can access a published conversation of their problem-solving efforts (Counsell, 2011a, 2011b; Fordham 2015a). Let us say that our head of history wishes to reflect, specifically, on students' causation essays. It is likely that her quest, like that of the literature she will consult, will embrace two closely woven goals: not just to *nurture* more powerful causal argument but to define *what causal argument is*, that is, what makes for explanatory power in history and how it might be characterized as a curricular goal. Our head of history may examine history teachers' challenges to reductive construals of long- and short-term causes (e.g. Howells, 1998), critiques of the atomization of causal reasoning into skills or increments of skill (Counsell, 2000, 2004b) and associated critiques of pedagogic or assessment practices associated with such increments (e.g. Burnham and Brown, 2004; Evans and Pate, 2007). She might consider teachers' explorations of counterfactual reasoning (e.g. Chapman, 2003; Woodcock, 2005; Buxton, 2010). She might also consider changing approaches to causal argument adopted by academic historians. She might, for example, have read Clark's *The Sleepwalkers* and there encountered his challenge to the 'distorting effect' of all this 'analytic clarity' with its 'illusion of a steadily building causal pressure' (2013, p. xxix). She might consult the work of history teachers such as Holliss (2014) who have read Clark's scholarship and, following their example, build more contingency into her students' causal arguments or, as Kemp (2011) had done earlier, consider the properties of narrative as a means of doing so.

How might our head of history's efforts to use such professional knowledge fare when faced with a senior leadership team's (SLT) decision to implement a whole-school approach to lesson planning, using a generic framework such as one derived from Bloom's taxonomy of educational objectives (Anderson and Krathwohl, 2001)? Let us imagine three such heads of history conversing with their respective senior leaders in three different schools.

In Scenario 1, lesson objectives commencing with the verbs 'describe'/'understand', 'explain' and 'analyse'/'evaluate' must match successive stages of a lesson. Pedagogies associated with these verbs are assumed to foster the increments of demand that their hierarchy is deemed to embody. These pedagogies form a menu on which teachers are expected to draw. The conversation our head of history has with an SLT member is confused, stressful and culminates in *impasse* on two fronts: first, over the term 'explain'; second, over the status of the verbs. The head of history insists that she is indeed privileging explanation, but *causal* explanation, that this is a particular style of disciplinary reasoning, that it amounts to an argument in response to a certain kind of 'Why?' question for which students will prepare across three or four lessons and that 'explain', in such a context, does not match the everyday meaning of 'explicate', 'set out' or 'expand'. It certainly has little to do with explaining the process of photosynthesis or explaining how a bicycle works. To force an 'explain' (of either meaning) into the middle section of each lesson confuses the journey toward building a powerful, independent *causal* explanation, especially if, as SLT expects, the teacher must tell pupils that 'explain' is a step more demanding than 'describe', and even more damaging if teachers must distinguish it from 'analyse'. Causal explanation, in history, is necessarily analysis. Moreover, as the conversation unfolds, it appears that SLT is not only treating the verbs as proxies for learning processes, each with its attendant teaching method, but is reading the head of history's comments on 'explanation' through that lens. In other words, the SLT member reads the history department's curricular account *as if it were a pedagogy*. But causal explanation is a curricular object; it is neither learning process nor pedagogy. Causal explanation may, of course, command all kinds of learning process; some may even correlate with aspects of Bloom's taxonomy, but it is not, *in itself*, a learning process. It is a disciplinary end, a curricular 'what?' not a pedagogic 'how'.

To read curriculum as pedagogy is not to read a curriculum at all. The conversation is held entirely at cross purposes. The underlying difficulty is that this SLT is promoting an intransitive pedagogy, a pedagogy without an object. Thus our head of history and SLT continue to talk past each other.

In Scenario 2, by contrast, our second SLT does treat Bloom's taxonomy as a property of curriculum, but the conversation with the head of history is just as vexed. In this school, a derivative of the taxonomy is used to capture generic 'thinking skills for the twenty-first century'. In this construal, the verbs describe processes, but processes to be learned rather than processes of learning – a crucial distinction, for it renders them a curricular object. Underpinning SLT's desire to add these into the curriculum is a perception of deficit. History is construed by SLT as a body of facts or information; students must therefore be taught, as an addition, to think critically and creatively. Yet our head of history knows that history is not a body of *information* but a distinctively structured field of *knowledge*, a system of meanings. Moreover, in addition to building security with its disciplinary products, history teaching addresses the origin, structure and status of that knowledge: students learn to re-arrange and re-construe, to argue and analyse, to examine and evaluate. A history teacher therefore shuttles between collective representations of the material that the discipline studies (substantive knowledge) and induction into the tradition of epistemic rules that made such representations possible (disciplinary knowledge). Our head of history's resistance therefore now arises not just from clashing nomenclature but from her view that the required curricular addition is redundant. It is also epistemically weaker than the one her department has taken care to build.

Scenario 3 yields a happier conversation, but the result of its harmony is tragic. This time our SLT member listens well to the head of history's account. She realizes that the school's history curriculum already sees students carrying out all the complex moves in Bloom's taxonomy and its variants. Students in history do, indeed, apply and create, analyse and argue, evaluate and explain. Delighted at this surprising, if accidental, compliance, all SLT need ask our head of history to do is to show where in her history curriculum these accomplishments will be secured, and to evidence the result. Thus, in Scenario 3, curricular by-product has become product. A *faux* curricular narrative has been created, and now becomes the narrative that will hold the head of history to account. As price for being left in peace, this third head of history will now complete audits against these categories, fill columns on work-schemes and boxes on lesson plans, in order to satisfy a management narrative. She will engage in concomitant casuistry in assessment. It is not that the head of history does not value creativity and criticality, but these outputs do not correspond with the means of their nurture; they are not resolvable into objectives of the same name. The tragedy is that SLT investigation of the history department has not improved SLT's grasp of the nature of historical knowledge, its relational properties and epistemic structures; it has converted these things into a superficial and misleading curricular narrative, and in order to retain professional harmony, the head of history must pretend her curricular decisions are governed by it. She must be complicit in a lie.

These three conversations, about a non-curriculum, a redundant curriculum and a usurper curriculum, illustrate various types of communication breakdown between generi-cist and subject-specialist. They are not mutually exclusive, and they do no more than imper-fectly exemplify a stream of *cri de coeurs* in my in-box from desperate heads of history, but I share them here in order to illustrate a clash of cultures in many of England's secondary schools, that between curriculum construed as strongly bounded domains of 'specialized knowledge' (Young, this volume, p. 186) and curriculum construed as sets of aims deriving from assorted perceptions of utility. It is a divide between two views of what is emancipatory for students. It may also reflect a wider, international 'crisis in curriculum theory' charac-terized by an absence of curricular reflection on knowledge structures and their epistemic power and therefore a vacuum into which genericism flows (Young, 2013).

The dominant genericist culture may make history's teacher-authored, subject-specific, published discourse seem remarkable, but it may also, in part, explain its continued vibrancy. Monaghan, for example, described the disciplinary derivation of his history department's work using Dickens' *Great Expectations* as a reaction against pressure to introduce 'watered-down teaching, generic thinking skills and the loss of any kind of intellectual framework' (2010, p. 3). Whatever its current drivers, what seems to sustain history teacher publication as a coherent discourse is a relentless curiosity about the curricular, 'what?'. I have argued elsewhere that it gains its currency from this pull in a curricular direction:

> [A] professional conversation's curricular artefacts are more portable than its pedagogic products. Activities deemed a short cut to success . . . once packaged and stripped of the disciplinary purposes that framed them, might not only fail but become harmful. What makes the product living and usable is the intellectual framework to which it refers and the elements of that framework that its designer deemed critical. Without this, we are forever condemned to erstwhile excellent products that go wrong in transit. They become a twisted proxy for the deeper learning they were designed to express. Similarly, if we create staging posts towards an outcome we need to be even more care-ful lest its increments become ends in themselves – empty, algorithmic moves serving only technicist ends . . . curricular curiosity keeps professional focus on what sits behind those moves. (Counsell, 2011b, pp. 77–78)

History teachers' published curricular theorizing is a continuous 'recontextualizing' of the discipline (Bernstein, 1988). These teachers treat the properties of the curricular 'what?' as an open question rather than as a given. Just as trainee history teachers, selecting content and a question angle, often find themselves moving from choosing the ontic to examining the ontological (Counsell, 2014), so do many published authors end up examining attrib-utes of the discipline. Curricular theorizing allows history teachers' contributions to join up and gives the combined conversation theoretical power (Counsell, 2011a, 2011b; Fordham, 2015a). Very often, teachers find themselves defining the boundaries of a feature within the curriculum and arguing for the disciplinary function of that feature, what secures or detracts from its rigour and how it might converge or diverge from other curricular features. A good example of this is the narrative of teacher debates on 'interpretations of history' (Counsell, 2011a, 2011b). Howells (2005) for example, challenged a tendency to veer towards an epistemology of voice when teaching pupils to examine scholarly interpretations. His solution was to make stronger connection with historical causation. Some years later, Brown and Massey (2014) explored ways in which study of interpretations both intersects with and is distinct from evidential thinking, yet in contrasting ways from Hammond's (2007) treatment of the same. Each begins with a context-specific challenge, but moves into wrestling with a curricular goal which involves, as Foster puts it in this volume, 'searching for an analytical language' (p. 10).

Yet if it is the *curricular* dimension that allows these teachers' writings to create a theoretical currency, why does it matter so much that teachers themselves continue to drive it? After all, the power of theory is that it leaves context behind (Wheelahan, 2010). Two answers are suggested in this volume. First, the pedagogic setting is perpetually revelatory of curricular issues that may not surface if framed only in the realms of (say) cognitive psychology, the sociology of knowledge, assessment theory or even historical scholarship. As Elliott shows, a teacher's pedagogic enquiry can invite a sustained, determined questioning about the validity of categories. For example, Worth's argument, in this volume, for integration of comprehension and evaluation, and her exploration of contextual knowledge, calls into question a common assumption that is latent in some historical reading assessments, namely that asking students '*simply* [my emphasis] . . . to summarise or explain the substance of historical documents' is a lower level accomplishment than, or even distinct from, critical analysis (Reisman, 2015, p. 37). Second, inclusion of pedagogic moorings in the account draws in other teachers. In her comment on Worth's sharing of detail, Jones remarks, 'It allows us to arrive *with* her, at her curricular re-think about the interplay, and therefore the relative status, of components of evidential thinking' (Jones, this volume, p. 216).

Where might history teachers' published curricular theorizing turn next? An issue to which history teachers are giving renewed attention is that of substantive knowledge (e.g. Donaghy, 2014; Hammond, 2014; Palek, 2015). In this final section I will reflect on why teacher-generated, subject-specific discourse about substantive knowledge is particularly important in a climate of educational genericism.

My own first efforts to theorize substantive knowledge were those of a practising history teacher. I was increasingly convinced that 'lower-attaining' students stayed 'lower-attaining' chiefly for want of sufficient content security to move about freely within narratives and to recognize recurring abstract references when introduced to new historical accounts. Constantly having to look up events central to a narrative made analysis confusing or impossible; terms such as 'political power' or 'civilization' remained thin and meaningless rather than thick with the meaning that accrues from having stories attached to them in one's head through successive prior encounter (Counsell, 2001). Contrary to then-emerging orthodoxies wherein skills or processes were considered transferable, and knowledge (in the sense of content) was deemed 'inert' and 'non-functioning' (Fines, 1987), it was *knowledge* that seemed to me functional and 'transferable' from topic to topic, but in unexamined ways: 'Knowledge is an enabler. Yet we have scarcely begun to examine how, exactly, it can be harnessed to enable those pupils who find history hard' (Counsell, 2000, p. 71). Conceptualizing lower-attainer difficulties *only* in second-order terms felt inadequate both as diagnosis of deficit and as prescription for remedy.

A common remark among history education professionals in the 1990s was that substantive knowledge and second-order thinking supported one another, but it seemed to me, first, that there were specific ways in which this could be better exploited; and, second, that we needed a way of talking about systematic planning for growing substantive knowledge confidence. Working on the latter, I found inspiration in Rogers' notion of 'the past as a frame of reference' (1987, p. 3). I argued that history teachers might plan, proactively, for an intensification of 'resonance', so that recognition and instant meaning-making (of events such as 'Reformation' or terms such as 'religious practice') would be enabled through association with earlier stories and would render subsequent allusions or proximal concepts in other topics easier to assimilate:

> One way of analysing a teacher's work is to examine what the teacher does to highlight resonance, to 'warm it up', and to prepare for future resonance . . . The more pupils know the more they are in a position to learn. To say that the learning of content is unimportant is to ignore its subtle role in future learning. (2000, p. 62)

My own tentative early efforts tended to rest, however, with the projective, that is, how a history teacher might plan to realize the potential of knowledge in immediate and future planning. In 2000, I argued that attention to historical knowledge could be given curricular function on two temporal scales: first, knowledge needed at the 'fingertips' in order to engage in immediate debate and, second, 'residue' knowledge. The 'residue' is the sense of period and chronological reference points that are left behind by fingertip knowledge, and which improve students' access to subsequent topics (Counsell, 2000, p. 67). Hammond (2014), also drawing on her own practice, has recently gone much further by using a retrospective analysis. Hammond worked backwards from the possible manifestations of such knowledge. Examining subtle differences between arguments written by GCSE students performing securely at 'A' grade and those whose 'A' grade answers appear fragile, she looked not for direct deployment and substantiation but for indirect evidence of student awareness of 'ways in which the past worked' which somehow colour or 'flavour' use of terms and so render students' analyses more historically mature (Hammond, 2014). Going beyond the topic at hand (Nazi Germany), she then related these accomplishments to scales and types of prior knowledge that might be enabling her students to use a term such as 'the public' with greater flexibility than a student operating with a thinner definition.

Hammond's explicit theorizing is new in important ways, but a glance at a range of work by history teachers in the last twenty years actually yields a variety of nascent curricular theories, many of them all the more interesting for being closely entwined with second-order purposes. Perhaps the most influential (see Gadd, 2009 and Jones, 2009), has been Banham's notion of the 'overview lurking in the depth' (2000, p. 23). Banham defended an eight-week-long depth study of one medieval monarch, not as an *alternative* to gaining outline knowledge of changing monarchy across the medieval period, but as a device for making such an overview possible:

> The value of depth consists not merely in its intrinsic learning outcomes but in its role as a kind of mental investment for later. During the subsequent overview, the return on that investment is substantial. (2000, p. 27)

I suspect that many other history teachers do this tacitly, with attention to *disciplinary* knowledge such as second-order concepts perhaps obscuring the import of the *substantive* dimension. In search of such tacit progression models, I once conducted a small-scale study of three history teachers 'weaving content into memorable shapes ready for future use . . . These teachers were similarity spotters and the function of the lessons was to turn the pupils, bit by bit, into similarity spotters, too' (2000, p. 68). An element of this is likely to be present even in those approaches that privilege the second-order dimension. Advocates of 'Big History' who recommend teaching a 'provisional factual scaffold' (Howson and Shemilt, 2011), such as the framework used by Rogers in this volume, require students to become familiar with the time-bound, thematic generalizations afforded by that framework. What does it mean to be 'familiar' with those substantive generalizations? Which parts must be carried forward in memory precisely so that students can critique and transform them as they encounter evidence that demands their revision?

As I write this, I scratch about for a generative language – shapes, types, layers, structures – that would capture the mutable form and function of knowledge as it is carried, *via* a curriculum, across the timespan of a students' learning. What survives from 'fingertip' knowledge that I once had of Gladstone's and Disraeli's ministries (once, when teaching it at A Level, I knew copious details), is now a usable residue (what remains are layers of period-grounded meaning that help me to navigate any new reading on late nineteenth-century politics). Not all the dates and details remain in long-term memory, but once having them at my 'fingertips' has played a long-term role. A curricular model cannot be merely aggregative (Lee and Shemilt, 2003) but the fact that it cannot be aggregative is no reason to neglect the function of substantive knowledge in opening up both the past worlds to which it directly refers and others to which it can be transferred by association.

Yet this long-term, enabling function of knowledge *is* invariably neglected. Instead, debates about *which* substantive knowledge frequently dominate curricular debate. Of course, such debates are vital. Content choices have to be made from a vast canvas of world history. These choices can profoundly affect students' experience (Whitburn and Yemoh, 2012). Detailed choices will always entail myriad considerations when unnumbered options for content (such as local history) are interchangeable in serving the same curricular function. Debates about what should be the net content 'takeaway' from a curriculum matter greatly (e.g. Harris, 2013; Wilkinson, 2015). But having made decisions as to *which* 'what?', the nature of the 'what?' to be attended to at any one time, its role as a component in growing substantive knowledge, that is, a meaningful system held by the pupil held in the head and not 'outsourced', needs to be examined if adequate fluency in its currency is to be secured.

Recent turns in wider debates about curriculum and pedagogy now make the knowledge question pressing for subject communities. A wider, more general interest in knowledge and memory is gaining ground (e.g. Christodoulou, 2014), often drawing on the cognitive psychology of memory (e.g. Willingham, 2009). I welcome this emphasis on the curricular 'what?' and on memory but the 'what?' must be examined in terms of the epistemic traditions that give disciplinary products (substantive knowledge) their structure and that allow students to examine those traditions and structures (disciplinary knowledge). If 'knowledge' is construed only generically, for example by treating 'facts' as similar curricular entities across subjects, then a new, even more alarming version of the confusions and missed opportunities set out at the start of this chapter, could take hold.

I see three dangers here. Each arises from genericism. Each might be obviated by subject teachers expanding and then mobilizing their curricular theorizing about substantive knowledge. The first danger echoes that of Scenario 1 at the start of this chapter. If a focus on knowledge collapses into pedagogy at the expense of curriculum, then the type, status or interplay of *what* needs to be encountered and the form in which it needs later to be manifested will not be properly examined. Acts of deliberate memorization are extremely useful, not to mention motivating, satisfying and strengthening of analysis and debate (see Carr and Counsell, 2014), but generic, non-subject-specific demand for memorization that fails to attend to the *nature* of what is being remembered and its role in subsequent learning will lead to confusions equivalent to those emerging from generic skills. Boundaries between subjects matter. The relationship between abstract substantive concepts and their particular instantiations differ profoundly between science and history, between music and languages. The distinctive ways in which facts interrelate to become new knowledge, the peculiar ways in which narrative 'carries' knowledge (Counsell and Mastin, 2015) differ in epistemic role and in their means of nurture. We need a subject-specific taxonomy of historical knowledge that relates to curricular function. A subject-specific approach to theorizing substantive knowledge demands not just an accumulation of stuff but the interplay of one kind of stuff with another over time.

A second danger could arise from an unfortunate conjunction of a *genericist* interest in substantive knowledge, a high-stakes assessment culture and a managerialist drive to track overt student improvement through data. This could result in an alarming narrowing of historical content. Hammond (2014) has explored what may be missing in the support of students who struggle to perform well in examinations but far from arguing for a narrowing of focus onto examination content, her argument for the 'indirect manifestation of knowledge' is a case for the opposite. Her subject-specific case leads her to argue for spending time on material outside the examination specification, as well as an argument, echoing that of Laffin (1998) over a decade earlier, that drilling in examination questions may bypass the problem. It points to a case for teaching to the domain, rather than to the test (Koretz, 2009). Buxton (this volume), for example, wants her students to produce rigorous arguments about the French Revolution and key to her distinctive approach is to study an additional country, not to limit study to France. To understand how domain-led teaching might be the best way to perform better in the test requires theoretical grasp of how each subject community uses curriculum to operationalize its domain.

The third danger, one that Young warns against, is that of 'sloganizing' (Young, this volume, p. 193). Slogans, despite our best intentions, lead easily to triumphalism. If the story of all our strivings to teach history well has anything to teach us it is that a sustained spirit of questioning and humility is essential. Notions of a 'return to knowledge' have political cachet but they are dangerous. A 'return' would suggest Young's 'Future 1'. Young's 'Future 3', by contrast, blends a concern for secure knowledge of disciplinary products with a critical meta-knowledge about the discipline itself, what the history education community traditionally calls second-order thinking and what I have termed here 'disciplinary knowledge'. And this is not a 'return'. Contrary to myths of a golden age, the majority of the attainment range never had this knowledge, whether substantive or disciplinary (Cannadine, Keating and Sheldon, 2011). Those history teachers, such as the authors contributing to this volume, who strive to bring both substantive and disciplinary knowledge to the full attainment range, as history's Future 3, are pioneers. We are still in the earliest decades of the effort, with a great deal to find out.

Notes

Chapter 1

1   AS (Advanced Subsidiary) level qualifications are offered primarily to 16–18-year-olds and are administered through five examination boards. They are studied either as a stand-alone qualification or as the first part of an A level course. History AS level consists of two examined units: the unit upon which this study was based is Edexcel's Unit 1 Historical Themes in Depth *Pursuing Life and Liberty: Equality in the USA, 1945–68*. See http://www.edexcel.com/migrationdocuments/GCE%20New%20GCE/UA033545_GCE_08_History_Issue_4.pdf

2   All students' names have been changed.

3   The Schools Council History Project (SCHP) was founded in 1972. In 1984 it was renamed the Schools History Project.

4   The General Certification of Secondary Education (GCSE) and the General Certificate of Education (GCE) Advanced Level are the public examinations normally taken at ages 16+ and 18+ respectively, in England, Wales and Northern Ireland.

Chapter 3

1   In relation to their research-based models of progression (as opposed to the NC model), Lee and Shemilt (2003) had been similarly clear in stating that a progression model is not the same as a mark scheme, and they were very critical of attempts to convert the former into the latter.

Chapter 4

1   World History for Us All can be accessed at http://worldhistoryforusall.sdsu.edu/bigeras.php.

2   History of Medicine has been part of the Schools History Project (SHP) specification – one syllabus option for the 16+ General Certificate of Secondary Education (GCSE) examination in England for nearly forty years. At the time of publication, about one-third of those pupils entered for GCSE history follow this option.

3   The International Big History Association has its own website at http://www.ibhanet.org/ and held its inaugural conference in August 2012 in the United States.

4   The pupils for the first Magna Carta project were from a 'top' set. They were therefore more academically able than all those pupils who experienced the synoptic framework teaching described in this chapter.

Chapter 5

1   General Certificate of Secondary Education (GCSE) is the 16+ public examination in England, Wales and Northern Ireland. In England, schools usually select one of three awarding bodies. These students were preparing for the History B: Modern World examination set by OCR (2009).

2 I differentiate between 'sources' and 'evidence' as follows: sources are what have survived from the past; information is what is derived from interrogating the source; information becomes evidence when used to answer a particular question.

Chapter 6

1 This paper reports on the second iteration of The Beatles Project, which took place in 2012. In the original iteration, which took place in 2011, the students were required to analyse The Beatles' 'changing attitudes to love'. The concept and definition of 'love' proved a problematic distraction for the students, with discussions often moving away from the methodological discourse that we wanted to encourage. In 2012 the question posed was broadened to 'attitudes and values' generally, in the hope that this might focus discussions more clearly on methodology and that it would have greater potential to reveal the paradigms that were driving the students' analyses.
2 All unattributed quotes are from unpublished History Virtual Academy (HVA) 2012 Beatles discussion forum data sets. Student responses have been edited where necessary for spelling and grammatical errors.
3 Thirty-four students answered Task 1 and students often offered more than one type of explanation.
4 This is an erroneous interpretation of the song (MacDonald, 2008, pp. 358–360).
5 As Collins demonstrated in his responses to students, all of these assumptions about the social context of 1960s Britain are questionable.

Chapter 7

1 The Hypercities project can be accessed at: www.hypercities.com.

Chapter 10

1 I thus use the term 'interpretation' more broadly here than I do in *Historical Knowledge, Historical Error*, where I distinguish among 'description', 'explanation', 'interpretation', and 'argument' (Megill, 2007, pp. 96–98 and 101–103).
2 My account here is elliptical. Concerning historical experience, see Frank Ankersmit, *Sublime Historical Experience* (Ankersmit, 2005), especially chapters 2, 3 and 4. See also Eelco Runia on 'presence', including 'the presence of the past', in Runia (2006, 2014). The terms 'historical experience' and 'presence of the past', as well as Johan Huizinga's term (to which Ankersmit draws attention). 'historical sensation', refer to the same intuition – which is the foundation of, in my terminology, the 'aesthesis of history', which is, in turn, a central part of the 'science of history'. (I can only allude to, not thoroughly discuss, these matters here.)
3 See also Alon Confino (2009, 2012), who, inspired by Ankersmit and Huizinga, discovers elements of Huizinga's 'historical sensation' in Friedländer's *Nazi Germany and the Jews*, vol. 2, *The Years of Extermination* (2007).
4 Danto originally made this point as early as 1962, in an article contributing to the debate over the 'Covering Law Model' (Danto, 1962).
5 Although I am no fan of *What Is History?* on one matter Carr is correct, namely, in his insistence that facts are dependent on the dialectical relation between 'the historian and his facts' (Carr, 1961, p. 24). I never learned this in school.
6 I here draw from Butterfield (1965 [1931], p. 73).

Chapter 13

1 When stored on the Internet or in a textbook, Newton's famous Law of Motion is only *information*. It becomes *powerful knowledge* when it is part of how we understand the world, that is, when we have a relationship to it.

2 The issue of 'modes of knowledge' and the difference between Mode 1 (discipline-based) and Mode 2 (trans-discipline based) has led to an extensive literature in higher education. The issues have also been discussed in relation to the school curriculum (Whitty, 2010).

Chapter 18

1 Wineburg (2001 and 2004) has shown that the 'discovery' (and rediscovery) of the alarming ignorance of the young has been a perennial theme in North American education over the last 100 years. The scenario is the same in England too (see Field, 2009 and Matthews, 2009 for examples). It seems probable that in England, as in the USA, the one continuity for which we have compelling evidence is continuity in an adult tendency to diagnose and lament the ignorance of the young and to posit it as a new and alarming development (see Lee, 2011b, pp. 141–143 for a fuller discussion of these issues).

2 The influence on English policymakers of this polemical, non-peer-reviewed and self-published pamphlet, in the period 2009–2014 was, to say the least, remarkable (Haydn, 2011a).

3 For an outline of the 'first' and 'second-order' distinction, which has become increasingly widespread in the last decade in British history education, see Lee (2005b).

4 In Coffin's terms, Muriel is writing in one of the simplest of history's 'recording genres', the biographical 'recount', which consists of 'orientation, record of events (evaluation of person) (Coffin, 2006b, p. 418).

5 Advocates of history as identity engineering through narrative tend, rather problematically, to assume that mastery of such narratives (*knowing* the story) will lead to their appropriation (*identifying* with the story). It is not at all obvious that it should and there are good empirical reasons for doubting that it will, as Wertsch (1998 and 2002) has shown, through intergenerational studies of the mastery and appropriation of Soviet party history in Estonia in the early 1990s, and as Epstein has shown by exploring African American students' responses to dominant narratives of US history (Epstein, 2008). The political difficulties with a curriculum presenting a single narrative of national history in a pluralist democracy are self-evident and have been made manifestly so repeatedly (e.g. Hansard, 2009).

6 See Lee (2014) for a review of this tradition and its achievements.

7 See Aldrich (1984) for a review of the impact of the work of Keatinge and others on history education before the 'new history' and, for some qualifications, see Chapman (2014).

8 For an incisive discussion of the role and relative importance of content and conceptual knowledge and understanding in the learning of subject disciplines from a cognitive scientist's perspective see Howard Gardner's response to E. D. Hirsch in *The Disciplined Mind* (Gardner, 2000, pp. 252–260).

9 See Donovan and Bransford (2005, p. 1). In addition to researching the second-order conceptual underpinnings of knowledge-building, the 'form of knowledge' tradition has also explored ways of developing children's 'frame of reference' knowledge and understanding (Rogers, 1984, pp. 28–35; Rogers, 1987) and knowledge 'frameworks' and 'big picture' representations of the past (Shemilt, 2000, 2009; Lee, 2005a, 2011a and 2011b; Howson, 2007 and 2009; Howson and Shemilt, 2011; Rogers, 2008 and this volume; Blow et al., 2015). Unlike some more polemical contributors to debates on

knowledge and knowing, this tradition has been careful to recognize that developing children's large-scale representations of the past is a problem requiring innovation in theorizing, research, practice and reflection.

10 The counts reported here were inspired by Fordham (2015a). My analysis is much cruder than Fordham's and is more of a sketch than a completed picture. The totals count each item that our authors referenced and thus count a number of items more than once – Woodcock (2005), for example, was referenced by four of our authors.

11 There are exceptions to these generalizations, of course, as Shemilt's evaluation of the Schools Council History Project shows (Shemilt, 1980). The generalizations still stand.

12 See notes 2 and 5, above.

Chapter 19

1 The all-pervasive and pernicious influence of Bloom's taxonomy of cognitive objectives is discussed at greater length by Counsell in this volume. A further critique of its application in learning history can be found in Wineburg and Schneider (2010).

2 By 'enquiry sequences' I mean schemes of work constructed to allow students to answer a genuine historical question – as elaborated by Riley (2000) and Byrom and Riley (2003).

3 The distinction that Vygtosky (1986) drew between 'spontaneous' or everyday concepts and 'scientific' or disciplinary concepts is echoed in Wineburg's (2001) description of historical thinking as an 'unnatural act'.

4 Indeed, Chapman's analysis of the teacher-researcher chapters in this volume found that only 13 (3.6%) of their 363 references were to works reporting generic educational research.

5 For an explanation of these skills and their ubiquitous appearance in the education policies of the last Labour government, see Braun, Maguire and Ball (2012).

References

Acomb, F. (1950), *Anglophobia in France 1763–1789*. Duke, NC: Duke University Press.

Acton, E. (2008), *Lectures on Modern History*, ed. J. N. Figgis and R. V. Laurence. Truro: Dodo Press.

Ajegbo, K. (2007), *Diversity and Citizenship*. London: DfES.

Akhtar, J. and A. R. Rahman (songwriters) (2008a), *Azeem-O-Shan-Shahenshah* [Song], in R. Screwvala and A. Gowariker (producers), *Jodhaa/Akbar* [Motion Picture]. Mauritius: UTV Motion Pictures.

Akhtar, J. and A. R. Rahman (songwriters) (2008b), *Khwaja Mere Khwaja* [Song], in R. Screwvala and A. Gowariker (producers), *Jodhaa/Akbar* [Motion Picture]. Mauritius: UTV Motion Pictures.

Aldrich, R. E. (1984), 'New History: An Historical Perspective', in A. K. Dickinson, P. J. Lee and P. J. Rogers (eds), *Learning History*. London: Heinemann Educational Books, pp. 210–224.

Alexander, R. (2008), *Essays on Pedagogy*. London: Routledge.

Alkis, C. (2005), 'A Student's Perspective'. Paper given at the Institute of Historical Research's conference History in Schools and Higher Education: Issues of Common Concern, 29 September 2005. http://sas-space.sas.ac.uk/view/collections/ihr-events.html, accessed 17 December 2014.

Altrichter, H., P. Posch and B. Somekh (1993), *Teachers Investigate Their Work: An Introduction to the Methods of Action Research*. London: Routledge.

Anderson, B. (1983), *Imagined Communities: Reflections on the Origin and Spread of Nationalism*. London: Verso.

Anderson, L. W. and D. R. Krathwohl (eds) with P. W. Airasian, K. A. Cruikshank, R. E. Mayer, P. R. Pintrich, J. Raths and M. C. Wittrock (2001), *A Taxonomy for Learning, Teaching, and Assessing: A Revision of Bloom's Taxonomy of Educational Objectives*. New York: Longman.

Andrews, R. (1995), *Teaching and Learning Argument*. London: Cassell.

Ankersmit, F. R. (1994), *History and Tropology: The Rise and Fall of Metaphor*. Berkeley: University of California Press.

Ankersmit, F. R. (2005), *Sublime Historical Experience*. Stanford, CA: Stanford University Press.

Ashby, R. (2011), 'Understanding Historical Evidence: teaching and learning challenges' in I. Davies (ed.), *Debates in History Teaching*. London: Routledge, pp. 137–147.

Ashby, R. and P. Lee (2000), 'Progression in Historical Understanding Among Students Ages 7–14', in P. Stearns, P. Seixas and S. Wineburg (eds), *Knowing, Teaching and Learning History: National and International Perspectives*. New York: New York University Press, pp. 199–222.

Austin, J. L. (1980), *How to Do Things with Words*. Cambridge, MA: Harvard University Press.

Badiou, A. (2001), *Ethics: An Essay on the Understanding of Evil*, trans. P. Holworth. London: Verso.

Baert, P. (1998), *Social Theory in the Twentieth Century*. Oxford: Polity Press.

Ball, S. J., M. Maguire and A. Braun (2012), *How Schools Do Policy: Policy Enactment in Secondary Schools*. London: Routledge.

Banham, D. (1998), 'Getting Ready for the Grand Prix: Learning How to Build a Substantiated Argument in Year 7', *Teaching History*, 92, 6–15.

Banham, D. (2000), 'The Return of King John: Using Depth to Strengthen Overview in the Teaching of Political Change', *Teaching History*, 99, 22–31.

Banham, D. and R. Hall (2013), *Raising Attainment at GCSE & A Level: Using Recent Research to Inform Planning*. http://www.schoolshistoryproject.org.uk/ResourceBase/BanhamHallGCSE.htm#nav, accessed 30 July 2015.

Barca, I. (2005), ' "Till New Facts Are Discovered": Students' Ideas about Objectivity in History', in R. Ashby, P. Gordon and P. J. Lee (eds), *Understanding History: Recent Research in History Education, International Review of History Education, Volume 4*. London: Routledge Falmer, pp. 68–82.

Barnes, S. (2002), 'Revealing the Big Picture: Patterns, Shapes and Images at Key Stage 3', *Teaching History*, 107, 6–12.

Baronov, D. (2004), *Conceptual Foundations of Social Research Methods*. Boulder, CO: Paradigm Publishers.

Barrett, M. (1989), 'Some Different Meanings of the Concept of "Difference": Feminist Theory and the Concept of Ideology', in E. Meese and A. Parker (eds), *The Difference within: Feminism and Critical Theory*. Amsterdam: John Benjamin's Publishing Company, pp. 37–48.

Barrs, M. and V. Cork (2001), *The Reader in the Writer: The Links between the Study of Literature and Writing Development at Key Stage 2*. London: Centre for Language in Primary Education.

Barton, K. and A. McCully (2005), 'History, Identity and the School Curriculum in Northern Ireland: An Empirical Study of Secondary Students' Ideas and Perspectives', *Journal of Curriculum Studies*, 37 (1), 85–116.

Bassey, M. (1999), *Case Study Research in Educational Settings*. Buckingham: Open University Press.

Beck, J. (2013), 'Powerful Knowledge, Esoteric Knowledge, Curriculum Knowledge', *Cambridge Journal of Education*, 43 (2), 177–193.

Benjamin, T. (2005), 'Perceptions from a Student in Higher Education'. Paper given at the Institute of Historical Research Conference 'History in Schools and Higher Education: Issues of Common Concern'. London, 29 September 2005. http://sas-space.sas.ac.uk/view/collections/ihr-events.html, accessed 17 December 2014.

Bernstein. B. (1970), 'Education Cannot Compensate for Society', *New Society*, 26, 344–347.

Bernstein, B. (1988), *Class, Codes, and Control* (Vol. 3). London: Routledge.

Bernstein, B. (2000), *Pedagogy, Symbolic Control and Identity: Theory, Research, Critique*. New York: Rowan and Littlefield.

Bhabha, H. (1994), *The Location of Culture*. London: Routledge.

Bhabha, H. (2003), 'Signs Taken for Wonders', in B. Ashcroft, G. Griffiths and H. Tiffin (eds), *Post-Colonial Studies: The Key Concepts*. London: Routledge, pp. 29–35.

Biesta, G. J. J. and D. Egéa-Kuehne (eds) (2001), *Derrida and Education*. London: Routledge.

Black, P. and D. Wiliam (1998), 'Assessment and Classroom Learning', *Education: Principles, Policy and Practice*, 5 (1), 7–74.

Blommaert, J. and J. Verschueren (1998), *Debating Diversity: Analysing the Discourse of Tolerance*. London: Routledge.

Blow, F. (2011a), ' "Everything flows and nothing stays": How Students Make Sense of the Historical Concepts of Change, Continuity and Development', *Teaching History*, 145, 47–55.

Blow, F. (2011b), 'How Pupils' Conception of the Relationship between the Past and the Present Impact on the Ways That They Make Sense of the History Taught', in K. Nordgren, P. Eliasson and C. Ronnqvist (eds), *The Processes of Teaching History*. Karlstad: Karlstad University Press, pp. 125–154.

Blow, F., P. Lee and D. Shemilt (2012), 'Time and Chronology: Conjoined Twins or Distant Cousins?' *Teaching History*, 147, 26–35.

Blow, F., R. Rogers and D. Shemilt (2008), 'Framework Working Group Report'. Unpublished report submitted to the Qualifications and Curriculum Development Agency by the Framework Working Group (FWG). Leeds: FWG.

Blow, F., P. Lee, D. Shemilt and C. Smith (2015), '"Only Connect: How Students Form Connections within and between Historical Narratives', in A. Chapman and A. Wilschut (eds), *International Review of History Education: Joined-up History*, Vol. 8. Charlotte, NC: Information Age Publishing, pp. 277–314.

Bolstad, R. and J. Gilbert (2012), *Supporting Future-Oriented Learning and Teaching – a New Zealand Perspective*. Wellington: Ministry of Education.

Booth, A. (2005), 'Worlds in Collision: University Tutor and Student Perspectives on the Transition to Degree Level History', *Teaching History*, 121, 14–19.

Booth, M. (1987), 'Ages and Concepts: A Critique of the Piagetian Approach to History Teaching', in C. Portal (ed.), *The History Curriculum for Teachers*. Lewes: The Falmer Press, pp. 22–38.

Bourdieu, P. (1974), 'The School as a Conservative Force', in J. Egglestone (ed.), *Contemporary Research in the Sociology of Education*. London: Methuen, pp. 32–46.

Bourdieu, P. and J.-C. Passeron (1977), *Reproduction in Education, Society and Culture*. London: Sage.

Boyatzis, R. E. (1998), *Transforming Qualitative Information: Thematic Analysis and Code Development*. Thousand Oaks, CA: Sage.

Bracey, P., A. Gove-Humphries and D. Jackson (2011), 'Teaching Diversity in the History Classroom', in I. Davies (ed.), *Debates in History Teaching*. Abingdon: Routledge, pp. 137–147.

Bradshaw, M. (2006), 'Creating Controversy in the Classroom: Making Progress with Historical Significance', *Teaching History*, 125, 18–25.

Bradshaw, M. (2009), 'Drilling Down: How One History Department Is Working towards Progression in Pupils' Thinking about Diversity across Years 7, 8, and 9', *Teaching History*, 135, 5–11.

Braudel, F. (1972), *The Mediterranean and the Mediterranean World in the Age of Philip II*, trans. S. Reynolds. New York: Harper and Row.

Braun, A., M. Maguire and S. Ball (2010), 'Policy Enactments in the UK Secondary School: Examining Policy, Practice and School Positioning', *Journal of Education Policy*, 25, (4), 547–560.

Braun, V. and V. Clarke (2006), 'Using Thematic Analysis in Psychology', *Qualitative Research in Psychology*, 3, (2), 77–101.

British Educational Research Association-Royal Society of the encouragement of the Arts (BERA-RSA) (2014), *Research and the Teaching Profession: Building the Capacity for a Self-improving Education System*. https://www.bera.ac.uk/project/research-and-teacher-education, accessed 30 July 2015.

Brooker, E. (2009), 'Telling Tales: Developing Students' Own Thematic and Synoptic Understandings at Key Stage 3', *Teaching History*, 136, 45–52.

Brown, A. and P. Dowling (1998), *Doing Research/Reading Research: A Mode of Interrogation for Education*. London: Falmer Press.

Brown, G. and S. Burnham (2014), 'Assessment after Levels', *Teaching History*, 157, 8–17.

Brown, M. and C. Massey (2014), 'Teaching "the Lesson of Satire": Using *the Wipers Times* to Build an Enquiry on the First World War', *Teaching History*, 155, 20–28.

Brown, G. and J. Woodcock (2009), 'Relevant, Rigorous and Revisited: Using Local History to Make Meaning of Historical Significance', *Teaching History*, 134, 4–11.

Bruner, J. S. (1966), *Toward a Theory of Instruction*. Cambridge, MA: Belkapp Press.

Bruner, J. S. (1996), *The Culture of Education*. Cambridge, MA: Harvard University Press.

Burke III, E., D. Christian and R. Dunn (2012), *World History. The Big Eras: A Compact History of Humankind for Teachers' and Students*. Culver City, CA: Social Studies School Service.

Burke, P. (1990), *The French Historical Revolution: The Annales School 1929–89*. Cambridge: Polity Press.

Burke, P. (2002), 'Western Historical Thinking in a Global Perspective: 10 Theses', in J. Rüsen (ed.), *Western Historical Thinking: An Intercultural Debate*. New York: Berghahn Books, pp. 15–33.

Burn, K. (2012), '"If I Wasn't Learning Anything New about Teaching I Would Have Left It by Now!" How History Teachers Can Support Their Own and Others' Continued Professional Learning', *Teaching History*, 146, 40–49.

Burn, K. (2015), 'The Gove Legacy in the Curriculum: The Case of History', in M. Finn (ed.), *The Gove Legacy: Education in Britain after the Coalition*. Basingstoke: Palgrave Macmillan.

Burn, K., H. Hagger and T. Mutton (2015), *Beginning Teacher's Learning: Making Experience Count*. Northwich: Critical.

Burn, K. and R. Harris (2014), 'The Voice of the Profession in the "History Wars": What Teachers' Responses to the DfE's National Curriculum Proposals (2013) Reveal about Their Conceptions of the Nature and Purpose of History in Schools'. Paper presented at BERA conference, London, 24–26 September.

Burnham, S. and G. Brown (2004), 'Assessment without Level Descriptions', *Teaching History*, 115, 5–15.

Burr, V. (1995), *Introduction to Social Constructionism*. London: Routledge.

Burrow, J. (2009), *A History of Histories: Epics, Chronicles, Romances and Inquiries from Herodotus and Thucydides to the Twentieth Century*. Harmondsworth: Penguin.

Butler, C. (2002), *Postmodernism: A Very Short Introduction*. Oxford: Oxford University Press.

Butler, T. (2006), 'A Walk of Art: The Potential of the Sound Walk as a Practice in Cultural Geography', *Social and Cultural Geography*, 7, (6), 889–908.

Butler, T. (2007), 'Memoryscape: How Audio Walks Can Deepen Our Sense of Place by Integrating Art, Oral History and Cultural Geography', *Geography Compass*, 1, (3), 360–372.

Butterfield, H. (1965 [1931]), *The Whig Interpretation of History*. New York: Norton.

Buxton, E. (2010), '"Fog Over Channel; Continent Accessible"? Year 8 Use Counterfactual Reasoning to Explore Place and Social Upheaval in Eighteenth-Century France and Britain', *Teaching History*, 140, 4–15.

Byrom, J. (1998), 'Working with Sources: Scepticism or Cynicism? Putting the Story Back Together Again', *Teaching History*, 91, 32–35.

Byrom, J. and M. Riley (2003), 'Professional Wrestling in the History Department: A Case Study in Planning the Teaching of the British Empire at Key Stage 3', *Teaching History*, 112, 6–14.

Byrom, J. and M. Riley (2009), Video contribution to 'Dimensions of Diversity: How Do We Improve Our Teaching of Social Complexity in History?' Online e-CPD unit. Historical Association. http://www.history.org.uk/resources/secondary_resource_1326_11.html, accessed 26 July 2015.

Byrom, J., M. Riley and C. Culpin (2004), *Impact of Empire: Pupils' Book: Colonialism 1500–2000*. London: Hodder Murray.

Cain, T. and A. Chapman (2014), 'Dysfunctional Dichotomies? Deflating Bipolar Constructions of Curriculum and Pedagogy through Case Studies from Music and History', *The Curriculum Journal*, 25, (1), 111–129.

Cannadine, D. (2013), 'The Future of History', *The Times Literary Supplement*, 13 March 2013. http://www.the-tls.co.uk/tls/public/article1228938.ece, accessed 28 July 2015.

Cannadine, D., J. Keating and S. Sheldon (2011), *The Right Kind of History: Teaching the Past in Twentieth Century England*. Houndsmills: Palgrave Macmillan.

Card, J. (2004), 'How One Period Visualises Another', *Teaching History*, 117, 6–11.

Card, J. (2008), *History Pictures: Using Visual Sources to Build Better History Lessons*. London: Hodder Education.

Carey, J. (1990), *The Oxford Authors: John Donne*. Oxford: Oxford University Press.

Carlisle, J. (2000), Letters, *Teaching History*, 101, 3.

Carr, E. H. (1961), *What Is History?* London: Macmillan.

Carr, E. and C. Counsell (2014), 'Using Timelines in Assessment', *Teaching History*, 157, 54–62.

Carretero, M. and P. J. Lee (2014), 'Learning Historical Concepts', in R. K. Slater (ed.), *The Cambridge Handbook of the Learning Sciences*. Cambridge: Cambridge University Press, pp. 587–604.

Carter, A. (2015), *Carter Review of Initial Teacher Training (ITT)*. Department for Education. https://www.gov.uk/government/publications/carter-review-of-initial-teacher-training, accessed 30 July 2015.

Cercadillo, L. (2001), 'Significance in History: Students' Ideas in England and Spain', in A. Dickinson, P. Gordon and P. Lee (eds), *Raising Standards in History Education*. London: Woburn Press, pp. 116–145.

Cercadillo, L. (2006), '"Maybe they haven't decided yet what is right": English and Spanish Perspectives on Teaching Historical Significance', *Teaching History*, 125, 6–9.

Chapman, A. (2003), 'Camels, Diamonds and Counterfactuals: A Model for Teaching Causal Reasoning', *Teaching History*, 112, 46–53.

Chapman, A. (2009a), *Supporting High Achievement and Transition to Higher Education through History Virtual Academies*. Warwick: History Subject Centre. http://www2.warwick.ac.uk/fac/cross_fac/heahistory/elibrary/internal/cs_chapman_highachievement_20091001, accessed 17 December 2014.

Chapman, A. (2009b), 'Towards an Interpretations Heuristic: A Case Study Exploration of 16–19-Year-Old Students' Ideas about Explaining Variations in Historical Accounts'. Unpublished EdD thesis. University of London, Institute of Education.

Chapman, A. (2010), 'Reading P. J. Rogers' The New History 30 Years on', *International Journal of Historical Learning, Teaching and Research*, (9), 1, 50–61.

Chapman, A. (2011a), 'Historical Interpretations', in I. Davies (ed.), *Debates in History Teaching*. Abingdon: Routledge, pp. 96–108.

Chapman, A. (2011b), 'The History Curriculum 16–19', in I. Davies (ed.), *Debates in History Teaching*. Abingdon: Routledge, pp. 46–59.

Chapman, A. (2011c), 'Twist and Shout? Developing Sixth-Form Students' Thinking about Historical Interpretation', *Teaching History*, 142, 24–33.

Chapman, A. (2012), '"They have come to differing opinions because of their differing interpretations": Developing 16–19 Year-Old English Students' Understandings of Historical Interpretation through Online Inter-Institutional Discussion', *International Journal of Historical Learning Teaching and Research*, 11, (1), 188 – 214.

Chapman, A. (2014), 'The "Enormous Condescension of Posterity"? Maurice Keatinge and the Teaching of History'. Paper presented at BERA conference, London, 24–26 September.

Chapman, A. and B. Hibbert (2009), 'Advancing History Post-16: Using E-Learning, Collaboration and Assessment to Develop AS and A2 Students' Understanding of the Discipline of History', in H. Cooper and A. Chapman (eds), *Constructing History 11–19*. London: Sage, pp. 120–148.

Chapman, A., G. Elliott and R. Poole (2012), *The History Virtual Academy Project: Facilitating Inter and Intra-Sector Dialogue and Knowledge Transfer through Online Collaboration*. Warwick: History Subject

Centre. http://www2.warwick.ac.uk/fac/cross_fac/heahistory/elibrary/internal/br_chapman_hva_ 20120117, accessed 17 December 2014.

Chapman, A. and J. Facey (2009), 'Documentaries, Causal Linking and Hyper-Linking: Using Learner Collaboration, Peer and Expert Assessment and New Media to Enhance AS History Students' Causal Reasoning', in H. Cooper and A. Chapman (eds), *Constructing History 11–19*. London: Sage, pp. 88–119.

Chapman, A. and J. Woodcock (2006), 'Mussolini's missing marbles: simulating history at GCSE', *Teaching History*, 124, 17–27.

Charmaz, K. (2006), *Constructing Grounded Theory: A Practical Guide through Qualitative Analysis*. London: Sage.

Christian, D. (2005), *Maps of Time*. Berkeley: University of California Press.

Christodoulou, D. (2014), *Seven Myths about Education*. London: Routledge.

Cixous, H. and C. Clement (1986), *The Newly Born Woman*, trans. B. Wing. Minneapolis: University of Minnesota Press.

Clark, C. (2013), *The Sleepwalkers: How Europe Went to War in 1914*. London: Harper Collins.

Coffin, C. (2006a), *Historical Discourse: the Language of Time, Cause and Evaluation*. London: Continuum.

Coffin, C. (2006b), 'Learning the Language of School History: The Role of Linguistics in Mapping the Writing Demands of the Secondary School Curriculum', *Journal of Curriculum Studies*, (38), 4, 413–429.

Collingwood, R. G. (1994), *The Idea of History, Revised edition with Lectures 1926–1928*, ed. W. J. van der Dussen. Oxford: Oxford University Press.

Collins, M. (2011), 'Historiography from below: How Undergraduates Remember Learning History at School', *Teaching History*, 142, 34–39.

Coltham, J. B. (1960), 'Junior School Children's Understanding of Some Terms Commonly Used in the Teaching of History', Unpublished PhD thesis, University of Manchester.

Confino, A. (2009), 'Narrative Form and Historical Sensation: On Saul Friedländer's *the Years of Extermination*', *History and Theory* 48, (3) (Oct.), 199–219. Reprinted, with revisions, in Confino (2012).

Confino, A. (2012), *Foundational Pasts: The Holocaust as Historical Understanding*. New York: Cambridge University Press.

Connelly, F. M. and D. J. Clandinin (1990), 'Stories of Experience and Narrative Inquiry', *Educational Researcher*, 19, (5), 2–14.

Conway, D. (2005), 'Why History Remains the Best Form of Citizenship Education', *Civitas Review*, (2), 2, 1–9.

Cooper, D. (2004), *Challenging Diversity: Rethinking Equality and the Value of Difference*. Cambridge: Cambridge University Press.

Corfield, P. J. (2009), 'Teaching History's Big Pictures: Including Continuity as Well as Change', *Teaching History*, 136, 53–59.

Counsell, C. (1997), *Analytical and Discursive Writing at Key Stage 3*. London: Historical Association.

Counsell, C. (2000), 'Historical Knowledge and Historical Skill: The Distracting Dichotomy', in J. Arthur and R. Phillips (eds), *Issues in History Teaching*. Abingdon: Routledge.

Counsell, C. (2001), 'Knowledge, Writing and Delighting; Extending the Historical Thinking of 11 and 12-Year-Olds', *Welsh Historian*, 31, 7–13.

Counsell, C. (2002), 'Editorial', *Teaching History*, 107, 2.

Counsell, C. (2003), 'History for All', in R. Harris and M. Riley (eds), *Past Forward: A Vision for School History, 2002–2012: Conference Papers*. London: Historical Association.

Counsell, C. (2004a), 'Editorial', *Teaching History*, 115, 2.

Counsell, C. (2004b), *History and Literacy in Year 7: Building the Lesson around the Text*. London: Hodder Murray.

Counsell, C. (2004c), 'Looking through a Josephine-Butler-Shaped Window: Focusing Pupil's Thinking on Historical Significance', *Teaching History*, 114, 30–36.

Counsell, C. (2009a), 'Interpretivism: Meeting Ourselves in Research', in E. Wilson (ed.), *School-based Research: A Guide for Education Students*. London: Sage, pp. 112–124.

Counsell, C. (2009b), Video contribution to 'Dimensions of Diversity: How Do We Improve Our Teaching of Social Complexity in History?' Online e-CPD unit. Historical Association. http://www.history.org.uk/resources/secondary_resource_1326_11.html, accessed 26 July 2015.

Counsell, C. (2011a), 'Disciplinary Knowledge for All, the Secondary History Curriculum and History Teachers' Achievement', *The Curriculum Journal*, (22), 2, 201–225.

Counsell, C. (2011b), 'History Teachers as Curriculum Makers: Professional Problem-Solving in Secondary School History Education in England', in B. Schüllerquvist (ed.), *Patterns of Research in Civics, History, Geography and Religious Education*. Karlstad: University of Karlstad Press, pp. 53–88.

Counsell, C. (2011c), 'What Do We Want Students to Do with Historical Change and Continuity?', in I. Davies (ed.) *Debates in History Teaching*. Abingdon: Routledge, pp. 109–123.

Counsell, C. (2013), 'The Other Person in the Room: A Hermeneutic-Phenomenological Enquiry into Mentors' Experience of Using Academic and Professional Literature with Trainee History Teachers', in M. Evans (ed.), *Teacher Education and Pedagogy: Theory, Policy and Practice*. Cambridge: Cambridge University Press, pp. 134–182.

Counsell, C. (2014), 'The Uses of the 'Enquiry Question' in Mediating Content and Concept: Liminality and Hermeneutic Play in History Teachers' Curricular Realisation'. Paper presented at BERA conference, London, 24–26 September.

Counsell, C. and S. Mastin (2015), 'Narrating Continuity: Investigating Knowledge and Narrative in a Lower Secondary School Study of Sixteenth-Century Change', in A. Chapman and A. Wilschut (eds), *International Review of History Education: Joined-up History*, Vol. 8. Charlotte, NC: Information Age Publishing, pp. 315–348.

Cresswell, T. (2004), *Place: A Short Introduction*. Malden (USA), Oxford (UK), Carlton (AUST): Blackwell Publishing.

Crotty, M. (1998), *The Foundations of Social Research: Meaning and Perspective in the Research Process*. London: Sage.

Currie, M. (2004), *Difference*. London: Routledge.

Dalrymple, W. (2004), *White Mughals: Love and Betrayal in Eighteenth-Century India*. London: Harper Perennial.

Danto, A. C. (1962), 'Narrative Sentences', *History and Theory*, 2, (2), 146–179.

Danto, A. C. (1985 [1st edition, 1965]), *Narration and Knowledge* (including the integral text of *Analytical Philosophy of History*). New York: Columbia University Press.

Davison, M. (2010), 'The Case for Empathy in the History Classroom', *Curriculum Matters*, 6, 82–98.

Davison, M., P. Enright and M. Sheehan (2014), *History Matters 2: A Handbook for Teaching and Learning How to Think Historically*. Wellington: NZCER Press.

Dawson, I. (2004), 'Time for Chronology? Ideas for Developing Chronological Understanding', *Teaching History*, 117, 14–24.

Dawson, I. (2008), 'Thinking across Time: Planning and Teaching the Story of Power and Democracy at Key Stage 3', *Teaching History*, 130, 14–21.

Dawson, I. (2009), 'What time does the tune start?: from Thinking about "Sense of Period" to Modelling History at Key Stage 3', *Teaching History*, 135, 50–57.

Dawson, I. and D. Banham (2002), 'Thinking from the inside: je suis le roi!', *Teaching History*, 109, 12–18.

Department for Education (DfE) (1994), *History in the National Curriculum*: England. London: HMSO.

Department for Education (DfE) (2010), 'The Importance of Teaching: The Schools White Paper'. https://www.gov.uk/government/uploads/system/uploads/attachment_data/file/175429/CM-7980.pdf, accessed 30 July 2015.

Department for Education (DfE) (2011), *The National Strategies 1997–2011: A Brief Evaluation of the Impact and Effectiveness of the National Strategies*. https://www.gov.uk/government/uploads/system/uploads/attachment_data/file/175408/DFE-00032–2011.pdf, accessed 30 July 2015.

Department for Education (DfE) (2013), *National Curriculum in England: History Programmes of Study*. London: Department for Education. https://www.gov.uk/government/publications/national-curriculum-in-england-history-programmes-of-study, accessed 28 July 2015.

Department for Education and Employment (DFEE) (1999), *History in the National Curriculum: England*. London: HMSO.

Department of Education and Science (DES), (1990a) *National Curriculum History Working Group: Final Report*. London: HMSO.

Department of Education and Science (DES) (1990b), *History in the National Curriculum (England)*. London: HMSO.

Department for Education and Skills (DfES) (2007), *Diversity and Citizenship Curriculum Review*. London: DfES

Derrida, J. (1982), 'Différance', in J. Derrida (ed.), *Margins of Philosophy*. Chicago: University of Chicago Press, pp. 3–27.

Derrida, J. (1988), *Limited Inc.*, trans. S. Weber. Evanston, IL: Northwestern University Press.

Diamond, J. (1997), *Guns, Germs and Steel*. London: Jonathan Cape.

Diamond, J. (2005), *Collapse: How Societies Choose to Fail or Survive*. London: Allen Lane.

Dickinson, A. K., A. Gard and P. J. Lee (1978), 'Evidence in History in the Classroom', in A. K. Dickinson and P. J. Lee (eds), *History Teaching and Historical Understanding*. London: Heinemann Educational, pp. 1–20.

Donaghy, L. (2014), 'Using Regular, Low-Stakes Tests to Secure Pupils' Contextual Knowledge in Year 10', *Teaching History*, 157, 44–53.

Donovan, M. S. and J. D. Bransford (eds), (2005), *How Students Learn: History in the Classroom*. Washington, DC: National Academies Press.

Donovan, M. S., J. D. Bransford and J. W. Pellegrino (eds) (1999), *How People Learn: Bridging Research and Practice*. Washington, DC: National Academy Press.

Edexcel (2012a), 'History Advanced Unit 3 Option B: Politics, Protest and Revolution (6HI03/B), Tuesday 12 June 2012 – Morning'. London: Pearson Education. http://www.edexcel.com/migrationdocuments/QP%20GCE%20Curriculum%202000/June%202012%20-%20QP/6HI03_B_que_20120612.pdf, accessed 17 December 2014.

Edexcel (2012b), 'Mark Scheme (Results) Summer 2012 GCE History (6HI03/E), Unit 3: Depth Studies & Associated Historical Controversies Option E: War & Peace: 20th Century International

Relations'. London: Pearson Education. http://www.edexcel.com/migrationdocuments/QP%20 GCE%20Curriculum%202000/June%202012%20-%20MS/6HI03_E_rms_20120816.pdf, accessed 17 December 2014.

Eliasson, P., F. Alvén, C. Aselsson Yngvéus and D. Rosenlund (2015), 'Historical Consciousness and Historical Thinking Reflected in Large-Scale Assessment in Sweden', in K. Ercikan and P. Seixas (eds), *New Directions in Assessing Historical Thinking*. London: Routledge, pp. 171–182.

Elliott, J. (2007), 'A Curriculum for the Study of Human Affairs: The Contribution of Lawrence Stenhouse', in J. Elliott (ed.), *Reflecting Where the Action Is*. London and New York: Routledge. pp. 15–29.

Elton, G. R. (1967), *The Practice of History*. London: Methuen.

Epstein, T. (2008), *Interpreting National History: Race, Identity, and Pedagogy in Classrooms and Communities*. London and New York: Routledge.

Evans, J. and G. Pate (2007), 'Does Scaffolding Make Them Fall? Reflecting on Strategies for Developing Causal Argument in Years 8 and 11', *Teaching History*, 128, 18–29.

Evans, M. (2009), 'Reliability and Validity in Qualitative Research by Teacher Researchers', in E. Wilson (ed.), *School-based Research: A Guide for Education Students*. London: Sage, pp. 112–124.

Evans, R. J. (1997), *In Defence of History*. London: Granta.

Evans, R. J. (2011), 'The Wonderfulness of Us (the Tory Interpretation of History)', *London Review of Books*, (33), 6, 9–12. http://www.lrb.co.uk/v33/n06/richard-j-evans/the-wonderfulness-of-us, accessed 28 July 2015.

Evans, R. J. (2013), 'Michael Gove's History Wars', *The Guardian*. http://www.theguardian.com/books/2013/jul/13/michael-gove-teaching-history-wars, accessed 13 July 2013.

Evans, R. J. (2014), *Altered Pasts: Counterfactuals in History*. London: Little Brown.

Fairclough, A. (2002), *Better Day Coming: Blacks and Equality 1890–2000*. New York; London: Penguin.

Faulkner, K. (2010), 'Children Will Learn Poetry and Monarchs of England by Heart Under Tory Plans', *The Daily Mail*, 6 March 2010. http://www.dailymail.co.uk/news/article-1255899/Children-learn-poetry-monarchs-England-heart-Tory-plans.html#ixzz3hEIaH9Yj, 28 July 2015 accessed.

Feinberg, J. (2009), *Wordle* [online computer software]. http://www.wordle.net/, accessed 26 July 2015.

Ferguson, N. (1997), *Virtual History: Alternatives and Counterfactuals*. London: Picador.

Field, F. (2009), 'All Young People Deserve a Collective Memory of the Highs and Lows, Dangers, Failures as Well as the Triumphs of Britain', *Conservative Home*. http://www.conservativehome.com/platform/2009/08/frank-field-mp.html, accessed 31 July 2015.

Fielding, A. (2015), 'Transforming Year 11's Conceptual Understanding of Change', *Teaching History*, 158, 28–27.

Fines, J. (1987), 'Making Sense Out of the Content of the History Curriculum', in C. Portal (ed.), *The History Curriculum for Teachers*. London: The Falmer Press.

Firth, R. (2011), 'Making Geography Visible in the Secondary School Curriculum', *The Curriculum Journal*, 22, (3), 289–316.

Fordham, M. (2007), 'Slaying Dragons and Sorcerers in Year 12: In Search of Historical Argument', *Teaching History*, 129, 31–38.

Fordham, M. (2012), 'Out went Caesar and in came the Conqueror, though I'm sure something happened in between . . . a Case Study in Professional Thinking', *Teaching History*, 147, 38–45.

Fordham, M. (2013), 'O Brave New World without Those Levels In't: Where Now for Key Stage 3 Assessment in History?' *Teaching History Supplement*, 16–23.

Fordham, M. (2014a), '"But Why Then?" Chronological Context and Historical Interpretations', *Teaching History*, 156, 32–39.

Fordham, M. (2014b), 'What Does an Expert Teacher Need to Know?', Blogpost, 23 December 2014. http://clioetcetera.com/2014/12/23/what-does-an-expert-teacher-need-to-know/, accessed 27 July 2015.

Fordham, M. (2015a), 'Realising and Extending Stenhouse's Vision of Teacher Research: The Case of English History Teachers', *British Educational Research Journal*. doi: 10.1002/berj.3192.

Fordham, M. (2015b), 'Teachers and the Academic Disciplines', *Journal of Philosophy of Education*. doi: 10.1111/1467–9752.12145.

Foster, L. and P. Herzog (1994), *Contemporary Philosophical Perspectives on Pluralism and Multiculturalism*. Amherst, MA: University of Massachusetts Press.

Foster, R. (2008), 'Speed Cameras, Dead Ends, Drivers and Diversions: Year 9 Use a 'Road Map' to Problematize Change and Continuity', *Teaching History*, 131, 4–8.

Foster, R. (2011), 'Passive Receivers or Constructive Readers? Pupils' Experiences of an Encounter with Academic History', *Teaching History*, 142, 4–13.

Foster, R. (2013), 'The More Things Change, the More They Stay the Same: Developing Students' Thinking about Change and Continuity', *Teaching History*, 151, 8–17.

Foster, R. (2015), 'Pipes' Punctuation and Making Complex Historical Claims: How the Direct Teaching of Punctuation Can Improve Students' Historical Thinking and Argument', *Teaching History*, 159, 8–13.

Foster, R. and S. Gadd (2013), 'Let's Play Supermarket "Evidential" Sweep: Developing Students' Awareness of the Need to Select Evidence', *Teaching History*, 152, 24–29.

Foster, S., R. Ashby, P. Lee and J. Howson (2008), *Usable Historical Pasts: A Study of Students' Frameworks of the Past*. Economic and Social Research Council (ESRC) End of Award Report, RES-000–22–1676. Swindon: ESRC. http://www.esrc.ac.uk/my-esrc/grants/RES-000–22–1676/read, accessed 30 September 2014.

Fountain, G. (2012), 'Caught In-Between: The Impact of Different Forms of Mandated National Assessment for Qualifications on Teacher Decision-Making in Year 12 History in New Zealand, 1986–2005'. Unpublished MA dissertation, University of Wellington.

Friedländer, S. (1997), *Nazi Germany and the Jews, Vol. 1: The Years of Persecution, 1933–1939*. New York: HarperCollins.

Friedländer, S. (2007), *The Years of Extermination: Nazi Germany and the Jews, 1939–1945*. New York: HarperCollins.

Fulbrook, M. (2002), *Historical Theory*. London: Routledge.

Furlong, J. (2013), *Education: An Anatomy of the Discipline: Rescuing the University Project*. London: Routledge.

Gadamer, H.-G. (1975), *Truth and Method*. London: Sheed and Ward.

Gadd, S. (2009), 'Building Memory and Meaning: Supporting Year 8 in Shaping Their Own Big Narratives', *Teaching History*, 136, 34–41.

Gardner, H. (1985), *The Mind's New Science: A History of the Cognitive Revolution*. New York: Basic Books.

Gardner, H. (2000), *The Disciplined Mind: Beyond Facts and Standardized Tests, the K-12 Education that Every Child Deserves*. New York: Penguin Group.

Gardner, P. (2010), *Hermeneutics, History and Memory*. Abingdon: Routledge.

Garner, R. (2013), '100 Academics Savage Education Secretary Michael Gove for "Conveyor-Belt Curriculum" for Schools', *The Independent*, 19 March 2013. http://www.independent.co.uk/news/education/education-news/100-academics-savage-education-secretary-michael-gove-for-conveyorbelt-curriculum-for-schools-8541262.html, accessed 29 July 2014.

Gaze, R. (2005), 'Uncovering the Hidden Histories: Black and Asian People in the Two World Wars', *Teaching History*, 120, 46–53.

Gibb, N. (2015), 'Knowledge Is Power: The Social Justice Case for an Academic Curriculum'. http://www.policyexchange.org.uk/modevents/item/nick-gibb-mp-knowledge-is-power-the-social-justice-case-for-an-academic-curriculum, accessed 4 August 2015.

Gibbons, M., C. Limoges, H. Nowotny, S. Schwartzman, P. Scott and M. Trow (1994), *The New Production of Knowledge: the Dynamics of Science and Research in Contemporary Societies*. London: Sage.

Glaser, B. and A. Strauss (1967), *The Discovery of Grounded Theory*. Chicago: Aldine.

Glynn, S., and D. Booth (1985), 'Building Counterfactual Pyramids', *The Economic History Review*, 38, (1), 89–94.

Goldstein, L. J. (1976), *Historical Knowing*. Austin and London: The University of Texas Press.

Gorman, M. (1998), 'The "Structured Enquiry" Is Not a Contradiction in Terms: Focused Teaching for Independent Learning', *Teaching History*, 92, 20–25.

Gove, M. (2010), Speech to the National College Annual Conference, Birmingham. https://www.gov.uk/government/speeches/michael-gove-at-the-national-college-annual-conference, accessed 17 December 2014.

Gowariker, A. (dir.) (2008), *Jodhaa/Akbar* [Motion Picture], produced by R. Screwvala and A. Gowariker. Mauritius: UTV Motion Pictures.

Grant, C. A. and C. E. Sleeter (2007), *Doing Multicultural Education for Achievement and Equity*. New York: Routledge.

Grant, S. G. (2007), 'Understanding What Children Know about History: Exploring the Representation and Testing Dilemmas', *Social Studies Research and Practice*, 2, (2), 89–106.

Grever, M., P. De Bruijn and C. Van Boxtel (2012), 'Negotiating Historical Distance: Or, How to Deal with the Past as a Foreign Country in Heritage Education', *Paedagogica Historica: International Journal of the History of Education*, 48, (6), 873–887.

Gruenewald, D. A. (2003), 'Foundations of Place: A Multidisciplinary Framework for Place-Conscious Education', *American Education Research Journal*, 40, (3), 619–654.

Guyver, R. (2006), 'More Than just The Henries: Britishness and British history at Key Stage 3', *Teaching History*, 122, 15–23.

Guyver, R. and T. Taylor (eds) (2011), *History Wars in the Classroom: A Global Perspective*. Charlotte, NC: Information Age Publishing, pp. 104–127.

Haenen, J. and H. Schrijnemakers (2000), 'Suffrage, Feudal, Democracy, Treaty . . . History's Building Blocks: Learning to Teach Historical Concepts', *Teaching History*, 98, 22–29.

Haenen, J., H. Schrijnemakers, and J. Stufkens (2003), 'Transforming Year 7's understanding of the concept of imperialism: a case study on the Roman Empire', *Teaching History*, 112, 28–34.

Hallam, R. N. (1970), 'Piaget and Thinking in History', in M. Ballard (ed.), *New Movements in the Study and Teaching of History*. London: Temple Smith, pp. 162–178.

Hallam, R. N. (1975), 'Study of the Effect of Teaching Method on the Growth of Logical Thought with Special Reference to the Teaching of History', Unpublished PhD thesis, University of Leeds.

Hammond, K. (1999), 'And Joe Arrives . . . : Stretching the Very Able Pupil in the Mixed-Ability Classroom', *Teaching History*, 94, 23–31.

Hammond, K. (2007), 'Teaching Year 9 about Historical Theories and Methods'. *Teaching History*, 128, 4–10.

Hammond, K. (2014), 'The Knowledge That "Flavours" a Claim: Towards Building and Assessing Historical Knowledge on Three Scales', *Teaching History* 157, 18–25.

Hansard (2009), 'Teaching of British History in Schools, Motion for Leave to Introduce a Bill, Standing Order No. 23', *Hansard*, Column 850, The House of Commons, 4 March 2009. http://www.publications. parliament.uk/pa/cm200809/cmhansrd/cm090304/debtext/90304-0003.htm, accessed 28 July 2015.

Harcourt, M., G. Fountain and M. Sheehan (2011), 'Historical Significance and Sites of Memory', *SET*, 2, 26–31.

Harcourt, M. and M. Sheehan (eds) (2012), *History Matters: Teaching and Learning History in 21st Century New Zealand*. Wellington: NZCER Press.

Harris, R. (2001), 'Why Essay Writing Remains Central to Learning History at AS Level', *Teaching History*, 103, 13–16.

Harris, R. (2013), 'The Place of Diversity within History and the Challenge of Policy and Curriculum', *Oxford Review of Education*, 39, (3), 400–419.

Harris, R. and A. Rea (2006), 'Making History Meaningful: Helping Pupils See Why History Matters', *Teaching History*, 125, 28–36.

Harris, R., K. Burn and M. Woolley (2014), *The Guided Reader to Teaching and Learning History*. London: Routledge.

Havekes, H., A. Aardema and J. De Vries (2010), 'Active Historical Thinking: Designing Learning Activities to Stimulate Domain-Specific Thinking', *Teaching History*, 139, 52–59.

Hawthorne, S. (2008), 'Jacques Derrida: Deconstruction and Différance'. Lecture notes given at the School of Oriental and African Studies, November 2008.

Haydn, T. (2005), *Pupil Perceptions of History at Key Stage 3*. http://www.uea.ac.uk/~m242/historypgce/ qcafinalreport.pdf, accessed 30 September 2014.

Haydn, T. (2011a), 'The Place of the Journal Article in Presenting Research', *Cambridge Journal of Education*, (41), 2, 117–120.

Haydn, T. (2011b), 'Secondary History: Current Themes', in I. Davies (ed.), *Debates in History Teaching*. Abingdon: Routledge, pp. 30–45.

Hibbert, B. (2006), 'The Articulation of the Study of History at General Certificate of Education Advanced Level with the Study of History for an Honours Degree'. Unpublished PhD thesis, University of Leeds.

Hirsch, E. D. (1988), *Cultural Literacy: What Every American Needs to Know*. New York: Houghton Mifflin.

Hirst, P. H. (1974), *Knowledge and the Curriculum*. London: Routledge and Kegan Paul.

Historical Association (HA) (2005), *History 14–19: Report and Recommendations to the Secretary of State*. London: Historical Association.

Historical Association (2014), 'Concerns Over Future of Teacher Training'. http://www.history.org.uk/ resources/secondary_news_2294.html, accessed 30 July 2015.

Hobsbawm, E. (1962), *The Age of Revolutions*. London: Penguin.

Holliss, C. (2014), 'Waking Up to Complexity: Using Christopher Clark's *The Sleepwalkers* to Challenge Over-Determined Causal Explanations', *Teaching History*, 154, 48–54.

Howells, G. (1998), 'Being Ambitious with the Causes of the First World War: Interrogating Inevitability', *Teaching History*, 92, 16–19.

Howells, G. (2005), 'Interpretations and History Teaching: Why Ronald Hutton's *Debates in Stuart History* Matters', *Teaching History*, 121, 29–35.

Howells, G. (2011), 'Why Was Pitt Not a Mince Pie? Enjoying Argument without End: Creating Confident Historical Readers at a Level', *Teaching History*, 143, 4–14.

Howson, J. (2007), '"Is It the Tuarts and Then the Studors or the Other Was Round?" the Importance of Developing a Usable Big Picture of the Past', *Teaching History*, 127, 40–47.

Howson, J. (2009), 'Potential and Pitfalls in Teaching "Big Pictures" of the Past', *Teaching History*, 136, 24–33.

Howson, J. and D. Shemilt (2011), 'Frameworks of Knowledge: Dilemmas and Debates', in I. Davies (ed.), *Debates in History Teaching*. Abingdon: Routledge, pp. 73–83.

Hughes, A. (1998), *The Causes of the Civil War*. London: Macmillan.

Hughes, T. (1967), *Poetry in the Making*. London: Falmer & Falmer.

Hunt, M. (2000), 'Teaching Historical Significance', in J. Arthur and R. Phillips (eds), *Issues in History Teaching*. London: Routledge, pp. 39–53.

Husbands, C., A. Kitson and A. Pendry (2003), *Understanding History Teaching: Teaching and Learning about the Past in Secondary Schools*. Maidenhead: Open University Press.

Irigaray, L. (1993), *An Ethics of Sexual Difference*, trans. C. Burke and G. C. Gill. London: Athlone Press.

Jack, P. and E. Fearnhamm (1999), 'Ants and the Tet Offensive: Teaching Year 11 to Tell the Difference', *Teaching History*, 94, 32–37.

Jarman, B. (2009), 'When Were Jews in Medieval England Most in Danger? Exploring Change and Continuity with Year 7', *Teaching History*, 136, 4–12.

Jasanoff, M. (2005), *Edge of Empire: Lives, Culture, and Conquest in the East, 1750–1850*. New York: Alfred A. Knopf.

Jenkins, K. (1991), *Re-thinking History*. London: Routledge.

Jenner, T. (2010), 'From Human Scale to Abstract Analysis: Year 7 Analyse the Changing Relationship of Henry II and Becket', *Teaching History*, 139, 4–10.

Johnson, L. and P. Morris (2010), 'Towards a Framework for Critical Citizenship Education', *Curriculum Journal*, 21, (1), 77–96.

Jones, H. (2009), 'Shaping Macro-Analysis from Micro-History: Developing a Reflexive Narrative of Change in School History', *Teaching History*, 136, 13–21.

Joseph, M. (2002), *Against the Romance of Community*. Minneapolis: University of Minnesota Press.

Kahneman, D. (2012), *Thinking, Fast and Slow*. London: Penguin.

Kearney, R. (1994), *Modern Movements in European Philosophy*. Manchester: Manchester University Press.

Keatinge, M. W. (1913) *Studies in the Teaching of History*. London: Adam and Charles Black.

Kelly, A. (2004), 'Diachronic Dancing', workshop outline. http://www.thinkinghistory.co.uk/Issues/downloads/DiachronicDancing.pdf, accessed 30 September 2014.

Kemp, R. (2011), 'Thematic or Sequential Analysis in Causal Explanations? Investigating the Kinds of Historical Understanding That Year 8 and Year 10 Demonstrate in Their Efforts to Construct Narrative', *Teaching History*, 145, 32–43.

King, M. (2015), 'The Role of Secure Knowledge in Enabling Year 7 to Write Essays on Magna Carta', *Teaching History*, 159, 18–24.

Kinloch, N., A. Kitson and T. McConnell (2005), 'Editorial', *Teaching History*, 120.

Kipling, R. (1995), *Kim* (edition copied from original 1901 version). London: The Folio Society.

Kitson, A., C. Husbands and S. Steward (2011), *Teaching and Learning History 11–18: Understanding the Past*. Maidenhead: Open University Press.

Koretz, D. (2009), *Measuring Up: What Educational Testing Really Tells Us*. Harvard: Harvard University Press

Laffin, D. (1998), '"My essays could go on forever": Using Key Stage 3 to Improve Performance at GCSE', *Teaching History*, 98, 14–21.

Laffin, D. (2000), 'A Poodle with Bite: Using ICT to Make AS Level More Rigorous', *Teaching History*, 100, 8–17.

Laffin, D. (2009), *Better Lessons in A Level History*. London: Hodder Murray.

Laffin, D. (2012), 'Marr: Magpie or Marsh Harrier? The Quest for the Common Characteristics of the Genus "Historian" with 16- to 19-Year-Olds', *Teaching History*, 149, 18–25.

Lambert, D. (2011), 'Reviewing the Case for Geography, and the 'Knowledge Turn' in the English National Curriculum', *The Curriculum Journal*, 22, (2), 243–264.

Lang, S. (1993), 'What Is Bias?', *Teaching History*, 73, 9–13.

Lang, S. (2003), 'Narrative: The Under-rated Skill', *Teaching History*, 110, 8–13.

Lather, P. (1993), 'Fertile Obsessions: Validity after Poststructuralism', *The Sociological Quarterly*, 34, (4), 673–693.

Leat, D., A. Reid and R. Lofthouse (2015), 'Teachers' Experiences of Engagement with and in Educational Research: What Can Be Learned from Teachers' Views?', *Oxford Review of Education*, 41, (2), 270–286.

LeCocq, H. (2000), 'Beyond Bias: Making Source Evaluation Meaningful to Year 7', *Teaching History*, 99, 50–55.

Lee, P. J. (1984), 'Why Learn History?', in A. K. Dickinson, P. J. Lee and P. J. Rogers (eds), *Learning History*. London: Heinemann Educational, pp. 1–19.

Lee, P. J. (1991), 'Historical Knowledge and the National Curriculum', in R. Aldrich (ed.), *History in the National Curriculum*. London: Kogan Page, pp. 35–65.

Lee, P. J. (1992), 'History in Schools: Aims, Purposes and Approaches. A Reply to John White', in P. Lee, J. Slater, P. Walsh and J. White (eds), *The Aims of School History: The National Curriculum and Beyond*. London: Tufnell Press, pp. 20–34.

Lee, P. J. (2004), '"Walking Backwards into Tomorrow": Historical Consciousness and Understanding History', *International Journal of Historical Learning, Teaching and Research*, 4, (1). http://centres.exeter.ac.uk/historyresource/journal7/lee.pdf, accessed 30 September 2014.

Lee, P. J. (2005a), 'Historical Literacy: Theory and Research', *International Journal of Historical Learning, Teaching and Research*, 5 (2). http://centres.exeter.ac.uk/historyresource/journal9/papers/lee.pdf, accessed 30 September 2014.

Lee, P. J. (2005b), 'Putting Principles into Practice: Understanding History', in M. S. Donovan and J. D. Bransford (eds), *How Students Learn: History in the Classroom*. Washington, DC: National Academies Press, pp. 29–78.

Lee, P. J. (2011a), 'History Education and Historical Literacy', in I. Davies (ed.), *Debates in History Teaching*. Abingdon: Routledge, pp. 63–72.

Lee, P. J. (2011b), 'Historical Literacy and Transformative History', in L. Perikleous and D. Shemilt (eds), *The Future of the Past: Why history Education Matters*. Nicosia: UNDP-ACT / AHDR, pp. 129–168.

Lee, P. J. (2014) 'Fused Horizons? UK Research into Students' Second-Order Ideas in History: A Perspective from London', in M. Köster, H. Thünemann and M. Zülsdorf-Kersting (eds), *Researching History Education: International Perspectives and Disciplinary Traditions*. Schwalbach: Wochenschau Verlag, pp. 170–194.

Lee, P. J. and R. Ashby (2000), 'Progression in Historical Understanding Among Students Aged 7–14', in P. N. Stearns, P. Seixas and S. Wineburg (eds), *Knowing, Teaching and Learning History*. New York: New York University Press.

Lee, P. J., R. Ashby and A. K. Dickinson (1995), 'Progression in Children's Ideas about History', in M. Hughes (ed.), *Progression in Learning*. Clevedon: Multilingual Matters.

Lee, P. J. and D. Shemilt (2003), 'A Scaffold Not a Cage: Progression and Progression Models in History', *Teaching History,* 113, 13–23.

Lee, P. J. and D. Shemilt (2004), '"I just wish we could go back in the past and find out what really happened": Progression in Understanding about Historical Accounts', *Teaching History*, 117, 25–31.

Lee, P. J. and D. Shemilt (2009), 'Is Any Explanation Better Than None? Over-Determined Narratives, Senseless Agencies and One-Way Streets in Students' Learning about Cause and Consequence in History', *Teaching History*, 137, 42–49.

Lee, P. J. and D. Shemilt (2011), 'The Concept That Dares Not Speak Its Name: Should Empathy Come Out of the Closet?', *Teaching History*, 143, 39–49.

Lenso, K. (1995), 'Validity and Self-Reflexivity Meets Poststructuralism: Scientific Ethos and the Transgressive Self', *Educational Researcher*, 24, (4), 17–45.

Lévesque, S. (2008), *Thinking Historically: Educating Student for the Twenty-First Century*. Toronto: University of Toronto Press.

Levstik, L. (2001), 'Crossing the Empty Spaces: Perspective Taking in New Zealand Adolescents' Understanding of National History', in O. L Davis, E. A Yeager and S. J Foster (eds), *Historical Empathy and Perspective Taking in the Social Studies*. Lanham, MD: Rowman and Littlefield, pp. 69–96.

Limerick, B., T. Burgess-Limerick and M. Grace (1996), 'The Politics of Interviewing: Power Relations and Accepting the Gift', *International Journal of Qualitative Studies in Education*, 9, (4), 449–460.

Lomas, T. (1990), *Teaching and Assessing Historical Understanding*. London: The Historical Association.

Loomba, A. (1998), *Colonialism/Postcolonialism*. London: Routledge.

Lowenthal, D. (1985), *The Past Is a Foreign Country*. Cambridge: Cambridge University Press.

Lowenthal, D. (1996), *Possessed by the Past: The Heritage Crusade and the Spoils of History*. New York: Free Press.

Lowenthal, D. (1998), *The Heritage Crusade and the Spoils of History*. Cambridge: Cambridge University Press.

MacDonald, I. (2008), *Revolution in the Head: The Beatles' Records and the Sixties*. London: Vintage.

MacIntyre, A. (2007), *After Virtue*. Notre Dame: University of Notre Dame Press.

MacNaughton, G. (2005), *Doing Foucault in Early Childhood Studies: Applying Poststructural Ideas*. London: Routledge.

Maggioni, L., B. VanSledright and P. A. Alexander (2009), 'Walking on the Borders: A Measure of Epistemic Cognition in History', *Journal of Experimental Education,* 77, (3), 187–213.

Martin, D. (2008), 'What Do You Think? Using Online Forums to Improve Students' Historical Knowledge and Understanding', *Teaching History* 133, 31–38.

Martin, D., C. Coffin and S. North (2007), 'What's Your Claim? Developing Pupils Historical Argument Skills Using Asynchronous Text Based Computer Conferencing', *Teaching History,* 126, 32–7.

Matthews, D. (2009). *The Strange Death of History Teaching (Fully Explained in Seven Easy to Follow Lessons)*. Cardiff: Self-published.

Mattsson, M., T. Eilertson and D. Rorrison (eds) (2011), *A Practicum Turn in Teacher Education*. Rotterdam: Sense.

McAleavy, T. (1993), 'Using the Attainment Targets in Key Stage 3: Interpretations of History', *Teaching History*, 72, 14–17.

McAleavy, T. (1998), 'The Use of Sources in History Teaching 1910–1998: A Critical Perspective', *Teaching History*, 91, 10–16.

McCrory, C. (2013), 'How Many People Does It Take to Make an Essex Man? Year 9 Face Up to Historical Difference', *Teaching History*, 152, 8–19.

McCullagh, C. B. (1984), *Justifying Historical Descriptions*. Cambridge: Cambridge University Press.

McCutcheon, R. T. (2003), 'The Category "Religion" and the Politics of Tolerance', in L. Greil and D. G. Bromley (eds), *Defining Religion: Investigating the Boundaries Between the Sacred and Secular*. London: Elsevier Press, pp. 139–162.

McGrane, B. (1989), *Beyond Anthropology: Society and the Other*. New York: Columbia University Press.

McLaughlin, C., K. Black-Hawkins and D. McIntyre with A. Townsend (2007), *Networking Practitioner Research*. Abingdon: Routledge.

McNeill, J. R. and W. H. McNeill (2003), *The Human Web*. New York: W. W. Norton.

McQuillan, M. (2001), *Paul de Man*. London: Routledge.

Megill, A. (2007), *Historical Knowledge, Historical Error: A Contemporary Guide to Practice*. Chicago: The University of Chicago Press.

Megill, A. (2008), 'Historical Representation, Identity, Allegiance', Chapter 1 in S. Berger, L. Eriksonas, and A. Mycock (eds), *Narrating the Nation: Representations in History, Media and the Arts*. Oxford and New York: Berghahn, pp. 19–34.

Megill, A. (2015), '"Big History" Old and New: Presuppositions, Limits, Alternatives', *Journal of the Philosophy of History* 9, (2), 306–326.

Ministry of Education (2007), *The New Zealand Curriculum*. Wellington: Learning Media.

Mintrop, H. (2004), 'Fostering Constructivist Communities of Learners in the Amalgamated Multi-Discipline of Social Studies', *Journal of Curriculum Studies*, 36, (2), 141–158.

Monaghan, M. (2010), 'Having "Great Expectations" of Year 9. Interdisciplinary Work between English and History to Improve Pupils' Historical Thinking', *Teaching History*, 138, 13–19.

Moorhouse, D. (2006), 'When Computers Don't Give You a Headache: The Most Able Lead a Debate on Medicine through Time', *Teaching History*, 124, 30–36.

Munslow, A. (1997), *Deconstructing History*. New York: Routledge.

Murray, H., R. Burney and A. Stacey-Chapman (2013), 'Where's the Other "C"? Year 9 Examine Continuity in the Treatment of Mental Health through Time', *Teaching History*, 151, 45–54.

Nakou, I. and I. Barca (eds) (2010), *Contemporary Public Debates Over History Education*. Charlotte, NC: Information Age Publishing.

National Curriculum Council (NCC) (1993), *Teaching History at Key Stage 3*. London: HMSO.

Nietzsche, F. (1983), 'On the Uses and Disadvantages of History for Life', in R. J. Hollindale (trans.), *Untimely Mediations*. Cambridge: Cambridge University Press, pp. 7–124.

O'Hagan, S. (2011), 'Unreal Cities: Sohei Nishino's Magical Photographic Maps of London, Tokyo and Utopia', *Guardian*, [online] 24 February 2011. http://www.guardian.co.uk/artanddesign/2011/feb/24/sohei-nishino-diorama-maps, accessed 30 September 2014.

OCR (2009), *GCSE: History B (Modern World)*. Cambridge: Cambridge Assessment.

Office for Standards in Education (Ofsted), (2007), *History in the Balance: History in English Schools 2003–07*. London: Ofsted. http://www.ofsted.gov.uk/resources/history-balance, accessed 30 September 2014.

Office of Qualifications and Examinations Regulation (Ofqual) (2011), *GCE AS and A Level Subject Criteria for History*. Coventry: Ofqual. http://webarchive.nationalarchives.gov.uk/20141031163546/http://ofqual.gov.uk/documents/gce-as-and-a-level-subject-criteria-for-history/all-versions/, accessed 17 December 2014.

Office of Qualifications and Examinations Regulation (Ofqual) (2012), *GCSE Subject Criteria for History*. Coventry: Ofqual. http://ofqual.gov.uk/documents/gcse-subject-criteria-for-history/, accessed 17 December 2014.

Osowiecki, M. (2006), ' "Miss, Now I Can See Why That Was So Important". Using ICT to Enrich Overview at GCSE', *Teaching History*, 126, 37–42.

Oxford, Cambridge and Royal Society of Arts (OCR) (2013), *AS/A2 Level GCE, GCE History B Specification, Version 3, September 2013*. http://www.ocr.org.uk/Images/68665-specification.pdf, accessed 17 December 2014.

Palek, D. (2013), 'Was the Great Depression Always Depressing? Examining Diachronic Diversity in Students' Historical Learning', *International Journal for Lesson and Learning Studies*, 2 (2), 168–187.

Palek, D. (2015), ' "What Exactly Is Parliament?" Finding the Place of Substantive Knowledge in History', *Teaching History*, 158, 18–25.

Palmer, R. E. (1969), *Hermeneutics*. Evanston: Northwestern University Press.

Parekh, B. (2006), *Rethinking Multiculturalism: Cultural Diversity and Political Theory*. Basingstoke: Palgrave Macmillan.

Park, G. (1995), *Nga Uruora: Ecology and History in a New Zealand Landscape*. Victoria University Press: Wellington.

Parkes, R. J. and D. Donnelly (2014), 'Changing Conceptions of Historical Thinking in History Education: An Australian Case Study', *Revista Tempo e Argumento*, (6), 11, 113–136.

Partington, G. (1980), *The Idea of an Historical Education*. Slough: NFER.

Peck, C. (2010), ' "It's not like I'm Chinese and Canadian. I'm in between": Ethnicity and Students' Conceptions of Historical Significance', *Theory and Research in Social Education*, 38, (4), 574–618.

Peel, E. A. (1967), 'Some Problems in the Psychology of History Teaching: Historical Ideas and Concepts', in W. H. Burston and D. Thompson (eds), *Studies in the Nature and Teaching of History*. London: Routledge, pp. 173–190.

Phillips, R. (2002), 'Historical Significance – the Forgotten Key Element?', *Teaching History*, 106, 14–19.

Philpott, J. (2008), 'Would a Centenarian Recognise Norwich in the New Millennium? Helping Pupils with Special Educational Needs to Develop a Lifelong Curiosity for the Past', *Teaching History*, 131, 44–50.

Pickles, E. (2010), 'Assessment of Students' Uses of Evidence: Shifting the Focus from Processes to Historical Reasoning', *Teaching History*, 143, 52–59.

Pickles, E. (2011), 'How Can the Use of Historical Evidence Be Enhanced? a Research Study of the Role of Knowledge in Year 8 to Year 13 Students' Interpretations of Historical Sources'. *Teaching History*, 139, 41–51.

Plinder, D. (2001), 'Ghostly Footsteps: Voices, Memories and Walks in the City', *Cultural Geographies*, 8, (1), 1–19.

Pomeranz, K. and D. A. Segal (2012), 'World History: Departures and Variations', in D. Northrop (ed.), *A Companion to World History*. Oxford: Wiley-Blackwell, pp. 15–31.

Popper, K. (2003), *The Open Society and its Enemies, Volume II: Hegel and Marx*. Oxford: Routledge.

Portal, C. (1987), *The History Curriculum for Teachers*. London: Falmer.

Portal, C. (1990), *Sources in History: From Definition to Assessment*. Harlow: Longman.

Presner, T. (2011), 'HyperCities: Using Social Media and GIS to Archive and Map Time Layers', Coalition for Networked Information Spring 2011 Membership Meeting, San Diego, CA, 4–5 April 2011. http://www.youtube.com/watch?v=WS-SLGAWxHY&feature=player_Embedded#, accessed 30 July 2015.

Qualifications and Curriculum Authority (QCA) (1999), *History. The National Curriculum for England. Key Stages 1–3*. London: DFEE/QCA.

Qualifications and Curriculum Authority (QCA)/Department of Children, Schools and Families (DCSF) (2007), *Secondary National Curriculum History*. London: QCA. http://webarchive.nationalarchives.gov.uk/20130802151252/https://www.education.gov.uk/schools/teachingandlearning/curriculum/secondary/b00199545/history, accessed 30 September 2014.

Ramsey, P. G. and L. R. Williams (2003), *Multicultural Education: A Source Book*. London: Routledge Falmer.

Ranke, L. von (1981), *The Secret of World History: Selected Writings on the Art and Science of History*, ed. R. Wines. New York: Fordham University Press.

Redlich, F. (1965), '"New" and Traditional Approaches to Economic History and Their Interdependence', *The Journal of Economic History*, 25, (4), 480–495.

Reisman, A. (2012), 'Reading Like a Historian: A Document-Based History Curriculum Intervention in Urban High Schools', *Cognition and Instruction*, (30), 1, 86–112.

Reisman, A. (2015), 'The Difficulty of Assessing Disciplinary Historical Reading', in K. Ercikan and P. Seixas (eds), *New Directions in Assessing Historical Thinking*. London: Routledge, pp. 29–39.

Richards, K. (2012), 'Avoiding a Din at Dinner, or Teaching Students to Argue for Themselves: Year 13 Plan a Historians' Dinner Party', *Teaching History*, 148, 18–27.

Rigby, S. (1995), 'Historical Causation: Is One Thing More Important Than Another?' *History*, 80, 227–242.

Riley, M. (2000), 'Into the Key Stage 3 History Garden: Choosing and Planting Your Enquiry Questions', *Teaching History*, 99, 8–13.

Rimmon-Kenan, S. (1983), *Narrative Fiction: Contemporary Poetics*. London and New York: Routledge.

Rogers, P. J. (1979), *The New History: Theory into Practice*. London: The Historical Association.

Rogers, P. J. (1984), 'Why Teach History?', in A. K. Dickinson, P. J.Lee and P. J. Rogers (eds), *Learning History*. London: Heinemann Educational Books, Ltd, pp. 20–38.

Rogers, P. J. (1987), 'History – The Past as a Frame of Reference', in C. Portal (ed.), *The History Curriculum for Teachers*. Lewes: The Falmer Press, pp. 3–21.

Rogers, R. (2008), 'Raising the Bar: Developing Meaningful Historical Consciousness at KS3', *Teaching History* 133, 24–30.

Rogers, R. (2011), '"Isn't the trigger the thing that sets the rest of it on fire?" Causation Maps: Emphasising Chronology in Causation Exercises', *Teaching History*, 142, 50–55.

Runia, E. (2006), 'Presence', *History and Theory* 45, (1), 1–29. Reprinted, with revisions, in Runia (2014).

Runia, E. (2014), *Moved by the Past: Discontinuity and Historical Mutation*. New York: Columbia University Press.

Rüsen, J. (2002), 'Introduction: Historical Thinking as Intercultural Discourse', in J. Rüsen (ed.), *Western Historical Thinking: An Intercultural Debate*. New York: Berghahn Books, pp. 15–33.

Rüsen, J. (2005), *History: Narration, Interpretation, Orientation*. Oxford: Berghahn Books.

Said, E. (1979), *Orientalism*. New York: Vintage Books.

Saussure, F. de. (1983), *Course in General Linguistics*, trans. R. Harris. London: Duckworth.

Savenije G., C. Van Boxtel and M. Grever (2014), 'Sensitive "Heritage" of Slavery in a Multicultural Classroom: Pupils' Ideas Regarding Significance', *British Journal of Educational Studies*, 62, (2), 127–148.

Savenije, G. (2014), 'Sensitive History Under Negotiation. Pupils' Historical Imagination and Attribution of Significance while Engaged in Heritage Projects'. Unpublished dissertation, Erasmus University, Rotterdam.

Scheurich, J. J. (1997), *Research Method in the Postmodern*. London: The Falmer Press.

School Curriculum and Assessment Authority (SCAA) (1996), *History: Optional Tests and Tasks: Key Stage 3*. London: SCAA.

Schwab, J. (1978), 'Education and the Structure of the Disciplines' in I. Westbury and N. J. Wilkof (eds), *Science, Curriculum and Liberal Education: Selected Essays*. NJ, Chicago: University of Chicago Press, pp. 229–272.

Scott, J. (ed.) (1990), *Understanding Cause and Effect: Learning and Teaching about Causation and Consequence in History*. Harlow: Longman, Teaching History Research Group.

Seixas, P. (2000), ' "Schweigen! die Kinder!" Or, Does Postmodern History Have a Place in Schools?', in P. Stearns, P. Seixas and S. Wineburg (eds), *Knowing, Teaching and Learning History*. New York: New York University Press, pp. 19–38.

Seixas, P. and T. Morton (2013), *The Big Six Historical Thinking Concepts*. Toronto: Nelson Education.

Sellar, W. C. and R. J. Yeatman (1975), *1066 and All That*. London: Magnum Books.

Shemilt, D. (1980), *Evaluation Study: Schools Council History 13–16 Project*. Edinburgh: Holmes McDougall.

Shemilt, D. (1983), 'The Devil's Locomotive', *History and Theory*, 22 (4), Beiheft 22, The Philosophy of History Teaching, pp. 1–18.

Shemilt, D. (1987), 'Adolescent Ideas about Evidence and Methodology in History', in C. Portal (ed.), *The History Curriculum for Teachers*. London: Heinemann, pp. 29–61.

Shemilt, D. (2000), 'The Caliph's Coin: The Currency of Narrative Frameworks in History Teaching', in P. N. Stearns, P. Seixas and S. Wineburg (eds), *Knowing, Teaching and Learning History: National and International Perspectives*. New York: New York University Press, pp. 83–101.

Shemilt, D. (2009), ' "Drinking an Ocean and Pissing a Cupful": How Adolescents Make Sense of History', in L. Symcox and A. Wilschut (eds), *National History Standards: The Problem of the Canon and the Future of Teaching History. International Review of History Education, Volume 5*. Charlotte, NC: Information Age Publishing, pp. 141–210.

Shryock, A. and D. L. Smail (eds) (2011), *Deep History: the Architecture of Past and Present*. Berkeley, CA: University of California Press.

Shulman, L. (1986), 'Those Who Understand: Knowledge Growth in Teaching', *Educational Researcher*, 15, (2), 4–14.

Skinner, Q. (2002), *Visions of Politics, Volume 1: Regarding Method*. Cambridge: Cambridge University Press.

Smith, D. (2014), 'Period, Place and Mental Space: Using Historical Scholarship to Develop Year 7 Pupils' Sense of Period', in *Teaching History*, 145, 8–16.

Smith, P. (2001), 'Why Gerry Now Likes Evidential Work', *Teaching History*, 102, 8–13.

Somers, R. (2009), 'Unmasking Diversity: Deconstructing the Rhetoric on Diversity in the History Classroom and History Education Community'. Unpublished MEd Dissertation, University of Cambridge.

Spier, F. (2011), *Big History and The Future of Humanity*. Oxford: Wiley-Blackwell.

Spier, F. (2012), 'Interpreting the History of "Big History" ', *Teaching History*, 146, 50–51.

Spivak, G. C. (1976), 'Translator's Preface', in J. Derrida, *Of Grammatology*. Baltimore, MD: The Johns Hopkins University Press.

Spivak, G. C. (1988), 'Can the Subaltern Speak?', in C. Nelson and L. Grossberg (eds), *Marxism and the Interpretation of Culture*, Urbana: University of Illinois Press, pp. 271–313.

Stacey-Chapman, A. (2015), 'From a Compartmentalised to a Complicated Past: Developing Transferable Knowledge at a-Level', *Teaching History*, 158, 8–15.

Stack, T. (2007), 'A Higher Ground: The Secular Knowledge of Objects of Religious Devotion', in T. Fitzgerald (ed.), *Religion and the Secular: Historical and Cultural Formations*. London: Routledge, pp. 47–70.

Stake, R. (1995), *The Art of Case Study Research*. Thousand Oaks: Sage.

Stake, R. E. (2005), 'Qualitative Case Studies', in N. K. Denzin and Y. S. Lincoln (eds), *The Sage Handbook of Qualitative Research* (3rd edition). London: Sage, pp. 443–466.

Stanhope, P., 4th Earl of Chesterfield (1905), *Letters*. London: Walter Scott.

Stenhouse, L. (1975), *An Introduction to Curriculum Research and Development*. London: Heinemann.

Stenhouse, L. and the Humanities Curriculum Project Team (1983 edition revised by Jean Rudduck), *The Humanities Curriculum Project: An Introduction*. Norwich: University of East Anglia School of Education.

Stoel, G., J. Van Drie and C. Van Boxtel (2015), 'Teaching towards Historical Expertise: Developing a Pedagogy for Fostering Causal Reasoning in History', *Journal of Curriculum Studies*, 47, (1), 49–76.

Strauss, A. and J. Corbin (1998), *Basics of Qualitative Research: Techniques and Processes for Developing Grounded Theory*. London: Sage.

Stutchbury, E. (2013), 'Ethics in Educational Research', in E. Wilson (ed.), *School Based-Research*. London: Sage.

Suzuki, D. (2010), 'The Legacy: An Elder's Vision for our Sustainable Future', *Auckland Writers and Readers Festival*. 11 November 2011, The Embassy Theatre, Wellington.

Sylvester, D. (1994), 'Change and Continuity in History Teaching 1900–93', in H. Bourdillon (ed.), *Teaching History*. London: Routledge, pp. 9–26.

Taylor, C. (1992), 'The Politics of Recognition', in A. Guttmann (ed.), *Multiculturalism: Examining the Politics of Recognition*. Princeton, NJ: Princeton University Press.

Taylor, L. (2004), 'Sense, Relationship and Power: Uncommon Views of Place', *Teaching History*, 116, 6–8.

Taylor, T. and C. Young (2003), *Making History: A Guide for the Teaching and Learning of History in Australian Schools*. Carlton South, VIC: Curriculum Corporation.

Thompson, D and N. Cole (2003), 'Keeping the Kids on Message . . . One School's Attempt at Helping Sixth Form Students to Engage in Historical Debate Using ICT', *Teaching History*, 113, 8–42.

Timmins, G., K. Vernon and C. Kinealy (2005), *Teaching and Learning History*. London: Sage.

Tombs, R. and I. Tombs (2006), *That Sweet Enemy: The French and the British from the Sun King to the Present*. London: Heinemann.

Tosh, J. (2006), *The Pursuit of History* (4th edition). Harlow: Pearson Education.

Traille, K. (2007), '"You should be proud of your history. They made me feel ashamed": Teaching History Hurts', *Teaching History*, 127, 32–37.

Tuan, Y. (1977), *Space and Place: The Perspective of Experience*. University of Minnesota Press: Minneapolis.

Tuck, S. (2010), *We ain't what we ought to be: The Black Freedom Struggle from Emancipation to Obama*. Cambridge, MA; London: Belknap Press of Harvard University Press.

Tuckett, A. G. (2005), 'Applying Thematic Analysis Theory to Practice: A Researcher's Experience', *Contemporary Nurse*, 19, (1–2), 75–87.

Tversky, A., and D. Kahneman (1973), 'Availability: A Heuristic for Judging Frequency and Probability', *Cognitive Psychology*, 5, 207–232.

Tze Kwang, T. (2015), 'What Made Your Essay Successful? I T.A.C.K.L.E.D. the Essay Question!' *Teaching History*, 159, 36–43.

Van Boxtel, C. A. M. and M. C. R. Grever (2011), 'between Disenchantment and High Expectations. History Education in the Netherlands, 1968–2008', in E. Erdmann and W. Hasberg (eds), *Facing, Mapping, Bridging Diversity. Foundation of a European Discourse on History Education, Volume 2*. Schwalbach, Germany: Wochenschau Verlag. pp. 83–116.

Van Boxtel, C. and J. Van Drie (2012), '"That's in the time of the Romans!" Knowledge and Strategies Students Use to Contextualize Historical Images and Documents', *Cognition and Instruction*, 30, (2), 113–145.

Van Boxtel, C. and J. Van Drie (2013), 'Historical Reasoning in the Classroom: What Does It Look Like and How Can We Enhance It?' *Teaching History*, 150, 32–40.

Van Drie, J. and C. Van Boxtel (2003), 'Developing Conceptual Understanding Though Talk and Mapping', *Teaching History*, 110, 27–31.

Van Drie, J. and C. Van Boxtel (2008), 'Historical Reasoning: Towards a Framework for Analyzing Students' Reasoning about the Past', *Educational Psychology Review*, 20, (2), 87–110.

Van Drie, J., C. Van Boxtel and B. Stam (2013), '"But why is this so important?" Discussing Historical Significance in the Classroom', *International Journal of Historical Learning, Teaching and Research*, 12, (1), 146–168.

Van Drie, J., M. Van Riessen, A. Logtenberg and B. van der Meijden (2009), '"When was that date?" Building and Assessing a Frame of Reference in the Netherlands', *Teaching History*, 137, 14–21.

Van Manen, M. (1990), *Researching Lived Experience: Human Science for an Action Sensitive Pedagogy*. Ontario: State University of New York Press.

Vygotsky, L. S. (1986), *Thought and Language*, trans. A. Kozulin. Cambridge, MA: MIT Press.

Walsh, B. (2003), 'A Complex Empire: National Archives Learning Curve Takes on the British Empire', *Teaching History*, 112, 22–57.

Ward, R. (2006), 'Duffy's Devices: Teaching Year 13 to Read and Write', *Teaching History*, 124, 9–15.

Wertsch, J. V. (1998), *Mind as Action*. Cambridge: Cambridge University Press.

Wertsch, J. V. (2002), *Voices of Collective Remembering*. Cambridge: Cambridge University Press.

Wheelahan, L. (2010), 'The Structure of Pedagogic Discourse as a Relay for Power: The Case of Competency-Based Training', in P.Singh, A. Sadovnik and S. Semel (eds), *Toolkits, Translations and Conceptual Accounts: Essays on Basil Bernstein*. New York: Peter Lang.

Whitburn, R., M. Hussain and A. Mohamud (2012), '"Doing Justice to History": The Learning of African History in a North London Secondary School and Teacher Development in the Spirit of Ubuntu', *Teaching History,* 146, 18–27.

Whitburn, R. and S. Yemoh (2012), '"My People Struggled Too": Hidden Histories and Heroism – a School-Designed, Post-14 Course on Multi-Cultural Britain Since 1945', *Teaching History*, 147, 16–25.

White, H. (1985), *Tropics of Discourse*. London: The Johns Hopkins University Press.

White, H. (1984), 'The Question of Narrative in Contemporary Historical Theory', *History and Theory*, 23, (1), 1–33.

White, R. and R. Gunstone (1994), *Probing Understanding*. New York: Falmer Press.

Whitty, G. (2010), 'Revisiting School Knowledge: Some Sociological Perspectives on New School Curricula', *European Journal of Education*, 45, (1), 28–45.

Wilkinson, M. L. N. (2015), *A Fresh Look at Islam in a Multi-Faith World: A Philosophy for Success through Education*. London: Routledge.

Willingham, D. T. (2009), *Why Don't Students Like School? A Cognitive Scientist Answers Questions about How the Mind Works and What It Means for the Classroom*. San Francisco, CA: Jossey-Bass.

Wiltshire, T. (2000), 'Telling and Suggesting in the Conwy Valley', *Teaching History*, 100, 32–35.

Wineburg, S. (1991), 'On the Reading of Historical Texts: Notes on the Breach between School and Academy', *American Educational Research Journal*, 28, (3), 495–519.

Wineburg, S. (1999), 'Historical Thinking and Other Unnatural Acts', *Phi Delta Kappan*, 80, (7), 488–499.

Wineburg, S. (2001), *Historical Thinking and Other Unnatural Acts: Charting the Future of Teaching the Past*, Philadelphia, PA: Temple University Press.

Wineburg, S. (2004), 'Crazy for History', *Journal of American History*, 90, (4), 1401–1414.

Wineburg, S. (2007), 'Unnatural and Essential: The Nature of Historical Thinking', *Teaching History*, 129, 6–11.

Wineburg, S. and S. Schneider (2010), 'Was Bloom's Taxonomy Pointed in the Wrong Direction?' *The Phi Delta Kappan*, 94, (4), 56–61.

Wittgenstein, L. (1972), *Philosophical Investigations* (2nd edition). Oxford: Blackwell.

Wood, D. M. (1964), 'Some Concepts of Social Relations in Childhood and Adolescence Investigated by Means of the Analysis of the Definitions', Unpublished MEd thesis, University of Nottingham.

Woodcock, J. (2005), 'Does the Linguistic Release the Conceptual? Helping Year 10 to Improve Their Causal Reasoning', *Teaching History*, 119, 5–14.

Woodcock, J. (2011), 'Causal explanation', in I. Davies (ed), *Debates in History Teaching*. London: Routledge.

Woolley, M. (2003), ' "Really weird and freaky": Using a Thomas Hardy Short Story as a Source of Evidence in the Year 8 Classroom', *Teaching History*, 111, 6–11.

Wong, R. B. (2012), 'Causation', in U. Rublack (ed.), *A Concise Companion to History*. Oxford: Oxford University Press, pp. 27–54.

Worth, P. (2013), ' "English King Frederick I won at Arsuf, then took Acre, then they all went home": Exploring the Challenges Involved in Reading and Writing Historical Narrative', *Teaching History*, 156, 8–19.

Wrenn, A. (1998), 'What if . . . What if . . . What if we had all been less sniffy about counterfactual history in the classroom?' *Teaching History*, 92, 46–48.

Wrenn, A. (1999), 'Build It in, Don't Bolt It on: History's Opportunity to Support Critical Citizenship', *Teaching History*, 96, 6–12.

Yin, R. K. (2003), *Case Study Research: Design and Methods* (3rd edition). Thousand Oaks, CA: Sage.

Young, M. (1971), *Knowledge and Control*. London: Collier MacMillan.

Young, M. (2007), *Bringing Knowledge Back In: From Social Constructivism to Social Realism in the Sociology of Education*. London: Routledge.

Young. M. (2008a), 'Curriculum Theory and the Problem of Knowledge: A Personal Project and an Unfinished Journey', in L. Waks. and E. Short (eds), *Leaders in Curriculum Studies: Intellectual Self-Portraits*. Rotterdam: SENSE Books.

Young, M. (2008b), 'From Constructivism to Realism in the Sociology of the Curriculum', in G. Kelly, A. Luke and J. Green (eds), *What Counts as Knowledge in Educational Settings*. Washington: American Educational Research Association.

Young, M. (2010), 'The Future of Education in a Knowledge Society: The Radical Case for a Subject-Based Curriculum', *Journal of the Pacific Circle Consortium for Education*, 22, (1), 21–32.

Young, M. (2013), 'Overcoming the Crisis in Curriculum Theory: A Knowledge-Based Approach', *Journal of Curriculum Studies*, 45, (2), 101–118.

Young, M. and D. Lambert with C. Roberts and M. Roberts (2014), *Knowledge and the Future School: Curriculum and Social Justice*. London: Bloomsbury.

Young, M. and Muller, J. (2010), 'Three Educational Scenarios for the Future: Lessons from the Sociology of Knowledge', *European Journal of Education*, 45, (1), 11–27.

Young, M. and Muller, J. (2014), 'On Powers of Powerful Knowledge', in B.Barrett and E. Rata (eds), *Knowledge and the Future of the Curriculum: International Studies in Social Realism*. Basingstoke: Palgrave Macmillan, pp. 41–64.

Index

Note numbers are denoted by 'n', figures are denoted by 'f' and tables are denoted by 't'.